# Project Management 3e

Selected Chapters from
*Project Management: A Managerial Approach*

Jack R. Meredith
Samuel J. Mantel, Jr.

**For use by ESI International, Arlington, VA**

ESI
international

**WILEY**
EXECUTIVE RESOURCE PROGRAM

# PROJECT MANAGEMENT
## A Managerial Approach

JACK R. MEREDITH
SAMUEL J. MANTEL, JR.
University of Cincinnati

John Wiley & Sons, Inc.
New York • Chichester • Brisbane • Toronto • Singapore

Cover Photos: Alaskan Pipeline, G. Martin/Superstock
Inset Photo, The Rivera Collection/Superstock

| | |
|---|---|
| Acquisitions Editor | Beth L. Golub |
| Marketing Manager | Debra Riegert |
| Senior Production Editor | John Rousselle |
| Senior Freelance Production Editor | Lois Lombardo |
| Designer | Laura Nicholls |
| Manufacturing Manager | Susan Stetzer |
| Photo Researcher | Lisa Passmore |
| Freelance Illustration Coordinator | Jaime Perea |

This book was set in 10/12 Novarese Book by TCSystems and printed and bound by R.R. Donnelley (Crawfordsville). The cover was printed by Lehigh.

Recognizing the importance of preserving what has been written, it is a policy of John Wiley & Sons, Inc. to have books of enduring value published in the United States printed on acid-free paper, and we exert our best efforts to that end.

The paper in this book was manufactured by a mill whose forest management programs include sustained yield harvesting of its timberlands. Sustained yield harvesting principles ensure that the number of trees cut each year does not exceed the amount of new growth.

*Library of Congress Cataloging in Publication Data:*
Meredith, Jack R.
    Project management : a managerial approach / Jack R. Meredith, Samuel J. Mantel, Jr.—3rd ed.
        p.    cm.—(Wiley series in production/operations management)
    Includes bibliographical references and indexes.
    ISBN 0-471-01626-8
    1. Industrial project management.    I. Mantel, Samuel J.
II. Title.    III. Series.

HD69.P75M47  1995
658.4'04—dc20                                                    94-33876
                                                                    CIP

Printed in the United States of America
10  9  8  7  6  5  4  3  2  1

# Contents

**CHAPTER 1 / Projects in Contemporary Organizations** — 1

1.1 The Definition of a "Project" — 7
1.2 Why Project Management? — 9
1.3 The Project Life Cycle — 13
1.4 The Structure of This Text — 17

*Project Management in Practice* - The Undersea England–France Chunnel — 5

*Project Management in Practice* - The Endicott, Alaska Oil Project — 11

*Project Management in Practice* - Project Management Style and the Challenger Disaster — 16

CASE - Peerless Laser Processors — 23

Classic Reading · Making Project Management Work — 28

**PART I / PROJECT INITIATION** — 37

**CHAPTER 2 / Project Selection** — 39

2.1 Criteria for Project Selection Models — 41
2.2 The Nature of Project Selection Models — 43
2.3 Types of Project Selection Models — 47
2.4 Analysis Under High Uncertainty — 67
2.5 Comments on the Information Base for Selection — 71
2.6 Project Proposals — 74
2.7 The Past and Future of Project Evaluation/Selection Models — 78

*Project Management in Practice* - Estimating Electronic Systems Costs for Future Projects — 54

*Project Management in Practice* - The Military Mobile Communication System—A Procurement Innovation — 77

CASE I - Westfield, Inc.: Packaging Alternatives — 88

CASE II - Planning and Budgeting a Social Service System — 93

READING - Justification Techniques for Advanced Manufacturing Technologies — 98

**CHAPTER 3 / The Project Manager** — 108

3.1 Some Comments on Project Management and the Project Manager — 110
3.2 Special Demands on the Project Manager — 119
3.3 Selecting the Project Manager — 128

*Project Management in Practice* - The Wreckmaster at a New York Subway Accident — 115

*Project Management in Practice* - Selecting Project Managers at GTE Telecom, Inc. — 132

CASE - Geartrain International: Medina, Ohio — 138

READING - What It Takes to Be a Good Project Manager — 146

**CHAPTER 4 / Project Organization** — 150

4.1 The Project as Part of the Functional Organization — 153
4.2 Pure Project Organization — 155
4.3 The Matrix Organization — 158
4.4 Mixed Organizational Systems — 163
4.5 Choosing an Organizational Form — 165
4.6 The Project Team — 170
4.7 Human Factors and the Project Team — 173

*Project Management in Practice* - Reorganizing for Project Management at AT&T — 151

*Project Management in Practice* - Chrysler's Platform Team for New Auto Development   163

CASE - Oilwell Cable Company, Inc.   183

READING - Matrix Management: Contradictions and Insights   187

## CHAPTER 5 / Project Planning   196

5.1   Initial Project Coordination   200
5.2   Systems Integration   205
5.3   Sorting Out the Project   207
5.4   The Work Breakdown Structure and Linear Responsibility Charts   215
5.5   Interface Management   221

*Project Management in Practice* - Planning Anchorage's Bid for the Winter Olympics   198

*Project Management in Practice* - Integrating Company Policy with Company Strategy   201

*Project Management in Practice* - Planning for Public Project Management: Milwaukee's Sewerage Renovation/Expansion   213

CASE - A Project Management and Control System for Capital Projects   229

READING - Balancing Strategy and Tactics in Project Implementation   240

## CHAPTER 6 / Negotiation and Conflict Resolution   250

6.1   The Nature of Negotiation   252
6.2   Partnering, Chartering, and Change   254
6.3   Conflict and the Project Life Cycle   257
6.4   Some Requirements and Principles of Negotiation   265
6.5   Negotiation in Action—The Quad Sensor Project   268

*Project Management in Practice* - Using Project Management to Avoid Conflicts During the AT&T/NCR Merger   252

*Project Management in Practice* - A Consensus Feasibility Study for Montreal's Archipel Dam   254

CASE - Cincinnati Milacron Inc.: Robot Welding   274

Classic Reading - Methods of Resolving Interpersonal Conflict   278

## ▶ PART II / PROJECT IMPLEMENTATION   285

## CHAPTER 7 / Budgeting and Cost Estimation   287

7.1   Estimating Project Budgets   289
7.2   Improving the Process of Cost Estimation   303

*Project Management in Practice* - Financing the Flight of the Voyager   288

*Project Management in Practice* - Completing the Limerick Nuclear Facility Under Budget   301

CASE - Automotive Builders, Inc.: The Stanhope Project   319

READING - Three Perceptions of Project Cost—Cost Is More Than a Four Letter Word   325

## CHAPTER 8 / Scheduling   332

8.1   Background   332
8.2   Network Techniques: PERT and CPM   336
8.3   Gantt Charts   354
8.4   Extensions and Applications   362

*Project Management in Practice* - Replacing the Atigun Section of the TransAlaska Pipeline   334

*Project Management in Practice* - Hosting the Annual Project Management Institute Symposium   359

CASE - The Sharon Construction Corporation   381

READING - "On Time" Project Completion— Managing the Critical Path   382

## CHAPTER 9 / Resource Allocation   389

9.1   Critical Path Method   390
9.2   The Resource Allocation Problem   395
9.3   Resource Loading   398

9.4    Resource Leveling    400
9.5    Constrained Resource Scheduling    404
9.6    Multiproject Scheduling and
       Resource Allocation    412
*Project Management in Practice* - A Resource
    Leveling Information System for
    Scheduling at Sacramento Municipal
    Utility District    403
*Project Management in Practice* - Benefits of
    Resource Constraining at Pennsylvania
    Electric    411
*Project Management in Practice* - Tying
    Projects to Resources and Constraints
    at the Minnesota Department of
    Transportation    422
**CASE** - D.U. Singer Hospital Products
    Corp.    430
**READING** - Resource Constrained
    Scheduling Capabilities of Commercial
    Project Management Software    434

**CHAPTER 10 / Monitoring and
Information Systems    441**

10.1    The Planning-Monitoring-
        Controlling Cycle    444
10.2    Information Needs and the
        Reporting Process    452
10.3    Computerized PMIS (Project
        Management Information
        Systems)    466
*Project Management in Practice* - Using
    Project Management Software to
    Schedule the 1988 Olympic Winter
    Games in Calgary    442
*Project Management in Practice* - Applying
    the BCWP Concept at the U.S.
    Environmental Protection Agency    461
*Project Management in Practice* - Developing
    an Integrated Project Management
    System at Lederle Laboratories    481
**CASE** - Riverview Children's Hospital    487
**READING** - Project Management Control
    Problems: An Information Systems
    Focus    501

**CHAPTER 11 / Project Control    508**

11.1    The Fundamental Purposes of
        Control    510
11.2    Three Types of Control Processes    513
11.3    Comments on the Design of
        Control Systems    522
11.4    Control as a Function of
        Management    529
11.5    Balance in a Control System    532
11.6    Control of Creative Activities    534
11.7    Control of Change    536
*Project Management in Practice* - Formalizing
    the Program Control System at Battelle
    Laboratories    512
*Project Management in Practice* - Schedule
    and Cost Control for Australia's
    Immense New Parliament House    527
*Project Management in Practice* - Better
    Control of Product Development
    Projects at Johnson Controls    538
**CASE** - Corning Glass Works: The Z-Glass
    Project    544
**READING** - Criteria for Controlling
    Projects According to Plan    556

▶ **PART III / PROJECT
TERMINATION,
MULTICULTURAL PROJECTS,
AND UNSOLVED PROBLEMS    565**

**CHAPTER 12 / Project Auditing    567**

12.1    Purposes of Evaluation - Goals of
        the System    568
12.2    The Project Audit    571
12.3    Construction and Use of the Audit
        Report    574
12.4    The Project Audit Life Cycle    578
12.5    Some Essentials of an Audit/
        Evaluation    581
12.6    Measurement    583
*Project Management in Practice* - Evaluating
    the Results of a Sewerage Project in
    Barbados    570

*Project Management in Practice* - Auditing a
Troubled Project at Atlantic States
Chemical Laboratories 577

**CASE** - Delta Electronics, Inc. 590

**READING** - The Project Management Audit:
Its Role and Conduct 604

**CHAPTER 13 /** Project
Termination 611

13.1 The Varieties of Project Termination 612
13.2 When to Terminate a Project 616
13.3 The Termination Process 621
13.4 The Final Report - A Project History 629

*Project Management in Practice* - Nucor's
Approach to Termination by Addition 614

*Project Management in Practice* - A Smooth
Termination-Transition for Suncor's
Ontario Refinery 628

**CASE I** - Cincinnati Milacron Inc.: Casting
Cleaning 635

**CASE II** - Beta Company: The Z15 Engine
Program (A) 644

**Classic Reading** - Knowing When to Pull
the Plug 654

**CHAPTER 14 /** Multicultural,
Environmental, and Unsolved
Issues 661

14.1 Problems of Cultural Differences 662
14.2 Impact of Institutional
Environments 666
14.3 Multicultural Communications and
Managerial Behavior 674
14.4 Three Critical, Unsolved Problems 678

*Project Management in Practice* - A Project
Emergency Due to International Politics 662

*Project Management in Practice* - Energo-
project Holding Integrates Two Diverse
Cultures to Achieve Project Success 665

*Project Management in Practice* - Project
Management in Brazil During Unstable
Political and Monetary Environments 670

*Project Management in Practice* - Boeing's Key
to Future Project Management Success—
Multi-Discipline Teams 680

**CASE** - Supernet 684

**READING** - The Age of Project
Management 686

**APPENDIX A /** Creativity and
Idea Generation 695

A.1 Creativity and the Competitive Firm 696
A.2 Creativity Management 698
A.3 Individual Creativity 699
A.4 Group Creativity 701
A.5 Evaluation of Creativity Methods 706
A.6 Organizing to Allow and Assist
Creativity 707

**APPENDIX B /** Technological
Forecasting 711

B.1 Characteristics, History, and
Importance of Technological
Forecasting 712
B.2 Technological Forecasting Methods 714
B.3 Technological Forecasting in Use 728

**APPENDIX C /** The Normal
Probability Distribution 733

**APPENDIX D /** Matrix
Multiplication 735

**APPENDIX E /** Probability and
Statistics 738

E.1 Probability 738
E.2 Event Relationships and Probability
Laws 739
E.3 Statistics 742

**SOURCENOTES** 749

**NAME INDEX** 753

**SUBJECT INDEX** 760

**PHOTO CREDITS** 767

# CHAPTER

# 2

# Project Selection

Project selection is the process of evaluating individual projects or groups of projects, and then choosing to implement some set of them so that the objectives of the parent organization will be achieved. This same systematic process can be applied to any area of the organization's business in which choices must be made between competing alternatives. For example, a manufacturing firm can use evaluation/selection techniques to choose which machine to adopt in a part-fabrication process; a TV station can pick out which of several syndicated comedy shows to rerun in its 7:30 PM weekday time-slot; a trucking firm can use these methods to decide which of several tractors to purchase; a construction firm can select the best subset of a large group of potential projects on which to bid; a hospital can find the best mix of psychiatric, orthopedic, obstetric, pediatric, and other beds for a new wing; or a research lab can choose the set of R & D projects that holds the best promise of reaching a technological goal.

In this chapter we look at the procedures firms use to decide which creative idea to support, which new technology to develop, which repair to authorize. Each project will have different costs, benefits, and risks. Rarely are these known with certainty. In the face of such differences, the selection of one project out of a set is a difficult task. Choosing a number of different projects, a *portfolio*, is even more complex.

This chapter, like Appendixes A and B, may cover a subject not customarily covered in books on project management. Though the project manager often enters the picture at the stage of the project life cycle following selection, in many situations the project manager is the person who has worked and lobbied for the selection of this specific project, particularly if an RFP (Request For Proposal) was involved. Moreover, though project evaluation and selection is usually a task for senior management, this is an important part of the project life cycle because project success is judged by the degree to which the project meets its goals. Since project selection is based on a direct statement of those goals, the project manager needs to know them in order to perform effectively.

In this chapter we discuss several techniques that can be used to help decision makers select projects. Project selection is only one of many decisions associated with project management. To deal with all of these problems, we use *decision-aiding models*. We need such models because they abstract the relevant issues about a problem from the welter of detail in which the problem is embedded.

Realists cannot solve problems, only idealists can do that. Reality is far too complex to deal with in its entirety. The reality of this page, for instance, includes the weight of ink imprinted on it as well as the number of atoms in the period at the end of this sentence. Those aspects of reality are not relevant to a decision about the proper width of the left margin or the precise position of the page number. An "idealist" is needed to strip away almost all the reality from a problem, leaving only the aspects of the "real" situation with which he or she wishes to deal. This process of carving away the unwanted reality from the bones of a problem is called *modeling the problem*. The idealized version of the problem that results is called a *model*.

The model represents the problem's *structure*, its form. Every problem has a form, though often we may not understand a problem well enough to describe its structure. Several different types of models are available to make the job of modeling the problem easier. *Iconic* models are physical representations of systems. The category includes everything from teddy bears to the dowel rod and styrofoam model of an atom hanging from the ceiling of a high school chemistry lab. *Analogue* models are similar to reality in some respects and different in others. Traditionally, every student of elementary physics was exposed to the hydraulic analogy to explain electricity. This model emphasized the similarities between water pressure and voltage, between the flow of water and the flow of electrical current, between the reservoir and the capacitor. *Verbal* models use words to describe systems—George Orwell's novel *Animal Farm*, for example. *Diagrammatic* models may be used to explain the hierarchical command structure of an army battalion or a business firm, just as *graphic* models may be used to illustrate the equilibrium solution to problems of supply and demand. We will use all these models in this book, as well as *flow graph* and *network* models to help solve scheduling problems, *matrix* models to aid in project evaluation, and *symbolic* (mathematical) models for a number of purposes.

This wide variety of models allows the decision maker considerable choice. Most problems can be modeled in several different ways, and it is often not difficult to transform a problem from one model to another—the transformation from matrix to network to mathematical models, for instance, is usually straightforward. The decision maker usually has some leeway in selecting the model form.

Models may be quite simple to understand, or they may be extremely complex. In general, introducing more reality into a model tends to make the model more difficult to manipulate. If the input data for a model are not known precisely, we often use probabalistic information; that is, the model is said to be *stochastic* rather than *deterministic*. Again, in general, stochastic models are more difficult to manipulate. (Readers who are not familiar with the fundamentals of decision making might find a book such as *The New Science of Management Decisions* [57] or *Fundamentals of Management Science* [65] useful.) A few of the models we discuss employ mathematical programming techniques for solution. These procedures are rarely used, but they illustrate a logic that can be useful; and it is not necessary to understand mathematical programming to profit from the discussion.

This chapter relies heavily on the use of models for project evaluation and selection. First, we examine fundamental types of project selection models and the characteristics that make any model more or less acceptable. Next we consider the limitations, strengths, and weaknesses of project selection models, including some suggestions of factors to consider when making a decision about which, if any, of the selection models to use (see also the end of Section 2.3). We then discuss the problem of selecting projects when high levels of uncertainty about outcomes, costs, schedules, or technology are present. Finally, we comment on some special aspects of the information base required for project selection.

One might argue that we should discuss the *project proposal*, its contents and construction, before considering project selection models. It is, however, useful to understand how an idea will be evaluated before deciding on how best to present the idea. Further, we set aside the issue of where ideas come from and how they are introduced into the process that, sooner or later, results in a proposal. The subject is certainly of consequence, but project managers are rarely directly involved. As a result, consideration of idea generation is relegated to Appendix A. As noted, project proposals are discussed later in this chapter. We finish the chapter with a guess about the future of project selection models.

## ▶ 2.1 CRITERIA FOR PROJECT SELECTION MODELS

We live in the midst of what has been called the "knowledge explosion." We frequently hear such comments as "90 percent of all we know about physics has been discovered since Albert Einstein published his original work on special relativity"; and "80 percent of what we know about the human body has been discovered in the past 50 years." In addition, evidence is cited to show that knowledge is growing exponentially. Such statements emphasize the importance of the *management of change*. To survive, firms must develop strategies for assessing and reassessing the use of their resources. Every allocation of resources is an investment in the future. Because of the complex nature of most strategies, many of these investments are in projects.

To cite one of many possible examples, special visual effects accomplished through computer animation are common in the movies and television shows we watch daily. A few years ago they were unknown. When the capability was in its idea stage, computer companies as well as the firms producing movies and TV shows faced the decision whether or not to invest in the development of these techniques. Obviously valuable as the idea seems today, the choice was not quite so clear a decade ago when an entertainment company compared investment in computer animation to alternative investments in a new star, a new rock group, or a new theme park—or when the computer firm considered alternative investments in a new business software package, a higher resolution color monitor, or a faster processor.

The proper choice of investment projects is crucial to the long-run survival of every firm. Daily we witness the results of both good and bad investment choices. In our daily newspapers we read of Ashland Oil's decision to reformulate its automotive fuel in order to lower pollution at a cost of $0.03 to $0.05 per gallon—at the same time that British Petroleum decides to lower the volatility of its automotive fuel to lower pollution at a cost of $0.01 per gallon. We read of Chrysler's decision to make a major alteration in its passenger car line, of IBM's decision to make significant cuts in the prices of its personal computers, and of the United States congressional decision to withdraw funding from the Super Conducting Super Collider project. But can such important choices be made rationally? Once made, do they ever change, and if so, how? These questions reflect the need for effective selection models.

Within the limits of their capabilities, such models can be used to increase profits, to select investments for limited capital resources, or to improve the competitive position of the organization. They can be used for ongoing evaluation as well as initial selection, and thus are a key to the allocation and reallocation of the organization's scarce resources.

When a firm chooses a project selection model, the following criteria, based on Souder [60], are most important.

1. **Realism**   The model should reflect the reality of the manager's decision situation, including the multiple objectives of both the firm and its managers. Without a common measurement system, direct comparison of different projects is impossible. For example, Project A may strengthen a firm's market share by extending its facilities, and Project B might improve its competitive position by strengthening its technical staff. Other things being equal, which is better? The model should take into account the realities of the firm's limitations on facilities, capital, personnel, etc. The model should also include factors for risk—both the technical risks of performance, cost, and time and the market risk of customer rejection.

2. **Capability**   The model should be sophisticated enough to deal with multiple time periods, simulate various situations both internal and external to the project (e.g., strikes, interest rate changes, etc.), and *optimize* the decision. An optimizing model will make the comparisons that management deems important, consider major risks and constraints on the projects, and then select the best overall project or set of projects.

3. **Flexibility**   The model should give valid results within the range of conditions that the firm might experience. It should have the ability to be easily modified, or to be self-adjusting in response to changes in the firm's environment; for example, tax laws change, new technological advancements alter risk levels, and, above all, the organization's goals change.

4. **Ease of Use**   The model should be reasonably convenient, not take a long time to execute, and be easy to use and understand. It should not require special interpretation, data that are hard to acquire, excessive personnel, or unavailable equipment. The model's variables should also relate one to one with those real-world parameters the managers believe significant to the project. Finally, it should be easy to simulate the expected outcomes associated with investments in different project portfolios.

5. **Cost**   Data-gathering and modeling costs should be low relative to the cost of the project and must surely be less than the potential benefits of the project. All costs should be considered, including the costs of data management and of running the model.

We would add a sixth criterion:

6. ***Easy Computerization***   It must be easy and convenient to gather and store the information in a computer data base, and to manipulate data in the model through use of a widely available, standard computer package such as Lotus 1-2-3®, Quattro Pro®, Excel®, and like programs.

## ▶ 2.2   THE NATURE OF PROJECT SELECTION MODELS

There are two basic types of project selection models, numeric and nonnumeric. Both are widely used. Many organizations use both at the same time, or they use models that are combinations of the two. Nonnumeric models, as the name implies, do not use numbers as inputs. Numeric models do, but the criteria being measured may be either objective or subjective. It is important to remember that the *qualities* of a project may be represented by numbers, and that *subjective* measures are not necessarily less useful or reliable than so-called *objective* measures. (We will discuss these matters in more detail in Section 2.5.)

Before examining specific kinds of models within the two basic types, let us consider just what we wish the model to do for us, never forgetting two critically important, but often overlooked, facts.

- Models do not make decisions; people do. The manager, not the model, bears responsibility for the decision. The manager may "delegate" the task of making the decision to a model, but the responsibility cannot be abdicated.

- All models, however sophisticated, are only partial representations of the reality they are meant to reflect. Reality is far too complex for us to capture more than a small fraction of it in any model. Therefore, no model can yield an optimal decision except within its own, possibly inadequate, framework.

We seek a model to assist us in making project selection decisions. This model should possess the characteristics discussed previously: ease of use, flexibility, low cost, and so on. Above all, it must evaluate potential projects by the degree to which they will meet the firm's objectives. (In general, we will not differentiate between such terms as *goals*, *objectives*, *aims*, etc.) To construct a selection/evaluation model, therefore, it is necessary to develop a list of the firm's objectives.

Such a list should be generated by the organization's top management. It is a direct expression of organizational philosophy and policy. The list should go beyond the typical clichés about "survival" and "maximizing profits," which are certainly real goals but are just as certainly not the only goals of the firm. Others might include maintenance of share of specific markets, development of an improved image with specific clients or competitors, expansion into a new line of business, decrease in sensitivity to business cycles, maintenance of employment for specific categories of workers, and maintenance of system loading at or above some percent of capacity, just to mention a few.

A model of some sort is implied by any conscious decision. The choice between two or more alternative courses of action requires reference to some objective(s), and the choice is thus made in accord with some, possibly subjective, "model."

In the past two or three decades, largely since the development of computers and the establishment of operations research as an academic subject area, the use of formal, numeric models to assist in decision making has expanded. A large majority of such models use financial measures of the "goodness" of a decision. Project selection decisions are no exception, being based primarily on the degree to which the financial goals of the organization are met [35]. As we will see later, this stress on financial goals, largely to the exclusion of other criteria, raises some serious problems for the firm, irrespective of whether the firm is for-profit or not-for-profit.

When the list of objectives has been developed, an additional refinement is recommended. The elements in the list should be weighted. Each item is added to the list because it represents a contribution to the success of the organization, but each item does not make an equal contribution. The weights reflect the different degree of contribution of each element in the set of goals.

Once the list of goals has been developed, one more task remains. A project is selected or rejected because it is predicted to have certain outcomes if implemented. These outcomes are expected to contribute to goal achievement. If the estimated level of goal achievement is sufficiently large, the project is selected. If not, it is rejected. The relationship between the project's expected results and the organization's goals must be understood. In general, the kinds of information required to evaluate a project can be listed under production, marketing, financial, personnel, administrative, and other such categories.

The following is a list of factors that contribute, positively or negatively, to these categories. In order to give focus to this list, we assume that the projects in question involve the possible substitution of a new production process for an existing one. The list is meant to be illustrative. It certainly is not exhaustive.

**Production Factors**

1. Time until ready to install
2. Length of disruption during installation
3. Degree of disruption during installation
4. Learning curve—time until operating as desired
5. Effects on waste and rejects
6. Energy requirements
7. Facility and other equipment requirements
8. Safety of process
9. Other applications of technology
10. Consistency with current technological know-how
11. Change in cost to produce a unit output

**12.** Change in time to produce a unit output
**13.** Change in raw material usage
**14.** Availability of raw materials
**15.** Required development time and cost
**16.** Impact on current suppliers
**17.** Change in quality of output
**18.** Change in quality control procedures

## Marketing Factors

**1.** Size of potential market for output
**2.** Probable market share of output
**3.** Time until market share is acquired
**4.** Impact on current product line
**5.** Ability to control quality
**6.** Consumer acceptance
**7.** Impact on consumer safety
**8.** Estimated life of output
**9.** Shape of output life cycle curve
**10.** Spin-off project possibilities

## Financial Factors

**1.** Profitability, net present value of the investment
**2.** Impact on cash flows
**3.** Payout period
**4.** Cash requirements
**5.** Time until break-even
**6.** Size of investment required
**7.** Impact on seasonal and cyclical fluctuations
**8.** Cost of getting system up to speed
**9.** Level of financial risk

## Personnel Factors

**1.** Training requirements
**2.** Labor skill requirements
**3.** Availability of required labor skills
**4.** Level of resistance from current work force
**5.** Other worker reactions
**6.** Change in size of labor force
**7.** Change in sex, age, or racial distribution of labor force

8. Inter- and intra-group communication requirements
9. Support labor requirements
10. Impact on working conditions

**Administrative and Miscellaneous Factors**

1. Meet government safety standards
2. Meet government environmental standards
3. Impact on information system
4. Impact on computer usage
5. Need for consulting help, inside and outside
6. Reaction of stockholders and securities markets
7. Patent and trade secret protection
8. Impact on image with customers, suppliers, and competitors
9. Cost of maintaining skill in new technology
10. Vulnerability to single supplier
11. Degree to which we understand new technology
12. Elegance of new process
13. Degree to which new process differs from current process
14. Managerial capacity to direct and control new process

Some factors in this list have a one-time impact and some recur. Some are difficult to estimate and may be subject to considerable error. For these, it is helpful to identify a *range of uncertainty*. In addition, the factors may occur at different times. And some factors may have *thresholds*, critical values above or below which we might wish to reject the project.

Clearly, no single project decision need include all these factors. Moreover, not only is the list incomplete, but it contains redundant items. Perhaps more important, the factors are not at the same level of generality: *profitability* and *impact on organizational image* both affect the overall organization, but *impact on working conditions* is more oriented to the production system. Nor are all elements of equal importance. *Change in production cost* is usually considered more important than *impact on computer usage*. Later in this chapter we will deal with the problem of generating an acceptable list of factors and measuring their relative importance. At that time we will discuss the creation of a DSS (Decision Support System) for project evaluation and selection. The same subject will arise once more in Chapters 12 and 13 when we consider project auditing and termination.

Although the process of evaluating a potential project is time-consuming and difficult, its importance cannot be overstated. A major consulting firm has argued [37] that the primary cause for the failure of R & D projects is insufficient care in evaluating the proposal before the expenditure of funds. What is true of R & D projects also appears to be true for other kinds of projects. Careful analysis of a potential project is a *sine qua non* for profitability in the construction business. There are many horror stories [43] about firms that undertook projects for the installation of a computer information system without sufficient analysis of the time, cost, and disruption involved.

Later in this chapter we will consider the problem of conducting an evaluation under conditions of uncertainty about the outcomes associated with a project. Before dealing with this problem, however, it helps to examine several different evaluation/selection models and consider their strengths and weaknesses. Recall that the problem of choosing the project selection model itself will be discussed later in this chapter.

## ▶ 2.3  TYPES OF PROJECT SELECTION MODELS

Of the two basic types of selection models, numeric and nonnumeric, nonnumeric models are older and simpler and have only a few subtypes to consider. We examine them first.

### Nonnumeric Models

*The Sacred Cow*  The project is suggested by a senior and powerful official in the organization. Often the project is initiated with a simple comment such as, "If you have the chance, why don't you look into . . . ," and there follows an undeveloped idea for a new product, for the development of a new market, for the installation of a new decision support system, for the adoption of Material Requirements Planning, or for some other project requiring an investment of the firm's resources. The immediate result of this bland statement is the creation of a "project" to investigate whatever the boss has suggested. The project is "sacred" in the sense that it will be maintained until successfully concluded, or until the boss, personally, recognizes the idea as a failure and terminates it.

*The Operating Necessity*  If a flood is threatening the plant, a project to build a protective dike does not require much formal evaluation. Republic Steel Corporation (now a part of LTV Corp.) has used this criterion (and the following criterion also) in evaluating potential projects. If the project is required in order to keep the system operating, the primary question becomes: Is the system worth saving at the estimated cost of the project? If the answer is yes, project costs will be examined to make sure they are kept as low as is consistent with project success, but the project will be funded.

*The Competitive Necessity*  Using this criterion, Republic Steel undertook a major plant rebuilding project in the late 1960s in its steel-bar-manufacturing facilities near Chicago. It had become apparent to Republic's management that the company's bar mill needed modernization if the firm was to maintain its competitive position in the Chicago market area. Although the planning process for the project was quite sophisticated, the decision to undertake the project was based on a desire to maintain the company's competitive position in that market.

In a similar manner, many business schools are restructuring their undergraduate and MBA programs to stay competitive with the more forward-looking schools.

In large part, this action is driven by declining numbers of tuiton-paying students and the stronger competition to attract them.

Investment in an *operating necessity* project takes precedence over a *competitive necessity* project, but both types of projects may bypass the more careful numeric analysis used for projects deemed to be less urgent or less important to the survival of the firm.

***The Product Line Extension***    A project to develop and distribute new products would be judged on the degree to which it fits the firm's existing product line, fills a gap, strengthens a weak link, or extends the line in a new, desirable direction. Sometimes careful calculations of profitability are not required. Decision makers can act on their beliefs about what will be the likely impact on the total system performance if the new product is added to the line.

***Comparative Benefit Model***    Assume that an organization has many projects to consider, perhaps several dozen. Senior management would like to select a subset of the projects that would most benefit the firm, but the projects do not seem to be easily comparable. For example, some projects concern potential new products, some concern changes in production methods, others concern computerization of certain records, and still others cover a variety of subjects not easily categorized (e.g., a proposal to set up a daycare center for employees with small children). The organization has no formal method of selecting projects, but members of the Selection Committee do think that some projects will benefit the firm more than others, even if they have no precise way to define or measure "benefit."

The concept of comparative benefits, if not a formal model, is widely adopted for selection decisions on all sorts of projects. Most United Way organizations use the concept to make decisions about which of several social programs to fund. The comparative benefit concept is also commonly used when making funding decisions on fundamental research projects. Organizations such as the National Science Foundation, the Office of Naval Research, and a great many other governmental, private, and university sponsors of research usually send project proposals to outside experts in the relevant areas who serve as "referees," a process known as *peer review*. The proposal is evaluated according to the referee's technical criteria, and a recommendation is submitted. Senior management of the funding organization then examines all projects with positive recommendations and attempts to construct a portfolio that best fits the organization's aims and its budget.

Of the several techniques for ordering projects, the Q-Sort [26] is one of the most straightforward. First, the projects are divided into three groups—*good*, *fair*, and *poor*—according to their relative merits. If any group has more than eight members, it is subdivided into two categories, such as *fair-plus* and *fair-minus*. When all categories have eight or fewer members, the projects within each category are ordered from best to worst. Again, the order is determined on the basis of relative merit. The rater may use specific criteria to rank each project, or may simply use general overall judgment. See Figure 2-1 for an example of a Q-Sort.

The process described may be carried out by one person who is responsible for evaluation and selection, or it may be performed by a committee charged with the responsibility. If a committee handles the task, the individual rankings can be devel-

| **Steps** | **Results at Each Step** |
|---|---|
| 1. For each participant in the exercise, assemble a deck of cards, with the name and description of one project on each card. | 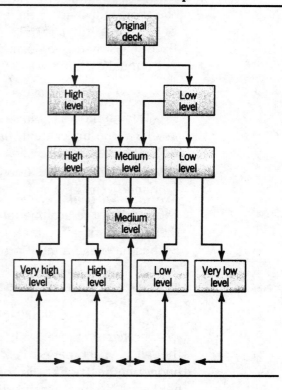 |
| 2. Instruct each participant to divide the deck into two piles, one representing a high priority, the other a low-priority level. (The piles need not be equal.) | |
| 3. Instruct each participant to select cards from each pile to form a third pile representing the medium-priority level. | |
| 4. Instruct each participant to select cards from the high-level pile to yield another pile representing the very high level of priority; select cards from the low-level pile representing the very low level of priority. | |
| 5. Finally, instruct each participant to survey the selections and shift any cards that seem out of place until the classifications are satisfactory. | |

**Figure 2-1:** The Q-sort method. *Source*: [61]

oped anonymously, and the set of anonymous rankings can be examined by the committee itself for consensus. It is common for such rankings to differ somewhat from rater to rater, but they do not often vary strikingly because the individuals chosen for such committees rarely differ widely on what they feel to be appropriate for the parent organization. Projects can then be selected in the order of preference, though they are usually evaluated financially before final selection.

There are other, similar nonnumeric models for accepting or rejecting projects. Although it is easy to dismiss such models as unscientific, they should not be discounted casually. These models are clearly goal-oriented and directly reflect the primary concerns of the organization. The sacred cow model, in particular, has an added feature; sacred cow projects are visibly supported by "the powers that be." Full support by top management is certainly an important contributor to project success [43]. Without such support, the probability of project success is sharply lowered.

## Numeric Models: Profit/Profitability

As noted earlier, a large majority of all firms using project evaluation and selection models use profit/profitability as the sole measure of acceptability. We will consider these models first, and then discuss models that go well beyond the profit test for acceptance.

***Payback Period***   The payback period for a project is the initial fixed investment in the project divided by the estimated annual cash inflows from the project. The ratio of these quantities is the number of years required for the project to repay its initial fixed investment. For example, assume a project costs $100,000 to implement and has annual cash inflows of $25,000. Then

$$\text{Payback period} = \$100,000/\$25,000 = 4 \text{ years}$$

This method assumes that the cash inflows will persist at least long enough to pay back the investment, and it ignores any cash inflows beyond the payback period. The method also serves as an inadequate proxy for risk. The faster the investment is recovered, the less the risk to which the firm is exposed.

***Average Rate of Return***   Often mistakenly taken to be the reciprocal of the payback period, the average rate of return is the ratio of the average annual profit (either before or after taxes) to the initial or average investment in the project. Because average annual profits are not equivalent to net cash inflows, the average rate of return does not equal the reciprocal of the payback period. Assume, in the example just given, that the average annual profits are $15,000:

$$\text{Average rate of return} = \$15,000/\$100,000 = 0.15$$

Neither of these evaluation methods is recommended for project selection, though payback period is widely used and does have a legitimate value for cash budgeting decisions. The major advantage of these models is their simplicity, but neither takes into account the time value of money. Unless interest rates are extremely low and the rate of inflation is nil, the failure to reduce future cash flows or profits to their present value will result in serious evaluation errors.

***Discounted Cash Flow***   Also referred to as the present value method, the discounted cash flow method determines the net present value of all cash flows by discounting them by the required rate of return (also known as the *hurdle rate, cutoff rate,* and similar terms) as follows,

$$\text{NPV (project)} = A_0 + \sum_{t=1}^{n} \frac{F_t}{(1+k)^t}$$

*where*

$F_t$ = the net cash flow in period $t$,

$k$ = the required rate of return, and

$A_0$ = initial cash investment (because this is an outflow, it will be negative).

To include the impact of inflation (or deflation) where $p_t$ is the predicted rate of inflation during period $t$, we have

$$\text{NPV (project)} = A_0 + \sum_{t=1}^{n} \frac{F_t}{(1+k+p_t)^t}$$

Early in the life of a project, net cash flow is likely to be negative, the major outflow being the initial investment in the project, $A_0$. If the project is successful, however, cash flows will become positive. The project is *acceptable* if the sum of the net present values of all estimated cash flows over the life of the project is positive. A simple example will suffice. Using our $100,000 investment with a net cash inflow of $25,000 per year for a period of eight years, a required rate of return of 15 percent, and an inflation rate of 3 percent per year, we have

$$\text{NPV (project)} = -\$100,000 + \sum_{t=1}^{8} \frac{\$25,000}{(1 + 0.15 + 0.03)^t}$$

$$= \$1939$$

Because the present value of the inflows is greater than the present value of the outflow—that is, the net present value is positive—the project is deemed acceptable.

---

## PsychoCeramic Sciences, Inc.

PsychoCeramic Sciences, Inc. (PSI), a large producer of cracked pots and other cracked items, is considering the installation of a new manufacturing line that will, it is hoped, allow more precise quality control on the size, shape, and location of the cracks in its pots as well as in vases designed to hold artificial flowers.

The plant engineering department has submitted a project proposal that estimates the investment requirements as follows: an initial investment of $125,000 to be paid up-front to the Pocketa-Pocketa Machine Corporation, an additional investment of $100,000 to install the machines, and another $90,000 to add new material handling systems and integrate the new equipment into the overall production system. Delivery and installation is estimated to take one year, and integrating the entire system should require an additional year. Thereafter, the engineers predict that scheduled machine overhauls will require further expenditures of about $15,000 every second year, beginning in the fourth year. They will not, however, overhaul the machinery in the last year of its life.

The project schedule calls for the line to begin production in the third year, and to be up-to-speed by the end of that year. Projected manufacturing cost savings and added profits resulting from higher quality are estimated to be $50,000 in the first year of operation and are expected to peak at $120,000 in the second year of operation, and then to follow the gradually declining pattern shown in the table at the end of this box.

Project life is expected to be 10 years from project inception, at which time the proposed system will be obsolete and will have to be replaced. It is estimated that the machinery will have a salvage value of $35,000.

PSI has a 12 percent hurdle rate for capital investments and expects the rate of inflation to be about 3 percent over the life of the project. Assuming that the initial expenditure occurs at the beginning of the year and that all other receipts and expenditures occur as lump sums at the end of the year, we can prepare the Net Present Value analysis for the project shown in the table.

The Net Present Value of the project is positive and, thus, the project can be accepted. (The project would have been rejected if the hurdle rate were 14 percent.)

Just for the intellectual exercise, note that the total inflow for the project is $759,000, or

$75,900 per year *on average* for the 10 year project. The required investment is $315,000 (ignoring the biennial overhaul charges). Assuming 10 year, straight line depreciation or $31,500 per year, the payback period would be

$$PB = \frac{\$315,000}{\$75,900 + 31,500} = 2.9 \text{ years}$$

A project with this payback period would probably be considered quite desirable.

| Year A | Inflow B | Outflow C | Net Flow D = (B – C) | Discount Factor $1/(1 + k + p)^t$ | Net Present Value D(Disc. Fact.) |
|---|---|---|---|---|---|
| 1996* | $ 0 | $125,000 | $−125,000 | 1.0000 | $−125,000 |
| 1996 | 0 | 100,000 | −100,000 | 0.8696 | −86,960 |
| 1997 | 0 | 90, 000 | − 90,000 | 0.7561 | −68,049 |
| 1998 | 50,000 | 0 | 50,000 | 0.6575 | 32,875 |
| 1999 | 120,000 | 15,000 | 105,000 | 0.5718 | 60,039 |
| 2000 | 115,000 | 0 | 115,000 | 0.4972 | 57,178 |
| 2001 | 105,000 | 15,000 | 90,000 | 0.4323 | 38,907 |
| 2002 | 97,000 | 0 | 97,000 | 0.3759 | 36,462 |
| 2003 | 90,000 | 15,000 | 75,000 | 0.3269 | 24,518 |
| 2004 | 82,000 | 0 | 82,000 | 0.2843 | 23,313 |
| 2005 | 65,000 | 0 | 65,000 | 0.2472 | 16,068 |
| 2005 | 35,000 | | 35,000 | 0.2472 | 8,652 |
| Total | $759,000 | $360,000 | $ 399,000 | | $ 18,003 |

*$t = 0$ at the beginning of 1996.

***Internal Rate of Return*** If we have a set of expected cash inflows and cash outflows, the internal rate of return is the discount rate that equates the present values of the two sets of flows. If $A_t$ is an expected cash outflow in the period $t$ and $R_t$ is the expected inflow for the period $t$, the internal rate of return is the value of $k$ that satisfies the following equation (note that the $A_0$ will be positive in this formulation of the problem):

$$A_0 + A_1/(1 + k) + A_2/(1 + k)^2 + \ldots + A_n/(1 + k)^n = R_1/(1 + k) + R_2/(1 + k)^2 + \ldots + R_n/(1 + k)^n \quad t = 1,2,3, \ldots ,n$$

The value of $k$ is found by trial and error.

***Profitability Index*** Also known as the benefit–cost ratio, the profitability index is the net present value of all future expected cash flows divided by the initial cash investment. (Some firms do not discount the cash flows in making this calculation.) If this ratio is greater than 1.0, the project may be accepted.

***Other Profitability Models*** There are a great many variations of the models just described. These variations fall into three general categories: (1) those that subdivide net cash flow into the elements that comprise the net flow, (2) those that include specific terms to introduce risk (or uncertainty, which is treated as risk) into the evaluation, and (3) those that extend the analysis to consider effects that the project might have on other projects or activities in the organization. Two product line extension models, taken from Dean [16], will illustrate these methods.

**Pacifico's Method**  PI is the profitability index of acceptability where

$$PI = rdpc\ SP\ \sqrt{L}/C,$$

   $r$ = probability of research success,

   $d$ = probability of development success, given research success,

   $p$ = probability of process success, given development success, and

   $c$ = probability of commercial success, given process success.

The investment, $C$, is the estimated total cost of the R & D effort for the project. Risk is incorporated in the $rdpc$ term.
The cash flow is $SP\ \sqrt{L}$ where

$S$ = estimated average annual sales volume in units of product,

$P$ = estimated average annual profit per unit, and

$L$ = estimated life of the product extension in years. (Note that although the profits are not formally discounted, they are "devalued" over time by multiplying them by $\sqrt{L}$ rather than by $L$.)

**Dean's Profitability Method**  Dean's model contains a term that subtracts the unit manufacturing cost and the unit selling and administrative costs from the unit price, multiplies the remainder by the expected number of units sold per year, and then subtracts tooling and development costs (a project risk factor is also included). All costs and revenues are time-indexed and discounted to the present. Dean modifies his model to deal with three distinct cases: (1) where the product extension has no significant impact on the existing system, (2) where the product extension may affect the profitability or the sales of existing products, or both, and (3) where the product extension is a replacement for an existing product.

Several comments are in order about all the profit–profitability numeric models. First, let us consider their advantages.

1. The undiscounted models are simple to use and understand.

2. All use readily available accounting data to determine the cash flows.

3. Model output is in terms familiar to business decision makers.

4. With a few exceptions, model output is on an "absolute" profit/profitability scale and allows "absolute" go/no-go decisions.

5. Some profit models account for project risk.

6. Dean's model includes the impact of the project on the rest of the organization.

The disadvantages of these models are the following.

1. These models ignore all nonmonetary factors except risk.

2. Models that do not include discounting ignore the timing of the cash flows and the time value of money.

3. Models that reduce cash flows to their present value are strongly biased toward the short run.

4. Payback-type models ignore cash flows beyond the payback period.

5. The IRR model can result in multiple solutions.

6. All are sensitive to errors in the input data for the early years of the project.

7. All discounting models are nonlinear, and the effects of changes (or errors) in the variables or parameters are generally not obvious to most decision makers.

8. Those models incorporating the risks of research and/or development and/or process (the commercial success risk factor is excluded from this comment) mislead the decision maker. It is not so much that the research–development–process success is risky as it is that the time and cost required to ensure project success is uncertain. The application of these risk terms applies mainly to R & D projects.

9. Some models, Dean's and Pacifico's, for example, are oriented only toward evaluation of projects that result in new products.

10. All these models depend for input on a determination of cash flows, but it is not clear exactly how the concept of cash flow is properly defined for the purpose of evaluating projects. (This problem is discussed later in this chapter.)

A complete discussion of profit/profitability models can be found in any standard work on financial management—see [1, 9, 67], for example. In general, the net present value models are preferred to the internal rate of return models.

In our experience the payback period model, occasionally using discounted cash flows, is one of the most commonly used models for evaluating projects and other investment opportunities. Managers generally feel that insistence on short payout periods tends to minimize the uncertainties associated with the passage of time. While this is certainly logical, we prefer evaluation methods that discount cash flows and deal with uncertainty more directly by considering specific risks. Using the payout period as a cash-budgeting tool aside, *its only virtue is simplicity*, a dubious virtue at best.

---

## Project Management in Practice
### *Estimating Electronic System Costs for Future Projects*

In the early 1980s, the U.S. Air Force found that it needed to be able to predict the flight test costs (one of eight cost predictions required for a full estimate) of electronic warfare systems such as radar warning receivers, electronic countermeasure radiating devices, and chaff dispensers. This task was an exceptionally difficult one due not only to the rapid technological advancements being made in the electronics field, but particularly because the estimates had to be made up to six years before the equipment would incur those costs; that is, even before the system was conceptualized or defined!

---

*Source*: J.R. Ward, "Project Management Cost Estimate: A Case Study in Electronic Warfare System Flight Test Costs," *Project Management Journal*, December 1984.

Cost estimating approaches based on estimating the costs of the system components could not be used because the components were often not even identified six years beforehand. Sometimes the only data available was the nature of the enemy system to be countered, or possibly, only the general type of equipment to be used. Thus, an approach was used based on independent variables with strong causal links to the dependent variable of interest: the flight test cost. Two general rules were employed to select variables to be included in a variety of statistical models available for test: (1) a logical, causal relationship must exist between the variable and the flight test cost, and (2) the variable must relate to an equipment characteristic that can be identified early in the equipment's conceptual phase. Based on these rules, the following variables were selected for testing:

weight, density, volume, input power, equipment type, whether new or modified equipment, and the phase of development for the flight tests.

Two statistical models offered good results (high correlations with actual flight test costs) but had problems unique to each of them. A linear regression model was unable to employ a number of key variables that would have offered good predictive ability. A principle components analysis model had two problems: (1) it used many cross-product variables whose causality was unclear, and (2) it only allowed a point estimate to be made without a confidence interval or trade-off figures.

Nevertheless, the study was considered highly successful, offering almost 90 percent explained variance for systems six years prior to actual use.

## Numeric Models: Scoring

In an attempt to overcome some of the disadvantages of profitability models, particularly their focus on a single decision criterion, a number of evaluation/selection models that use multiple criteria to evaluate a project have been developed. Such models vary widely in their complexity and information requirements. The examples discussed illustrate some of the different types.

***Unweighted 0–1 Factor Model***   A set of relevant factors is selected by management. These are usually listed in a preprinted form, and one or more raters score the project on each factor depending on whether or not it qualifies for that individual criterion. The raters are chosen by senior managers, for the most part from the rolls of senior management. The criteria for choice are a clear understanding of organizational goals and a good knowledge of the firm's potential project *portfolio*. Figure 2-2 shows an example of the rating sheet for an unweighted, 0–1 factor model.

The columns of Figure 2-2 are summed and those projects with a sufficient number of qualifying factors may be selected. The main advantage of such a model is that it uses several criteria in the decision process. The major disadvantages are that it assumes all criteria are of equal importance and it allows for no gradation of the degree to which a specific project meets the various criteria.

***Unweighted Factor Scoring Model***   The second disadvantage of the 0–1 factor model can be dealt with by constructing a simple linear measure of the degree to which the project being evaluated meets each of the criteria contained in the list.

Project _____

Rater _____ Date _____

| | Qualifies | Does Not Qualify |
|---|---|---|
| No increase in energy requirements | x | |
| Potential market size, dollars | x | |
| Potential market share, percent | x | |
| No new facility required | x | |
| No new technical expertise required | | x |
| No decrease in quality of final product | x | |
| Ability to manage project with current personnel | | x |
| No requirement for reorganization | x | |
| Impact on work force safety | x | |
| Impact on environmental standards | x | |
| Profitability | | |
|   Rate of return more than 15% after tax | x | |
|   Estimated annual profits more than $250,000 | x | |
| Time to break-even less than 3 years | x | |
| Need for external consultants | | x |
| Consistency with current lines of business | | x |
| Impact on company image | | |
|   With customers | x | |
|   With our industry | | x |
| Totals | 12 | 5 |

*Figure* **2-2:** Sample project evaluation form.

The x marks in Figure 2-2 would be replaced by numbers. Often a five-point scale is used, where 5 is very good, 4 is good, 3 is fair, 2 is poor, 1 is very poor. (Three-, seven-, and 10-point scales are also common.) The second column of Figure 2-2 would not be needed. The column of scores is summed, and those projects with a total score exceeding some critical value are selected. A variant of this selection process might select the highest-scoring projects (still assuming they are all above some critical score) until the estimated costs of the set of projects equaled the resource limit. The criticism that the criteria are all assumed to be of equal importance still holds.

The use of a discrete numeric scale to represent the degree to which a criterion is satisfied is widely accepted. To construct such measures for project evaluation, we proceed in the following manner. Select a criterion, say, "estimated annual profits in dollars." For this criterion, determine five ranges of performance so that a typical project, chosen at random, would have a roughly equal chance of being in any one of the five performance ranges. (Another way of describing this condition is: Take a large number of projects that were selected for support in the past, regardless of whether they were actually successful or not, and create five levels of predicted performance so that about one-fifth of the projects fall into each level.) This procedure will usually create unequal ranges, which may offend our sense of symmetry but need not concern us otherwise. It ensures that each criterion performance measure utilizes the full scale of possible values, a desirable characteristic for performance measures.

Consider the following two simple examples. Using the criterion just mentioned, "estimated annual profits in dollars," we might construct the following scale:

| Score | Performance Level |
|-------|-------------------|
| 5 | Above $1,100,000 |
| 4 | $750,001 to $1,100,000 |
| 3 | $500,001 to $750,000 |
| 2 | $200,000 to $500,000 |
| 1 | Less than $200,000 |

As suggested, these ranges might have been chosen so that about 20 percent of the projects considered for funding would fall into each of the five ranges.

The criterion "no decrease in quality of the final product" would have to be restated to be scored on a five-point scale, perhaps as follows:

| Score | Performance Level |
|-------|-------------------|
| | The quality of the final product is: |
| 5 | significantly and visibly improved |
| 4 | significantly improved, but not visible to buyer |
| 3 | not significantly changed |
| 2 | significantly lowered, but not visible to buyer |
| 1 | significantly and visibly lowered |

This scale is an example of scoring cells that represent opinion rather than objective (even if "estimated") fact, as was the case in the profit scale.

***Weighted Factor Scoring Model***  When numeric weights reflecting the relative importance of each individual factor are added, we have a weighted factor scoring model. In general, it takes the form

$$S_i = \sum_{j=1}^{n} s_{ij} w_j \qquad j = 1, 2, 3, \ldots, n$$

*where*

$S_i$ = the total score of the *i*th project,
$s_{ij}$ = the score of the *i*th project on the *j*th criterion, and
$w_j$ = the weight of the *j*th criterion.

The weights, $w_j$, may be generated by any technique that is acceptable to the organization's policy makers. There are several techniques available to generate such numbers, but the most effective and most widely used is the Delphi technique. The Delphi technique was developed by Brown and Dalkey of the Rand Corporation during the 1950s and 1960s [15]. It is a technique for developing numeric values that are equivalent to subjective, verbal measures of relative value. (The method is also useful for developing technological forecasts. For a description of the technique see Appendix B and also reference [31] in the bibliography to that appendix.) The method of successive comparisons (or pairwise comparisons) may also be used for the same purpose. Originally described by Churchman, Ackoff, and Arnoff in their classic text on operations research [10], this technique asks the decision maker to make a series of choices between several different sets of alternatives. A set of numbers is then found that is consistent with the choices. These numbers can serve as weights in the scoring model. For an example of the use of this method, see [18]. Another popular and quite similar approach is the Analytic Hierarchy Process, developed by Saaty, see [54, 65] for details.

When numeric weights have been generated, it is helpful (but not necessary) to scale the weights so that

$$0 \leq w_j \leq 1 \qquad j = 1,2,3, \ldots, n$$

$$\sum_{j=1}^{n} w_j = 1$$

The weight of each criterion can be interpreted as the "percent of the total weight accorded to that particular criterion."

A special caveat is in order. It is quite possible with this type of model to include a large number of criteria. It is not particularly difficult to develop scoring scales and weights, and the ease of gathering and processing the required information makes it tempting to include marginally relevant criteria along with the obviously important items. Resist this temptation! After the important factors have been weighted, there usually is little residual weight to be distributed among the remaining elements. The result is that the evaluation is simply insensitive to major differences in the scores on trivial criteria. A good rule of thumb is to discard elements with weights less than 0.02 or 0.03. (If elements are discarded, and if you wish $\sum w_j = 1$, the weights must be rescaled to 1.0.) As with any linear model, the user should be aware that the elements in the model are assumed to be independent. This presents no particular problems for these scoring models because they are used to make estimates in a "steady state" system, and we are not concerned with transitions between states.

It is useful to note that if one uses a weighted scoring model to aid in project selection, the model can also serve as an aid to project *improvement*. For any given criterion, the difference between the criterion's score and the highest possible score on that criterion, multiplied by the weight of the criterion, is a measure of the potential improvement in the project score that would result were the project's performance on that criterion sufficiently improved. It may be that such improvement is not feasible, or is more costly than the improvement warrants. On the other hand, such an analysis of each project yields a valuable statement of the comparative benefits of project improvements. Viewing a project in this way is a type of *sensitivity analysis*. We examine the degree to which a project's score is sensitive to attempts to improve it—usually by adding resources. We will use sensitivity analysis several times in this book. It is a powerful managerial technique.

It is not particularly difficult to computerize a weighted scoring model by creating a template on Lotus 1-2-3 or one of the other standard computer spreadsheets. In Chapter 13, Section 13.3 we discuss an example of a computerized scoring model used for the project termination decision. The model is, in fact, a project selection model. The logic of using a "selection" model for the termination decision is straightforward: Given the time and resources required to take a project from its current state to completion, should we make the investment? A "Yes" answer to that question "selects" for funding the partially completed project from the set of all partially finished and not-yet-started projects.

---

## Gettin' Wheels

Rather than using an example in which actual projects are selected for funding with a weighted factor scoring model (hereafter "scoring model") which would require tediously long descriptions of the projects, we can demonstrate the use of the model in a simple, common problem that many readers will have faced—the choice of an automobile for purchase. This problem is nicely suited to use of the scoring model because the purchaser is trying to satisfy multiple objectives in making the purchase and is typically faced with several different alternative cars from which to choose.

Our model must have the following elements:

1. A set of criteria on which to judge the value of any alternative;

2. A numeric estimate of the relative importance (i.e., the "weight") of each criterion in the set; and

3. Scales by which to measure or score the performance or contribution to value of each alternative on each criterion.

The criteria weights and measures of performance must be numeric in form, but this does not mean that they must be either "objective" or "quantitative." (If you find this confusing, look ahead in this chapter and read the subsection entitled "Comments on Measurement" in Section 2.5.) Criteria weights, obviously, are subjective by their nature, being an expression of what the decision maker thinks is important. The development of performance scales is more easily dealt with in the context of our example, and we will develop them shortly.

Assume that we have chosen the criteria and weights shown in Table A to be used in our evaluations.* The weights represent the relative importance of the criteria measured on a 10-point scale. The numbers in parentheses show the proportion of the total weight carried by each criterion. (They add to only .99 due to rounding.) Raw weights work just as well for decision making as their percentage counterparts, but the latter are usually preferred because they are a constant reminder to the decision maker of the impact of each of the criteria.

---

* The criteria and weights were picked arbitrarily for this example. Because this is typically an individual or family decision, techniques like Delphi or successive comparisons are not required.

**Table A** Criteria and Weights for
Automobile Purchase

| | | |
|---|---|---|
| Appearance | 4 | (.10) |
| Braking | 3 | (.07) |
| Comfort | 7 | (.17) |
| Cost, operating | 5 | (.12) |
| Cost, original | 10 | (.24) |
| Handling | 7 | (.17) |
| Reliability | 5 | (.12) |
| Total | 41 | 99 |

Prior to consideration of performance standards and sources of information for the criteria we have chosen, we must ask, "Are there any characteristics that must be present (or absent) in a candidate automobile for it to be acceptable?" Assume, for this example, that to be acceptable, an alternative must not be green, must have air conditioning, must be able to carry at least four adults, must have at least 10 cubic feet of luggage space, and must be priced less than $33,000. If an alternative violates any of these conditions, it is immediately rejected.

For each criterion, we need some way of measuring the estimated performance of each alternative. In this case, we might adopt the measures shown in Table B. Our purpose is to transform a measure of the degree to which an alternative meets a criterion into a score, the $s_{ij}$, that is a general measure of the utility or value of the alternative with respect to that criterion. Note that this requires us to define the criterion precisely as well as to specify a source for the information.

Figure A shows the scores for each criterion transformed to a 5-point scale, which will suffice for our ratings.

Using the performance scores shown in Figure A, we can evaluate the cars we have identified as our alternatives: the Leviathan 8, the NuevoEcon, the Maxivan, the Sporticar 100, and the Ritzy 300. Each car is scored on each criterion according to the categories shown in Figure A. Then each score is multiplied by the criterion weight and the result is entered into the appropriate box in Figure B. Last, the results for each alternative are summed to represent the weighted score.

According to this set of measures, we prefer the Ritzy 300, but while it is a clear winner over the Leviathan 8 and the Maxivan, and scores about 8 percent better than the Sporticar, it rates only about 0.13 points or 4 percent above the NuevoEcon. Note that if we overrated the Ritzy by one point on Comfort or Handling, or if we underrated the NuevoEcon by one point on either of these criteria, the result would have been reversed. (We assume that the original cost data are accurate.) With the scores this close, we might want to evaluate these two cars by additional criteria (e.g., ease of carrying children, status,

**Table B** Automobile Selection Criteria, Measures and Data Sources

| | |
|---|---|
| Appearance | Subjective judgment, personal |
| Braking | Distance in feet, 60–0 mph, automotive magazine[a] |
| Comfort | Subjective judgment, 30 min. road test |
| Cost, operating | Annual insurance cost plus fuel cost[b] |
| Cost, original | Dealer cost, auto-cost service[c] |
| Handling | Average speed through standard slalom, automotive magazine[a] |
| Reliability | Score on *Consumer Reports*, "Frequency-of-Repair" data (average of 2 previous years) |

[a]Many automotive periodicals conduct standardized performance tests of new cars.

[b]Annual fuel cost is calculated as (17,500 mi/DOE ave. mpg) × $1.25/gal.

[c]There are several sources for dealer-cost data (e.g., AAA, which provides a stable data base on which to estimate the price of each alternative).

| Criteria | Scores | | | | |
|---|---|---|---|---|---|
| | 1 | 2 | 3 | 4 | 5 |
| Appearance | Ugh | Poor | Adequate | Good | WOW |
| Braking | >165 | 165–150 | 150–140 | 140–130 | <130 |
| Comfort | Bad | Poor | Adequate | Good | Excellent |
| Cost, operating* | >$2.5 | $2.1–2.5 | $1.9–2.1 | $1.6–1.9 | <$1.6 |
| Cost, original* | >$26.5 | $19–26.5 | $14.5–19 | $10–14.5 | < $10 |
| Handling | <45 | 45–49.5 | 49.5–55 | 55–59 | >59 |
| Reliability | Worst | Poor | Adequate | Good | Excellent |

*Cost data in $1000s

**Figure A:** Performance measures and equivalent scores for selection of an automobile.

safety features like dual airbags or ABS, etc.) prior to making a firm decision.

All in all, if the decision maker has well delineated objectives, and can determine how specific kinds of performance contribute to those criteria, and finally, can measure those kinds of performance for each of the alternative courses of action, then the scoring model is a powerful and flexible tool. To the extent that criteria are not carefully defined, performance is not well linked to the criteria, and is carelessly or wrongly measured, the scoring model rests on a faulty foundation and is merely a convenient path to error.

| Alternatives | Criteria and Weights | | | | | | | |
|---|---|---|---|---|---|---|---|---|
| | Appearance (0.10) | Braking (0.07) | Comfort (0.17) | Cost, operating (0.12) | Cost, original (0.24) | Handling (0.17) | Reliability (0.12) | $\sum s_{ij} w_j$ |
| Leviathan 8 | 3×0.1 =0.30 | 1×0.07 =0.07 | 4×0.17 =0.68 | 2×0.12 =0.24 | 1×0.24 =0.24 | 2×0.17 =0.34 | 3×0.12 =0.36 | 2.23 |
| NuevoEcon | 3×0.1 =0.30 | 3×.07 =.21 | 2×0.17 =0.34 | 5×0.12 =0.60 | 4×0.24 =0.96 | 2×0.17 =0.34 | 4×0.12 =0.48 | 3.23 |
| Maxivan | 2×0.1 =0.20 | 1×0.07 =0.07 | 4×0.17 =0.68 | 4×0.12 =0.48 | 3×0.24 =0.72 | 1×0.17 =0.17 | 3×0.12 =0.36 | 2.68 |
| Sporticar 100 | 5×0.1 =0.50 | 4×0.07 =0.28 | 3×0.17 =0.51 | 2×0.12 =0.24 | 2×0.24 =0.48 | 5×0.17 =0.85 | 2×0.12 =0.24 | 3.10 |
| Ritzy 300 | 4×0.1 =0.40 | 5×0.07 =0.35 | 5×0.17 =0.85 | 2×0.12 =0.24 | 1×0.24 =0.24 | 4×0.17 =0.68 | 5×0.12 =0.60 | 3.36 |

**Figure B:** Scores for alternative cars on selection criteria.

***Constrained Weighted Factor Scoring Model*** The temptation to include marginal criteria can be partially overcome by allowing additional criteria to enter the model as constraints rather than weighted factors. These constraints represent project characteristics that *must* be present or absent in order for the project to be acceptable. In our example concerning a product, we might have specified that we would not undertake any project that would significantly lower the quality of the final product (visible to the buyer or not).

We would amend the weighted scoring model to take the form:

$$S_i = \sum_{j=1}^{n} s_{ij} w_j \prod_{k=1}^{v} c_{ik}$$

where $c_{ik} = 1$ if the $i$th project satisfies the $k$th of $v$ constraints, and 0 if it does not. Other elements in the model are as defined earlier.

Although this model is analytically tidy, in practice we would not bother to evaluate projects that are so unsuitable in some ways that we would not consider supporting them regardless of their expected performance against other criteria. For example, except under extraordinary circumstances, Procter & Gamble would not consider a project for adding a new consumer product or product line:

- that cannot be marketed nationally,
- that cannot be distributed through mass outlets (grocery stores, drugstores),
- that will not generate gross revenues in excess of $ ———— million,
- for which Procter & Gamble's potential market share is not at least 50 percent,
- that does not utilize Procter & Gamble's scientific expertise, manufacturing expertise, advertising expertise, or packaging and distribution expertise.

Again, a caveat is in order. Exercise care when adopting constraints. It may seem obvious that we should not consider any project if it has no reasonable assurance of long-run profitability. But such a constraint can force us to overlook a project that, though unprofitable itself, might have a strong, positive impact on the profitability of other projects in which we are interested.

***Dean and Nishry's Model*** Beginning with the weighted factor scoring model, Dean and Nishry [16] cast the project selection decision in the form of an integer programming problem. In the problem

$$S_i = \sum_{j=1}^{n} w_j s_{ij}$$

$$\max x_i \left\{ \sum_{i=1}^{n} x_i S_i \right\}$$

such that

$$x_i = 0 \text{ or } 1$$

and

$$\sum_{i=1}^{n} x_i m_i \leq M$$

where $m_i$ is the resource (labor, capital, etc.) requirement for the $i$th project, and $M$ is the total amount of the resource available for use. The value of $x_i = 0$ or 1 depends on whether or not the $i$th project is selected.

In essence, the Dean and Nishry approach selects the highest-scoring project candidates from the scoring model, and selects them one after another until the available resources have been depleted. If there are several scarce resources, the selection problem can be recast and solved by dynamic programming methods. There are several other R & D project evaluation/selection models described in this excellent work [16]. Many are adaptable to a wide variety of project types.

***Goal Programming with Multiple Objectives***  Goal programming is a variation of the general linear programming method that can optimize an objective function with multiple objectives. In order to apply this method to project selection, we adopt a linear, 0–1 goal program.

First, establish a set of objectives such as "maximize equipment utilization," "minimize idle labor crews," "maximize profits," and "satisfy investment budget constraints." Alternative sets of projects are adopted or rejected based on their impact on goal achievement. A detailed discussion of goal programming is beyond the scope of this book. The interested reader should consult any modern text on management science, for example, [63, 65].

Because most real-world problems are too large for analytic solutions, heuristic solutions are necessary. Ignizio [30, pp. 202–206] has developed a heuristic approach that is easily applied to project selection.

As was the case with profitability models, scoring models have their own characteristic advantages and disadvantages. These are the advantages.

1. These models allow multiple criteria to be used for evaluation and decision, including profit/profitability models and both tangible and intangible criteria.

2. They are structurally simple and therefore easy to understand and use.

3. They are a direct reflection of managerial policy.

4. They are easily altered to accommodate changes in the environment or managerial policy.

5. Weighted scoring models allow for the fact that some criteria are more important than others.

6. These models allow easy sensitivity analysis. The trade-offs between the several criteria are readily observable.

The disadvantages are the following.

1. The output of a scoring model is strictly a relative measure. Project scores do not represent the value or "utility" associated with a project and thus do not directly indicate whether or not the project should be supported.

2. In general, scoring models are linear in form and the elements of such models are assumed to be independent.

3. The ease of use of these models is conducive to the inclusion of a large number of criteria, most of which have such small weights that they have little impact on the total project score.

4. Unweighted scoring models assume all criteria are of equal importance, which is almost certainly contrary to fact.

5.  To the extent that profit/profitability is included as an element in the scoring model, this element has the advantages and disadvantages noted earlier for the profitability models themselves.

## Selecting Projects within a Program

This project selection technique is a special type of weighted scoring model. Let us pose a more complex selection problem. Presume that one of a drug firm's three R & D laboratories has adopted a research program aimed at the development of a family of compounds for the treatment of a related set of diseases. An individual project is created for each compound in the family in order to test the compound's efficacy, to test for side effects, to find and install efficient methods for producing the compound in quantity, and to develop marketing strategies for each separate member of the drug family. Assume further that many aspects of the research work on any one compound both profits from and contributes to the work done on other members of the family. In such a case, how does one evaluate a project associated with any given member of the family? *One doesn't!*

To evaluate each project–drug family combination would require a separation of costs and revenues that would be quite impossible except when based on the most arbitrary allocations. Instead of inviting the political bloodletting that would inevitably accompany any such approach, let us attempt to evaluate the performance of *all* the projects as well as the laboratory that directed and carried out the entire program—and that may be conducting other programs at the same time.

B. V. Dean has developed an ingenious technique for accomplishing such an evaluation [17]. This tool not only helps identify the most desirable projects but can also be used as a planning tool to identify resource needs, especially for *large* projects. Consider Figure 2-3. R & D Laboratory A is conducting a set of interrelated projects in Program 1. Project $i$ contributes to technology $j$, one of a set of desirable technologies that, in turn, makes a contribution to requirement $k$, one of a desired set of end requirements with some value $V_k$, the sum of all values being 1.0.

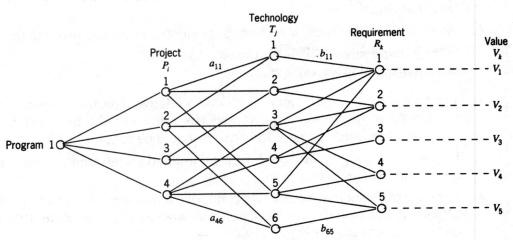

**Figure 2-3:** Evaluation of a related set of projects for R & D lab A.

Now consider the set of projects, $P_i$, and the technologies, $T_j$. We can form the transfer matrix

$$\mathbf{A} = [a_{ij}]$$

composed of ones and zeros as follows:

$$a_{ij} = \begin{cases} 1, \text{ if } P_i \text{ contributes to } T_j \\ 0, \text{ if } P_i \text{ does not contribute to } T_j \end{cases}$$

Similarly, we form the transfer matrix

$$\mathbf{B} = [b_{jk}]$$

composed of ones and zeros as follows:

$$b_{jk} = \begin{cases} 1, \text{ if } T_j \text{ contributes to } R_k \\ 0, \text{ if not} \end{cases}$$

Now find

$$\mathbf{C} = [c_{ik}]$$

where

$$\mathbf{C} = \mathbf{AB}$$

The resultant matrix will link $P_i$ directly to $R_k$, thus indicating which projects contribute to which requirements.*

Now consider the value set $V_k$. "Normalize" $V_k$ so that

$$\sum_k V_k = 1$$

Each normalized $V_k$ will represent the *relative* value of $R_k$ in the set $\{R_k\}$. The values can be written as a column matrix

$$\mathbf{V} = [V_k]$$

Note that a project, $P_i$, that contributes to a requirement, $R_k$, in $c_{ik}$ ways will have a value

$$c_{ik} V_k$$

and that the *total* value of $P_i$ is thus

$$e_i = \sum_k c_{ik} V_k$$

The column matrix $\mathbf{E} = [e_i]$ is the set of values for all projects in the laboratory, and the sum of all project values,

$$\mathbf{E}^* = \sum_i e_i = \mathbf{JE}$$

where **J** is a row matrix consisting of ones.

$$\begin{aligned} \mathbf{E}^* &= \mathbf{JE} \\ &= \mathbf{JCV} \\ &= \mathbf{JABV} \end{aligned}$$

---

*This step requires the arithmetic process of matrix multiplication. The process is not difficult. An explanation of the methods together with a short example is presented in Appendix D. The method is further illustrated in Case II of this chapter.

***Example*** An R & D program consists of two projects, four technologies, and three requirements. Project 1 contributes to technologies 1 and 4 only but project 2 contributes to technologies 2, 3, and 4. Technology 1 contributes to requirement 2 only and technology 4 contributes to requirement 1 only. Technologies 2 and 3 contribute to requirements 1 and 3 and requirements 1 and 2, respectively. Requirements 1, 2, and 3 have relative values of 0.2, 0.5, and 0.3, respectively. What is the overall value of the program and which project is most important?

$$A = \begin{bmatrix} 1001 \\ 0111 \end{bmatrix} \quad B = \begin{bmatrix} 010 \\ 101 \\ 110 \\ 100 \end{bmatrix} \quad V = \begin{bmatrix} 0.2 \\ 0.5 \\ 0.3 \end{bmatrix}$$

The contribution of each project to each requirement is

$$C = AB = \begin{bmatrix} 110 \\ 311 \end{bmatrix}$$

The value of each project is

$$E = CV = \begin{bmatrix} .7 \\ 1.4 \end{bmatrix}$$

The value of the program is

$$E^* = JE = 2.1$$

Thus, project 2 is twice as important (valuable) as project 1.

If, in the preparation of matrix **A**, it seems desirable to differentiate between the different degrees by which a project contributes to a technology or a technology to a requirement, this is easily accomplished. Instead of a one-zero measure of contribution, one might use the following:

$$a = \begin{cases} 2, \text{ if } P_i \text{ makes a "major" contribution to } T_j \\ 1, \text{ if } P_i \text{ makes a "minor" contribution to } T_j \\ 0, \text{ if } P_i \text{ makes none} \end{cases}$$

Matrix **B** could also accommodate a more sensitive measure of the contributions of a technology to a requirement if the evaluator wishes.

Dean's method has wide applicability for evaluation of programs composed of multiple interdependent projects. Scores can be compared for several programs. When program life is extended over several time periods and generates outputs in these successive time periods, program performance can be compared between periods.

## Choosing a Project Selection Model

Selecting the type of model to aid the evaluation/selection process depends on the philosophy and wishes of management. Liberatore and Titus [35] conducted a survey of 40 high-level staff persons from 29 *Fortune 500* firms. Eighty percent of their respondents report the use of one or more financial models for R & D project decision making. Although their sample is small and nonrandom, their findings are quite consistent with the present authors' experience. None of the respondent firms used mathematical programming techniques for project selection or resource allocation.

We strongly favor weighted scoring models for three fundamental reasons. First, they allow the multiple objectives of all organizations to be reflected in the important decision about which projects will be supported and which will be rejected. Second, scoring models are easily adapted to changes in managerial philosophy or changes in the environment. Third, they do not suffer from the bias toward the short run that is inherent in profitability models that discount future cash flows. This is not a prejudice against discounting and most certainly does not argue against the inclusion of profits/profitability as an important factor in selection, but rather *it is an argument against the exclusion of nonfinancial factors* that may require a longer-run view of the costs and benefits of a project. For a powerful statement of this point, see [25].

It is also interesting to note that Liberatore and Titus found that firms with a significant amount of contract research funded from outside the organization used scoring models for project screening much more frequently than firms with negligible levels of outside funding. It was also found that firms with significant levels of outside funding were much less likely to use a payback period [35, p. 969].

The structure of a weighted scoring model is quite straightforward. Its virtues are many. Nonetheless, the actual use of scoring models is not as easy as it might seem. Decision makers are forced to make difficult choices and they are not always comfortable doing so. They are forced to reduce often vague feelings to quite specific words or numbers. The Delphi method mentioned above and described in Appendix B is helpful, and is a satisfying process for decision makers. Even so, multiattribute, multiperson decision making is not simple. (For an interesting discussion of this process, see [31] as well as reference [31] in Appendix B.)

## ▶ 2.4 ANALYSIS UNDER HIGH UNCERTAINTY

At times an organization may wish to evaluate a project about which there is little information. Research and development projects sometimes fall into this general class. But even in the comparative mysteries of research and development activities, the level of uncertainty about the outcomes of R & D is not beyond analysis. As we noted when discussing Dean's profitability model, there is actually not much uncertainty about whether a product, process, or service can be developed, but there can be considerable uncertainty about *when* it will be developed and at *what* cost.

As they are with R & D projects, time and cost are also often uncertain in other types of projects. When the organization undertakes projects in which it has little or no recent experience—for example, the installation of a new computer, investment in an unfamiliar business, engaging in international trade, and a myriad of other projects common enough to organizations in general but uncommon to any single organization—there are three distinct areas of uncertainty. First, there is uncertainty about the timing of the project and the cash flows it is expected to generate.

Second, though not as common as generally believed, there may be uncertainty about the direct outcomes of the project—that is, what it will accomplish. Third, there is uncertainty about the side effects of the project, its unforeseen consequences.

Typically, we try to reduce such uncertainty by the preparation of *pro forma* documents. *Pro forma* profit and loss statements and break-even charts are examples of such documents. The results, however, are not very satisfactory unless the amount of uncertainty is reflected in the data that go into the documents. When relationships between inputs and outputs in the projects are complex, Monte Carlo simulation [34, 65] can handle such uncertainty by exposing the many possible consequences of embarking on a project. *Risk analysis* is a method based on such a procedure. With the great availability of microcomputers and user-friendly software, these procedures are becoming very common.

## Risk Analysis

The term risk analysis is generally credited to David Hertz in his classic *Harvard Business Review* article, "Risk Analysis in Capital Investment" [27]. The principal contribution of this procedure is to focus the decision maker's attention on understanding the nature and extent of the uncertainty associated with some variables used in a decision-making process. Although the method can be used with almost any kind of variable and decision problem, risk analysis is usually understood to use financial measures in determining the desirability of an investment project.

Hertz [28] differentiates risk analysis from both traditional financial analysis and more general decision analysis with the diagrams in Figure 2-4. Figure 2-4a illustrates traditional financial analysis, Figure 2-4b risk analysis. The primary difference is that risk analysis incorporates uncertainty in the decision input data. Instead of point estimates of the variables, probability distributions are determined or subjectively estimated for each of the "uncertain" variables. With such inputs, the probability distribution for the rate of return (or NPV) is then usually found by simulation. The decision maker not only has probabilistic information about the rate of return and future cash flows but also gains knowledge about the *variability* of such estimates as measured by the standard deviation of the financial returns. Both the expectation and its variability are important decision criteria in the evaluation of the project. For an example, see the Reading at the end of this chapter.

When most managers refer to risk analysis, they are usually speaking of what Hertz and Thomas call "decision analysis." As Figure 2-4c shows, for decision analysis the manager's "utility function" for money must be determined. If the decision maker is seeking a decision that achieves several different objectives simultaneously, this method (utilizing a weighted factor scoring model, for example, rather than simulation) would be appropriate.

This approach is useful for a wide range of project-related decisions. For example, simulation risk analysis was used to select the best method of moving a computer to a new facility [64]. The major task elements and their required sequences were identified. Cost and time distributions were then programmed for analysis and a computer run of 2000 trials was made, simulating various failures and variations in cost and time for each of three methods of moving the computer. A cost–probability distribution was constructed (see Figure 2-5) to help identify the lowest-cost alternative and also the alternative with the lowest risk of a high cost, alternatives that are often not the same. As seen in the illustration, alternative 3 has the lowest expected cost (of 9) but also has the highest likelihood for a cost of 20 or more.

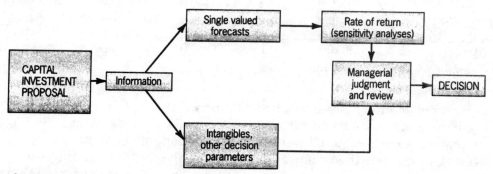

**Figure 2-4a:** Traditional financial analysis.

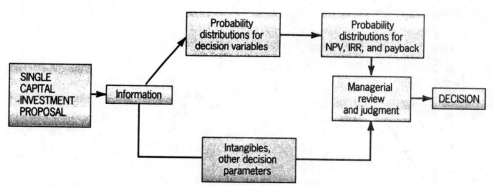

**Figure 2-4b:** Risk analysis.

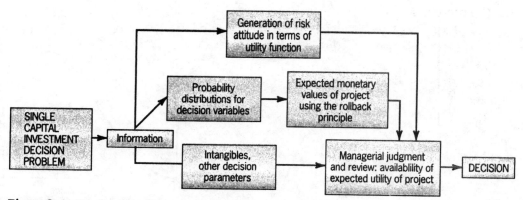

**Figure 2-4c:** Decision analysis. *Source:* [28]

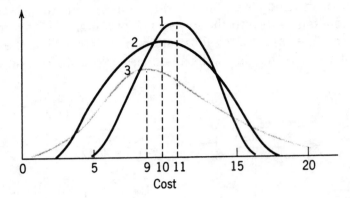

*Figure* **2-5**: Probability density for three alternatives. *Note*: Alternative 3 has the lowest mean, but alternative 1 has a smaller variance and thus less risk.

A public utility faced with deciding between several R & D projects [21] used four separate cost-related distributions in a risk analysis simulation (Figure 2-6). (Total wage costs required two separate distributions, as shown in the figure.) The distributions were then combined to generate the distribution of a cost overrun for each potential project. In addition, sensitivity analysis was conducted to determine the effect of court rulings and specific task failures on project costs. High-risk projects were identified in this way, and tasks that posed high risk could then be moni-

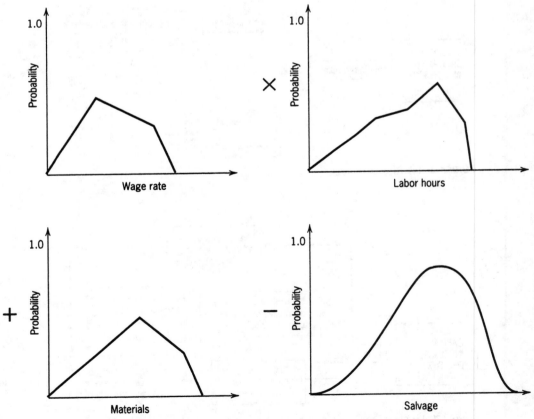

**Figure 2-6:** Probability distributions for elements of project cost for a utility.

tored with tight managerial controls. Following the cost analysis, project schedules were analyzed in the same way. Finally, time and cost analyses were combined to determine interactions and overall project effects.

### General Simulation Analysis

Simulation combined with sensitivity analysis is also useful for evaluating R & D projects while they are still in the conceptual stage. Using the net present value approach, for example, we would support an R & D project if the net present value of the cash flows (including the initial cash investment) is positive and represents the best available alternative use of the funds. When these flows are estimated for purposes of the analyses, it is well to avoid the *full-cost* philosophy that is usually adopted. The full-cost approach to estimating cash flows forces the inclusion of arbitrarily determined overheads in the calculation—overheads which, by definition, are not affected by the change in product or process and thus are not relevant to the decision. The only relevant costs are those that will be changed by the implementation of the new process or product.

The determination of such costs is not simple. If the concept being considered involves a new process, it is necessary to go to the detailed *route sheet*, or *operations sequence sheet*, describing the operation in which the new process would be used. Proceeding systematically through the operating sequence step by step, one asks whether the present time and cost required for this step are likely to be altered if the new process concept is installed. If and only if the answer is yes, three estimates (optimistic, most likely, and pessimistic) are made of the size of the expected change. These individual estimated changes in the production cost and time, together with upstream or downstream time and cost changes that might also result (e.g., a production method change on a part might also alter the cost of inspecting the final product), are used to generate the required cash flow information—presuming that the time savings have been properly costed. This estimation process will be explained in detail in Chapter 8.

The analysis gives a picture of the proposed change in terms of the costs and times that will be affected. The uncertainty associated with each individual element of the process is included. Simulation runs will then indicate the likelihood of achieving various levels of savings. Note also that investigation of the simulation model will expose the major sources of uncertainty in the final cost distributions. If the project itself is near the margin of acceptability, the uncertainty may be reduced by doing some preliminary research aimed at reducing uncertainty in the areas of project cost estimation where it was highest. This preliminary research can be subjected to a cost–benefit analysis when the benefit is reduced uncertainty. For an example of such an approach see [41].

## ▶ 2.5   COMMENTS ON THE INFORMATION BASE FOR SELECTION

Our bias in favor of weighted scoring models is quite clear, but irrespective of which model is chosen for project selection, an annual or computerized data base must be created and maintained to furnish input data for the model. Directions for the actual construction of the data base go beyond the scope of this book, but some comments about the task are in order.

The use of either scoring models or profit/profitability models assume that the decision-making procedure takes place in a reasonably rational organizational environment. Such is not always the case. In some organizations, project selection seems to be the result of a political process, and sometimes involving questionable ethics, complete with winners and losers. In others, the organization is so rigid in its approach to decision making that it attempts to reduce all decisions to an algorithmic proceeding in which predetermined programs make choices so that humans have minimal involvement—and responsibility. In an interesting paper, Huber examines the impact that the organizational environment has on the design of decision support systems [29].

The remainder of this section deals with three special problems affecting the data used in project selection models.

## Comments on Accounting Data

Whether managers are familiar with accounting systems or not, they can find it useful to reflect on the methods and assumptions used in the preparation of accounting data. Among the most crucial are the following.

1.  Accountants live in a linear world. With few exceptions, cost and revenue data are assumed to vary linearly with associated changes in inputs and outputs.

2.  The accounting system often provides cost–revenue information that is derived from standard cost analyses and equally standardized assumptions regarding revenues. These standards may or may not be accurate representations of the cost–revenue structure of the physical system they purport to represent.

3.  As noted in the previous section, the data furnished by the accounting system may or may not include overhead costs. In most cases, the decision maker is concerned solely with cost–revenue elements that will be changed as a result of the project under consideration. Incremental analysis is called for, and great care must be exercised when using *pro forma* data in decision problems. Remember that the assignment of overhead cost is always arbitrary. The accounting system is the richest source of information in the organization, and it should be used—but with great care and understanding.

## Comment on Measurements

It is common for those who oppose a project, for whatever reason, to complain that information supporting the project is "subjective." This epithet appears to mean that the data are biased and therefore untrustworthy.

To use the scoring methods discussed, we need to *represent* though not necessarily *collect* expected project performance for each criterion in numeric form. If a performance characteristic cannot be measured directly as a number, it may be useful to characterize performance verbally and then, through a word/number equivalency scale, use the numeric equivalents of verbal characterizations as model inputs.

***Subjective versus Objective***   The distinction between subjective and objective is generally misunderstood. All too often the word *objective* is held to be synonymous with *fact* and *subjective* is taken to be a synonym for *opinion*—where fact = true and opinion = false. The distinction in measurement theory is quite different, referring to the location of the standard for measurement. A measurement taken by reference to an external standard is said to be "objective." Reference to a standard that is internal to the system is said to be "subjective." A yardstick, incorrectly divided into 100 divisions and labeled "meter," would be an objective but inaccurate measure. The eye of an experienced judge is a subjective measure that may be quite accurate.

***Quantitative versus Qualitative***   The distinction between quantitative and qualitative is also misunderstood. It is not the same as numeric and nonnumeric. Both quantity and quality may be measured numerically. The number of words on this page is a quantity. The color of a red rose is a quality, but it is also a wavelength that can be measured numerically, in terms of microns. The true distinction is that one may apply the law of addition to quantities but not to qualities [66]. Water, for example, has a volumetric measure and a density measure. The former is quantitative and the latter qualitative. Two one-gallon containers of water poured into one container give us two gallons, but the density of the water, before and after joining the two gallons, is still 1.0.

***Reliable versus Unreliable***   A data source is said to be reliable if repetitions of a measurement produce results that vary from one another by less than a prespecified amount. The distinction is important when we consider the use of statistical data in our selection models.

***Valid versus Invalid***   Validity measures the extent to which a piece of information means what we believe it to mean. A measure may be reliable but not valid. Consider our mismarked yardstick 36 inches long but pretending to be a meter. It performs consistently, so it is reliable. It does not, however, match up well with other meter rules, so it would not be judged valid.

To be satisfactory when used in the previous project selection models, the measures may be either subjective or objective, quantitative or qualitative, but they must be numeric, reliable, and valid. Avoiding information merely because it is subjective or qualitative is an error and weakens our decisions. On the other hand, including information of questionable reliability or validity in selection models, even though it may be numeric, is dangerous. It is doubly dangerous if decision makers in the organization are comfortable dealing with the selection model but are unaware of the doubtful character of some input data. A condition a colleague has referred to as GIGO—garbage in, *gospel* out—may prevail.

## Comment on Technological Shock

If the parent organization is not experienced in the type of project being considered for selection, performance measures such as time to installation, time to achieve

80 percent efficiency, cost to install, and the like are often underestimated. It is interesting to observe that an almost certain, immediate result of installing a new, cost–saving technology is that costs rise. Sometimes we blame the cost increases on resistance to change, but a more sensible explanation is that when we alter a system, we disturb it and it reacts in ways we did not predict. A steelmaker recalling the installation of the then new technology for manufacturing tinplate by electrolysis remarked: "We discovered and installed the world's first electrolytic method for making scrap. It took a year before we had that line running the way it was designed."

Of course, if the organization is experienced, underestimation is not likely to be a serious problem. The Reliance Electric Company undertook several "18-month" plant construction projects that they predicted, accurately, would require 36 months to build from decision to the point when the plant was capable of operating at or above three-fourths capacity. (Note the potential for ethical problems here.)

To the extent possible, past knowledge of system actions and reactions should be built into estimates of future project performance.

## ▶ 2.6 PROJECT PROPOSALS

Now that project selection methods have been discussed, it is appropriate to consider what documentation is needed to evaluate a project that is being considered. The set of documents submitted for evaluation is called the project proposal, whether it is brief (a page or two) or extensive, and regardless of the formality with which it is presented.

Several issues face firms preparing proposals, particularly firms in the aerospace, construction, defense, and consulting industries.

1.  Which projects should be bid on?
2.  How should the proposal-preparation process be organized and staffed?
3.  How much should be spent on preparing proposals for bids?
4.  How should the bid prices be set? What is the bidding strategy? Is it ethical?

Generally, these decisions are made on the basis of their overall expected values, perhaps as reflected in a scoring model.

In-house proposals submitted by a firm's personnel to that firm's top management do not usually require the extensive treatment given to proposals submitted to outside clients or such agencies as the Department of Defense. For the Department of Defense, a proposal must be precisely structured, meeting the requirements contained in the official RFP (Request for Proposal) or, more specifically, in the TPR (Technical Proposal Requirements) that is part of the RFP. The construction and preparation of a proposal to be submitted to the government or other outside funder is beyond the scope of this book. However, the subject has been well treated by Roman [52] and the interested reader is referred to his work as well as [24 and 53].

All proposals should begin with a short summary statement (an "Executive Summary") covering the fundamental nature of the proposal *in nontechnical language,* as well as the general benefits that are expected to accrue to its implementation. All proposals should be accompanied by a "cover letter." Roman [52, pp. 67–68] emphasizes that the cover letter is a key marketing document and is worthy of careful attention. In addition to the Executive Summary and the cover letter, every proposal should deal with four distinct issues: (1) the nature of the technical problem and how it is to be approached; (2) the plan for implementing the project once it has been accepted; (3) the plan for logistic support and administration of the project; and (4) a description of the group proposing to do the work, plus its past experience in similar work.

The precise way in which the contents of a proposal are organized usually follows the directions found in the TPR or RFP, the stated requirements of a specific potential funder, the traditional form used by the organization issuing the proposal, or, occasionally, the whim of the writer. As is the case with most products, the highest probability of acceptance will occur when the proposal meets the expectations of the "buyer," as to form and contents.

At times there is a tendency to feel that so-called "nontechnical" projects (by which is usually meant projects that are not concerned with the physical sciences or a physical product) are somehow exempt from the need to describe how the problem will be approached and how the project will be implemented—including such details as milestones, schedules, and budgets. To deal with nontechnical projects so casually is folly and casts considerable doubt on the proposer's ability to deliver on promises. (It is all too common for projects concerned with the development of art, music, drama, and computer software, among other "nontechnical" areas, to be quite vague as to what will be delivered, when, and at what cost.) On the other hand, when the proposal is aimed at another division or department of the same parent organization, the technical requirements of the proposal may be greatly relaxed, but the technical approach and implementation plan are still required—even if their form is quite informal.

## The Technical Approach

The proposal begins with a general description of the problem to be attacked or project to be undertaken. If the problem is complex, the major subsystems of the problem or project are noted, together with the organization's approach to each. The presentation is in sufficient detail that a knowledgeable reader can understand what the proposer intends to do. The general method of resolving critical problems is outlined. If there are several subsystems, the proposed methods for interfacing them are covered.

In addition, any special client requirements are listed along with proposed ways of meeting them. All test and inspection procedures to assure performance, quality, reliability, and compliance with specifications are noted.

## The Implementation Plan

The implementation plan for the project contains estimates of the time required, the cost, and the materials used. Each major subsystem of the project is listed along with estimates of its cost. These costs are aggregated for the whole project, and totals are shown for each cost category. Hours of work and quantities of material used are shown (along with the wage rates and unit material costs). A list of all equipment costs is added, as is a list of all overhead and administrative costs.

Depending on the wishes of the parent organization and the needs of the project, time charts, PERT/CPM, or Gantt charts are given for each subsystem and for the system as a whole. Personnel, equipment, and resource usages are estimated on a period-by-period basis in order to ensure that resource constraints are not violated. Major milestones are indicated on the time charts. Contingency plans are specifically noted. For any facility that might be critical, load charts are prepared to make sure that the facility will be available when needed.

## The Plan for Logistic Support and Administration

The proposal includes a description of the ability of the proposer to supply the routine facilities, equipment, and skills needed now and then during any project. Having the means to furnish artist's renderings, special signs, meeting rooms, stenographic assistance, reproduction of oversized documents, computer graphics, word processing, conference telephone calls, and many other occasionally required capabilities provides a "touch of class." Indeed, their unavailability can be irritating. Attention to detail in all aspects of project planning increases the probability of success for the project—and impresses the potential funder.

It is important that the proposal contain a section explaining how the project will be administered. Of particular interest will be an explanation of how control over subcontractors will be administered, including an explanation of how proper subcontractor performance is to be insured and evaluated. The nature and timing of all progress reports, budgetary reports, audits, and evaluations are covered, together with a description of the final documentation to be prepared for users. Termination procedures are described, clearly indicating the disposition of project personnel, materials, and equipment at project end.

A critical issue, often overlooked, that should be addressed in the administrative section of the proposal is a reasonably detailed description of how change orders will be handled and how their costs will be estimated. Change orders are a significant source of friction (and lawsuits) between the organization doing the project and the client. The client rarely understands the chaos that can be created in a project by the introduction of a seemingly simple change. To make matters worse, the group proposing the project seems to have a penchant for misleading the potential client about the ease with which "minor" changes can be adopted during the process of implementing the project. Control of change orders is covered in Chapter 11.

## Past Experience

All proposals are strengthened by including a section that describes the past experience of the proposing group. It contains a list of key project personnel together with their titles and qualifications. For outside clients, a full résumé for each principal should be attached to the proposal. When preparing this and the other sections of a proposal, the proposing group should remember that the basic purpose of the document is to convince a potential funder that the group and the project are worthy of support. The proposal should be written accordingly.

# Project Management in Practice
## *The Military Mobile Communication System—A Procurement Innovation*

In 1981, the U.S. military was using a hodge-podge of communication equipment that largely didn't intercommunicate. Different services used different vendors, each with their own protocol, and equipment for voice communication was completely different from that for data, facsimile, or e-mail. James Ambrose, then Undersecretary of the Army, thus initiated a $4.2 billion project to completely revamp the entire Army communications system, the largest communications program ever placed by the Army. His conception of the need included six unique acquisition guidelines that led to an extremely successful project:

1. The contractor is responsible for all aspects of systems acquisition, production, integration, fielding, training, logistics, and maintenance.

2. The contractor will satisfy 19 required design and functional features and as many of 82 desired features as possible.

3. The contractor will provide only fully developed, working equipment; there is to be virtually no engineering development.

4. Delivery of the system will start after 22 months and be completed 60 months after basic operations.

5. The contractor will buy every piece of equipment needed for each system, even if that equipment is already in use.

*Source*: A. A. Dettbarn, et al. "Excellence in Cost, Schedule and Quality Performance," PM *Network*, January 1992.

Depending on the new communications system during the Gulf War.

6. The contract is firm fixed price with the contractor accepting all cost risks.

In 1985, GTE won the bidding with a proposal $3 billion lower than the next competitor's. GTE has developed and refined their program management capabilities over a period of 35 years. A project team was assembled consisting of 32 subcontractors and 700 vendors to supply over 8000 mobile radios, 1400 telephone switching centers, and 25,000 telephones. This system can send and receive calls, electronic mail, data, and facsimiles to mobile units without interruption over an area of 37,500 square kilometers, even while the connective elements of the system are on the move. The system interconnects with the existing U.S. Army communications equipment as well as that of the other military services, NATO, and commercial satellite and landline telephone networks around the world. The system was tested in late 1985 for 10 slushy days during winter in eastern France. Mobile units crossed fields and roads, reconnecting between coverage areas, while switching centers jumped from location to location, just as would a regular Army corps during combat.

The final system met the requirement of 19 necessary features and 69 of the 82 desired features. The project also met the strict delivery deadlines and realized $21.7 million in cost savings as well. In 1991, the system was very successfully employed in the Persian Gulf for Operation Desert Shield/Storm. During the war period, the system operated for two straight weeks with only 45 minutes of downtime. It also was able to be set up and taken down in just the 30 minutes specified (completed in five minutes in one instance). It truly achieved the goal of "Effective communications from the foxhole to the theater commander to the President." This outstanding performance has been honored in four separate U.S. Army awards, including the DOD Value Engineering Contractor of the Year Award.

## ▶ 2.7   THE PAST AND FUTURE OF PROJECT EVALUATION/SELECTION MODELS

In 1964, Baker and Pound [6] surveyed the state of the art of evaluating and selecting R & D projects. Although their investigation focused solely on R & D projects, their findings, and the subsequent findings of Baker and Freeland [4, 5] lead to some tentative conclusions about the past, present, and future use of project selection methods.

The use of formal, numeric procedures for the evaluation and selection of projects is a recent phenomenon, largely post-World War II. At first, payback period (and the related "average annual rate of return") was widely used. It is still used by those who feel that the uncertainties surrounding project selection are so great that a higher level of sophistication is unwarranted.

The use of formal models slowly increased during the 1950s and 1960s, and a large majority of the models employed were strictly profit/profitability models. As we have noted, the emphasis on profitability models tended to shorten the time horizon of project investment decisions. This effect and the results of several studies on the use of project selection models are reported in Mansfield [39, App. A]; also see [40, pp. 15–16].

A similar effect on non-R & D projects is easily observed by noting the sharp decline of investment in long-term projects. The increasing interest rates seen during the 1970s forced cutoff ("hurdle") rates of return higher, which cut back investment in projects for which the time gap between investment and return was more than a very few years. For example, neither new steelmaking capacity nor copper-refining capacity was expanded nearly as rapidly as long-run growth in the demand for steel and copper seemed to justify during this period. Producers tended to blame the lack of investment on foreign competition, but given the aging capacity in the United States, it may well be that the level of foreign competition is as much a result of the lack of growth (that is, our failure to invest in newer technology) as it is a cause. Again, the reader is referred to Hayes and Abernathy [25].

A decade later, Baker [4] and Souder [60] reassessed R & D project selection. In this decade there was considerable growth in the use of formal models, again with great emphasis on profitability models. But Baker reported significant growth in the literature on models that use multiple criteria for decision making. He observed a trend away from decision models *per se*, and toward the use of decision information systems. Among other reasons for this change, he notes [4] that "the decision problem is characterized by multiple criteria, many of which are not easily quantified, and the typical approaches to quantifying subjective preferences are far from satisfactory." He also notes the development of interactive decision systems that allow users to examine the effects of different mixes of possible projects.

More than two decades have passed since Baker's 1974 study. Considerable progress has been made in the development of processes for measuring preferences that yield suitable input data for sophisticated scoring models, models which serve, in turn, as data for goal programming and other resource allocation models. Because it is easy to enter all the parts (data base, decision model, and list of potential projects) in a computer, it is feasible to simulate many solutions to the project selection problem. The decision maker can easily change the criteria being used, as well as the criteria weights. Decision makers can even investigate the sensitivity of their decisions to changes in the estimates of subjective input data, thus directly examining the potential impact of errors in their opinions. In spite of all these capabilities, Liberatore and Titus [35] have found that mathematical programming models are not used for project selection or resource allocation, at least in the firms they interviewed. They did find, however, that scoring models were used for selection—particularly when the firm dealt with outside funding agencies.

We believe that use of these techniques will be extended in the future. As we become more familiar with the construction and use of decision support and expert systems (see [65]), the simulation of project selection decisions will grow in popularity. It seems to us that two concurrent events will support this trend. First is the rapid growth in the ownership and use of microcomputers by organizational executives. The operation of a computer is no longer seen as restricted to computer specialists. Second is the growing realization that profitability alone is not a sufficient test for the quality of an investment.

Almost everyone who has studied project selection in recent years has noted the need for selection processes using multiple criteria. The writings of Michael

Porter [47, 48] and others have emphasized the role of innovation in the maintenance or improvement of a competitive position. Indeed, it is now clear that the firm's portfolio of projects is a key element in its competitive strategy. Suresh and Meredith [62] have added a "strategic approach" to the problem of selecting process technologies for implementation. In sum, the methodology and technology for multiple-criteria project selection not only exist but are widely available. Perhaps more important, we are beginning to understand the necessity for using them.

# ▶ SUMMARY

This chapter initiated our discussion of the project management process by describing procedures for evaluating and selecting projects. We first outlined some criteria for project selection models and then discussed the general nature of these models. From this basic overview, the chapter then described the types of models in use and their advantages and disadvantages. Considering the degree of uncertainty associated with many projects, a section was devoted to selection models concerned with risk and uncertainty. Concluding the discussion, some general comments were made about data requirements and the use of these models. Finally, two sections discussed the documentation of the evaluation/selection process via project proposals and the general trend of selection models in the past and for the probable future.

The following specific points were made in the chapter.

- Primary model selection criteria are realism, capability, flexibility, ease of use, and cost.

- Preparatory steps in using a model include identifying the firm's objectives, weighting them relative to each other, and determining the probable impacts of the project on the firm's competitive abilities.

- Project selection models can generally be classified as either numeric or nonnumeric; numeric models are further subdivided into profitability and scoring categories.

- Nonnumeric models include the sacred cow, the operating necessity, the competitive necessity, and comparative benefit.

- Profitability models include such standard forms as payback period, rate of return, discounted cash flow, and profitability index.

- Scoring models, the authors' preference, include the unweighted 0–1 factor model, the unweighted factor scoring model, the weighted factor scoring model, the constrained weighted factor scoring model, Dean and Nishry's model, and goal programming with multiple objectives.

- For handling uncertainty, *pro forma* documents, risk analysis, and simulation with sensitivity analyses are all helpful.

- Special care should be taken with the data used in project selection models. Of concern are data taken from an accounting data base, how data are measured and conceived, and the effect of technological shock.

- Project proposals generally consist of a number of sections: the technical approach, the implementation plan, the plan for logistic support and administration, and past experience.

- The history of project selection models has shown an increase in the use of formal models, particularly profitability models. We feel the future will extend the use of multiple criteria and simulation models, especially with the wide use of the microcomputer.

In the next chapter we consider the selection of the appropriate manager for a project and what characteristics are most helpful for such a position. We also address the issue of the project manager's special role, and the demands and responsibilities of this critical position.

# ► GLOSSARY

**Decision Support System**—A computer package and data base to aid managers in making decisions. It may include simulation programs, mathematical programming routines, and decision rules.

**Delphi**—A formalized method of group decision making that facilitates drawing on the knowledge of experts in the group (described in Appendix B of this book).

**Deterministic**—Predetermined, with no possibility of an alternate outcome. Compare with stochastic.

**Expert System**—A computer package that captures the knowledge of recognized experts in an area and can make inferences about a problem based on decision rules and data input to the package.

**Matrix**—A table of numbers or other items with each row and column having a particular definition.

**Model**—A way of looking at reality, usually for the purpose of abstracting and simplifying it to make it understandable in a particular context.

**Network**—A group of items connected by some common mechanism.

**Portfolio**—A group or set of projects with varying characteristics.

**Pro Forma**—Projected or anticipated, usually applied to financial data such as balance sheets and income statements.

**Programming**—An algorithmic methodology for solving a particular type of complex problem, usually conducted on a computer.

**Sensitivity Analysis**—Investigation of the effect on the outcome of changing some parameters in the procedure or model.

**Simulation**—A technique for emulating a process, usually conducted a considerable number of times to understand the process better and measure its outcomes under different policies.

**Stochastic**—Probabilistic, or not deterministic.

# ► MATERIAL REVIEW QUESTIONS

1. What are the four parts of a technical proposal?

2. By what criteria do you think managers judge selection models? What criteria *should* they use?

3. Contrast the competitive necessity model with the operating necessity model. What are the advantages and disadvantages of each?

4. What is a sacred cow? Give some examples.

5. Give an example of a Q-Sort process for project selection.

6. What are some of the limitations of project selection models?

7. What is the distinction between a qualitative and a quantitative measure?

8. How does the discounted cash flow method answer some of the criticisms of the payback period and average rate of return methods?

9. What are some advantages and disadvantages of the profit/profitability numeric models?

10. How is sensitivity analysis used in project selection?

11. How does Dean's program evaluation method work?

12. What ethical issues can arise when proposing an 18 month project that you know will require 36 months to complete?

# ► CLASS DISCUSSION QUESTIONS

1. Explain why goal programming is classified as a scoring model. What is the real difference between profitability and scoring models? Describe a model that could fit both categories.

2. Can risk analysis be used for nonproject business decision making? Explain how.

3. Discuss how the following project selection models are used in real-world applications.

(a) Capital investment with discounted cash flow.

(b) Goal programming models.

(c) Simulation models.

4. Why do you think managers underutilize project selection models?

5. Would uncertainty models be classified as profitability models, scoring models, or some other type of model?

6. Contrast validity with reliability. What aspects, if any, are the same?

7. Contrast subjective and objective measures. Give examples of the proper use of each type of measure when evaluating competing projects.

8. Can a measure be reliable, yet invalid? Explain.

9. What are some possible extensions of project evaluation models for the future?

10. Are there certain types of projects that are better suited for nonnumeric selection methods as opposed to numeric ones?

11. Identify some of the ethical issues that can arise in a bid response to an RFP.

# ▶ PROBLEMS

1. Two projects are proposed to a company. Project A will cost $250,000 to implement and will have annual cash flows of $75,000. Project B will cost $150,000 to implement and will have annual cash flows of $52,000. The company is very concerned about their cash flow. Using the payback period, which project is better, from a cash flow standpoint?

2. What is the average rate of return for a project that costs $200,000 to implement and has an average annual profit of $30,000?

3. A three-year project has net cash flows of $20,000; $25,000; and $30,000 in the next three years. It will cost $75,000 to implement the project. If the required rate of return is 0.2, what is the NPV?

4. What would happen to the NPV of the above project if the inflation rate was expected to be 7 percent in each of the next three years?

5. Given: An information systems program to develop a set of financial accounts systems consists of two projects, three packages, and three required deliverables, as shown (a contribution of 2 is twice that of 1).

$$A = \begin{bmatrix} 1 & 0 & 2 \\ 2 & 1 & 0 \end{bmatrix}$$

$$B = \begin{bmatrix} 0 & 2 & 1 \\ 0 & 1 & 2 \\ 1 & 2 & 0 \end{bmatrix}$$

$$V = \begin{bmatrix} 0.3 \\ 0.6 \\ 0.1 \end{bmatrix}$$

(a) Interpret the matrices **A**, **B**, and **V**.

(b) Calculate **C** and interpret it.

(c) Calculate **E** and interpret it.

(d) Calculate **E\*** and interpret it.

6. Given the following military weapons program:

$$A = \begin{bmatrix} 0 & 0 & 1 & 1 & 0 \\ 1 & 0 & 1 & 0 & 1 \\ 0 & & 0 & 1 & 0 \\ 1 & 0 & 1 & 1 & 0 \\ 0 & 1 & 1 & 0 & 0 \\ 0 & 0 & 0 & 0 & 0 \end{bmatrix}$$

$$B = \begin{bmatrix} 1 & 0 \\ 0 & 1 \\ 0 & 1 \\ 0 & 1 \\ 1 & 0 \end{bmatrix} \qquad V = \begin{bmatrix} 0.6 \\ 0.4 \end{bmatrix}$$

Calculate **C, E,** and **E\*** and interpret the meaning of all the matrices.

7. Use a weighted score model to choose between three locations (A, B, C) for setting up a factory. The relative weights for each criterion are shown in the following table. A score of 1 represents unfavorable, 2 satisfactory, and 3 favorable.

| Category | Weight | Location A | B | C |
|---|---|---|---|---|
| Labor costs | 20 | 1 | 2 | 3 |
| Labor productivity | 20 | 2 | 3 | 1 |
| Labor supply | 10 | 2 | 1 | 3 |
| Union relations | 10 | 3 | 3 | 2 |
| Material supply | 10 | 2 | 1 | 1 |
| Transport costs | 25 | 1 | 2 | 3 |
| Infrastructure | 10 | 2 | 2 | 2 |

**8.** Given:

$$A = \begin{bmatrix} 1 \\ 0 \\ 0 \\ 1 \\ 1 \end{bmatrix}$$

$$B = \begin{bmatrix} 0 & 0 & 1 & 1 & 1 & 0 & 0 \end{bmatrix}$$

$$V = \begin{bmatrix} 0.1 \\ 0.2 \\ 0.1 \\ 0.1 \\ 0.2 \\ 0.1 \\ 0.2 \end{bmatrix}$$

Describe the situation. Calculate **C**, **E**, and **E***.

**9.** Compare the value of the programs in Problems 5, 6, and 8.

**10.** Recompute the program value in Problem 6 if the unit values in **B** were each replaced with 2. Now how does the answer to Problem 6 compare to those of Problems 5 and 8?

**11.** A major consumer products company is determining the value of its program which includes two projects, A and B. There are three technologies that are affected: 1, 2, and 3. Project A has a major contribution to technology 1, no contribution to technology 2, and a major contribution to technology 3. Project B has no contribution to technology 1 and a minor contribution to technologies 2 and 3. There are two requirements, *a* and *b*, that are affected by these three technologies. Requirement *a* has a relative value of 0.6 and requirement *b* of 0.4. Technology 1 makes a contribution to requirement *a* but not to *b*. Technology 2 makes no contribution to requirement *a* but does to requirement *b*. Technology 3 makes a contribution to both requirements *a* and *b*. What is the overall value of this company's program?

**12.** Nina is trying to decide in which of four shopping centers to locate her new boutique. Some cater to a higher class of clientele than others, some are in an indoor mall, some have a much greater volume than others, and, of course, rent varies considerably. Because of the nature of her store, she has decided that the class of clientele is the most important consideration. Following this, however, she *must* pay attention to her expenses and rent is a major item, probably 90 percent as important as clientele. An indoor, temperature-controlled mall is a big help, however, for stores such as hers where 70 percent of sales are from passersby slowly strolling and window shopping. Thus, she rates this as about 95 percent as important as rent. Last, a higher volume of shoppers means more potential sales; she thus rates this factor as 80 percent as important as rent.

As an aid in visualizing her location alternatives, she has constructed the following table. A "good" is scored as 3, "fair" as 2, and "poor" as 1. Use a weighted score model to help Nina come to a decision.

| | Location 1 | 2 | 3 | 4 |
|---|---|---|---|---|
| Class of clientele | Fair | Good | Poor | Good |
| Rent | Good | Fair | Poor | Good |
| Indoor mall | Good | Poor | Good | Poor |
| Volume | Good | Fair | Good | Poor |

# ▶ INCIDENTS FOR DISCUSSION

## Multiplex Company

Multiplex Company is in its third year of using a rather complex and comprehensive strategic planning process. Billi Chase, CEO of Multiplex, is very pleased with the output of the planning process. Plans are logical, organized, and pertinent to the firm's business environment. However, implementation of the plans leaves something to be desired. Billi is convinced that her managers do a poor job of estimating the amount of resources and time required to complete the strategic projects associated with the plan.

This fiscal year, eleven new strategic projects were identified. There were six major types of projects: new products, modifications of existing products, research and development, new applications studies, manufacturing process improvements, and reorganization of the sales department. Each project is sponsored by one of the functional department managers, who is required to prepare a simple cost–benefit analysis and a Gantt chart (see Chapter 8, Section 8.3) showing the aggregate time required to finish a project. This sponsor usually, but not always, winds up being assigned as the project manager.

Tomorrow is the final day of the current year's strategic planning session. Ms. Chase plans to make a strong pitch to her managers to prioritize the strategic projects to ensure that those most important to the company get done. In the past it seemed as though all the projects lagged behind when resource problems arose. In the future she wants a consensus from the managers about which projects will go on the back burner and which are to proceed on schedule when problems are encountered.

*Question:* Ms. Chase is not sure how to go about ranking the projects. Will the managers be able to achieve consensus? Should they use the cost–benefit analysis done by the project sponsor? Perhaps the planning group could use their collective experience to rank the projects subjectively. What method would you recommend to Ms. Chase? Support your recommendation.

## L & M Power

In the next two years a large municipal gas and electric company must begin construction on a new electric generating plant to accommodate the increased demand for electricity and to replace one of the existing plants that is fast becoming obsolete. The vice-president in charge of the new project believes there are two options. One is a new coal-fired steam plant and the other is a new nuclear plant. The vice-president has developed a project selection model and will use it in presenting the project to the president. For the models she has gathered the following information:

|  | Initial Cost | Generating Cost/KW | Exp. Life | Salv. Value |
|---|---|---|---|---|
| Steam plant | $10,000,000 | $0.004 | 20 yr | 10% |
| Nuclear plant | 25,000,000 | $0.002 | 15 yr | 5% |

Since the vice-president's background is in finance, she believes the best model to use is a financial one, net present value analysis.

*Questions:* Would you use this model? Why or why not? Base your answer on the five criteria developed by Souder and evaluate this model in terms of the criteria.

## Billboard Publications

Billboard's top management, located in New York, has recently authorized a large number of data processing projects. However, when under pressure, they ask Bruce Johnson, manager of data processing, to reassign programmers to the latest "squeaky wheel." This situation was causing such turmoil that it was becoming impossible to manage the various projects, and staff morale was deteriorating rapidly.

Johnson's immediate project manager in Cincinnati agreed with him that this situation needed to be resolved, so a project evaluation and selection meeting was arranged. The meeting was held off-site to get away from the immediate pressures of business. It was attended by vice-presidents and department managers who had outstanding requests for data processing services or personnel assigned to such projects. In preparation for the meeting, Johnson gathered a portfolio of all project requests for data processing services with their labor and equipment requirements.

The meeting was held all day Monday and Tuesday. After the two long days and many discussions, all the projects had been evaluated and ranked. However, no one was truly pleased; there were not enough resources to go around, and no one received what he or she really wanted. But they had been heard and all agreed that, given the demands and the resources available, they would abide by the decisions of the group.

Johnson was exhausted after the meetings, but he returned to the office Wednesday and went right to work implementing the plans agreed to the day before. He held meetings with the project managers, programmers, and project personnel from user departments, explaining the "new" priorities. Much patience and persuasion was required, as some projects were placed on hold, staffing reduced on some and increased on others, and entirely new projects formed. The big selling point was that the working environment should be much more stable and professional because these assignments represented the consen-

sus of management on projects to be pursued for the next several months.

Thursday morning, Johnson was looking forward to a calm, peaceful day in which to tackle the pile on his desk and contribute his individual expertise to some of the projects to which he was personally assigned. Before Johnson had made much progress, a call came from Bill Evans, vice-president of finance in New York, the functional manager to whom Johnson reported. Several managers had complained to Evans about the ranking of their pet projects and he had agreed to call Johnson and "discuss" how they could be "fit in." Johnson reminded Evans of the priorities that they had begun to implement only yesterday, and of the two-day meeting earlier that week that Evans had attended and chaired. All to no avail.

Johnson was now not only faced with reassigning personnel to deal with Evans's latest "squeaky wheels," but knew that it would most likely have to be done again tomorrow and then again on Monday. He asked himself, "Had anything really been accomplished?"

*Questions*: What project evaluation and selection methods do you think were used during the meeting? What should Johnson do? Do you think that hiring more personnel would help?

## ▶ INDIVIDUAL EXERCISE

Consider the purchase of a house. Develop a profitability model to compare alternative houses. Include depreciation, expenses, repairs, insurance, initial costs, and so on.

Next, devise a scoring model to evaluate the alternative purchases. How should you weight the various factors, and how do you decide?

Last, how would a risk analysis be used to make a decision? What factors would require distributions, and how might these be obtained? Which data are subjective and which objective? Which are qualitative and which are quantitative?

## ▶ PROJECT TEAM CONTINUING EXERCISE

For this topic, the project team is to develop a project proposal, as described in the chapter. *Pro forma* documents (e.g., a projected income statement) should be included, as well as a justification of the project. The team should endeavor to apply as many of the project

selection methods as may be applicable, including both numeric and nonnumeric models. Both profitability and scoring models should certainly be included. How might goal programming or simulation models be useful here?

## ▶ BIBLIOGRAPHY

1. ALLEN, D. E. *Finance: A Theoretical Introduction.* New York: St. Martins Press, 1983.

2. ARCHIBALD, R. D. *Managing High Technology Programs and Projects.* New York: Wiley, 1976.

3. ATKINSON, A. C., and A. H. BOBIS. "A Mathematical Basis for the Selection of Research Projects." *IEEE Transactions on Engineering Management,* Jan. 1969.

4. BAKER, N. R. "R & D Project Selection Models: An Assessment." *IEEE Transactions on Engineering Management,* Nov. 1974.

5. BAKER, N. R., and J. FREELAND. "Recent Advances in R & D Benefit Measurement and Project Selection Models." *Management Science* June 1975.

6. BAKER, N. R., and W. H. POUND. "R & D Project Selection: Where We Stand." *IEEE Transactions on Engineering Management,* Dec. 1964.

7. BEALE, P., and M. FREEMAN. "Successful Project Execution: A Model," *Project Management Journal,* Dec. 1991.

8. BECKER, R. H. "Project Selection for Research, Product Development and Process Development." *Research Management,* Sept. 1980.

9. BLOCK, S., and G. HIRT. *Foundations of Financial Management.* 5th ed. Homewood, IL: Irwin, 1988.

10. CHURCHMAN, C. W., R. L. ACKOFF, and E. L. ARNOFF. *Introduction to Operations Research.* New York: Wiley, 1957.

11. CLARK, P. "A Profitability Project Selection Method." *Research Management,* Nov. 1977.

12. CLAYTON, R. "A Convergent Approach to R & D Planning and Project Selection." *Research Management,* Sept. 1971.

13. CLIFTON, D. S., JR., and D. E. FYFFE. *Project Feasibility Analysis: A Guide to Profitable Ventures.* New York: Wiley, 1977.

14. COCHRAN, M., E. B. PYLE, III, L. C. GREENE, H. A. CLYMER, and A. D. BENDER. "Investment Model for R & D Project Evaluation and Selection." *IEEE Transactions on Engineering Management,* Aug. 1971.

15. DALKEY, N. C. *The Delphi Method: An Experimental Study of Group Opinion* (RM-5888-PR). Santa Monica, CA: The Rand Corporation, June 1969.

16. DEAN, B. V. *Evaluating, Selecting, and Controlling R & D Projects.* New York: American Management Association 1968.

17. DEAN, B. V. "A Research Laboratory Performance Model." In *Quantitative Decision Aiding Techniques for Research and Development,* M. J. Cetron, H. Davidson, and A. H. Rubenstein, eds. New York: Gordon and Breach, 1972.

18. DEAN, B. V., and S. J. MANTEL, JR. "A Model for Evaluating Costs of Implementing Community Projects," *Analysis for Planning Programming Budgeting,* M. Alfandary-Alexander, ed. Potomac, MD: Washington Operations Research Council, 1968.

19. ENRICK, N. L. "Value Analysis for Priority Setting and Resource Allocation." *Industrial Management,* Sept.–Oct. 1980.

20. European Industrial Research Management Association. "Top–Down and Bottom–Up Approaches to Project Selection." *Research Management,* March 1978.

21. GARCIA, A., and W. COWDREY. "Information Systems: A Long Way from Wall-Carvings to CRTs." *Industrial Engineering,* April 1978.

22. GEE, R. E. "A Survey of Current Project Selection Practices." *Research Management,* Sept. 1971.

23. GOLABI, K., G. W. KIRKWOOD, and A. SICHERMAN. "Selecting a Portfolio of Solar Energy Projects Using Multi-Attribute Preference Theory." *Management Science,* Feb. 1981.

24. HAJEK, V. G. *Management of Engineering Projects,* 3rd ed. New York: McGraw-Hill, 1984.

25. HAYES, R., and W. J. ABERNATHY, "Managing Our Way to Economic Decline." *Harvard Business Review,* July–Aug. 1980.

26. HELIN, A. F., and W. E. SOUDER. "Experimental Test of a Q-Sort Procedure for Prioritizing R & D Projects." *IEEE Transactions on Engineering Management,* Nov. 1974.

27. HERTZ, D. B. "Risk Analysis in Capital Investment." *Harvard Business Review,* Sept.–Oct. 1979.

28. HERTZ, D. B., and H. THOMAS, *Risk Analysis and Its Applications.* New York: Wiley, 1983.

29. HUBER, G. P. "The Nature of Organizational Decision Making and the Design of Decision Support Systems," MIS *Quarterly*, June 1981.

30. IGNIZIO, J. P. *Goal Programming and Extensions*. Lexington, MA: Lexington Books, 1976.

31. IRVING, R. H., and D. W. CONRATH, "The Social Context of Multiperson, Multiattribute Decision-making," *IEEE Transactions on Systems, Man, and Cybernetics*, May–June 1988.

32. JOHNSTON, R. D. "Project Selection and Evaluating." *Long Range Planning*, Sept. 1972.

33. KHORRAMSHAHGOL, R., H. AZANI, and Y. GOUSTY. "An Integrated Approach to Project Evaluation and Selection," *IEEE Transactions on Engineering Management*, Nov. 1988.

34. LAW, A. M., and W. KELTON. *Simulation Modeling and Analysis*, 2nd ed. New York: McGraw-Hill, 1990.

35. LIBERATORE, M. J., and G. J. TITUS. "The Practice of Management Science in R & D Project Management." *Management Science*, Aug. 1983.

36. MAHER, P. M., and A. H. RUBENSTEIN. "Factors Affecting Adoption of a Quantitative Method for R & D Project Selection." *Management Science*, Oct. 1974.

37. *Management of New Products*. New York: Booz, Allen, and Hamilton, Inc., 1966.

38. MANN, G. A. "VERT: A Risk Analysis Tool for Program Management." *Defense Management*, May–June 1979.

39. MANSFIELD, E. *Industrial Research and Technological Innovation*. New York: Norton, 1968.

40. MANSFIELD, E., J. RAPOPORT, J. SCHNEE, S. WAGNER, and M. HAMBURGER. *Research and Innovation in the Modern Corporation*. New York: Norton, 1971.

41. MANTEL, S. J., JR., J. R. EVANS, and V. A. TIPNIS. "Decision Analysis for New Process Technology," in B. V. Dean, ed., *Project Management: Methods and Studies*. Amsterdam: North-Holland, 1985.

42. MASON, B. M., W. E. SOUDER, and E. P. WINKOFSKY. "R & D Budgeting and Project Selection: A Review of Practices and Models" ISMS, 1980.

43. MEREDITH, J. "The Implementation of Computer Based Systems." *Journal of Operations Management*, Oct. 1981.

44. MERRIFIELD, D. B. "How to Select Successful R & D Projects." *Management Review*, Dec. 1978.

45. MOORE, J. R., JR., and N. R. BAKER. "Computational Analysis of Scoring Models for R & D Project Selection." *Management Science*, Dec. 1969.

46. PAOLINI, A., JR., and M. A. GLASER. "Project Selection Methods That Pick Winners." *Research Management*, May 1977.

47. PORTER, M. E. *Competitive Strategy*. New York: Free Press, 1980.

48. PORTER, M. E. *Competitive Advantage*. New York: Free Press, 1985.

49. RAMSEY, J. E. "Selecting R & D Projects for Development." *Long Range Planning*, Feb. 1981.

50. REYNARD, E. L. "A Method for Relating Research Spending to Net Profit." *Research Management*, Dec. 1979.

51. ROBINSON, B., and C. LAKHANI. "Dynamic Models for New Product Planning." *Management Science*, June 1975.

52. ROMAN, D. D. *Managing Projects: A Systems Approach*. New York: Elsevier, 1986.

53. ROSENAU, M. D., JR. *Successful Project Management*, 2nd ed. New York: Van Nostrand Reinhold, 1991.

54. SAATY, T. S. *Decision for Leaders: The Analytic Hierarchy Process*. Pittsburgh, PA: University of Pittsburgh, 1990.

55. SCHMIDT, R. L. "A Model for R & D Project Selection with Combined Benefit, Outcome and Resource Interactions," *IEEE Transactions on Engineering Management*, Nov. 1993.

56. SCHWARTZ, S. L., and I. VERTINSKY. "Multi-Attribute Investment Decisions: A Study of R & D Project Selection." *Management Science*, Nov. 1977.

57. SIMON, H. *The New Science of Management Decisions*, rev. ed. Englewood Cliffs, NJ: Prentice Hall, 1977.

58. SOUDER, W. E. "Comparative Analysis of R & D Investment Models." *AIIE Transactions*, April 1972.

59. SOUDER, W. E. "Analytical Effectiveness of Mathematical Models for R & D Project Selection." *Management Science*, April 1973.

60. SOUDER, W. E. "Utility and Perceived Acceptability of R & D Project Selection Models." *Management Science*, Aug. 1973.

61. SOUDER, W. E. "Project Evaluation and Selection," in D. I. Cleland, and W. R. King, eds., *Project Management Handbook*. New York: Van Nostrand Reinhold, 1983.

**62.** SURESH, N. C., and J. R. MEREDITH. "Justifying Multimachine Systems: An Integrated Strategic Approach." *Journal of Manufacturing Systems*, Nov. 1985.

**63.** THOMPSON, G. E. *Management Science: An Introduction to Modern Quantitative Analysis and Decision Making.* Huntington, NY: Krieger, 1982.

**64.** TOWNSEND, H. W. R., and G. E. WHITEHOUSE. "We Used Risk Analysis to Move Our Computer." *Industrial Engineering*, May 1977.

**65.** TURBAN, E., and J. R. MEREDITH, *Fundamentals of Management Science*, 6th ed. Homewood, IL: Irwin, 1994.

**66.** VAN GIGCH, J. P. *Applied General Systems Theory*, 2nd ed. New York: Harper & Row, 1978.

**67.** VAN HORNE, J. C. *Fundamentals of Financial Management.* Englewood Cliffs, NJ: Prentice Hall, 1971.

**68.** WHALEY, W. M., and R. A. WILLIAMS. "A Profits-Oriented Approach to Project Selection." *Research Management*, Sept. 1971.

**69.** WILLIAMS, D. J. "A Study of a Decision Model for R & D Project Selection" *Operational Research Quarterly*, Sept. 1969.

**70.** ZALOON, V. A. "Project Selection Methods," *Journal of Systems Management*, Aug. 1973.

# CASE 1

## WESTFIELD, INC.: PACKAGING ALTERNATIVES*

William McRay, project manager for the Consumer Packaging Group at Westfield, Inc. had just begun work on the 1988 Strategic Plan for the frozen concentrate juice business segment. These juices were currently packed in Westfield's traditional line of containers. However, this traditional line was being threatened by a host of alternative packaging technologies. Westfield had already experienced the painful effects of substitution when its largest segment of traditional container users switched to a new-material container in 1986. Bill wanted to do whatever was necessary to anticipate and minimize the negative effects of this substitution trend as it related to the frozen concentrate juice segment.

Westfield had recently licensed a new container technology called Formatek. The company's exclusive rights to this revolutionary process could provide Westfield with an answer to the substitution threat and a sustainable competitive advantage. But the technology was expensive, and there was no guarantee that the powerful customers within the frozen concentrate juice market would adopt the new containers. On the other hand, failure to innovate on Westfield's part could cause a reversal of fortunes for this container manufacturer that had been able to maintain a 13 percent compound annual growth rate over the last three years.

### Company

Founded in 1903 in Georgia, Westfield began as a manufacturer of disposable paper cones for the growing textile industry. In its first year of operations, it generated sales of $17,000 and profits of $2000. The company projected sales of $739.6 million and net income of $42.4 million for the end of the current fiscal year, 1987, and employed more than 10,000 persons throughout the U.S. (see Exhibits 1 and 2 for recent financial data).

While Westfield had previously been considered strictly a paper company, acquisitions and internal developments transformed the firm into a packaging company. In fact, paper cones, once the company's mainstay, by 1987 represented only 5 percent of the business. Westfield was the leading manufacturer of paper tubes for the paper industry, the third largest manufacturer of traditional containers, and one of the country's largest users of waste paper.

When evaluating new projects, Westfield used an IRR analysis and required a 15 percent after-tax return on investment. Pricing for all new products was expected to cover the following costs: variable manufac-

| | 1987E | 1986 | 1985 | 1984 | 1983 |
|---|---|---|---|---|---|
| Net Sales | $739.6 | $629.6 | $568.3 | $457.8 | $453.3 |
| Cost & Expenses | | | | | |
| Cost of Products Sold | 585.3 | 500.8 | 456.5 | 368.2 | 349.8 |
| Sell., Gen., & Admin. | 71.4 | 60.7 | 53.9 | 46.8 | 42.2 |
| Interest Expense | 7.4 | 3.7 | 4.3 | 3.9 | 3.1 |
| Profit Before Tax | 75.5 | 64.4 | 53.6 | 38.9 | 58.2 |
| Taxes on Income | 35.6 | 30.0 | 23.9 | 16.5 | 26.6 |
| Profit After Tax | 39.9 | 34.4 | 29.7 | 22.4 | 31.6 |
| Equity Earnings of Affiliates | 2.5 | 1.6 | 1.9 | 2.3 | 1.3 |
| Income from Continuing Operations | 42.4 | 36.0 | 31.6 | 24.7 | 32.9 |
| Discontinued Operations | | | (3.1) | (0.4) | (0.2) |
| Net Income | $42.4 | $36.0 | $28.5 | $24.3 | $32.7 |

Note: E 5 Estimated

**Exhibit 1: Westfield, Inc.: Packaging Alternatives—Income Statement (dollars in millions)**

turing costs; plant fixed costs; marketing, technical, and administrative costs (MTA); changes in working capital; and recovery of the initial capital outlay. Westfield used a straight-line depreciation period of eight years and allocated MTA as 5 percent of net sales. While MTA for most other companies was a fixed cost, it was considered variable by Westfield because of the company's exceptional growth rates. Accounts receivable and inventory averaged 25 days of sales and 50 days of sales, respectively.

## Traditional Container Industry

The majority of the company's containers were made from a single type of material, one that was relatively easy and inexpensive to manufacture but that still met customers' needs. The containers were available in a wide range of sizes (circumferences measured in increments of $\frac{1}{16}$ of an inch) and with a choice of closure, either rigid or flexible.

These containers were an outgrowth of tube manufacturing in the late 1800s when such tubes were used for gun powder, oatmeal, and salt. Container use

| | 1987E | 1986 | 1985 | 1984 | 1983 |
|---|---|---|---|---|---|
| Cash and Equivalent | $16.2 | $15.1 | $8.2 | $7.7 | $20.6 |
| Accounts Receivable | 75.3 | 60.1 | 58.3 | 41.6 | 39.3 |
| Inventories | 75.0 | 61.5 | 54.0 | 50.2 | 38.8 |
| Prepaid Expenses | 3.0 | 6.5 | 4.9 | 2.5 | 1.1 |
| Current Assets | 169.5 | 143.2 | 125.4 | 102.0 | 99.8 |
| Prop., Plant, & Equip. | 209.1 | 171.0 | 169.7 | 171.7 | 154.5 |
| Investment in Affiliate | 12.3 | 12.6 | 11.7 | 11.6 | 12.1 |
| Goodwill | 30.6 | 16.6 | 15.5 | 16.7 | 12.1 |
| Other Assets | 4.2 | 3.5 | 3.4 | 3.2 | 2.7 |
| TOTAL ASSETS | $425.7 | $346.9 | $325.7 | $305.2 | $281.2 |
| Accounts Payable | $ 65.7 | $ 47.0 | $ 43.9 | $ 35.4 | $ 35.7 |
| Short-Term Debt | 8.1 | 9.3 | 10.5 | 26.2 | 8.2 |
| Taxes | 6.5 | 10.2 | 3.9 | 1.0 | 10.2 |
| Current Liabilities | 80.3 | 66.5 | 58.3 | 62.6 | 54.1 |
| Long-Term Debt | 62.4 | 26.8 | 35.8 | 29.5 | 25.3 |
| Deferred Taxes | 31.7 | 32.3 | 30.6 | 28.1 | 23.0 |
| Stockholders' Equity | 251.3 | 221.3 | 201.0 | 185.0 | 178.8 |
| TOTAL LIABS. & EQUITY | $425.7 | $346.9 | $325.7 | 305.2 | $281.2 |

Note: E = Estimated

**Exhibit 2: Westfield, Inc.: Packaging Alternatives—Balance Sheet (dollars in millions)**

grew steadily through the early 1950s, and advances in technology spurred additional applications including use for cleansers, caulk, frozen fruit juices, and refrigerated dough. During the 1950s, three significant manufacturing advances laid the groundwork for future growth of traditional containers:

- the development of higher speed winding and cut-off equipment;

- improved lining materials such as aluminum foil for greater product protection; and

- specially designed metal ends for improved seaming techniques.

Use of the traditional container for frozen concentrate juices, or FCJ (FCJ refers to all types of frozen concentrate juices), in 6- and 12-ounce sizes increased significantly during the 1960s. During this same period, the motor oil container gradually became the largest product segment within this industry.

While a limited number of major new markets were on the horizon, technical innovations and imaginative new applications offered good opportunities to convert several of these major segments. Such innovations included aseptic packaging, hot-filled cans, improved liner technology, and new advancements in end-seaming technologies. Potential applications for the future included coffees, peanuts and other snack foods, meat products, and institutional foods.

## Competition

Traditional-container manufacturers had steadily been nibbling away at the metal can and glass markets by offering definite cost advantages. Still, the threat of substitutes remained very high. Since no proprietary technology was used in manufacturing, traditional containers were commodities. Companies competed on quality, service, and packaging innovation. Prices were already low—less than one-half cent per can so there was little room for price wars. Packaging innovation was either developed internally or at the insistence of a customer. Providing a new innovative package that solved a problem, offered a cost advantage, or differentiated the customer's product gave the manufacturer a competitive advantage. Companies were committed to research and development, and most were testing the potential of new technologies for their container lines.

## Customer

Packaging provided a key marketing tool for customers. Customers tried to differentiate their products from competitors' products with eye-catching, attractive, informative labels or with a new, unique container. The outside package was usually the first thing the end user saw of the product, and many believed that packaging influenced buying behavior. Even though the container represented but a small portion of the total cost of the product, it needed to be appealing, functional, easy-to-fill, and long-lasting.

Westfield's product line satisfied these requirements. These traditional holders were strong, lightweight alternatives to metal and glass containers that could take advantage of high-speed filling equipment with minimal changeover costs. Additionally, the manufacturing process for these containers eliminated the side seam, giving the customer an unimpaired 360-degree billboard for graphics. Graphic quality was sharp and eye-catching for easy identification. Finally, the containers satisfied end users' demand for convenient resealable packaging.

Customers were large and extremely powerful, and few exhibited loyalty to a particular container manufacturer. Price was the key attribute in the decision-making process, followed by quality of both the service provided and the product, as well as the previous experience with a particular manufacturer. Customers often looked to container manufacturers that were innovators.

A revolutionary new container material on the market was receiving much attention. Until very recently, for example, motor oil had been packaged in the traditional containers supplied by Westfield and its competitors. But in late 1986, motor oil packaging was converted to this new container material. The switch was not cost driven; but rather the new material, molded with a spout, made pouring the oil easier and neater. Westfield feared further conversions from traditional containers to these new ones in other key market segments such as frozen concentrate juices.

## Consumer Packaging Group

In 1986, the container unit was renamed the "Consumer Packaging Group" to emphasize, primarily internally, Westfield's desire to think beyond traditional containers to additional product lines that it might market to some of its existing customers. The Consumer Packaging Group had 16 plants strategically located near customers in order to be responsive to their needs and to save shipping costs. (See Exhibit 3 for a map of the plant locations.)

When the motor oil container market—the largest user of all segments—switched from the traditional material to the new material, the Consumer Packaging Group's sales declined because some of its customers switched to container manufacturers capable of producing the new material. Westfield reacted

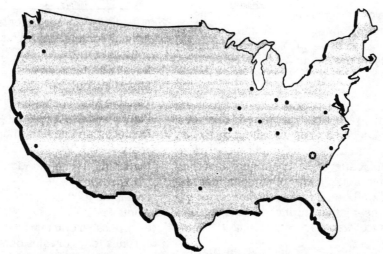

**Exhibit 3: Westfield, Inc.: Packaging Alternatives—Consumer Packaging Group Plant Locations**

by moving into production of these new containers. But because the conversion to the new material was capital intensive and because the company wanted to iron out any production problems before attempting large volume production, Westfield agreed to produce these new containers for only one of its major oil packer accounts. But the seriousness of the substitution threat hit home when the loss of sales was so extensive that one of the production lines for traditional motor oil containers was cut below a full shift.

## Situation

Realizing that the decline of traditional containers to the motor oil market was likely the precursor to similar declines in other markets, Westfield sought to be proactive in its conversion of other key segments to the new containers. Bill McRay focused his attention on the frozen concentrate juices (FCJ) segment because it represented 19 percent of the division's sales and currently used only traditional containers. Westfield's reaction to this situation would likely influence the direction, and perhaps even the fate, of the firm.

Adding to the threat of substitution were the following factors: commodity product, basic technology, low price, low switching costs for customers, little brand loyalty, high bargaining leverage of customers. Mitigating the threat was the capital intensiveness of the industry.

The size of the FCJ market was an estimated 2.4 billion units, representing approximately $105 million

in sales (see Exhibit 4 for a list of the major FCJ customers). Wesfield had a 23 percent unit market share of the 2.4 billion unit market. Sales had been flat over recent years because of a consumer trend to drink chilled ready-to-serve juices, packed in cartons, instead of FCJ. Annual market growth was projected to be 3 percent for the next few years.

The net price of the traditional FCJ container was $52.35 with variable manufacturing costs of $43.79 (figures per thousand). In investigating alternative

| Major Customers | Total Usage (in millions) | |
|---|---|---|
| | Units | Total Cost* |
| Coca-Cola Company | 700 | $37.0 |
| Ventura Coastal Company | 96 | 8.0 |
| McCain's | 60 | 4.3 |
| Welch Foods | 96 | 5.3 |
| Seneca Foods | 80 | 4.5 |

**Others**

Procter & Gamble
Treesweet
Bodiness

*Note that unit costs vary per customer because of differences in such factors as volume, length of time as customer, degree of customization required, special delivery arrangements, etc. The $52.34 price quoted in the case is an average across all customers.

**Exhibit 4: Westfield Inc.: Packaging Alternatives—Major FCJ Customers**

technologies, Westfield ran across a new material and manufacturing process, Formatek, that could offer substantial cost savings as its variable manufacturing costs were only $38.40 per thousand.

## The Alternative

In July 1985, Westfield first uncovered this new process, Formatek, which was developed by an Australian company. Formatek introduced control in the high-speed manufacture of containers that had never before been achievable with other container materials. Uniformity of wall and base thickness, for example, was key to the manufacturing process, and Formatek's performance was excellent along those lines.

The fixed capital investment in this process (for one line) would be $2,099,000, and the annual volume output (operating 7 days a week, 3 shifts) would be 81 million units. These units would replace an equal number of traditional containers. In line with company practices, any currently operating equipment that would be replaced by the Formatek investment would be shipped to Westfield's overseas operations instead of being sold or disposed of. The terminal (book) value for the old equipment would be approximately $500,000 at the time of the installation of the new machine, and the Consumer Packaging Group would receive credit for the book value. The Formatek technology was not expected to become obsolete before 1995.

The plant's fixed costs for the Formatek machine would be $330,000, and the variable manufacturing costs would be $38.40 per thousand. Inflation was expected to average 5 percent a year over the life of the new licensed technology. (See Exhibit 5 for a summary of the costs and other assumptions for Formatek.)

An off-set printing technique was assumed in calculating the costs, but Bill wondered if the quality of the graphics would be an issue because multicolored inks were applied directly to the container and heat dried, so the quality depended on the surface and the inks. Slower printing speeds reduced blurred labels. The detail of off-set printing was not equivalent to that of paper labels used on traditional containers, but temperature extremes in filling and transporting FCJ limited labeling alternatives.

Formatek would give Westfield a proprietary technological competitive advantage and provide its customers with a container that Westfield's competitors could not offer. Westfield licensed this technology in early 1986 (agreeing to pay a royalty fee of 2.5 percent of sales) and had begun testing potential applications

| | |
|---|---|
| Westfield's ROI Target (after tax) | 15% |
| Annual Volume Estimated for 1988[a] (000s of units) | 81,000 |
| Royalty Deduction (% of sales) | 2.5% |
| Miscellaneous Deduction (% of sales) | 1.0% |
| Variable Mfg. Costs (per 000) | $38.40 |
| Plant Fixed Costs ($000) | $330 |
| Depreciation Life (straight line) years | 8 |
| Marketing, Technical, & Administrative Expenses (% of sales) | 5% |
| Fixed Capital ($000) | $2099 |
| Accounts Receivable (days of sales outstanding) | 25 |
| Inventories (days of sales outstanding) | 50 |
| Expected Inflation for Sales and Fixed Costs | 5% |
| Expected Inflation for Variable Costs | 5% |
| Tax Rate | 34% |

*Note:* All costs were estimates of those expected with the Formatek project.

[a]The 81 million units would replace an equal number of traditional containers.

**Exhibit 5: Westfield, Inc.: Packaging Alternative— Summary of Formatek Machine Data.**

in its pilot plant. Westfield's exclusive rights to the new technology would expire within two years if the technology were not put into operation before then.

In Bill's mind, the evaluation of the Formatek project had to be done on a stand-alone basis. Economically, the process for traditional containers was too entrenched to make an apples-to-apples comparison: the machines were fully depreciated; the workers had come quite a way down the learning curve; and the traditional containers were so profitable that Westfield would be extremely hard-pressed to find any new technology that could beat the traditional containers' margins. Even more importantly, though, the project had important *strategic* implications for the firm. Bill was far less interested in the incremental pennies per container that could be won or lost here than he was with the continuing viability of Westfield as a container manufacturer. For these reasons, the project needed to be evaluated as a stand-alone alternative.

To be consistent within this stand-alone analysis, Bill wanted to consider all the key factors—terminal value of old equipment; variable manufacturing costs; plant fixed costs; marketing, technical, and administrative costs (MTA); changes in working capital; and recovery of the initial capital outlay—as though this line were starting from scratch. Specifically, 25 days of accounts receivable and the 50 days of inventory would need to be built up the first year, and changes would be reflected in years thereafter. Bill also wanted to separate inflation for sales and fixed costs in his spreadsheet from inflation for variable costs to facilitate his sensitivity analysis.

Bill identified the following questions as key to his evaluation of the Formatek project:

- What would the IRR be over the life of the project if the new containers were introduced at the prevailing price of the traditional containers?

- What would the IRR be if the Formatek equipment was stretched two years past its estimated eight year life?

- What prices would Westfield have to charge to achieve the 15 percent hurdle rate required of all of Westfield's capital expenditures under both the eight-year and 10-year scenarios?

- What are the key value drivers in the analysis? Could small changes in several drivers lead to big changes in the IRR? For example, what would happen if variable costs rose only 4.5 percent per year (because of learning curve improvements), the royalty fee could be negotiated down to 2.25 percent and/or the price could be raised to $52.84?

- Assume future technology improvements allow 2 percent annual increases in output. What would be the effect?

- What strategic factors should be considered?

Bill knew he had to move quickly if Westfield was to enter 1988 with Formatek capacity on line.

# Project Planning

In the previous chapter we discussed the problem of structuring the interface between the project and its parent organization. We then introduced several issues bearing on the formation and management of the project team. It is now time to consider how to plan the work of the project and to examine how the project plan impacts on the structure of the project team as well as on its relationship to its parent.

There is an extensive literature on project planning. Some of it is concerned with the strategic aspects of planning, being focused on the choice of projects that are consistent with the organization's goals (e.g., [3, 9, 13, 19, 25, and 42]). Another group of works is aimed at the process of planning individual projects, given that they have been chosen as strategically acceptable (e.g., [1, 6, 12, 13, 19, 21, 27, 30, 32, 35, and 44]). Laufer [23], in particular, offers an interesting discussion on the theory of planning that includes some practical implications. Most fields have their own accepted set of project planning processes, though they are all similar, as we shall soon see. For example, in the field of Information Systems they refer to the standard "systems development cycle" for software projects, consisting of four or six or seven "phases", depending on which author is being consulted (e.g., see [36]). It is even standard to use the example of building a house to communicate the activities involved in each phase, as illustrated below:

- **Definition Phase**  Here the problem is defined in a Requirements Document. A house would need heating, plumbing, lighting, space, storage, etc.
- **Analysis Phase**  This phase produces the Functional Specifications ("deliverables") for the house such as the location of vents for central heating and air conditioning or outlets for phone service.

- **Design Phase**   Here a system is proposed to solve the problem. The system is divided into functional components and the components are intercon-nected. These would include the rooms, ventilation, wiring.
- **Programming Phase**   This is the actual work that is conducted to bring the system into being. It is the building of the house.
- **System Test Phase**   This phase brings the pieces together and tests them as a whole. In the house, we test the plumbing, the electricity, the roof, and so on.
- **Acceptance Phase**   The customer now tests the completed system for ac-ceptance and payment. Minor problems are fixed at the time; major prob-lems require negotiation (see Chapter 6). The house buyer may ask for re-pairs to cracked plaster, or an outlet. A major problem would be if the buyer had specified two fireplaces and the contractor had only built one.
- **Operation Phase**   This includes installation and use. The house buyer moves in and lives in the house. If problems develop or are found upon use, the contractor fixes them during the warranty period. This does not include maintenance, or upgrades and extensions.

Prentis [35] breaks the general planning process into seven steps, while Roman [38] describes it as a set of six planning sequences. First comes preliminary coordi-nation where the various parties involved in the project get together and make pre-liminary decisions about what will be achieved (project objectives) and by whom. These preliminary plans serve as the basis for the second step: a detailed descrip-tion of the various tasks that must be undertaken and accomplished in order to achieve the objectives of the project. In addition, the very act of engaging in the pre-liminary planning process increases member commitment to the project.

These work plans are used for the third and fourth sequences, deriving the pro-ject budget and schedule. Both the budget and the schedule directly reflect the de-tail (or lack of it) in the project work plan, the detailed description of project tasks. The fifth planning sequence is a precise description of all project status reports, when they are to be produced, what they must contain, and to whom they will be sent. Finally, plans must be developed that deal with project termination, explain-ing in advance how the project pieces will be redistributed once its purpose has been completed.

This chapter deals only with the first two of Roman's six planning sequences, or the first three of Prentis', but we develop planning techniques that link the first two stages to each of the other sequences, which are covered in later chapters. Project budgets are discussed in Chapter 7, schedules in Chapter 8, status reports in Chapter 10, and project termination in Chapter 13.

Before we begin, we assume in this chapter that the purpose of planning is to facilitate later accomplishment. The world is full of plans that never become deeds. The planning techniques covered here are intended to smooth the path from idea to accomplishment. It is a complicated process to manage a project, and plans act as a map of this process. The map must have sufficient detail to determine what must be done next but be simple enough that workers are not lost in a welter of minutiae.

In the pages that follow we discuss a somewhat formal method for the development of a project plan. Almost all project planning techniques lead to plans that contain the same basic elements. They differ only in the ways they approach the process of planning. We have adopted an approach that we think makes the planning process straightforward and fairly systematic, but it is never as systematic and straightforward as planning theorists would like you to believe. At its best, planning is tortuous. It is an iterative process yielding better plans from not-so-good plans, and the iterative process of improvement seems to take place in fits and starts. The process may be described formally, but it does not occur formally. Bits and pieces of plans are developed by individuals, by informal group meetings, or by formalized

# Project Management in Practice
## Planning Anchorage's Bid for the Winter Olympics

Hosting the Olympic Games is always a massive project, but even the preparation of the bid proposal is a major project itself, involving the conceptualization and selling of the Olympics project. Just before the 1984 Winter Olympics in Sarajevo, a group of managers of the Alyeska Ski Resort, while meeting for lunch, wondered aloud, "Why couldn't we host a Winter Olympics in Anchorage?" Anchorage was already studying the construction of Olympic-caliber sports facilities and being an Olympic training site. Why not the Olympics themselves? As public discussion of the idea grew, a steering committee was formed to investigate the issue. Some members went to observe the Winter Games, some visited former winter sites, and some visited the U.S. Olympic Headquarters. Assessing their information, the steering committee decided that it was feasible for Anchorage to make a bid by 1989 to host the 1996 Winter Olympic Games, so in late 1984 the Anchorage Organizing Committee (AOC) was incorporated as a nonprofit organization.

The project was planned to be slow and deliberate, gaining the inside track over time. However, in March 1985, the United States Olympic Committee (USOC) asked the AOC and four other interested cities to bid in June for the 1992 winter games. The winning USOC bid would be forwarded to the International Olympic Committee (IOC) for the final selection decision in September. With only 90 days to prepare their bid, the AOC, as well as the citizens of Anchorage, were galvanized into action. A number of committees were formed and a fund-raiser was hired. The bid was completed in 30 days but the preparation of the presentation took another 45 days. The project garnered wide public support and volunteers. On June 15, the USOC selected Anchorage's bid to forward to the International Committee! In October 1986, the AOC made its bid

*Source*: Mystrom, R., D. Baumeister, and R. Nerland. "Anchorage Organizing Committee for the 1994 Olympics," *Project Management Journal*, June 1988.

Anchorage Organizing Committee Logo

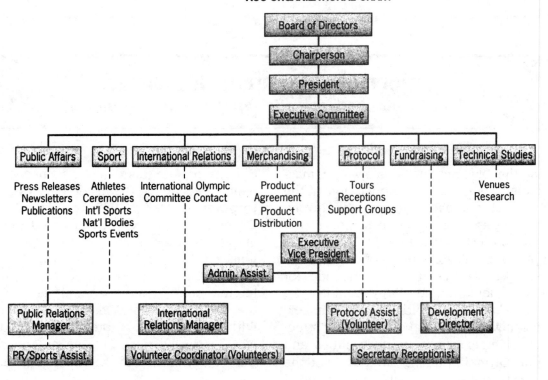

presentation to the International Committee. More than 200 Anchorage residents traveled at their own expense to Lausanne, Switzerland for the presentation, but the selection went to Albertville, France. The Anchorage presentation had been impressive, however, and established the serious Olympic credentials of the city. Thus, when the IOC announced a month later that future winter games would be staggered from the summer games, beginning with the winter games in 1994 (rather than 1996), the USOC, with little debate, reselected Anchorage as its bid.

Again, the AOC began the preparations to make a serious bid for the next winter games. Cost of the bid effort was estimated to be $2.8 million, one of the least expensive bids ever (Paris' bid cost $22 million) due to the massive community volunteer effort and support. Two-thirds of all Alaskans (158,000) made a $5 contribution from their 1986 "dividend" checks to support the bid effort, and the 1987 contributions are expected to double that. In addition, corporate and private donations are expected to bring in $1 million and merchandise marketing should earn another $600,000.

The committee formalized its organization (see chart) and did an extensive economic analysis. One study on the long-term impact concluded that the Alaskan economy would receive between $150 and $750 million in net value from the games. The financial plan was to stage the games without any government funding. Television revenues would bring in two-thirds of the cost; sponsorships and ticket sales would provide most of the rest. The biggest expense would be the cost of facilities while the major operating expense during the games would be the cost of communications.

(*Note*: Anchorage was not selected by the IOC for the 1994 Winter Olympics.)

planning teams [32], and then improved by other individuals, groups, or teams, and improved again, and again.

If the appropriate end product is kept firmly in mind, this untidy process yields a project *master plan*. In this chapter and several following chapters, we discuss the end product, defining the parts of the plan and describing the characteristics each of the parts must have to be most useful in making sure that the project is completed and achieves its objectives.

## ▶ 5.1 INITIAL PROJECT COORDINATION

It is crucial that the project's objectives be clearly tied to the overall mission of the firm. Senior management should define the firm's intent in undertaking the project, outline the scope of the project, and describe the project's desired results. Without a clear beginning, project planning can easily go astray. It is also vital that a senior manager call and be present at an initial coordinating meeting as a visible symbol of top management's commitment to the project.

At the meeting, the project is discussed in sufficient detail that potential contributors develop a general understanding of what is needed. If the project is one of many similar projects, the meeting will be quite short and routine, a sort of "touching base" with other interested units. If the project is unique in most of its aspects, extensive discussion may be required.

Whatever the process, the outcome must be that: (1) technical objectives are established (though perhaps not "cast in concrete"), (2) basic areas of performance responsibility are accepted by the participants, and (3) some tentative schedules and budgets are spelled out. Each individual/unit accepting responsibility for a portion of the project should agree to deliver, by the next project meeting, a preliminary but detailed plan about how that responsibility will be accomplished. Such plans should contain descriptions of the required tasks, budgets, and schedules.

These plans are then reviewed by the group and combined into a composite *project plan*. The composite plan, still not completely firm, is approved by each participating group, by the project manager, and then by senior organizational management. Each subsequent approval hardens the plan somewhat, and when senior management has endorsed it, any further changes must be made by processing a formal *change order*. However, if the project is not large or complex, informal written memoranda can substitute for the change order. The main point is that no *significant* changes in the project are made, without written notice, following top management's approval. The definition of "significant" depends on the specific situation and the people involved.

The PM generally takes responsibility for gathering the necessary approvals and assuring that any changes incorporated into the plan at higher levels are communicated to, and approved by, the units that have already signed off on the plan. Nothing is as sure to enrage functional unit managers as to find that they have been committed by someone else to alterations in their carefully considered plans without being informed. Violation of this procedure is considered a betrayal of trust. Several incidents of this kind occurred in a firm during a project to design a line of children's clothing. The anger at this *change without communication* was so great that two chief designers resigned and took jobs with a competitor.

Because senior managers are almost certain to exercise their prerogative to change the plan, the PM should always return to the contributing units for consideration and reapproval of the plan as modified. The final, approved result of this procedure is the project plan, also known as the *master plan*, or the *baseline plan*.

## Project Management in Practice
### Integrating Company Policy with Company Strategy

A major insurance company decided, as a matter of corporate strategy, that they should embark on a campaign of new product development. Further, they wished to make some other significant changes in their operation, for example, computerization of all forms and records. In order to accomplish these objectives, the Research and Development group, working with senior executives, developed a methodology that formalized the developmental process from the examination of a new idea, through its definition, design, production, and implementation stages. The following flow chart was developed that spelled out the entire process and denoted a series of "check points" at which progress could be measured and controlled. Company management felt that this methodology for new product project development would help make sure that corporate strategy could be embodied in projects—as well as ensure that projects were consistent with and advanced corporate strategy.

*Source:* Mantel, S. J., Jr. Consulting Project.

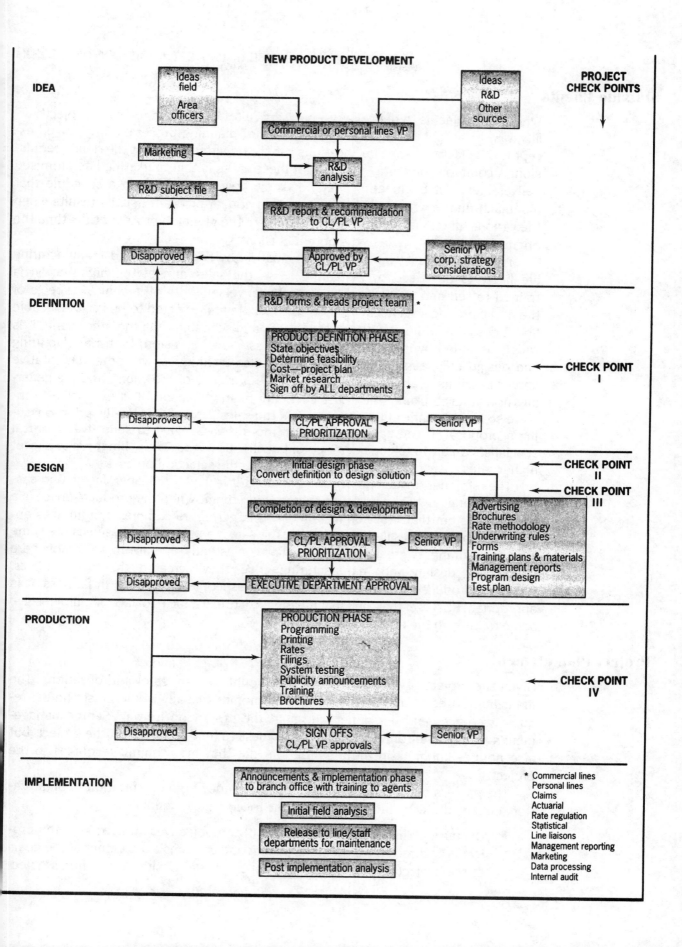

# NEW PRODUCT DEVELOPMENT

**PROJECT CHECK POINTS** ↓

**IDEA**

- Ideas field / Area officers
- Ideas R&D / Other sources

→ Commercial or personal lines VP

Marketing ← R&D analysis

R&D subject file ← R&D analysis

R&D report & recommendation to CL/PL VP

Disapproved ← Approved by CL/PL VP ← Senior VP corp. strategy considerations

**DEFINITION**

R&D forms & heads project team *

**PRODUCT DEFINITION PHASE**
- State objectives
- Determine feasibility
- Cost—project plan
- Market research
- Sign off by ALL departments *

← **CHECK POINT I**

Disapproved ← CL/PL APPROVAL PRIORITIZATION ← Senior VP

**DESIGN**

Initial design phase
Convert definition to design solution  ← **CHECK POINT II**

← **CHECK POINT III**

Completion of design & development

Disapproved ← CL/PL APPROVAL PRIORITIZATION → Senior VP

Disapproved ← EXECUTIVE DEPARTMENT APPROVAL

- Advertising
- Brochures
- Rate methodology
- Underwriting rules
- Forms
- Training plans & materials
- Management reports
- Program design
- Test plan

**PRODUCTION**

**PRODUCTION PHASE**
- Programming
- Printing
- Rates
- Filings
- System testing
- Publicity announcements
- Training
- Brochures

← **CHECK POINT IV**

Disapproved ← SIGN OFFS CL/PL VP approvals → Senior VP

**IMPLEMENTATION**

Announcements & implementation phase to branch office with training to agents

Initial field analysis

Release to line/staff departments for maintenance

Post implementation analysis

\* Commercial lines
Personal lines
Claims
Actuarial
Rate regulation
Statistical
Line liaisons
Management reporting
Marketing
Data processing
Internal audit

## Outside Clients

When the project is to deliver a product/service (often referred to as the project's *deliverables*) to an outside client, the fundamental planning process is unchanged except for the fact that the specifications cannot be altered without the *client's* permission. A common "planning" problem in these cases is that marketing has promised deliverables that engineering may not know how to produce on a schedule that manufacturing may be unable to meet. This sort of problem usually results when the various functional areas are not involved in the planning process at the time the original proposal is made to the potential client.

Two objections to such early participation by engineering and manufacturing are likely to be raised by marketing. First, the sales arm of the organization is trained to sell and is expected to be fully conversant with all technical aspects of the firm's products/services. Further, salespeople are expected to be knowledgeable about design and manufacturing lead times and schedules. On the other hand, it is widely assumed by marketing (with some justice on occasion) that manufacturing and design engineers do not understand sales techniques, will be argumentative and/or pessimistic about client needs in the presence of the client, and are generally not "housebroken" when customers are nearby. Second, it is expensive to involve so much technical talent so early in the sales process—typically, prior to issuing a proposal. It can easily cost a firm more than $10,000 to send five technical specialists on a trip to consider a potential client's needs. The willingness to accept higher sales costs puts even more emphasis on the selection process.

The rejoinder to such objections is simple. It is usually cheaper, faster, and easier to do things right the first time than to redo them. When the product/service is a complex system that must be installed in a larger, more complex system, it is appropriate to treat the sale like a project. The sale *is* a project and deserves the same kind of planning. A great many firms that consistently operate in an atmosphere typified by design and manufacturing crises have created their own panics. (Software producers and computer system salespeople take note!) In fairness, it is appropriate to urge that anyone meeting customers face to face should receive some training in the tactics of selling.

## Project Plan Elements

Given the project plan, approvals really amount to a series of authorizations. The PM is authorized to direct activities, spend monies (usually within preset limits) request resources and personnel, and start the project on its way. Senior management's approval not only signals its willingness to fund and support the project, but also notifies subunits in the organization that they may commit resources to the project.

The process of developing the project plan varies from organization to organization, but any project plan must contain the following elements:

- **Overview** This is a short summary of the objectives and scope of the project. It is directed to top management and contains a statement of the goals of the project, a brief explanation of their relationship to the firm's objectives, a description of the managerial structure that will be used for the project, and a list of the major milestones in the project schedule.

- **Objectives**  This contains a more detailed statement of the general goals noted in the overview section. The statement should include profit and competitive aims as well as technical goals.

- **General Approach**  This section describes both the managerial and the technical approaches to the work. The technical discussion describes the relationship of the project to available technologies. For example, it might note that this project is an extension of work done by the company for an earlier project. The subsection on the managerial approach takes note of any deviation from routine procedure—for instance, the use of subcontractors for some parts of the work.

- **Contractual Aspects**  This critical section of the plan includes a complete list and description of all reporting requirements, customer-supplied resources, liaison arrangements, advisory committees, project review and cancellation procedures, proprietary requirements, any specific management agreements (e.g., use of subcontractors), as well as the technical deliverables and their specifications, delivery schedules, and a specific procedure for changing any of the above. (Project change orders will be discussed in Chapter 11.) Completeness is a necessity in this section. If in doubt about whether an item should be included or not, the wise planner will include it.

- **Schedules**  This section outlines the various schedules and lists all milestone events. The estimated time for each task should be obtained from those who will do the work. The project master schedule is constructed from these inputs. The responsible person or department head should sign off on the final, agreed-on schedule.

- **Resources**  There are two primary aspects to this section. The first is the budget. Both capital and expense requirements are detailed by task, which makes this a *project budget* (discussed further in Chapter 7). One-time costs are separated from recurring project costs. Second, cost monitoring and control procedures should be described. In addition to the usual routine elements, the monitoring and control procedures must be designed to cover special resource requirements for the project, such as special machines, test equipment, laboratory usage or construction, logistics, field facilities, and special materials.

- **Personnel**  This section lists the expected personnel requirements of the project. Special skills, types of training needed, possible recruiting problems, legal or policy restrictions on work force composition, and any other special requirements, such as security clearances, should be noted here. (This reference to "security" includes the need to protect trade secrets and research targets from competitors as well as the need to protect the national security.) It is helpful to time-phase personnel needs to the project schedule. This makes clear when the various types of contributors are needed and in what numbers. These projections are an important element of the budget, so the personnel, schedule, and resources sections can be cross-checked with one another to ensure consistency.

- **Evaluation Methods** Every project should be evaluated against standards and by methods established at the project's inception. This section contains a brief description of the procedure to be followed in monitoring, collecting, storing, and evaluating the history of the project.

- **Potential Problems** Sometimes it is difficult to convince planners to make a serious attempt to anticipate potential difficulties. One or more such possible disasters such as subcontractor default, technical failure, strikes, bad weather, sudden required breakthroughs, critical sequences of tasks, tight deadlines, resource limitations, complex coordination requirements, insufficient authority in some areas, and new, complex, or unfamiliar tasks are certain to occur. The only uncertainties are which ones will occur and when. In fact, the timing of these disasters is not random. There are times, conditions, and events in the life of every project when progress depends on subcontractors, or the weather, or coordination, or resource availability, and plans to deal with unfavorable contingencies should be developed early in the project's life cycle. Some PMs disdain this section of the plan on the grounds that crises cannot be predicted. Further, they claim to be very effective firefighters. It is quite possible that when one finds such a PM, one has discovered an arsonist. No amount of current planning can solve the current crisis, but preplanning may avert some.

These are the elements that constitute the project plan and are the basis for a more detailed planning of the budgets, schedules, work plan, and general management of the project. Once this basic plan is fully developed and approved, it is disseminated to all interested parties. For an example of a project plan, see the case at the end of this chapter.

# ▶ 5.2 SYSTEMS INTEGRATION

*Systems integration* (sometimes called *systems engineering*) plays a crucial role in the performance aspect of the project. We are using this phrase to include any technical specialist in the science or art of the project who is capable of performing the role of integrating the technical disciplines to achieve the customer's objectives, and/or integrating the project into the customer's system. As such, systems integration is concerned with three major objectives.

1. **Performance** Performance is what a system does. It includes system design, reliability, quality, maintainability, and repairability. Obviously, these are not separate, independent elements of the system, but are highly interrelated qualities. Any of these system performance characteristics is subject to overdesign as well as underdesign but must fall within the design parameters established by the client. If the client approves, we may give the client more than the specifications require simply because we have already designed to some capability, and giving the client an overdesigned system is faster and less expensive than

delivering precisely to specification. At times, the esthetic qualities of a system may be specified, typically through a requirement that the appearance of the system must be acceptable to the client.

2.  **Effectiveness**   The objective is to design the individual components of a system to achieve the desired performance in an optimal manner. This is accomplished through the following guidelines:

    *   Require no component performance specifications unless necessary to meet one or more systems requirements.

    *   Every component requirement should be traceable to one or more systems requirements.

    *   Design components to optimize system performance, not the performance of a subsystem.

    It is not unusual for clients to violate any or all of these seemingly logical dicta. Tolerances specified to far closer limits than any possible system requirement, superfluous "bells and whistles," and "off the shelf" components that do not work well with the rest of the system are so common they seem to be taken for granted by both client and vendor. The causes of these strange occurrences are probably associated with some combination of inherent distrust between buyer and seller, the desire to overspecify in order "to be sure," and the feeling that "this part will do just as well." As we will see in Chapter 6, these attitudes can be softened and replaced with others that are more helpful to the process of systems integration.

3.  **Cost**   Systems integration considers cost to be a design parameter, and costs can be accumulated in several areas. Added design cost may lead to decreased component cost, leaving performance and effectiveness otherwise unchanged. Added design cost may yield decreased production costs, and production cost may be traded off against unit cost for materials. *Value engineering* (or *value analysis*) examines all these cost tradeoffs and is an important aspect of systems integration [31]. It can be used in any project where the relevant cost tradeoffs can be estimated. It is simply the consistent and thorough use of cost/effectiveness analysis. For an application of value engineering techniques applied to disease control projects, see [13].

Systems integration plays a major role in the success or failure of any project. If a risky approach is taken by systems integration, it may delay the project. If the approach is too conservative, we forego opportunities for enhanced project capabilities or advantageous project economics. A good design will take all these tradeoffs into account in the initial stages of the technical approach. A good design will also avoid locking the project into a rigid solution with little flexibility or adaptability in case problems occur later on or changes in the environment demand changes in project performance or effectiveness.

The details of systems integration are beyond the scope of this book. The interested reader is referred to [4, 7]. In any case, the ability to do systems integration or engineering depends on at least a minimal level of technical knowledge about most parts of the project. It is one of the reasons project managers are expected to have some understanding of the technology of the projects they head.

# ▶ 5.3 SORTING OUT THE PROJECT

In this and the following sections of this chapter, and in Chapters 7 and 8 on budgeting and scheduling, we move into a consideration of the details of the project. We need to know exactly what is to be done, by whom, and when. All activities required to complete the project must be precisely delineated and coordinated. The necessary resources must be available when and where they are needed, and in the correct amounts. Some activities must be done sequentially, but some may be done simultaneously. If a large project is to come in on time and within cost, a great many things must happen when and how they are supposed to happen. In this section, we propose a conceptually simple method to assist in sorting out and planning all this detail.

To accomplish any specified project, several major activities must be completed. First, list them in the general order in which they would normally occur. A reasonable number of major activities might be anywhere between two and 20. Break each of these major activities into two to 20 subtasks. There is nothing sacred about these limits. Two is the minimum possible breakdown and 20 is about the largest number of interrelated items that can be comfortably sorted and scheduled at a given level of task aggregation. Second, preparing a network from this information, as we will in Chapter 8, is much more difficult if the number of activities is significantly greater than 20.

It is important to be sure that all items in the list are at roughly the same level of task generality. In writing a book, for example, the various chapters tend to be at the same level of generality, but individual chapters are divided into finer detail. Indeed, subdivisions of a chapter may be divided into finer detail still. It is difficult to overstate the significance of this simple dictum. It is central to the preparation of most of the planning documents that will be described in this chapter and those that follow.

Sometimes a problem arises because some managers tend to think of outcomes (events) when planning and others think of specific tasks (activities). Many mix the two. The problem is to develop a list of both activities and outcomes that represents an exhaustive, nonredundant set of results to be accomplished (outcomes) and the work to be done (activities) in order to complete the project.

The procedure proposed here is a *hierarchical* planning system. First, the goals must be specified. This will aid the planner in identifying the set of required activities for the goals to be met, the *project action plan*. Each activity has an outcome (event) associated with it, and these activities and events can be decomposed into subactivities and subevents, which may, in turn, be subdivided again. The *project plan* is the set of these action plans. The advantage of the project plan is that it contains all planning information in one document.

Assume, for example, that we have a project whose purpose is to acquire and install a large machining center in an existing plant. In the hierarchy of work to be accomplished for the installation part of the project, we might find such tasks as "Develop a plan for preparation of the floor site" and "Develop a plan to maintain plant output during the installation and test period." These tasks are two of a larger set of jobs to be done. The task " . . . preparation of the floor site" is subdivided into its elemental parts, including such items as "Get specifics on machine center mounting points," "Check construction specifications on plant floor," and "Present final plan for floor preparation for approval." A form that may help to organize this information is shown in Figure 5-1. (Additional information about each element of the project will be added to the form later when budgeting and scheduling are discussed.) Figure 5-2 shows an action plan for a college "Career Day." (Clearly, Figure 5-2 is not complete. For example, the list of activities does not show such items as "setting and decorating the tables." In the interest of simplicity and in order to avoid doubling the length—and cost—of this book, the examples shown in this and following chapters are meant to be indicative, not exhaustive.)

A short digression is in order before continuing this discussion on action plans. The actual form the action plan takes is not sacrosanct. As we will show in this and the coming chapters, not even all elements of the action plan shown in Figure 5-1 are necessary in all cases. In some cases, for example, the amounts of specific resources required may not be relevant. In others, "due dates" may be substituted for activity durations. The appearance of action plans differs in different organizations, and may even differ between departments or divisions of the same organization (though standardization of format is usual, and probably desirable in any given firm). In some plans, numbers are used to identify activities; in others, letters. In still others, combinations of letters and numbers are used. In this chapter, we will illustrate several different forms of action plans drawn from "real life." Our purpose is not to confuse the reader, but to focus the reader's attention on the *content* of the plan, not its *form*.

A tree diagram can be used to represent a hierarchical plan as in Figure 5-3. Professor Andrew Vazsonyi has called this type of diagram a *Gozinto chart* after the famous Italian mathematician, Prof. Zepartzat Gozinto, of Vazsonyi's invention. (Readers familiar with the Bill of Materials in a Materials Requirements Planning—MRP—system will recognize the parallel to nested hierarchical planning.)

**ACTION PLAN**

Deliverables _____

_____

_____

Measure(s) of accomplishment _____

_____

Key constraints and assumptions _____

_____

| TASKS | ESTIMATED RESOURCES | IMMEDIATE PREDECESSOR TASKS | ESTIMATED TIME DURATION(S) | ASSIGNED TO |
|---|---|---|---|---|

*Figure 5-1:* A form to assist hierarchical planning.

**ACTION PLAN**

| Steps | Responsibility | Time (weeks) | Prec. | Resources |
|---|---|---|---|---|
| **Objective: Career Day** | | | | |
| **1. Contact Organizations** | | | | |
| a. Print forms | Secretary | 6 | – | Print shop |
| b. Contact organizations | Program manager | 15 | 1.a | Word processing |
| c. Collect display information | Office manager | 4 | 1.b | |
| d. Gather college particulars | Secretary | 4 | 1.b | |
| e. Print programs | Secretary | 6 | 1.d | Print shop |
| f. Print participants' certificates | Graduate Assistant | 8 | – | Print shop |
| | | | | |
| **2. Banquet and Refreshments** | | | | |
| a. Select guest speaker | Program manager | 14 | – | |
| b. Organize food | Program manager | 3 | 1.b | Caterer |
| c. Organize liquor | Director | 10 | 1.b | Dept. of Liquor Control |
| d. Organize refreshments | Graduate Assistant | 7 | 1.b | Purchasing |
| | | | | |
| **3. Publicity and Promotion** | | | | |
| a. Send invitations | Graduate Assistant | 2 | – | Word processing |
| b. Organize gift certificates | Graduate Assistant | 5.5 | – | |
| c. Arrange banner | Graduate Assistant | 5 | 1.d | Print shop |
| d. Contact faculty | Program manager | 1.5 | 1.d | Word processing |
| e. Advertise in college paper | Secretary | 5 | 1.d | Newspaper |
| f. Class announcements | Graduate Assistant | 1 | 3.d | Registrar's office |
| g. Organize posters | Secretary | 4.5 | 1.d | Print shop |
| | | | | |
| **4. Facilities** | | | | |
| a. Arrange facility for event | Program manager | 2.5 | 1.c | |
| b. Transport materials | Office manager | .5 | 4.a | Movers |

*Figure* 5-2: Partial action plan for college "Career Day."

If the project does not involve capital equipment and special materials, estimates may not be necessary. Some projects require a long chain of tasks that are mostly sequential—for example, the real estate syndication of an apartment complex or the development and licensing of a new drug. Other projects require the coordination of many concurrent tasks that finally come together—for example, the design and manufacture of an aircraft engine or the construction of a house. Still others have the characteristics of both. An example of a plan to acquire a subsidiary is illustrated in Figures 5-4a and 5-4b. A verbal "action plan" was written in the form of a memorandum, Figure 5-4a, and was followed by the more common, tabular plan shown in Figure 5-4b. Only one page of a five-page plan is shown. The individu-

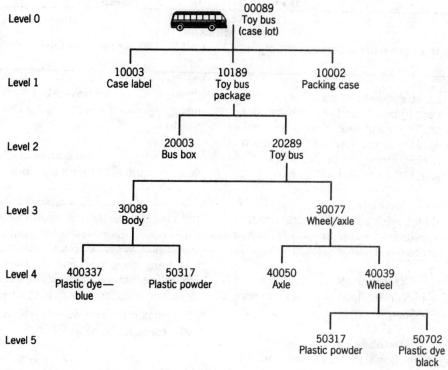

**Figure 5-3:** Gozinto chart for a toy bus. *Source:* [15]

als and groups mentioned developed similar plans at a greater level of detail. (Names have been changed at the request of the firm.)

The importance of careful planning can scarcely be overemphasized. Pinto and Slevin [33, 34] developed a list of ten factors that should be associated with success in implementation projects. The factors were split into strategic and tactical clusters. Of interest here are the strategic factors:

1. **Project mission.** It is important to spell out clearly defined and agreed-upon goals in the beginning of the project.

2. **Top management support.** It is necessary for top managers to get behind the project at the outset and make clear to all personnel involved that they support successful completion.

3. **Project schedule or plan.** A detailed plan of the required steps in the implementation process needs to be developed, including all resource requirements (money, raw materials, staff, and so forth).

Extensive empirical testing showed these factors to be required for implementation project success. (Tactical factors are also necessary for success, but they are not a consideration here.)

At this point, it might be helpful to sum up this section with a description of how the planning process actually works in many organizations. Assume that you, the PM, have been given responsibility for developing the computer software re-

**MEMO**

To allow Ajax to operate like a department of Instat by April 1, 1996, we must do the following by the dates indicated.

**September 24**

Ajax Management to be advised of coming under Instat operation. The Instat sales department will begin selling Ajax Consumer Division production effective Jan. 1, 1996. There will be two sales groups: (1) Instat, (2) Ajax Builder Group.

**October 15**

Instat Regional Managers advised—Instat sales department to assume sales responsibility for Ajax products to distribution channels, Jan. 1, 1986.

**October 15**

Ajax regional managers advised of sales changes effective Jan. 1, 1996.

**October 15**

Instat Management, Bob Carl, Van Baker, and Val Walters visit Ajax management and plant. Discuss how operations will merge into Instat.

**October 22**

Ajax regional managers advised Ajax sales personnel and agents of change effective Jan. 1, 1996.

**October 24**

Brent Sharp and Ken Roadway visit Instat to coordinate changeover.

**October 29**

Instat regional managers begin interviewing Ajax sales personnel for possible positions in Instat's sales organization.

**November 5**

Instat regional managers of Ajax for sales training session.

**November 26**

Walters visits Ajax to obtain more information.

**November 30**

Data Processing (Morrie Reddish) and Mfg. Engineering (Sam Newfield): Request DP tapes from Bob Cawley, Ajax, for conversion of Ajax to Instat eng. records: master inventory file, structure file, bill of materials file, where-used file, cross-reference Instat to Ajax part numbers, etc.

Allow maximum two weeks until December 14, 1995, for tapes to be at Instat.

**December 3**

ADMINISTRATIVE (Val Walters): Offer Norwood warehouse for sublease.

**December 3**

SALES (Abbott and Crutchfield): Week of sales meeting . . . instruction of salespeople in Ajax line . . . including procedure in writing Ajax orders on separate forms from Instat orders . . . temporarily, adding weight and shipping information, and procedure below:

Crutchfield to write procedure regarding transmission of orders to Instat, credit check, and transmission of order information to shipping point, whether Norwood, San Francisco, or, later, Instat Cincinnati.

*Figure 5-4a:* Action plan for merger of Ajax Hardware into Instat Corp. (page 1 of 5)

quired to transmit a medical X ray from one location to another over a telephone line. There are several problems that must be solved to accomplish this task. First, the X ray image must be translated into computer language. Second, the computerized image must be transmitted and received. Third, the image must be displayed (or printed) in a way that makes it intelligible to the person who must interpret it. You have a team of four programmers and a couple of assistant programmers as-

**ACTION PLAN**

| | Objective: Merger of Ajax Hardware into Instat Corp. by April 1, 1996 | | | |
|---|---|---|---|---|
| | **Steps** | **Due Date** | **Responsibility** | **Precedent** |
| **1.** | Ajax management advised of changes | September 24 | Bob Carl, Van Baker | – |
| **2.** | Begin preparing Instat sales dept. to sell Ajax Consumer Division products effective 1/1/96 | September 24 | Bob Carl | 1 |
| **3.** | Prepare to create two sales groups; (1) Instat, (2) Ajax Builder Group effective 1/1/96 | September 24 | Bob Carl | 1 |
| **4.** | Advise Instat regional managers of sales division changes | October 15 | Bob Carl | 2,3 |
| **5.** | Advise Ajax regional managers of sales division changes | October 15 | Van Baker | 2,3 |
| **6.** | Visit Ajax management and plan to discuss merger of operations | October 15 | Bob Carl, Van Baker, Val Walters | 4,5 |
| **7.** | Advise Ajax sales personnel and agents | October 22 | Van Baker | 6 |
| **8.** | Visit Instat to coordinate changeover | October 24 | Brent Sharp, Ken Roadway | 6 |
| **9.** | Interview Ajax sales personnel for possible positions | October 29 | Instat regional managers | 7 |
| **10.** | Sales training sessions for Ajax products | November 5 | Instat regional managers | 9 |
| **11.** | Visit Ajax again | November 26 | Val Walters | 8,10 |
| **12.** | Request DP tapes from Bob Cawley for conversion | November 30 | Morrie Reddish, Sam Newman | 6 |
| **13.** | Offer Norwood warehouse for sublease | December 3 | Val Walters | 11 |
| **14.** | Write order procedures | December 3 | Doug Crutchfield | 10 |
| **15.** | Sales meeting (instruction—product line and procedures) | December 3 | Fred Abbott, Doug Crutchfield | 14 |
| **16.** | DP tapes due for master inventory file, bill of materials, structure file | December 14 | Bob Cawley | 12 |
| | . . . | | | |
| | . . . | | | |
| | . . . | | | |

**Figure 5-4b:** Tabular action plan for Ajax-Instat merger based on Figure 5-4a.

signed to you. You also have a specialist in radiology assigned part-time as a medical advisor.

Your first action is to meet with the programmers and medical advisor in order to arrive at the technical requirements for the project. From these requirements, the project mission statement and detailed specifications will be derived. (Note that the original statement of your "responsibility" is too vague to act as an acceptable mission statement.) The basic actions needed to achieve the technical requirements for the project are then developed by the team. For example, one technical requirement would be to develop a method of measuring the density of the image at every point on the X ray and to represent this measurement as a numerical input for the computer. This is the first level of the project's action plan.

Responsibility for accomplishing the first level tasks is delegated to the project team members who are asked to develop their own action plans for each of the first level tasks. These are the second level action plans. The individual tasks listed in the second level plans are then divided further into third level action plans detailing how each second level task will be accomplished. The process continues until the lowest level tasks are perceived as "units" or "packages" of work.

Early in this section, we advised the planner to keep all items in an action plan at the same level of "generality" or detail. One reason for this is now evident. The tasks at any level of the action plan are usually monitored and controlled by the level just above. If senior managers attempt to monitor and control the highly detailed work packages several levels down, we have a classic case of micromanagement. Another reason for keeping all items in an action plan at the same level of detail is that planners have an unfortunate tendency to plan in great detail all activities they understand well, and to be dreadfully vague in planning activities they do not understand well. The result is that the detailed parts of the plan are apt to be carried out and the vague parts of the plan are apt to be given short shrift.

In practice, this process is iterative. Members of the project team who are assigned responsibility for working out a second, third, or lower-level action plan generate a tentative list of tasks, resource requirements, task durations, predecessors, etc., and bring it to the delegator for discussion, amendment, and approval. This may require several amendments and take several meetings before agreement is reached. The result is that delegator and delegatee both have the same idea about what is to be done, when, and at what cost. Not uncommonly, the individuals and groups that make commitments during the process of developing the action plan actually *sign-off* on their commitments. The whole process involves negotiation and will be further developed in the chapters to follow. Of course, like any managers, delegators can micromanage their delegatees, but micromanagement cannot be mistaken for negotiation—especially by the delegatee.

## Project Management in Practice
### Planning for Public Project Management: Milwaukee's Sewerage Renovation/Expansion

In 1977, by judicial and regulatory order, Milwaukee was ordered to renovate and expand their inadequate and outdated sewerage system. To do so would cost over $2 billion, involve 27 separate municipalities, and take approximately 20 years, all without disrupting existing sewerage services. To date, it has involved 306 construction and procurement

*Source*: H. F. Padgham, "The Milwaukee Water Pollution Abatement Program: Its Stakeholder Management," PM Network, April 1991.

Reconstructed treatment plant on the Milwaukee project.

contracts ranging from $100,000 to $200 million, 121 firms, and 1500 construction personnel. The project includes 20 miles of deep tunnels, ranging from 17 to 32 feet in diameter and 270 to 325 feet underground, and 62 miles of near-surface tunnels and sewers.

To manage this project, a Program Management Office (PMO) was established and given a set of seven physical objectives, seven community objectives, and five funding objectives. Overall, the PMO is responsible for six major functions: evaluation and planning, design management, cost/schedule management, construction, support service, and startup. Rather than PMO hiring all the workers needed for this project as city employees and bearing the costs of hiring, unemployment insurance, etc., an engineering consulting firm experienced in managing large municipal projects was engaged to "schedule, coordinate, and technically manage the various project elements of this program."

In addition to hiring construction and engineering contractors, a number of legal and public relations firms were also engaged to handle the many public conflicts that would invariably occur. One of these developed that seriously threatened the project when USA *Today* published a story that linked the Milwaukee Sewage Processing Plant with an illness contracted by three football players. The public relations firm engaged a number of medical authorities to study the data and offer opinions. They did, and discounted the possibility of any connection, a position affirmed by the national Environmental Protection Agency. The danger blew over.

Another critical point requiring political and public relations expertise concerned which of two major approaches were to be taken to the renovation: the separation of sewer and storm drains/tunnels (favored by excavators and pavers, plus newer communities who already had separate systems) versus the construction of deep underground storage facilities to allow the treatment plants time to process the polluted storm water (a much cheaper solution). Critical support from

Milwaukee community leadership organizations and public officials eventually led to selecting the second approach.

A more difficult problem, still not resolved, is how to pay for the project. Most of the suburbs preferred that the capital (investment) costs be paid through user charges based on the volume of wastewater entering the system. The city and other suburbs preferred that the capital costs be paid through property taxes, and operating costs be paid through user charges. The issue has been in and out of many courts, the state legislature, the state utility regulators, and the Public Service Commission.

In addition to the community leadership organizations, public agencies, and various engineering firms and contractors involved in the project, other stakeholders that need to be considered in the project's decisions include the EPA, the Wisconsin Department of Natural Resources, the U.S. Army Corps of Engineers, the operating staff of the Milwaukee Metropolitan Sewerage District (who will assume operating control of the new system when completed), local and state politicians, the governmental councils of the 27 municipalities, and the citizens and media of Milwaukee and its municipalities. As a tribute to the Milwaukee community, the contracting engineering firm designed a Milwaukee Riverwalk and solicited endorsements and funding for it. Today it is a reality.

## ▶ 5.4   THE WORK BREAKDOWN STRUCTURE AND LINEAR RESPONSIBILITY CHARTS

As was the case with project action plans and contrary to popular notion, the Work Breakdown Structure (WBS) is not one thing. It can take a wide variety of forms, which, in turn, serve a wide variety of purposes. It often pictures a project subdivided into hierarchical units of tasks, subtasks, work packages, etc., as a type of Gozinto chart or tree constructed directly from the project's action plans. Many of the project management software packages actually create WBSs automatically, given that the action plans have been input. These WBSs are usually in the form of outlines with the first level tasks at the left, and successive levels appropriately indented.

Another popular type of WBS shows the organizational elements associated with specific categories of tasks. Figure 5-5 is such a WBS. The project is to build a robot. The control group of the Electronics Department of the organization has responsibility for developing control systems for the robot. Five different control functions are shown, each of which is presumably broken down into more detailed tasks. In this case, the account numbers for each task are shown so that proper charges can be assigned to each piece of work done for the project.

Some writers recommend using the WBS as the fundamental tool for planning [16, for instance]. We find nothing logically wrong with this approach, but it seems overly structured when compared to the way that firms noted for high-quality planning actually proceed. If this approach is used, the PM is well advised to adopt the general philosophy of building the WBS that was used when building the action plan (see Section 5.3). Other writers pay scant attention to the WBS, giving the subject little more than a mention [4 and 26, among others]. We do not find this a fatal error as long as the planning activity is otherwise carried out to an appropriate level of detail.

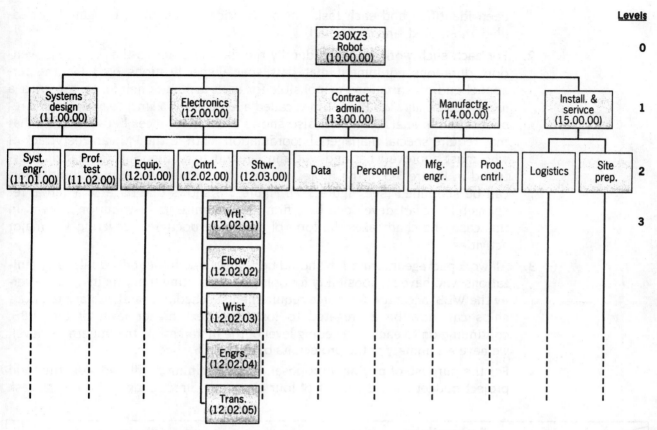

**Figure 5-5:** Work breakdown structure (account numbers shown).

In general, the WBS is an important document and can be tailored for use in a number of different ways. It may illustrate how each piece of the project contributes to the whole in terms of performance, responsibility, budget, and schedule. It may, if the PM wishes, list the vendors or subcontractors associated with specific tasks. It may be used to document that all parties have signed-off on their various commitments to the project. It may note detailed specifications for any work package, establish account numbers, specify hardware/software to be used, and identify resource needs. It may serve as the basis for making cost estimates (see Chapter 7) or estimates of task duration (see Chapter 8). Its uses are limited only by the needs of the project and the imagination of the PM. No one version of the WBS will suit all needs, so the WBS is not *a* document, but any given WBS is simply one of many possible documents.

The following general steps explain the procedure for designing and using the WBS. For small or moderate-size projects, and depending on the use for which the WBS is designed, some of the following steps might be skipped, combined, extended, and handled less formally than our explanation indicates, particularly if the project is of a type familiar to the organization.

1.  Using information from the action plan, list the task breakdown in successively finer levels of detail. Continue until all meaningful tasks or work packages have

been identified and each task can be individually planned, budgeted, scheduled, monitored, and controlled.

2.  For each such work package, identify the data relevant to the WBS (e.g., vendors, durations, equipment, materials, special specifications, etc.). List the personnel and organizations responsible for each task. It is helpful to construct a *linear responsibility chart* (sometimes called a *responsibility matrix*) to show who is responsible for what. This chart also shows critical interfaces between units that may require special managerial coordination. With it, the PM can keep track of who must approve what and who must report to whom. Such a chart is illustrated in Figure 5-6. If the project is not too complex, the responsibility chart can be simplified (see Figure 5-7). Figure 5-8 shows one page of a verbal responsibility chart developed by a firm to reorganize its distribution system. In this case, the chart takes the form of a 30-page document covering 116 major activities.

3.  All work package information should be reviewed with the individuals or organizations who have responsibility for doing or supporting the work in order to verify the WBS' accuracy. Resource requirements, schedules, and subtask relationships can now be aggregated to form the next higher level of the WBS, continuing on to each succeeding level of the hierarchy. At the uppermost level, we have a summary of the project, its budget, and schedule.

4.  For the purpose of pricing a proposal, or determining profit and loss, the total project budget should consist of four elements: direct budgets from each task

| WBS Subproject | Task | Project Manager | Contract Admin. | Project Eng. | Industrial Eng. | Field Manager | |
|---|---|---|---|---|---|---|---|
| Determine Need | A1 | ○ | | ● | ▲ | | |
| | A2 | ■ | ○ | ▲ | ● | | |
| Solicit Quotations | B1 | ○ | ■ | ▲ | | ● | |
| | | | | | | | |
| Write Approp. Request | C1 | ■ | ▲ | ○ | ● | | |
| | C2 | | ● | ○ | ▲ | | |
| | C3 | ● | ■ | ▲ | | ■ | |
| " | " | | | | | | |
| " | " | | | | | | |
| " | " | | | | | | |

*Responsibility* — *Project Office*: Project Manager, Contract Admin., Project Eng., Industrial Eng.; *Field Oper.*: Field Manager.

Legend:
▲  Responsible
●  Support
■  Notification
○  Approval

**Figure 5-6:** Linear responsibility chart.

| | Vice-president | General manager | Project manager | Manager engineering | Manager software | Manager manufacturing | Manager marketing | Subprogram manager manufacturing | Subprogram manager software | Subprogram manager hardware | Subprogram manager services |
|---|---|---|---|---|---|---|---|---|---|---|---|
| Establish project plan | 6 | 2 | 1 | 3 | 3 | 3 | 3 | 4 | 4 | 4 | 4 |
| Define WBS | | 5 | 1 | 3 | 3 | 3 | 3 | 3 | 3 | 3 | 3 |
| Establish hardware specs | | 2 | 3 | 1 | 4 | 4 | 4 | | | | |
| Establish software specs | | 2 | 3 | 4 | 1 | | 4 | | | | |
| Establish interface specs | | 2 | 3 | 1 | 4 | 4 | 4 | | | | |
| Establish manufacturing specs | | 2 | 3 | 4 | 4 | 1 | 4 | | | | |
| Define documentation | | 2 | 1 | 4 | 4 | 4 | 4 | | | | |
| Establish market plan | 5 | 3 | 5 | 4 | 4 | 4 | 1 | | | | |
| Prepare labor estimate | | | 3 | 1 | 1 | 1 | | 4 | 4 | 4 | 4 |
| Prepare equipment cost estimate | | | 3 | 1 | 1 | 1 | | 4 | 4 | 4 | 4 |
| Prepare material costs | | | 3 | 1 | 1 | 1 | | 4 | 4 | 4 | 4 |
| Make program assignments | | | 3 | 1 | 1 | 1 | | 4 | 4 | 4 | 4 |
| Establish time schedules | | 5 | 3 | 1 | 1 | 1 | 3 | 4 | 4 | 4 | 4 |

1 Actual responsibility 4 May be consulted
2 General supervision 5 Must be notified
3 Must be consulted 6 Final approval

*Figure* 5-7: Simplified linear responsibility chart.

as just described; an indirect cost budget for the project, which includes general and administrative overhead costs (G & A), marketing costs, potential penalty charges, and other expenses not attributable to particular tasks; a project "contingency" reserve for unexpected emergencies; and any residual, which includes the profit derived from the project, which may, on occasion, be intentionally negative. In Chapter 7 we argue that the budget used for pricing or calculation of profit should not be the same budget that the PM uses to control the project.

5. Similarly, schedule information and milestone (significant) events can be aggregated into a *project master schedule*. The master schedule integrates the many different schedules relevant to the various parts of the project. It is comprehensive and may include contractual commitments, key interfaces and sequencing, milestone events, and progress reports. In addition, a time contingency reserve for unforeseeable delays might be included. A graphic example of a master schedule is shown in Figure 5-9.

| Activities | Initiate Action | Responsible Individuals Work with | Clear Action with |
|---|---|---|---|
| **Distribution System and its Administration** | | | |
| 1. Recommend distribution system to be used. | Mktg Officers | ILI & IHI LOB MCs M-A Cttee VP &Agcy Dir | Sr VP Mktg |
| | Mktg Officers | Group LOB MC M-A Cttee VP & Agcy Dir | Sr VP Mktg |
| | Mktg Officers | IA LOB MC M-A Cttee VP & Agcy Dir | Sr VP Mktg |
| **Compensation** | | | |
| 2. Determine provisions of sales compensation programs (e.g., commissions, subsidies, fringes). | Compensation Task Force | Mktg, S&S & Eqty Prod Offrs | President |
| | Compensation Task Force | Mktg, S&S & Eqty Prod Offrs | |
| | Compensation Task Force | Mktg, S&S & Eqty Prod Offrs | President |
| 3. Ensure cost-effectiveness testing of sales compensation programs. | Compensation Task Force | Mktg, S&S & Eqty Prod Offrs | President |
| **Territory** | | | |
| 4. Establish territorial strategy for our primary distribution system. | VP & Agcy Dir | Dir MP&R M-A Cttee | Sr VP Mktg |
| 5. Determine territories for agency locations and establish priorities for starting new agencies. | VP & Agcy Dir | Dir MP&R M-A Cttee | Sr VP Mktg |
| 6. Determine agencies in which advanced sales personnel are to operate. | Dir Ret Pln Sls Dir Adv Sls | VP S&S | Sr VP Mktg |

Legend:   IA, ILI, IHI: Product lines
LOB: Line of business
MC: Management committee
M-A Cttee: Marketing administration committee
S&S: Sales and service
MP&R: Marketing planning and research

**Figure 5-8:** Verbal responsibility chart.

| Subproject | | Task | Responsible Dept. | Dependent Dept. | 19 x 4<br>J F M A M J J A S O N D | 19 x 5<br>J F M A M J J A S O N D |
|---|---|---|---|---|---|---|
| Determine Need | A1 | Find operations that benefit most | Industrial | | | |
| | A2 | Approx. size and type needed | Project Eng. | I.E. | | |
| Solicit Quotations | B1 | Contact vendors & review quotes | P.E. | Fin., I.E., Purch. | | |
| Write Appropriation Request | C1 | Determine tooling costs | Tool Design | I.E. | | |
| | C2 | Determine labor savings | I.E. | I.E. | | |
| | C3 | Actual writing | P.E. | Tool Dsgn, Fin., I.E. | | |
| Purchs. Mach. Tooling, and Gauges | D1 | Order robot | Purchasing | P.E. | | |
| | D2 | Design and order or manufacture tooling | Tool dsgn | Purch., Tooling | | |
| | D3 | Specify needed gauges and order or mfg. | Q.C. | Tool Dsgn., Purch. | | |
| Installation and Startup | E1 | Install robot | Plant Layout | Mill-wrights | | |
| | E2 | Train employees | Personnel | P.E. Mfg. | | |
| | E3 | Runoff | Mfg. | Q.C. | | |

Legend:
* Project completion
□ Contractual commitment
△ Planned completion
▲ Actual completion
< Status date
○ Milestone planned
● Milestone achieved
----- Planned progress
——— Actual progress

Note: As of Jan. 31, 19x5, the project is one month behind schedule. This is due mainly to the delay in task C1, which was caused by the late completion of A2.

**Figure 5-9:** Project master schedule.

Listed items 1 to 5 focus on the WBS as a planning tool. It may also be used as an aid in monitoring and controlling projects. Again, it is important to remember that no single WBS contains all of the elements described and any given WBS should be designed with specific uses in mind.

**6.** As the project is carried out, step by step, the PM can continually examine actual resource use, by work element, work package, task, and so on up to the full project level. By comparing actual against planned resource usage at a given time, the PM can identify problems, harden the estimates of final cost, and make sure that relevant corrective actions have been designed and are ready to implement if needed. It is necessary to examine resource usage in relation to results achieved because, while the project may be over budget, the results may be farther along than expected. Similarly, the expenses may be exactly as planned, or even lower, but actual progress may be much less than planned. Control charts showing these *earned values* are described in more detail in Chapter 10.

**7.** Finally, the project schedule may be subjected to the same comparisons as the project budget. Actual progress is compared to scheduled progress by work element, package, task, and complete project, to identify problems and take corrective action. Additional resources may be brought to those tasks behind schedule to expedite them. These added funds may come out of the budget reserve or from other tasks that are ahead of schedule. This topic is discussed further in Chapter 9.

## ▶ 5.5 INTERFACE MANAGEMENT

The most difficult aspect of implementing the project plan is the coordination of the various elements of the project so that they meet their joint goals of performance, schedule, and budget. The PM must control the process and timing of this coordination as a part of the everyday task of managing the project. The term *interface* is used to denote both the process and fact of this coordination. The linear responsibility chart discussed above is clearly a useful aid to the PM in performing this managerial task because it displays the multiple ways the project's people must interact and what the rights, duties, and responsibilities of each will be.

A more formal and detailed approach to this problem has been developed [6] by Benningson. This analytic approach is called TREND (Transformed Relationships Evolved from Network Data) and was designed to illustrate important relationships between work groups, to alert the project manager to potential problems associated with interfaces, and to aid in the design of effective ways to avoid or deal with the potential interface problems.

Three key concepts are added in Benningson's approach: interdependence, uncertainty, and prestige. The project master schedule, the WBS, and task networks can be used to provide some of the information required to delineate the nature of these concepts, to understand their potential impacts on the interface between individuals and groups, and to denote task and group interdependencies. Figure 5-10 is an organizational chart that has been modified according to TREND procedures.

Interdependencies are shown by lines, with the primary direction of the interdependence indicated by the arrows.

The uncertainty facing each task group or individual and the relative prestige levels of each of the task groups/individuals need to be established. Uncertainty levels are assumed to correlate with such factors as the length of the project time horizon, the level of reliance on formal authority, and the degree of task orientation of the work. If estimates are available, the spread between the optimistic and pessimistic time estimates reflects the level of uncertainty of the schedule. See the shaded boxes in Figure 5-10.

Prestige is inferred from organization charts or from known anecdotal information. See the right-hand scale in Figure 5-10. Although using position on the organization chart as a surrogate for organizational prestige is questionable, no better overall measure seems to be available. The analyst would be well advised to check this assumption for each particular case when employing this model. All three elements—prestige, uncertainty, and interdependence—can be depicted on an organization chart to illustrate potential coordination problems.

Dependence is shown by an arrow from the preceding task group/person to the following, dependent task group/person. Uncertainty is denoted by shading those groups/persons with high task uncertainty and not shading those with low uncertainty. Prestige is read directly off the chart by noting the level of the group/person in the organizational structure. See [6] for a detailed example.

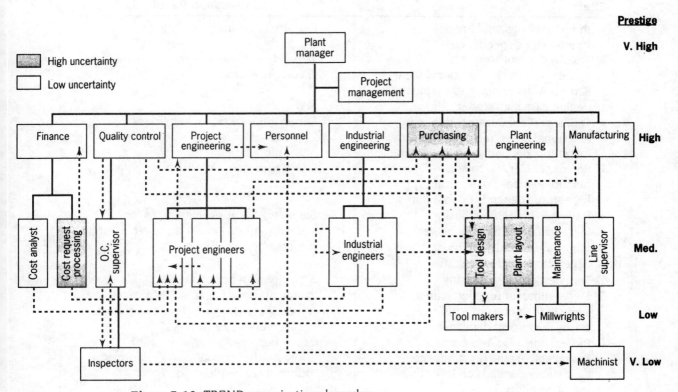

**Figure 5-10:** TREND organizational overlay.

A complete description of the project interfaces can be shown by mapping all dependencies in the project together with the average uncertainty faced by each group/person. Similarly, the different phases of the project life cycle can be displayed using TREND, and can be examined to see what problems might arise within particular time periods. For instance, the work of a particular group might consist mostly of work having low uncertainty, but at project startup, for example, the group may be assigned to some high uncertainty tasks. The PM would give this group special attention during startup in order to react quickly to problems that arose during that period, but could afford to relax attention to this specific group during other phases of the project's life cycle. This pattern of high uncertainty followed by low uncertainty is common. Design of the foundation for a large building may have high uncertainty until test borings are completed, and low uncertainty thereafter. The same is true for most R & D projects, there being high uncertainty until an approach is proven, and then low uncertainty.

Problems also tend to occur when a high-prestige group is dependent on a low-prestige group, when a high-uncertainty task follows another high-uncertainty task, when complex multiple uncertainties exist, and so on. The various combinations of uncertainty and group prestige differentials have various potentials for problems and can best be controlled by managerial strategies formulated specifically to deal with unique situations. Table 5-1 describes some potential interface problems in Figure 5-10 together with possible managerial solutions.

**Table 5-1**  Analysis of TREND Overlay

| Effect | Coordination Required |
|---|---|
| 1. Industrial Engs. and Project Engs.—self-dependencies. | Monitor internal coordination. |
| 2. Quality Control Mgr./Q.C. Supervisor—same functional areas, same low uncertainty, low status depends on high status. | Depend on planning, regular coordination. |
| 3. Q.C. Mgr./Tool Design—different functional areas, mixed uncertainty, low status depends on high status. | Set up interfunctional system for coordination. Monitor regularly. |
| 4. Personnel Mgr./Machinist—different functional area, low uncertainty, high status depends on low status. | Interface as coordinator and translator. |
| 5. Project Engineer/Purchasing Mgr.—different functional area, mixed uncertainty, reciprocal dependence, different status. | Set up regular review meetings for coordination. Project manager chairs meetings. |
| 6. Tool designers/Purchasing Mgr.—different functional area, same high uncertainty, different status, reciprocal dependence. | Set up regular review meetings. Plant eng. mgr. and purch. mgr. to rotate chairing meeting. Perhaps include the project engineers in the meeting. |
| 7. Project Eng. Mgr./Project Engineers—same functional area, high status depends on low, same low uncertainty. | Depend on regular authority and information structure. Stay informed. Encourage frequent discussion. |

TREND is hardly a complete system for interface management and its full-scale, formal use is rarely justified, but the conceptual approach is valuable. Experienced PMs are aware of many of the problems TREND exposes, but the technique provides an excellent framework for the inexperienced and a check for "old hands." For an excellent discussion of the behavioral problems in interface management as well as the entire project implementation process, see [29].

# ▶ SUMMARY

In this chapter we initiated planning for the project in terms of identifying and addressing the tasks required for project completion. We emphasized the importance of initial coordination of all parties involved and the smooth interpretation of the various systems required to achieve the project objectives. Last, we described some tools such as the Work Breakdown Structure (WBS), the linear responsibility chart, the action plan, TREND, and the Gozinto chart to aid in the planning process.

Specific points made in the chapter were these:

- The preliminary work plans are important because they serve as the basis for personnel selection, budgeting, scheduling, and control.

- Top management should be represented in the initial coordinating meeting where technical objectives are established, participant responsibility is accepted, and preliminary budgets and schedules are defined.

- The approval and change processes are complex and should be handled by the project manager.

- Common elements of the project plan are the overview, statement of objectives, general approach, contractual requirements, schedules, budget, cost control procedures, evaluation procedures, and potential problems.

- Systems integration concerns the smooth coordination of project systems in terms of cost, performance, and effectiveness.

- The hierarchical approach to project planning is most appropriate and can be aided by a tree diagram of project subsets, called a Gozinto chart, and a Work Breakdown Structure (WBS). The WBS relates the details of each subtask to its task and provides the final basis for the project budget, schedule, personnel, and control.

- A linear responsibility chart is often helpful to illustrate the relationship of personnel to project tasks and to identify where coordination is necessary.

- A tool particularly helpful in identifying potential interface and coordination problems is the TREND organization chart overlay, based on differences in status or prestige level, task dependence, and uncertainty.

Based on the now-established project plan and WBS, we can consider the task of negotiating for the resources to implement the project. This topic completes Part I of the text.

# ▶ GLOSSARY

Baseline Plan—The nominal plan to which deviations will be compared.

Bill of Materials—The set of physical elements required to build a product.

Control Chart—A graph showing how a statistic is changing over time compared to its average and extreme values.

Deliverables—The physical items to be delivered from a project. This typically includes reports and plans as well as physical objects.

Earned Value—A measure of project progress, frequently related to tasks accomplished and milestones achieved.

Effectiveness—Achieving the objectives set beforehand; to be distinguished from efficiency, which is measured by the output realized for the input used.

**Engineering Change Orders**—Product improvements that engineering has designed after the initial product design was released.

**Gozinto Chart**—A pictorial representation of a product that shows how the elements required to build a product fit together.

**Hierarchical Planning**—A planning approach that breaks the planning task down into the activities that must be done at each managerial level. Typically, the upper level sets the objectives for the next lower level.

**Interface Management**—Managing the problems that tend to occur between departments and disciplines, rather than within individual departments.

**Material Requirements Planning (MRP)**—A planning and material ordering approach based on the known or forecast final demand requirements, lead times for each fabricated or purchased item, and existing inventories of all items.

**Systems Engineering**—The engineering tasks involved in the complete system concerning the project and the integration of all the subsystems into the overall system.

**Value Engineering**—An approach that examines each element of a product or system to determine if there is a better or cheaper way of achieving the same function.

**Work Statement**—A description of a task that defines all the work required to accomplish it, including inputs and desired outputs.

## ▶ MATERIAL REVIEW QUESTIONS

1. List the six component planning sequences of project planning.

2. Any successful project plan must contain nine key elements. List these items and briefly describe the composition of each.

3. What are the basic guidelines for systems design which assure that individual components of the system are designed in an optimal manner?

4. What are the general steps for managing each work package within a specific project?

5. How may the three key concepts in the TREND approach be depicted on an organizational chart, and how are potential problems recognized and possibly averted using this method?

6. What is shown on a linear responsibility chart? How is it useful to a PM?

7. What should be accomplished at the initial coordination meeting?

8. Why is it important for the functional areas to be involved in the project from the time of the original proposal?

9. What are the three major objectives of systems integration?

10. What are the basic steps to design and use the Work Breakdown Structure?

11. What is the objective of interface management?

## ▶ CLASS DISCUSSION QUESTIONS

1. What percentage of the total project effort do you think should be devoted to planning? Why?

2. Why do you suppose that the coordination of the various elements of the project is considered the most difficult aspect of project implementation?

3. What kinds of problem areas might be included in the project plan?

4. What is the role of systems integration in project management? What are the three major objectives of systems integration?

5. In what ways may the WBS be used as a key document to monitor and control a project?

6. Describe the process of subdivision of activities and events that composes the tree diagram

known as the Work Breakdown Structure or Gozinto chart. Why is the input of responsible managers and workers so important an aspect of this process?

7. Why is project planning so important?

8. What are the pros and cons concerning the early participation of the various functional areas in the project plan?

9. What tradeoffs might exist among the three objectives of system integration?

10. Task 5-C is the critical, pacing task of a rush project. Fred always nitpicks anything that comes his way, slowing it down, driving up its costs, and irritating everyone concerned. Normally, Fred would be listed as "Notify" for task 5-C on the responsibility matrix but the PM is considering "forgetting" to make that notation on the chart. In this unethical, political, or just smart management?

# ▶ INCIDENTS FOR DISCUSSION

## Ringold's Pool and Patio Supply

John Ringold, Jr., just graduated from a local university with a degree in industrial management and joined his father's company as executive vice-president of operations. Dad wants to break John in slowly and has decided to see how he can do on a project that John Sr. has never had time to investigate. Twenty percent of the company's sales are derived from the sale of above-ground swimming pool kits. Ringold's does not install the pools. John Sr. has asked John Jr. to determine whether or not they should get into that business. John Jr. has decided that the easiest way to impress Dad and get the project done is personally to estimate the cost to the company of setting up a pool and then call some competitors and see how much they charge. That will show whether or not it is profitable.

John Jr. remembered a method called the work breakdown structure (WBS) that he thought might serve as a useful tool to estimate costs. Also, the use of such a tool could be passed along to the site supervisor to help evaluate the performance of work crews. John Jr.'s WBS is shown in Table 5-2. The total cost John Jr. calculated was $185.00, based on 12.33 labor-hours at $15.00/labor-hour. John Jr. found that, on average, Ringold's competitors charged $229.00 to install a similar pool. John Jr. thought he had a winner. He called his father and made an appointment to present his findings the next morning. Since he had never assembled a pool himself, he decided to increase the budget by 10 percent, "just in case."

*Questions*: Is John Jr.'s WBS projection reasonable? What aspects of the decision will John Sr. consider?

## HAC Computer Company

The board members of HAC Computer Company approved the building of a new facility approximately six months ago. The facility is to be constructed in South Carolina and will be used to manufacture a new line of microcomputers. The company is currently manufacturing only minicomputers and workstations but because of the tremendous market for the micro, they plan to enter this field also. The company has already selected the project manager and the project team. The project manager is ready to get the project under way and has begun work on the project master plan. The three aspects of the master plan that she is most concerned about are schedules, resources, and personnel. Since she is so concerned about scheduling, she decided to get a head start and do the project scheduling estimates for the milestone events herself. For the resource planning she developed some capital

**Table 5-2** Pool Installation WBS

| Work Tasks | | Labor-hours (estimated) |
|---|---|---|
| Prepare ground surface | | 2.67 |
|   Clear | 1 | |
|   Rake | 1/3 | |
|   Level | 1 | |
|   Sand bottom | 1/3 | |
| Lay out pool frame | | 2.50 |
|   Bottom ring | 1 | |
|   Side panels | 1/2 | |
|   Top ring | 1 | |
| Add plastic liner | | 0.50 |
| Assemble pool | | 1.66 |
| Build wooden support | | 3.00 |
|   Lay out | 1 | |
|   Assemble | 2 | |
| Fill and test | | 2.00 |
|   Total | | 12.33 |

requirements for the various parts of the project that would be continuing throughout the project, and for personnel she developed a preliminary forecast of what skills she felt might be needed, and when, over the life of the project.

*Questions:* If you were the project manager, would you handle these three aspects of the master plan the same or differently? Explain. What elements of resource planning and personnel planning should be included?

## ▶ INDIVIDUAL EXERCISE

Recall a recent or current project in a formal group, such as a church committee or social group, of which you are a member. Construct a detailed Gozinto chart and Work Breakdown Structure for the project. Then lay out a linear responsibility chart for the project along the lines of Figure 5-7. Next, design a general organization chart that includes all the parties identified on the linear responsibility chart.

## ▶ PROJECT TEAM CONTINUING EXERCISE

For this exercise, initial project planning must be conducted. To construct the overall project plan, start with the action plan and construct the work breakdown structure, a Gozinto chart, and determine a linear responsibility chart. Include the instructor in your plans as a representative of top management. From this set of information, build a preliminary project budget and determine a master schedule with major milestones. Finally, use the TREND procedure to build an organizational overlay, identify potential problem areas, and suggest possible remedies. Are there any missing information sets or aids that could be helpful for your specific project?

## ▶ BIBLIOGRAPHY

1. AGARWAL, J. C. "Project Planning at Kennecott." *Research Management.* May 1974.

2. ANDERSON, J., and R. NARASIMHAN. "Assessing Project Implementation Risk: A Methodical Approach." *Management Science,* June 1979.

3. ARCHIBALD, R. D. "Projects: Vehicles for Strategic Growth." *Project Management Journal,* Sept. 1988.

4. BADIRU, A. B. *Project Management in Manufacturing and High Technology Operations.* New York: Wiley, 1988.

5. BAUMGARTNER, J. S. *Project Management.* Homewood, IL: Irwin, 1963.

6. BENNINGSON, L. A. "TREND: A Project Management Tool." *Proceedings of the Project Management Conference,* Philadelphia, Oct. 1972.

7. BLANCHARD, B. S., and W. FABRYCKY. *Systems Engineering and Analysis,* 2nd ed. Englewood Cliffs, NJ.: Prentice Hall, 1990.

8. BLANNING, R. W. "How Managers Decide to Use Planning Models." *Long Range Planning,* April 1980.

9. CLELAND, D. I., and R. K. KIMBALL. "The Strategic Context of Projects." *Project Management Journal,* Aug. 1987.

10. DAVIS, E. W. *Project Management: Techniques, Applications, and Managerial Issues,* 2nd ed. Norcross, GA.: Institute of Industrial Engineers, 1983.

11. FRIEND, F. L. "Be A More Effective Program Manager." *Journal of Systems Management,* Feb. 1976.

12. GOODMAN, L. J., and R. N. LOVE, eds. *Project Planning Management.* New York: Pergamon Press Inc., 1980.

13. GROSS, R. N. "Cost–Benefit Analysis and Social Planning." M. Alfandary-Alexander, ed., *Analysis of Planning Programming Budgeting.* Potomac, MD.: Washington Operations Research Council, 1968.

14. GUNDERMAN, J. R., and F. R. MCMURRY. "Making Project Management Effective." *Journal of Systems Management,* Feb. 1975.

15. HARRIS, R. D., and R. F. GONZALEZ. *The Operations Manager.* St. Paul: West, 1981.

16. HUBBARD, D. G. "Work Structuring," in P. C. Dinsmore, ed., *The AMA Handbook of Project Management.* New York: AMACOM, 1993.

17. HUGHES, E. R. "Planning: The Essence of Control." *Managerial Planning*, June 1978.

18. JOHNSON, J. R. "Advanced Project Control." *Journal of Systems Management*, May 1977.

19. KAHERLAS, H. "A Look at Major Planning Methods: Development, Implementation, Strengths and Limitations." *Long Range Planning*, Aug. 1978.

20. KERZNER, H. *Project Management: A Systems Approach to Planning, Scheduling, and Controlling*, 3rd ed. New York: Van Nostrand Reinhold, 1984.

21. KNUTSON, J., and M. SCOTT. "Developing a Project Plan." *Journal of Systems Management*, Oct. 1978.

22. KONDINELL, D. A. "Planning Development Projects: Lessons from Developing Countries." *Long Range Planning*, June 1979.

23. LAUFER, A. "Project Planning: Timing Issues and Path of Progress." *Project Management Journal*, June 1991.

24. LAVOLD, G. D. "Developing and Using the Work Breakdown Structure," in Cleland, D. I., and W. R. King, *Project Management Handbook.* New York: Van Nostrand Reinhold, 1983.

25. LIBERATORE, M. J. "A Decision Support System Linking Research and Development Project Selection with Business Strategy." *Project Management Journal*, Nov. 1988.

26. LOVE, S. F. *Achieving Problem Free Project Management.* New York: Wiley, 1989.

27. MARTIN, J. "Planning: The Gap between Theory and Practice." *Long Range Planning*, Dec. 1979.

28. MARTYN, A. S. "Some Problems in Managing Complex Development Projects." *Long Range Planning*, April 1975.

29. MORRIS, W. T. *Implementation Strategies for Industrial Engineers.* Columbus, OH: Grid, 1979.

30. NUTT, P. C. "Hybrid Planning Methods." *Academy of Management Review*, July 1982.

31. PALEY, A. I. "Value Engineering and Project Management: Achieving Cost Optimization," in P. C. Dinsmore, ed., *The AMA Handbook of Project Management.* New York: AMACOM, 1993.

32. PELLS, D. L. "Project Management Plans: An Approach to Comprehensive Planning for Complex Projects," in P. C. Dinsmore, ed., *The AMA Handbook of Project Management.* New York: AMACOM 1993.

33. PINTO, J. K., and D. P. SLEVIN. "Critical Factors in Successful Project Implementation." *IEEE Transactions on Engineering Management*, Feb. 1987.

34. PINTO, J. K., and D. P. SLEVIN. "Project Success: Definitions and Measurement Techniques." *Project Management Journal*, Feb. 1988.

35. PRENTIS, E. L. "Master Project Planning: Scope, Time and Cost." *Project Management Journal*, Mar. 1989.

36. RAKOS, J. J. *Software Project Management.* Englewood Cliffs, NJ: Prentice Hall, 1990.

37. ROLEFSON, J. F. "Project Management—Six Critical Steps." *Journal of Systems Management*, April 1975.

38. ROMAN, D. *R & D Management.* New York: Appleton-Century-Crofts, 1968.

39. SCHULTZ, R. L., D. P. SLEVIN, and J. K. PINTO. "Strategy and Tactics in a Process Model of Project Implementation." *Interfaces*, May–June 1987.

40. SJOQUIST, P. *Program Management Handbook.* Bloomington, MN: Control Data Corporation (now Ceridian Corp.), undated.

41. STEWART, J. M. "Guides to Effective Project Management." *Management Review*, Jan. 1966.

42. WEBSTER, J. L., W. E. REIF, and J. S. BRACKER. "The Manager's Guide to Strategic Planning Tools and Techniques." *Planning Review*, Nov./Dec. 1989, reprinted in *Engineering Management Review*, Dec. 1990.

43. WEDLEY, W. C., and A. E. J. FERRIE. "Perceptual Differences and Effects of Managerial Participation on Project Implementation." *Operations Research*, March 1978.

44. WESTNEY, R. E., "Paradigms for Planning Productive Projects," in P. C. Dinsmore, ed., *The AMA Handbook of Project Management.* New York: AMACOM, 1993.

45. WHEELWRIGHT, S. C., and R. L. BLANK. "Involving Operating Managers in Planning Process Evaluation." *Sloan Management Review*, Summer 1979.

# CASE

## A PROJECT MANAGEMENT AND CONTROL SYSTEM FOR CAPITAL PROJECTS

### Herbert F. Spirer and A. G. Hulvey

## Introduction

Heublein, Inc., develops, manufactures, and markets consumer food and beverage products domestically and internationally. The business of Heublein, Inc., their sales revenue, and some of their better known products are shown in Figure 1. Highlights of Figure 1 include:

> The four major businesses ("Groups") use different manufacturing plants, equipment, and processes to produce their products. In the Spirits Group large, continuous-process bottling plants are the rule; in the Food Service and Franchising Group, small fast food restaurants are the "manufacturing plants."

> The amount of spending for capital projects and support varies greatly among the Groups, as would be expected from the differences in the magnitude of sales revenues.

> The engineering departments of the Groups have responsibility for operational planning and control of capital projects, a common feature of the Groups. However, the differences among the Groups are reflected in differences in the sizes of the engineering departments and their support services. Similarly, financial tracking support varies from full external support to self-maintained records.

Prior to the implementation of the Project Management and Control System (PM&C) described in this paper, the capital project process was chiefly concerned with the financial justification of the projects, as shown in Figure 2. Highlights include:

> A focus on cost–benefit analysis.

> Minimal emphasis on execution of the projects; no mechanism to assure that non-financial results were achieved.

In the late 1970s the following factors focused attention on the execution weaknesses of the process:

> Some major projects went over budget.

> The need for optimal utilization of capital funds intensified since depreciation legislation was not keeping pace with the inflationary rise in costs.

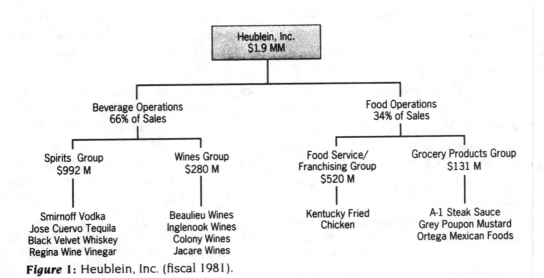

**Figure 1:** Heublein, Inc. (fiscal 1981).

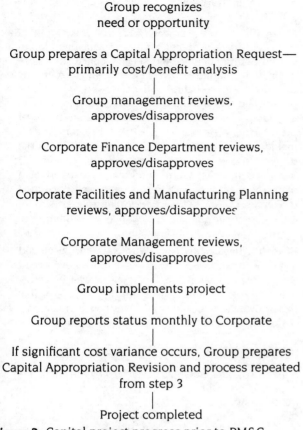

Group recognizes
need or opportunity

|

Group prepares a Capital Appropriation Request—
primarily cost/benefit analysis

|

Group management reviews,
approves/disapproves

|

Corporate Finance Department reviews,
approves/disapproves

|

Corporate Facilities and Manufacturing Planning
reviews, approves/disapproves

|

Corporate Management reviews,
approves/disapproves

|

Group implements project

|

Group reports status monthly to Corporate

|

If significant cost variance occurs, Group prepares
Capital Appropriation Revision and process repeated
from step 3

|

Project completed

**Figure 2:** Capital project progress prior to PM&C

Responding to these factors, Heublein's corporate management called for a program to improve execution of capital projects by implementing PM&C. Responsibility for this program was placed with the Corporate Facilities and Manufacturing Department, which, in addition to reviewing all Capital Appropriation Requests, provided technical consulting services to the corporation.

## Feasibility Study

Lacking specialized expertise in project management, the Director of Facilities and Manufacturing Planning decided to use a consultant in the field. Interviewing of three consultants was undertaken to select one who had the requisite knowledge, compatibility with the style and goals of the firm, and the ability to communicate to all levels and types of managers. The latter requirement was important because of the diversity of the engineering department structures and personnel involved. The first author was selected as the consultant.

With the consultant selected, an internal program manager for PM&C was selected. The deferral of this choice until after selection of the consultant was deliberate, to allow for development of interest and enthusiasm among candidates for this position and so that both the selected individual and the selection committee would have a clear picture of the nature of the program. A program manager was chosen from the corporate staff (the second author).

Having the key staff in place, ground rules were established as follows:

The PM&C program would be developed internally to tailor it to the specific needs of the Groups. A "canned" or packaged system would limit this flexibility, which was deemed essential in this application of project management principles.

The directors of the engineering departments of each of the Groups were to be directly involved in both the design and implementation of the PM&C system in total and for their particular Group. This would assure the commitment to its success that derives from ownership and guarantees that those who know the needs best determine the nature of the system.

To meet the above two ground rules, a thorough fundamental education in the basic principles of project management would be given to all involved in the system design.

The emphasis was to be project *planning* as opposed to project *control*. The purpose of PM&C was to achieve better performance on projects, not catch mistakes after they have occurred. Success was the goal, rather than accountability or identification of responsibility for failure.

## Program Design

The option of defining a uniform PM&C system, to be imposed on all engineering departments by corporate mandate was rejected. The diversity of projects put the weight in favor of individual systems, provided planning and control was such that success of the projects was facilitated. The advantage to corporate staff of uniform planning and reporting was given second place to accommodation of the unique needs of each Group and the wholehearted commitment of each engineering manager to the effective use of the adopted system. Thus, a phased implementation of PM&C within Heublein was planned in advance. These phases were:

**Phase 1. Educational overview for engineering department managers.**  A three-day seminar with two top-level educational objectives: (1) comprehension by participants of a maximal set of project management principles and (2) explanation of the corporate objectives and recommended approach for any PM&C system. Despite some expressed initial concern, the response to this session was positive. It was correctly perceived as the first step in a sincere attempt by corporate management to develop a jointly defined PM&C system that would be useful to the managers of projects, rather than to satisfy a corporate reporting need.

**Phase II. PM&C system design.**  A "gestation period" of three weeks was deliberately introduced between Phases I and II to allow for absorption, discussion, and review of the project management principles and objectives by the engineering department managers. At the end of this period a session was called for the explicit purpose of defining the system. The session was chaired by the consultant, a deliberate choice to achieve the "lightning rod" effect whereby any negative concern was directed to an outsider. Also, the consultant—as an outsider—could criticize and comment in ways that should not be done by the engineering department managers who will have long-term working relationships among each other. It was agreed in advance that a consensus would be sought to the greatest possible extent, avoiding any votes on how to handle particular issues which leaves the "nay" votes feeling that their interests have been overridden by the majority. If consensus could not be achieved, then the issue would be sidestepped to be deferred for later consideration; if sufficiently important then a joint solution could be developed outside the session without the pressure of a fixed closing time. The dynamics of this design session included the development of consensus statements which were displayed on overhead transparencies to be worked into shape. As soon as this was acceptable to the Group as a whole, one of two attending stenographers would record the agreement, leave the room and return later with a typed version for group consideration. The use of two group stenographers assured that one was always in attendance. The enthusiasm expressed by the engineering department managers for this meeting was high.

**Phase III. Project plan development.**  The output of Phase II (the set of consensus conclusions) represented both guidelines and specific conclusions concerning the nature of a PM&C system. Recognizing that the PM&C program will be viewed as a model project and that it should be used as such, serving as an example of what is desired, the program manager prepared a project plan for the PM&C program. The remainder of this paper is primarily concerned with the discussion of this plan, both as an example of how to introduce a PM&C system and how to make a project plan. The plan discussed in this paper and illustrated in Figures 3 to 11 is the type of plan that is now required before any capital project may be submitted to the approval process at Heublein.

**Phase IV. Implementation.**  With the plan developed in Phase III approved, it was possible to move ahead with implementation. Implementation was in accordance with the plan discussed in the balance of this paper. Evaluation of the results was considered a part of this implementation.

## Project Plan

A feature of the guidelines developed by the engineering managers in Phase II was that a "menu" of component parts of a project plan was to be established in the corporate PM&C system, and that elements of this menu were to be chosen to fit the situational or corporate tracking requirements. The menu is:

1.  Introduction
2.  Project Objectives
3.  Project/Program Structure
4.  Project/Program Costs
5.  Network
6.  Schedule
7.  Resource Allocation
8.  Organization and Accountability
9.  Control System
10.  Milestones or Project Subdivisions

In major or critical projects, the minimal set of choices from the menu is specified by corporate staff (the definition of a "major" or "critical" project is a part of the PM&C procedure). For "routine" projects, the choice from the menu is left to the project manager.

In the PM&C plan, items 6 and 7, Schedule and Resource Allocation, were combined into one section for reasons which will be described as part of the detailed discussions of the individual sections which follow.

## Introduction

In this PM&C system, the Introducton is an executive summary, with emphasis on the justification of the project. This can be seen from the PM&C Program Introduction shown in Figure 3. It is to the advantage of everyone concerned with a project to be fully aware of the reasons for its existence. It is as important to the technicians as it is to the engineers or the corporate financial department. When the project staff clearly comprehends the reason for the project's existence it is much easier to enlist and maintain their support and wholehearted efforts. In the Heublein PM&C system, it is expected that the introduction section of a project plan will include answers to these questions: What type of project is involved? What is the cost–benefit relationship? What are the contingency plans? Why is it being done this way (that is, why were alternatives rejected)? Figure 3 not only illustrates this approach, but is the executive summary for the Heublein PM&C system.

## Objectives

Both anecdotal and research inputs have established the importance of clearly stated objectives: von Clauswitz' "Principles of the Objective: A clearly defined, attainable goal" (*On War*, the Modern library, 1943), holds for projects in business. Goals for a project at Heublein must be stated in terms of *deliverable items*. To so state a project objective forces the definition of a clear, comprehensible, measurable and tangible objective. Often, deliverable items resulting from a project are documents. In constructing a residence, is the deliverable item "the house" or is it "the certificate of occupancy"? In the planning stages of a project (which can occur during the project as well as at the beginning), asking this question is as important as getting the answer. Also, defining the project in terms of the deliverables tends to reduce the number of items which are forgotten. Thus, the Heublein PM&C concept of objectives can be seen to be similar to a "statement of work" and is not meant to encompass specifications (detailed descriptions of the attributes of a deliverable item) which can be included as appendices to the objectives of the project.

Figure 4 shows the objectives stated for the Heublein PM&C program. It illustrates one of the principles set for objective statement: that they be hierarchically structured, starting with general statements

---

External and internal factors make it urgent to ensure most efficient use of capital funds. Implementation of a project management and control ("PM&C") system has been chosen as one way to improve the use of capital funds. In March 1979, the Corporate Management Committee defined this need.

Subsequently, Corporate Facilities and Manufacturing Planning performed a feasibility study on this subject. A major conclusion of the study was to develop the system internally rather than use a "canned" system. An internally developed system can be tailored to the individual Groups, giving flexibility which is felt to be essential to success. Another conclusion of the study was to involve Group engineering managers in the design and implementation of the system for better understanding and acceptance.

This is the detailed plan for the design and implementation of a corporate-wide PM&C System. The short term target of the system is major capital projects; the long term target is other types of projects, such as new product development and R&D projects. The schedule and cost are:
Completion Date: June 1980.
Cost: $200,000, of which $60,000 is out of pocket.

---

**Figure 3:** Introduction to PM&C program project plan.

### General Objectives

1. Enable better communication between Group and Corporate management with regard to the progress of major projects.
2. Enable Group management to more closely monitor the progress of major projects.
3. Provide the capability for Group personnel to better manage and control major projects.

### Specific Objectives[a]

1. Reporting and Control System
   - For communication of project activity within Group and between Group and Corporate.
   - Initially for high-cost capital projects, then for "critical," then all others.
2. Procedures Manual
   - Document procedures and policies.
   - Preliminary manual available by October 20, 1979, for use in general educational seminars.
3. Computer Support Systems
   - Survey with recommendations to establish need for and value of computer support.
4. General Educational Package
   - Provide basic project planning and control skills to personnel directly involved in project management, to be conducted by academic authority in field.
   - Technical seminars in construction, engineering, contract administration, and financial aspects of project management.

[a]Defined at the July 1979 PM&C Workshop, attended by representatives of Operating Groups.

**Figure 4:** Objectives of PM&C program.

and moving to increasingly more detailed particular statements. When both particular and general objectives are defined, it is imperative that there be a logical connection; the particular must be in support of the general. Ambiguity and confusion at this point is not unusual and where they exist, they are a source of considerable conflict among client, project management, and staff.

A project (the PM&C Program) satisfying the broadly expressed needs of the Introduction (Figure 3) is more precisely defined in Figure 4. Here we see first that the primary thrust of this system is *General Objectives* item number 3, to provide Group personnel with the ability to do their jobs better. We believe it is important that these general objectives, which were set in a Corporate Management Committee meeting, are not concerned with assigning blame or setting the stage for tighter corporate control, but are in fact positive goals which not only answer desires of Corporate and Group management, but also resolve issues often raised by the operational level personnel.

The specific objectives follow the general objectives in Figure 4, which is largely in accord with our own standards for expression of specific objectives in terms of deliverables. It is now apparent that this could have been carried further; but the success of the program supports the view that these objectives were good enough for their purpose.

### Project Structure

Having a definition of deliverables, the project manager needs explicit structuring of the project to:

Relate the specific objectives to the general.

Define the elements which comprise the deliverables.

Define the activities which yield the elements and deliverables as their output.

Show the hierarchical relationship among objectives, elements, and activities.

The WBS is the tool used to meet these needs. While the WBS may be represented in either indentured (textual) or tree (graphical) formats, the graphic tree format has the advantage of easy comprehension

| Work Breakdown Structure |
|---|

HEUBLEIN PM&C PROGRAM

1000 Program Plan

2000 PM&C System

  2100 Design-Phase Reports
    2101 Analyze Project Scope
    2102 Define Performance Reports
    2103 Define Project Planning
    2104 Define Revision Procedure
    2105 Define Approval/Signoff Procedure
    2106 Define Opening/Closing Procedure
    2107 Define Authority/Responsibility Procedure
    2108 Define Record-keeping Requirements
    2109 Define Estimating Requirements
    2110 Define Reporting and Control System
    2111 Determine Accounting Support Capabilities
    2112 Define Estimating Procedures
    2113 Define Record-keeping Procedures
    2114 Prepare Organization Impact Analysis (Include Ongoing training)
    2115 Define Policy Requirements
    2116 Define Public Relations Policy
    2117 Define Legal Policies—Environmental, OSHA, EEO, Government Agencies, Land Use
    2118 Define Personal Liability Policy
    2119 Define Financial Policy—Capital Expense, Cash Flow
    2120 Define Purchasing Policy—Contracts vs PO, Contractor Qualification, $ Approvals
    2121 Define Record Retention Policy
    2122 Define Computer Support Systems Requirements
  2200 Procedures Manual
    2201 Preliminary Manual
    2202 Final Manual
  2300 Reporting and Control System
  2400 Computer Support Survey
    2401 PERT/CPM
    2402 Scheduling
    2403 Accounting

3000 General Training

  3100 Project Planning and Control Seminar
    3101 Objective Setting
    3102 WBS
    3103 Networks
    3104 Scheduling
    3105 Cost Estimating
    3106 Record Keeping
    3107 Control
  3200 Technical Seminars
    3201 Construction Engineering
    3202 Contract Administration
    3203 Financial Aspects
  3300 Ongoing Training

**Figure 5:** Project structure.

at all levels. The tree version of the WBS also has the considerable advantage that entries may be made in the nodes ("boxes") to indicate charge account numbers, accountable staff, etc.

Figure 5 is the WBS for the PM&C Program, showing the nature of the WBS in general and the structure of the PM&C Program project in particular. At this point we can identify the component elements and the activities necessary to achieve them. A hierarchical numbering system was applied to the elements of the WBS, which is always a convenience. The 22 Design Phase Reports (2100 series in Figure 5) speak for themselves, but it is important to note that this WBS is the original WBS: All of these reports, analyses, and determinations were defined prior to starting the program and there were no requirements for additional items. In this area, there was no change of scope problem because the cooperation of all involved functions was obtained at the start of the program. The breadth of the definition task for this company, which does not contract or subcontract to public agencies (with their own special requirements), gives some idea of the considerations that must be taken into account when setting up a PM&C System. The rest of the WBS is self-explanatory and it is hoped that it can serve as a starting point for others wishing to implement similar programs.

### Project Costs

The WBS provides a listing of the tasks to be performed to achieve the project objectives; with only the WBS in hand it is possible to assemble a *preliminary* project estimate. The estimates based only on the WBS are preliminary because they reflect not only uncertainty (which varies considerably among types of projects), but because the allocation of resources to meet schedule difficulties cannot be determined until both the network and the schedule and resource evaluations have been completed. However, at this time the project planner can begin to hierarchically assemble costs for use at any level. First the lowest level activities of work (sometimes called "work packages") can be assigned values. These estimates can be aggregated in accordance with the WBS tree structure to give higher level totals. At the root of the tree there is only one element—the project—and the total preliminary estimated cost is available.

Figure 6 shows the costs as summarized for the PM&C program plan. This example is supplied to give the reader an idea of the nature of the costs to be ex-

pected in carrying out such a PM&C program in this type of situation. Since a project-oriented cost accounting system does not exist, out-of-pocket costs are the only incremental charges. Any organization wishing to cost a similar PM&C program will have to do so within the framework of the organizational approach to costing indirect labor. As a guide to such costs, it should be noted that in the Heublein PM&C Program, over 80 percent of the costs—both out-of-pocket and indirect—were in connection with the General Training (WBS code 3000).

Seminars were limited to two and two-and-a-half days to assure that the attendees perceived the educational process as efficient, tight, and not unduly interfering with their work; it was felt that it was much better to have them leaving with a feeling that they would have liked more rather than the opposite. Knowing the number of attendees, it is possible to determine the labor-days devoted to travel and seminar attendance; consultant/lecturer's fees can be obtained (expect preparation costs) and the incidentals (travel expenses, subsistence, printing, etc.) are easily estimated.

### Network

The PM&C system at Heublein requires networks only for major projects, but encourages their use for all projects. The project manager is allowed the choice of whatever type of network (activity-on-node or event-on-node) he or she prefers to use. For this reason, all educational activities provided instruction in both types of network.

Figure 7 shows a segment of the network for the PM&C Plan. All the usual principles of network cre-

| Labor costs | |
|---|---|
| Development & Design | $ 40,000 |
| Attendees' time in sessions | 60,000 |
| Startup time of PM&C in Group | 40,000 |
| **Basic Educational Package** | |
| Consultants' fees | 20,000 |
| Attendees' travel & expenses | 30,000 |
| Miscellaneous | 10,000 |
| **Total Program Cost** | $200,000 |

Out-of-pocket costs: $60,000

**Figure 6:** Program costs.

| Act'y Short Descr. | Time (weeks) | Immediate Predecessors |
|---|---|---|
| 4000 prepare final rpt | 2 | 2000, 2122, 3200 |
| 2000 monitor system | 6 | 2000: hold group workshops |
| 2000 hold group w'shps | 2 | 2000: obtain approval |
| 2000 prepare final proc | 2 | 2000: monitor system |
| 2000 prepare final proc manual, revise syst | 2 | 2116–2121: approvals |
| 2000 monitor system | 8 | 2000: hold group workshops |
| 2000 prepares for impl'n | 2 | 3100: hold PM&C seminar |
| 2122 get approval | 2 | 2122: define com'r supp needs |
| 2122 def comp supp needs | 4 | 3100: hold PM&C sem |
| 3200 hold tech seminars | 4 | 3200: prepare seminars |
| 3200 prepare seminars | 8 | 3200: obtain approvals |
| 3200 obtain approvals | 2 | 3200: def tech sem needs |
| 3200 def tech sem needs | 2 | 3100: hold PM&C sem |
| 3100 hold PM&C seminar | 3 | 3100: integrate proc man in sem; 2201: revise prel proc man |
| 3100 int. proc man in sem | 1 | 2201: prel. proc manual |
| 2201 revise prel proc man | .6 | 2201–2300: get approval |
| 2201–2300 get approval | 1 | 2214: org impact analysis |
| 2214 org impact analysis | .4 | 2201: prel. proc manual |
| 2201 prepare prel. pm | 1 | 2213: def recd kpng proc |
| 2213 def recd kpng proc | 1 | 2111: det acctg supp |
| 2111 det acctg supp | 2 | 2103, 2108, 2109 |
| 2112 def est proc | 2 | 2103, 2108, 2109 |
| 2300 revise rep cont sys | 6 | 2110: get approval |
| 2110 get approval | 1 | 2110: define rep/contr sys |
| 2110 def rep/con sys | 1 | 2101: analyze scopes; 1000: revise prog plan; 2104–7: def proc's; 2103, 2108, 2109 |
| 2116–21 get approval | 2 | 2116–21: define policies |
| 2116–21 define pol'y's | 8 | 2115: def pol'y req'ts |
| 2115 def pol'y req'ts | 3 | 1000: prep. program plan |
| 2101 analyze scopes | 1 | 1000: ditto |
| 1000 rev prog plan | .4 | 1000: get appr plan |
| 1000 get appr plan | 2 | 1000: prep. program plan |
| 2104-7 4-revision 5-appr/signoff 6-open/close 7-auth/resp'y | 1.8 | 2102: def perf repts |
| 2102 def perf repts | 1 | 1000: prep. program plan |
| 2103, 2108, 2109 3-proj planning 8-recd-kpng 9-estimating | 2 | 2102: def perf repts |
| 3100 prepare PM&C sem | 4 | 3100: get appr content |
| 3100 get appr content | 1 | 1000: prep. program plan |

Note: Because of space limitations, the network is given in the form of a precedence table. An activity-on-node diagram may be directly constructed from this table. Numerical designations refer to the WBS on Figure 5.

**Figure 7:** Network of PM&C program.

ation and analysis (for critical path, for example) may be applied by the project manager to the extent that it facilitates planning, implementation, and control. Considerable emphasis was placed on network creation and analysis techniques in the educational phases of the PM&C Program because the network is the basis of the scheduling methods presented, is potentially of great value and is one of the hardest concepts to communicate.

In the Heublein PM&C system, *managerial* networks are desired—networks which the individual project managers will use in their own management process and which the staff of the project can use to self-direct where appropriate. For this reason, the view toward the network is that no one network should exceed 50 nodes. The top-level network represents the highest level of aggregation. Each activity on that network may well represent someone else's next lower level network consisting of not more than 50 nodes; any activity on that second-level network may represent someone else's third-level network consisting of not more than 50 nodes; and so on. Networks with hundreds of nodes are to be avoided because of the difficulty of reading them and also because of the negative attitudes toward formal network planning methods generated by experiences with huge (over 5000 nodes, for example) networks in the past. This is not to say that there are not thousands of activities possible in a Heublein project, but that at the working managerial level, each manager or project staff person responsible for a networked activity is expected to work from a single network of a scope that can be easily comprehended. It is not an easy task to aggregate skillfully to reduce network size, but the exercise of this discipline has value in planning and execution in its own right.

The network shown reflects the interdependencies of activities for Heublein's PM&C Program; they are dependent on the design of the Program and the needs of the organization. Each organization must determine them for themselves. But what is important is that institution of a PM&C Program be planned this way. There is a great temptation in such programs to put all activities on one path and not to take advantage of parallel activities and/or not to see just what is the critical path and to focus efforts along it. Even where there is no special urgency in completion, it is important that all parts of the program work smoothly. If the PM&C Program team cannot assure that all necessary materials are on hand when the seminar attendees arrive to be instructed in methods of assuring timely completion of projects, the PM&C system will be viewed with great cynicism.

## Schedule and Resource Allocation

The network defines the mandatory interdependency relationships among the tasks on a project; the schedule is the realization of the *intent* of the project manager, as it shows when the manager has determined that tasks are to be done. The schedule is constrained in a way that the network is not, for the schedule must reflect calendar limitations (vacations, holidays, plant and vendor shutdowns, etc.) and also the limitations on resources. It is with the schedule that the project manager can develop the resource loadings and it is the schedule which ultimately is determined by both calendar and resource constraints.

## Organization and Accountability

Who is responsible for what? Without clear, unambiguous responses to this question there can be no assurance that the task will be done. In general, committees do not finish projects and there should be one organizational unit responsible for each element in the work breakdown structure and one person in that organizational unit who holds final responsibility. Thus responsibility implies a single name to be mapped to the task or element of the WBS, and it is good practice to place the name of the responsible entity or person in the appropriate node on the WBS.

However, accountability may have multiple levels below the top level of complete responsibility. Some individuals or functions may have approval power, veto power without approval power, others may be needed for information or advice, etc. Often, such multilevel accountability crosses functional and/or geographical boundaries and hence communication becomes of great importance.

A tool which has proved of considerable value to Heublein where multilevel accountability and geographical dispersion of project staff is common is the "accountability matrix." An accountability matrix for a part of the PM&C Program project is shown in Figure 8.

The accountability matrix reflects considerable thought about the *strategy* of the program. In fact, one of its great advantages is that it forces the originator (usually the project manager) to think through the process of implementation. Some individuals must be involved because their input is essential. For example, all engineering managers were essential inputs to establish the exact nature of their needs. On the other hand, some individuals or departments are formally involved to enlist their support, even though a satisfactory program could be defined without them.

| Activity | PM&C Mgr | Consultant | Mgrs. of Eng. FS/F GPG Wines Spirits | Dir F&MP |
|---|---|---|---|---|
| Program Plan | I | P | | A |
| Design-Phase Reports | I | P | P P P P | |
| Procedures Manual | I | | | A |
| Reporting & Control System | I | P | P P P P | |
| Computer Support Survey | I | P | | P |
| Project Planning & Control Seminar | A | I | | P |
| Technical Seminars | I | | P P P P | A |

Legend:  I:  Initiate/Responsibility
         A:  Approve
         P:  Provide input

**Figure 8:** Accountability matrix for PM&C program.

### Control System

The basic loop of feedback for control is shown in Figure 9. This rationale underlies all approaches to controlling projects. Given that a plan (or budget) exists, we then must know what is performance (or actual); a comparison of the two may give a variance. If a variance exists, then the cause of the variance must be sought. Note that any variance is a call for review; as experienced project managers are well aware, underspending or early completions may be as unsatisfactory as overspending and late completions.

The PM&C program did not involve large purchases, or for that matter, many purchases. Nor were large numbers of people working on different tasks to be kept track of and coordinated. These reasons of scale made it possible to control the PM&C Program through the use of Gantt conventions, using schedule bars to show plan and filling them in to show performance. Progress was tracked on a periodic basis, once a week.

Figure 10 shows the timing of the periodic reviews for control purpose and defines the nature of the reports used.

### Milestones and Schedule Subdivisions

Milestones and Schedule Subdivisions are a part of the control system. Of the set of events which can be defined (in the Event-on-Node network, or implicitly

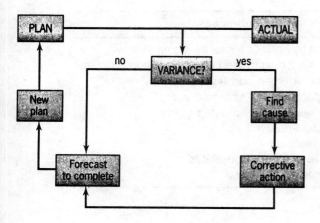

**Figure 9:** The basic feedback loop of control.

1. Periodic status checking will be performed monthly.
2. Labor costs will be collected manually and estimated where necessary from discussion with Group engineering management.
3. Out-of-pocket costs will be collected through commitments and/or invoice payment records.
4. Monthly status reports will be issued by the PM&C Program project manager including:
   a. Cost to date summaries.
   b. Cost variances.
   c. Schedule performance relative to schedule in Gantt format.
   d. Changes in scope or other modifications to plan.
5. Informal control will be exercised through milestone anticipation by the PM&C Program project manager.

**Figure 10:** Control system.

in the Activity-on-Node network), milestones form a limited subset of events, in practice rarely exceeding 20 at any given level. The milestones are predetermined times (or performance states) at which the feedback loop of control described above (Figure 9) should be exercised. Other subdivisions of the project are possible, milestones simply being a subdivision by events. Periodic time subdivisions may be made, or division into phases, one of the most common. Figure 11 shows the milestones for the PM&C Program.

## Summary

The Heublein PM&C Program met the conditions for a successful project in the sense that it was completed on time and within the budgeted funds. As is so often the case, the existence of a formal plan and continuing reference to it made it possible to deal with changes of scope. Initial reaction to the educational package was so favorable that the population of attendees was increased by Group executives and en-

gineering managers; by reference to the original plan it was possible to predict cost increases in advance. Thus, there was no overrun in any sense.

To deliver on time and within budget, but to deliver a product which does not serve the client's needs is also unsatisfactory. Did this PM&C Program achieve the "General Objectives" of Figure 5? We all know the difficulties of quantifying and measuring such objectives within the real-world environment, where the concept of a proper research design is not allowable: We rarely deliberately experiment with organizations. This is a similar problem to that faced in medical research; if we have a methodology that can save or make millions of dollars, can we deny it to any group, even if we are not absolutely certain of its value?

Thus, as is so often the case in managerial systems and educational programs, we are forced to rely on the perceptions of the clients. In this PM&C Program, the clients are Corporate Management, Group Management, and most importantly, the Managers of Engineering and their staffs. In the short

| Date | Description |
|---|---|
| 09/05/79 | Program plan approved by both Corporate & Groups |
| 09/26/79 | Reporting and control system approved by Corporate and Groups |
| 10/05/79 | Organizational impact analysis report issued |
| 11/07/79 | Basic project planning and control seminars completed |
| 01/07/80 | Reporting and control system implemented |
| 03/24/80 | Final procedures manual approved |
| 05/19/80 | Technical Seminars completed |
| | Computer support systems survey completed |
| 06/30/80 | Final impact assessment report issued |

**Figure 11:** Milestones.

run, the latter two operational clients are primary. In addition to informal feedback from them, formal feedback was obtained in the form of Impact Statements (item number 4000 in the WBS of Figure 5). The Impact Statements concerned the impact of the PM&C Program on the concerned organization ("How many labor-hours are expected to be devoted to the PM&C System?") and response to the PM&C Program ("Has this been of value to you in doing your job better?").

Clearly, the response of perceived value from the operating personnel was positive, or this paper would not have been written. Can we put any measure on it? We sought no formal instruments for measurement, relying instead on subjective, free form, and anecdotal responses. Can we measure the improvement which we believe to be taking place in the implementation of capital and other projects? It may be years before the impact (positive or negative) can be evaluated, and even then there may be such confounding with internal and external variables that no unequivocal, quantified response can be defined.

At this point we base our belief in the value of the PM&C Program on the continuing flow—starting with Impact Statements—of positive perceptions. The following is an example of such a response, occurring one year after the exposure of the respondent:

. . . find attached an R&D Project Tracking Diagram developed as a direct result of the [PM&C] seminar . . . last year. [In the seminar we called it] a Network Analysis Diagram. The Product Development Group has been using this exclusively to track projects. Its value has been immeasurable. Since its inception, fifteen new products have gone through the sequence. . . .

# ▶ QUESTIONS

1. Which of the project planning aids (WBS, etc.) described in the chapter was used in the case?

2. For each of the aids used in the case, describe how they were constructed and if there were any modifications in form.

3. How were each of the aids applied in the case?

4. Would a TREND organizational overlay have been useful in this situation? What potential problems might it have shown?

5. What was the purpose of the PM&C project? Was it successful?

6. What was wrong with the previous focus on cost–benefit? Does the PM&C system still include a cost–benefit analysis?

7. Why did lagging depreciation legislation increase the importance of using capital funds optimally?

## ▶ 6.2  PARTNERING, CHARTERING, AND CHANGE

Projects provide ample opportunity for the project manager (PM) to utilize her/his skills at negotiation. There are, however, three situations commonly arising during projects that call for the highest level of negotiating skill the PM can muster: the use of subcontractors, the development of the project's mission statement, and the management of changes ordered in the project's deliverables and/or priorities after the project is underway. The former probably accounts for more litigation than all other aspects of the project combined. The latter two are, in the authors' experience, by far the most common and most troublesome issues project managers report facing.

### Partnering

Generally, relations between the organization carrying out a project and a subcontractor working on the project are best characterized as adversarial. The parent organization's objectives are to get the deliverable at the lowest possible cost, as soon as possible. The subcontractor's objectives are to produce the deliverable at the highest possible profit with the least effort. These conflicting interests tend to lead both parties to work in an atmosphere of mutual suspicion and antagonism. Indeed, it is almost axiomatic that the two parties will have significantly different ideas about the exact nature of the deliverable, itself. The concept of "partnering" has been developed to replace this atmosphere with one of cooperation and mutual helpfulness.

In their excellent article on the subject, Cowan, Gray, and Larson define partnering as follows:

> *Project partnering is a method of transforming contractual relationships into a cohesive, cooperative project team with a single set of goals and established procedures for resolving disputes in a timely and effective manner.* [8, p. 5, italics in original]

They present a multistep process for building partnered projects. First, the parent firm must make a commitment to partnering, select subcontractors who will also make such a commitment, engage in joint team-building exercises, and develop a "charter" for the project. (See next subsection for a description of such a charter.) Second, both parties must implement the partnering process with a four-part agreement on: (1) "joint evaluation" of the project's progress, (2) a method for resolving any problems or disagreements, (3) acceptance of a goal for continuous improvement (also known as TQM) for the joint project, and (4) continuous support for the process of partnering from senior management of both parties. Finally, the parties commit to a joint review of "project execution" when the project is completed.

Clearly, each step in this process must be accompanied by negotiation, and just as clearly, the negotiations must be nonadversarial. The entire concept is firmly rooted in the assumption of mutual trust between the partners and this assumption, too, requires nonadversarial negotiation. Finally, the article focuses on partnering when the partners are members of different organizations. We think the issue is no less relevant when the partners are from different divisions or departments of the same parent organization. Identical assumptions hold, identical steps must be taken, and interparty agreements must be reached for partnering to succeed. (Also see [3].)

## Chartering

A project charter is simply a written agreement between the PM, senior management, and the functional managers who are committing resources and/or people to the project [20]. Like planning documents, WBSs, and responsibility charts, the charter may take many different forms. Typically, it details the expected project deliverables, often including the project's schedule and budget. It attests to the fact that senior management, functional managers, and the PM are "on the same page," agreeing about what is to be done, when, and at what cost. Note that if there is such an agreement, there is also an implication that none of the parties will change the agreement unilaterally, or, at least, without prior consultation with the other parties.

Most projects do not have charters, which is one reason for observing that most projects are not completed on specification, on time, and on budget. Also note the additional fact that project managers are among the most frustrated people in American industry.

In the previous chapter, we described an iterative process for developing project action plans wherein individuals responsible for a task or subtask provided an action plan for completing it. We noted that it is not uncommon for the individuals or groups who make commitments during the process of developing the projects's action plan to sign-off on their commitments. This signed-off set of action plans might constitute a project charter, particularly if senior management has signed-off on the overall mission statement, *and if it is recognized as a charter by all parties to the plan.*

A somewhat less specific charter appears in [8], in which the various members of the partnering team sign a commitment to

- Meet design intent
- Complete contract without need for litigation
- Finish project on schedule:
  - Timely resolution of issues
  - Manage joint schedule
- Keep cost growth to less than 2 percent . . . etc. [8 Figure 2, p. 8]

Of course, even this charter assumes some agreement on the "design intent," the schedule, and costs.

## Change

No matter how carefully a project is planned, it is almost certain to be changed before completion. There are three basic causes for change in projects. Some changes result because planners erred in their initial assessment about how to achieve a given end or erred in their choice of the proper goal for the project. Technological uncertainty is the fundamental causal factor for either error. The foundation for a building must be changed because a preliminary geological study did not reveal a weakness in the structure of the ground on which the building will stand. An R & D project must be altered because metallurgical test results indicate another approach should be adopted. The project team becomes aware of a recent innovation that allows a faster, cheaper solution to the conformation of a new computer.

Other changes result because the client/user or project team learns more about the nature of the project deliverable or about the setting in which it is to be used. An increase in user or team knowledge or sophistication is the primary factor leading to change. A computer program must be extended or rewritten because the user thinks of new uses for the software. Physicians request that intensive care units in a hospital be equipped with laminar air-flow control in order to accommodate patients highly subject to infection who might otherwise not be admissible in an ICU. The fledgling audio-addict upgrades the specifications for a system to include very high frequencies so that his/her dog can enjoy the music, too.

A third source of change is the mandate. A new law is passed. A government regulatory unit articulates a new policy. A trade association sets a new standard. The parent organization of the user applies a new criterion for its purchases. In other words, the rules of conduct for the project are altered. A state approved pollution control system must be adopted for each chemical refinery project. The state government requires all new insurance policies to conform to a revised law specifying that certain information must be given to potential purchasers. At times, mandates affect only priorities. The mandate in question might move a very important customer to the "head of the line" for some scarce resource or service.

In Chapter 11, we discuss some procedures for controlling the *process* of changing projects, but whatever the nature of the change, specifications of the deliverables must be altered, and the schedule and budget must be recalculated. Obviously, negotiation will be required to develop new agreements between the parties-at-interest to the project. These negotiations are difficult because most of the stakeholders will have a strong interest in maintaining the *status quo*. If the proposed change benefits the client and increases the cost of the project, the producer will try to sequester some of the user's potential benefit in the form of added charges to offset the added cost. The client will, of course, resist. All parties must, once again, seek a Pareto optimal solution—always a difficult task.

Change by mandate raises an additional problem. Not only are the project's deliverables, budget, and schedule usually changed, the *priorities* of other projects are typically changed, too. Suddenly, a PM loses access to key resources, because they are urgently required elsewhere. Key contributors to a project miss meetings or are unable to keep promised task-delivery dates. All too often, the PM's response to this state of affairs is anger and/or discouragement. Neither is appropriate.

After discussing priorities with both PMs and senior managers, it has become clear to us that most firms actually have only three levels of priority (no matter how ornate the procedure for setting project priorities might seem to be). First, there are the high-priority projects, that is the set of projects currently being supported. Second, there are the lower-priority projects, the projects "we would like to do when we have the time and money." Third, occasionally, there are urgent projects, mandates, that must be done immediately. "Customer `A's' project must be finished by the end of the month." "The state's mandate must be met by June 30th." Everything else is delayed to ensure that mandates are met. As noted above, we will have more to say on this subject in Chapter 11.

While project charters and partnerships would certainly help the PM deal with conflicts that naturally arise during a project, neither charters nor partnering are widely utilized at this time. It is understandably difficult to convince senior managers to make the firm commitments implied in a project charter in the face of a highly uncertain future. Functional managers are loath to make firm commitments for precisely the same reason. So, too, the client, aware of her/his own ignorance about the degree to which the project output will meet his/her needs, is cautious about commitment—even when a procedure for negotiating change exists.

Partnering is a recently developed concept, and in our litigious society any system for conflict resolution that asks parties to forego lawsuits is viewed with considerable suspicion. Indeed, we find that a great many organizations preach "team building," "TQM," and "employee involvement," but comparatively few practice what they preach. For each participative manager you find, we can show you a dozen micromanagers. For each team player ready to share responsibility, we can show you a dozen "blame placers." The era of project charters and partnering is approaching, but it is not yet here.

# CHAPTER 7

# Budgeting and Cost Estimation

In Chapter 5 we reviewed the planning process, gave some guidelines for designing the project plan, and then discussed the art of negotiation to achieve that plan in Chapter 6. We are now ready to begin implementation. First priority is, of course, obtaining resources with which to do the work. Senior management approval of the project budget does exactly that. A budget is a plan for allocating resources. Thus, the act of budgeting is the allocation of scarce resources to the various endeavors of an organization. The outcomes of the allocation process often do not satisfy managers of the organization who must live and work under budget constraints. It is, however, precisely the pattern of constraints in a budget that embodies organizational policy. The degree to which the different activities of an organization are fully supported by an allocation of resources is one measure of the importance placed on the outcome of the activity. Most of the senior managers we know try hard to be evenhanded in the budgetary process, funding each planned activity at the "right" level—neither overfunding, which produces waste and encourages slack management, nor underfunding, which inhibits accomplishment and frustrates the committed.

The budget is not simply one facet of a plan, nor is it merely an expression of organizational policy; it is also a control mechanism. The budget serves as a standard for comparison, a baseline from which to measure the difference between the actual and planned uses of resources. As the manager directs the deployment of resources to accomplish some desired objective, resource usage should be monitored carefully. This allows deviations from planned usage to be checked against the progress of the project, and exception reports can be generated if resource expenditures are not consistent with accomplishments. Indeed, the pattern of deviations (variances) can be examined to see if it is possible, or reasonable, to forecast significant departures from budget. With sufficient warning, it is sometimes possible to

**287**

implement corrective actions. In any event, such forecasting helps to decrease the number of undesirable surprises for senior management.

Budgets play an important role in the entire process of management. It is clear that budgeting procedures must associate resource use with the achievement of organizational goals or the planning/control process becomes useless. If budgets are not tied to achievement, management may ignore situations where funds are being spent far in advance of accomplishment but are within budget when viewed by time period. Similarly, management may misinterpret the true state of affairs when the budget is overspent for a given time period but outlays are appropriate for the level of task completion. Data must be collected and reported in a timely manner, or the value of the budget in identifying and reporting current problems or anticipating upcoming problems will be lost. The reporting process must be carefully designed and controlled. It is of no value if the data are sent to the wrong person or the reports take an inordinately long time to be processed through the system. For example, one manager of a large computer company complained that, based on third-quarter reports, he was instructed to act so as to alter the fourth-quarter results. However, he did not receive the instructions until the first quarter of the following year.

In Chapter 5 we described a planning process that integrated the planning done at different levels of the project. At the top level is the overall project plan, which is then divided and divided again and, perhaps, still again into a "nest" of plans. Project plans were shown to be the verbal equivalents of the WBS. If we cost the WBS, step by step, we develop a project budget. If we cost project plans, we achieve exactly the same end. Viewed in this way, *the budget is simply the project plan in another form*.

Let us now consider some of the various budgeting methods used in organizations. These are described in general first, then with respect to projects. We also address some problems of cost estimation, with attention to the details and pitfalls. We consider some of the special demands and concerns with budgeting for projects. Finally, we present a method for improving one's skills at budget estimation, or estimation and forecasting of any kind. Printouts of project budgets from PM software packages will be shown in Chapter 10 where we cover project management information systems.

# Project Management in Practice
## *Financing the Flight of the Voyager*

On the morning of December 23, 1986, Dick Rutan and Jeana Yeager landed their strange-looking canard aircraft at Edwards Air Force Base in California, culminating an historic 9-day, 25,000 mile nonstop circumnavigation of the globe without refueling. The plane is as stunning as the flight itself: an enormous flexible wing with a span of over 110 feet whose tips can move 30 feet up or down and has a

---

Source: D. E. Swanton, "The Voyager Aircraft Odyssey," *Project Management Journal*, April 1988.

surface area equivalent to that of a Boeing 727 airliner, a structural weight of only 2250 pounds but with a capacity for over 7000 pounds of fuel, a pusher and a puller engine, but the puller engine is turned off in flight, and numerous other such unexpected characteristics.

The flight itself was just as unusual. The noise level in the cockpit was too deafening for the two pilots to tolerate for nine days so a sine wave generator was installed to cancel the engine noise and piped into their earphones. A special oxygen supply was added to allow the plane to climb to the necessary 20,000 feet to fly over Africa. And the plane had a tendency to "porpoise" early in the flight and had to be continuously fought by the pilots for the first three days.

Yet, during the entire first two years of the project most of the time was not spent working on the plane, nor even on the flight plans—80 percent of the time was spent trying to raise funds! Volunteer project participants struggled from week to week for funding. With such a revolutionary concept and goal, the team thought it would be easy to secure corporate funding to back their efforts. With only one exception, no one, including Lee Iacocca and Ross Perot, was willing to help them—the exception was a Japanese firm, whose offer was politely declined. As flight tests began, however, media coverage increased and the public awareness brought donations as well as some corporate sponsors for the plane's components. The primary reason the plane could be built at a minimal cost was the focus on simplicity and essentials. Eliminating the nonessential items saved time and money, and possibly weight, and may have been the real reason the project was able to be completed successfully!

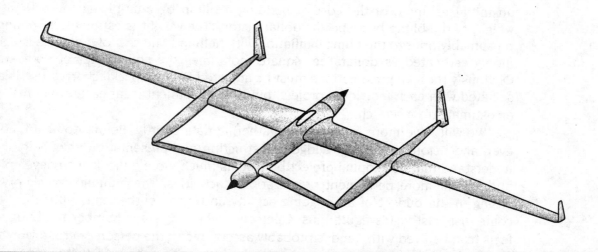

# ▶ 7.1 ESTIMATING PROJECT BUDGETS

In order to develop a budget, we must forecast what resources the project will require, the required quantity of each, when they will be needed, and how much they will cost—including the effects of potential price inflation. Uncertainty is involved in any forecast, though some forecasts have less uncertainty than others. An experienced cost estimator can forecast the number of bricks that will be used to construct a brick wall of known dimensions within 1 to 2 percent. (The estimator knows almost exactly how many bricks are needed to build the wall and must simply add a small allowance for some faulty (broken or discolored) bricks and a few more being broken during the construction process.) On the other hand, the errors are apt to be much larger for an estimate of the number of programmer hours or lines of code that will be required to produce a specific piece of software (see Section 7.2). While the field of software science makes such estimations quite possible, the level of uncertainty is considerably higher and the typical error size is much larger.

In many fields, cost estimation methods are well codified. The office walls of organizational purchasing departments are lined with catalogues detailing what materials, services, and machines are available, from whom, and at what prices. Also on the book shelves are volumes devoted to the techniques of estimating the quantities of materials and labor required to accomplish specific jobs. Every business has its own rules of thumb for cost estimation. These usually distill the collective experience gained by many estimators over many years. An experienced producer of books, for example, can leaf through a manuscript and, after asking a few questions about the number and type of illustrations and the quality of paper to be used, can make a fairly accurate estimate of what it will cost to produce a book.

At times, the job of cost estimation for entire complex projects may be relatively simple because experience has shown that some formula gives a good *first approximation* of the project's cost. For example, the Goodyear Aircraft Company makes an initial estimate of the cost of building a blimp by multiplying the estimated weight of the blimp by a specific dollar factor. (The weight is estimated in pounds, presumably prior to the blimp's inflation with helium.) The cost of buildings is commonly estimated as dollars per square foot times the square feet of floor area. Obviously these approximations must be adjusted for any special characteristics associated with each individual project, but this adjustment is far easier than making an estimate from scratch.

We will have more to say about gathering data shortly. Before doing so, however, and before discussing budget construction and presentation, it is helpful to understand that developing project budgets is much more difficult than developing budgets for more permanent organizational activities. The influence of history is strong in the budget of an ongoing activity and many entries may ultimately become just "last year's figure plus X percent," where X is any number the budgeter feels "can be lived with," and is probably acceptable to the person or group who approves the budgets. No single item in the budget for an ongoing activity is apt to be crucial, because over the course of years the budget has gained sufficient slack that internal adjustments will probably take care of minor shortages in the key accounts.

But the project budgeter cannot depend on tradition. At project inception, there are no past budgets to use as a base. At times, the budgeter may have budgets and audit reports for similar projects to serve as guides, but these are rough guides at best. Tradition, however, has another impact on budgeting, this time a helpful one. In the special case of R & D projects, it has been found [12] that project budgets are stable over time when measured as a percent of the total allocation to R & D from the parent firm, though within the project the budget may be reallocated among activities. There is no reason to believe that the situation is different for other kinds of projects, and we have some evidence that shows stability similar to R & D projects.

For multiyear projects, another problem is raised. The plans and schedules for such projects are set at the beginning of project life, but over the years, the forecast resource usage may be altered by the availability of alternate or new materials, machinery, or personnel—available at different costs than were estimated. The longer the project life, the less the PM can trust that traditional methods and costs will be relevant. As if that were not enough, the degree of executive oversight and review is usually much higher for projects than for ongoing operations, so the budgeter must expect to defend any and all budget entries.

Tradition has still another impact on project budgeting. Every organization has its idiosyncrasies. One firm charges the project's R & D budget with the cost of training sales representatives on the technical aspects of a new product. Another adopts special property accounting practices for contracts with the government. Unless the PM understands the organizational accounting system, there is no way to exercise budgetary control over the project. The methods for project budgeting described below are intended to avoid these problems as much as possible, but complete avoidance is out of the question. Further, it is not politically feasible for the PM to plead a special case with the accountants, who have their own problems. The PM simply must be familiar with the organization's accounting system!

One aspect of cost estimation and budgeting that is not often discussed has to do with the *actual* use of resources as opposed to the accounting department's assumptions about how and when the resources will be used. For instance, presume that you have estimated that $5000 of a given resource will be used in accomplishing a task that is estimated to require five weeks. The actual use of the resource may be none in the first week, $3000 worth in the second week, none in the third week, $1500 in the fourth week, and the remaining $500 in the last week. Unless this pattern of expenditure is detailed in the plan, the accounting department, which takes a linear view of the world, will spread the expenditure equally over the five-week period. This may not affect the project's budget, but it most certainly affects the project's cash flow. The PM must be aware of both the resource requirements and the specific time pattern of resource usage. The subject will be mentioned again in Chapter 9.

Another aspect of preparing budgets is especially important for project budgeting. Every expenditure (or receipt) must be identified with a specific project task (and with its associated milestone, as we will see in the next chapter). Referring back to Figure 5-5, we see that each element in the WBS has a unique account number to which charges are accrued as work is done. These identifiers are needed for the PM to exercise budgetary control.

With these things in mind, the issue of how to gather input data for the budget becomes a matter of some concern. There are two fundamentally different strategies for data gathering, top–down and bottom–up.

## Top–Down Budgeting

This strategy is based on collecting the judgments and experiences of top and middle managers, and available past data concerning similar activities. These managers estimate overall project cost as well as the costs of the major subprojects that comprise it. These cost estimates are then given to lower-level managers, who are expected to continue the breakdown into budget estimates for the specific tasks and work packages that comprise the subprojects. This process continues to the lowest level.

The process parallels the hierarchical planning process described in the last chapter. The budget, like the project, is broken down into successively finer detail, starting from the top, or most aggregated level following the WBS. It is presumed that lower-level managers will argue for more funds if the budget allocation they have been granted is, in their judgment, insufficient for the tasks assigned. However, this presumption is often incorrect. Instead of reasoned debate, argument sometimes ensues, or simply sullen silence. When senior managers insist on maintaining their budgetary positions—based on "considerable past experience"—junior managers feel forced to accept what they perceive to be insufficient allocations to achieve the objectives to which they must commit.

Discussions between the authors and a large number of managers support the contention that lower-level managers often treat the entire budgeting process as if it were a zero-sum game, a game in which any individual's gain is another individual's loss. Competition among junior managers is often quite intense.

The advantage of this top–down process is that aggregate budgets can often be developed quite accurately, though a few individual elements may be significantly in error. Not only are budgets stable as a percent of total allocation, the statistical distribution of the budgets is also stable, making for high predictability [12]. Another advantage of the top–down process is that small yet costly tasks need not be individually identified, nor need it be feared that some small but important aspect has been overlooked. The experience and judgment of the executive is presumed automatically to factor all such elements into the overall estimate.

## Bottom–Up Budgeting

In this method, elemental tasks, their schedules, and their individual budgets are constructed, again following the WBS. The people doing the work are consulted regarding times and budgets for the tasks to ensure the best level of accuracy. Initially, estimates are made in terms of resources, such as labor hours and materials. These are later converted to dollar equivalents. Standard analytic tools such as learning curve analysis (discussed in the next section) and work sampling are employed where appropriate to improve the estimates. Differences of opinion are resolved by the usual discussions between senior and junior managers. If necessary, the project manager and the functional manager(s) may enter the discussion in order to ensure the accuracy of the estimates. The resulting task budgets are aggregated to give the total direct costs of the project. The PM adds such indirect costs as general and administrative (G & A), a project reserve for contingencies, and a profit figure to arrive at the final project budget.

Bottom–up budgets should be, and usually are, more accurate in the detailed tasks, but it is critical that all elements be included. It is far more difficult to develop a complete list of tasks when constructing that list from the bottom up than from the top down. Just as the top–down method may lead to budgetary game playing, the bottom–up process has its unique managerial budget games. For example, individuals overstate their resource needs because they suspect that higher management will probably cut all budgets by some percentage. Their suspicion is, of course, quite justified, as Gagnon [15, 16] and others have shown. Managers who are particularly persuasive sometimes win, but those who are consistently honest and have high credibility win more often.

The advantages of the bottom–up process are those generally associated with participative management. Individuals closer to the work are apt to have a more accurate idea of resource requirements than their superiors or others not personally involved. In addition, the direct involvement of low-level managers in budget preparation increases the likelihood that they will accept the result with a minimum of grumbling. Involvement also is a good managerial training technique, giving junior managers valuable experience in budget preparation as well as the knowledge of the operations required to generate a budget.

While top–down budgeting is common, true bottom–up budgets are rare. Senior managers see the bottom–up process as risky. They tend not to be particularly trusting of ambitious subordinates who may overstate resource requirements in an attempt to ensure success and build empires. Besides, as senior managers note with some justification, the budget is the most important tool for control of the organization. They are understandably reluctant to hand over that control to subordinates whose experience and motives are questionable. This attitude is carried to an extreme in one large corporation that conducts several dozen projects simultaneously, each of which may last five to eight years and cost in excess of $1 million. Project managers do not participate in the budgeting process in this company, nor do they have access to project budgets during their tenure as PMs. (In the past few years, the firm has decided to give PMs access to project budgets but they are still not allowed to participate in the budgetary process.)

## An Iterative Budgeting Process—Negotiation-in-Action

In Chapter 5, we recommended an iterative planning process with subordinates* developing action plans for the tasks for which they were responsible. Superiors review these plans, perhaps suggesting amendments. (See also the latter part of Section 5.3.) The strength of this planning technique is that primary responsibility for the design of a task is delegated to the individual accountable for its completion, and thus it utilizes participative management (or "employee involvement"). If done correctly, estimated resource usage and schedules are a normal part of the planning process at all planning levels. Therefore, the individual concocting an action plan at the highest level would estimate resource requirements and durations for each of the steps in the highest level action plan. Let us refer to these as $r_i$ and $t_i$, the resource and task time requirements for the $i^{th}$ task respectively. Similarly, the

---

*We use the terms "superior" and "subordinate" here for the sole purpose of identifying individuals working on different relative levels of a project's set of action plans. We recognize that in a matrix organization it is not uncommon for PMs ("superiors") to delegate work to individuals ("subordinates") who do not report to the PM and who may be senior to the PM on the parent firm's organizational chart.

subordinate estimates the resource and time requirements for each step of the lower-level action plan. Let us denote the *aggregate* resource and time requirements for the lower level action plan as $r_i'$ and $t_i'$, respectively.

In a perfect world, $r_i$ would equal $r_i'$. (As regards $t_i$ and $t_i'$, our argument holds for duration estimates as well as resource estimates.) We do not, however, live in a perfect world. As a matter of fact, the probable relationship between the original estimates made at the different levels is $r_i << r_i'$. This is true for several reasons, three of which are practically universal. First, as Gagnon has found [15], the farther one moves up the organizational chart away from immediate responsibility for doing the work, the easier, faster, and cheaper the job looks to the superior than to the one who has to do it. This is because the superior either does not know the details of the task, or has conveniently forgotten the details, as well as how long the job takes and how many problems can arise. Second, wishful thinking leads the superior to underestimate cost (and time), because the superior has a stake in representing the project to senior management as a profitable venture. Third, the subordinate is led to build-in some level of protection against failure by adding an allowance for "Murphy's Law" onto a budget that already has a healthy contingency allowance.

Assuming that the superior and subordinate are reasonably honest with one another (any other assumption leads to a failure in win–win negotiations), the two parties meet and review the subordinate's action plan. Usually, the initial step toward reducing the difference in cost estimates is made by the superior who is "educated" by the subordinate in the realities of the job. The result is that $r_i$ rises. The next step is typically made by the subordinate. Encouraged by the boss's positive response to reason, the subordinate surrenders some of protection provided for by the budgetary "slop," and $r_i'$ falls. The subordinate's cost estimate is still greater than the superior's, but the difference is considerably decreased.

The pair now turn their attention to the technology of the task at hand. They carefully inspect the subordinate's work plan, trying to find a more efficient way to accomplish the desired end; that is, they practice total quality management (TQM) and/or value engineering. It may be that a major change can be made that allows a lower resource commitment than either originally imagined. It may be that little or no further improvement is possible. Let us assume that moderate improvement is made, but that $r_i'$ is still somewhat greater than $r_i$, although both have been altered by the negotiations thus far. What should the superior do, accept the subordinate's estimate or insist that the subordinate make do with $r_i$? In order to answer this question, we must digress and reconsider the concept of the project life cycle.

In Chapter 1, we presented the usual view of the project life cycle in Figure 1-2, shown here as Figure 7-1 for convenience. It is important to note that this figure shows "Percent project completion" as a function of "Time." The life-cycle function is essentially unchanged if, for the horizontal axis, we use "Resources" instead. In effect, the life cycle shows what an economist might call "return on input"; that is, the amount of project completion resulting from inputs of time and/or resources.

While this view of the life cycle reflects reality on many projects, it is seriously misleading for others. To understand the difference, let us consider the baking of a cake. Once the ingredients are mixed, we are instructed to bake the cake in a 350° (F) oven for 35 minutes. At what point in the baking process do we have "cake"?

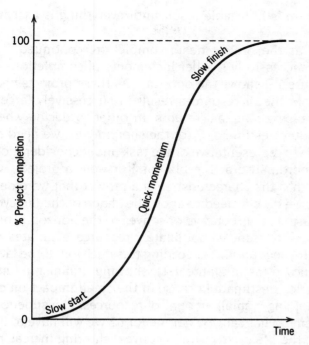

**Figure 7-1:** The project life cycle (Figure 1-2 reproduced).

Experienced bakers know that the mixture changes from "goop" (a technical term well-known to bakers and cooks) to "cake" quite rapidly in the last few minutes of the baking process. The life cycle of this process looks like the curve shown in Figure 7-2. A number of actual projects have a similar life cycle; for example, some projects devoted to the development of computer software, or some projects in chemistry and chemical engineering. In general, this life cycle may exist for projects in which the output is composed or constructed of several subunits (or subroutines) that have little use in and of themselves, but are quite useful when put together. It would also be typical for projects where a chemical-type reaction occurs that rapidly transforms the project from useless to useful. For example, the preparation of the manuscript for the current edition of this book is such a project. A great deal of information must be collected, a great deal of rewriting must be done, new materials

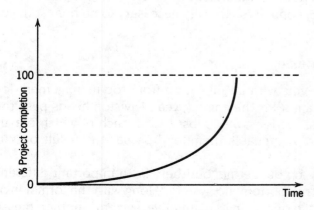

**Figure 7-2:** Another possible project life cycle.

have to be gathered, but there is no visible result until everything is assembled at the last minute.

Figure 7-1 shows that, as the project nears completion, continued inputs of time or resources result in successively smaller increments of completion—diminishing marginal returns. Figure 7-2 shows the opposite. As these projects near completion, successive inputs of time or resources result in successively larger increments of completion—increasing marginal returns. In order to decide whether to adopt the subordinate's resource estimate, $r_i'$, or the superior's, $r_i$, we need to know which picture of the life cycle is representative of the task under consideration. Note that we are treating the subordinate's action plan as if it were a project, which is perfectly all right because it has the characteristics of a project that were described in Chapter 1. Also note that we do not need to know the shape of the life cycle with any precision, merely if its last stage is concave or convex to the horizontal axis.

Remember that the superior's and subordinate's resource estimates are not very far apart as a result of the negotiations preceding this decision. If the latter part of the life-cycle curve is concave (as in Figure 7-1), showing diminishing marginal returns, we opt for the superior's estimate because of the small impact on completion that results from withholding a small amount of resources. The superior might say to the subordinate, "Jeremy, what can you get me for $r_i$? We will have to live with that." If, on the other hand, the life cycle curve is convex, showing increasing marginal returns, the subordinate's estimate should be chosen because of the potentially drastic effect a resource shortage would have on project completion. In this event, the superior might say, "OK, Brandon, we have got to be sure of this job. We'll go with your numbers." If the disagreement had concerned schedule (duration) instead of resources, the negotiation process and underlying logic would be unaltered.

This is a time-consuming process. At the same time the PM is negotiating with the several subordinates responsible for the pieces of the PM's action plan, each of the subordinates are negotiating with their subordinates, and so on. This multilevel process is messy and not particularly efficient, but it allows a free-flow of ideas up and down the system at all levels.

It is worth noting that ethics is just as important in negotiations within an organization as in negotiations between an organization and an outside party. In this case, the superior and subordinate have the responsibility to be honest with each other. For one thing, they must continue to work together in the future under the conditions of mutual trust. Second, it is ethically necessary to be honest in such negotiations.

## Comments on the Budget Request Process

The budget process often begins with an invitation from top management for each division to submit a *budget request* for the coming year. Division heads pass the invitation along to departments, sections, and subsections, each of which presumably collects requests from below, aggregates them, and passes the result back up the organizational ladder.

This sounds like bottom–up budgeting, but there is an important difference between this procedure and a true bottom–up system. Along with the formal invitation for submission of a budget request, in the iterative system another message is passed down—a much less formal message that carries the following kinds of information: the percent by which the wage bill of the organization will be allowed to be increased, organizational policy on adding to the work force, the general attitude toward capital expenditures, knowledge about which projects and activities are considered to be high priority and which are not, and a number of other matters that, in effect, prescribe a set of limits on lower-level managers. As the budget requests are passed back up the organization, they are carefully inspected for conformity to guidelines. If they do not conform, they are "adjusted," often with little or no consultation with the originating units.

The less autocratic the organization (and the less pressured it is by current financial exigencies), the greater the probability that this process will allow dialogue and some compromise between managerial levels. Even the most *participative* firms, however, will not long tolerate lower-level managers who are not sensitive to messages relating to budget limitations. It makes little difference whether budget policy is passed down the system by means of formal, written policy statements or as a haphazard set of oral comments informally transmitted by some senior managers and practically neglected by others; the PM's budget request is expected to conform to policy. Ignorance of the policy is no excuse. Repeated failure to conform will be rewarded with a ticket to corporate Siberia. It is the budget originator's responsibility to find out about budget policy. Again we see the importance of political sensitivity. The PM's channels of communication must be sensitive enough to receive policy signals even in the event that a noncommunicative superior blocks those signals.

## Activity Budgeting vs. Program Budgeting

Thus far we have discussed one facet of an organization's philosophy of budgeting. Another facet has to do with the degree to which a budget is activity-oriented or program-oriented, a distinction we have mentioned before. The traditional organizational budget is activity-oriented. Individual expenses are classified and assigned to basic budget *lines* such as phone, materials, personnel–clerical, utilities, direct labor, etc. These expense lines are gathered into more inclusive categories, and are reported by organizational unit—for example, by section, department, and division. In other words, the budget can be overlaid on the organizational chart. Table 7-1 shows one page of a typical, activity-oriented monthly budget report for a real estate project.

With the advent of project organization, it became necessary to organize the budget in ways that conformed more closely to the actual pattern of fiscal responsibility. Under traditional budgeting methods, the budget for a project could be split up among many different organizational units, which diffused control so widely that it was frequently nonexistent. It was often almost impossible to determine the actual size of major expenditure categories in a project's budget. In light of this problem, ways were sought to alter the budgeting process so that budgets could be associated directly with the projects that used them. This need gave rise to *program budgeting*. Table 7-2 shows a program-oriented project budget divided by task and expected time of expenditure. In an interesting paper, Brimson [6] critiques both systems separately, and then combines them.

**Table 7-1** Typical Monthly Budget for a Real Estate Project (Page 1 of 6)

| | Current | | | |
|---|---|---|---|---|
| | **Actual** | **Budget** | **Variance** | **Pct.** |
| *Corporate—Income Statement* | | | | |
| Revenue | | | | |
| 8430 Management fees | | | | |
| 8491 Prtnsp reimb—property mgmt | 7,410.00 | 6,222.00 | 1,188.00 | 119.0 |
| 8492 Prtnsp reimb—owner acquisition | .00 | 3,750.00 | 3,750.00— | .0 |
| 8493 Prtnsp reimb—rehab | .00 | .00 | .00 | .0 |
| 8494 Other income | .00 | .00 | .00 | .0 |
| 8495 Reimbursements—other | .00 | .00 | .00 | .0 |
| Total revenue | 7,410.00 | 9,972.00 | 2,562.00— | 74.3 |
| | | | | |
| *Operating expenses* | | | | |
| Payroll & P/R benefits | | | | |
| 8511 Salaries | 29,425.75 | 34,583.00 | 5,157.25 | 85.0 |
| 8512 Payroll taxes | 1,789.88 | 3,458.00 | 1,668.12 | 51.7 |
| 8513 Group ins & med reimb | 1,407.45 | 1,040.00 | 387.45— | 135.3 |
| 8515 Workmens compensation | 43.04 | 43.00 | .04— | 100.0 |
| 8516 Staff apartments | .00 | .00 | .00 | .0 |
| 8517 Bonus | .00 | .00 | .00 | .0 |
| Total payroll & P/R benefits | 32,668.12 | 39,124.00 | 6,457.88 | 83.5 |
| | | | | |
| Travel & entertainment expenses | | | | |
| 8512 Travel | 456.65 | 300.00 | 156.65— | 152.2 |
| 8522 Promotion, entertainment & gift | 69.52 | 500.00 | 430.48 | 13.9 |
| 8523 Auto | 1,295.90 | 1,729.00 | 433.10 | 75.0 |
| Total travel & entertainment exp | 1,822.07 | 2,529.00 | 706.93 | 72.1 |
| | | | | |
| Professional fees | | | | |
| 8531 Legal fees | 419.00 | 50.00 | 369.00— | 838.0 |
| 8532 Accounting fees | 289.00 | .00 | 289.00— | .0 |
| 8534 Temporary help | 234.58 | 200.00 | 34.58— | 117.2 |
| 8535 Commissions & consulting | 4,398.50 | 2,532.00 | 1,866.50— | 173.7 |
| 8536 Data processing services | 61.46 | 125.00 | 63.54 | 49.1 |
| Total professional fees | 5,402.54 | 2,907.00 | 2,495.54— | 185.8 |
| | | | | |
| Facility expense | | | | |
| 8541 Rent & parking | 8,860.60 | 8,816.00 | 44.60— | 100.5 |
| 8542 Telephone | 1,306.26 | 800.00 | 506.26— | 163.2 |
| 8543 Office supplies & expense | 664.62 | 700.00 | 35.38 | 94.9 |
| 8544 Photocopy | .00 | .00 | .00 | .0 |
| 8545 Postage | 302.45 | 200.00 | 102.45— | 151.2 |
| 8546 Repairs & maintenance | 440.00 | 350.00 | 90.00— | 125.7 |
| 8547 Insurance | 67.50 | .00 | 67.50— | .0 |

**Table 7-2**  Project Budget by Task and Month

| Task | I | J | Estimate | Monthly Budget (£) | | | | | | | |
|------|---|---|----------|------|------|------|------|------|------|------|------|
|      |   |   |          | 1    | 2    | 3    | 4    | 5    | 6    | 7    | 8    |
| A | 1 | 2 | 7000 | 5600 | 1400 |      |      |      |      |      |      |
| B | 2 | 3 | 9000 |      | 3857 | 5143 |      |      |      |      |      |
| C | 2 | 4 | 10000 |      | 3750 | 5000 | 1250 |      |      |      |      |
| D | 2 | 5 | 6000 |      | 3600 | 2400 |      |      |      |      |      |
| E | 3 | 7 | 12000 |      |      |      | 4800 | 4800 | 2400 |      |      |
| F | 4 | 7 | 3000 |      |      |      | 3000 |      |      |      |      |
| G | 5 | 6 | 9000 |      |      | 2571 | 5143 | 1286 |      |      |      |
| H | 6 | 7 | 5000 |      |      |      |      | 3750 | 1250 |      |      |
| I | 7 | 8 | 8000 |      |      |      |      |      | 2667 | 5333 |      |
| J | 8 | 9 | 6000 |      |      |      |      |      |      |      | 6000 |
|   |   |   | 75000 | 5600 | 12607 | 15114 | 14192 | 9836 | 6317 | 5333 | 6000 |

*Source:* [17]

Program budgeting is the generic name given to a budgeting system that aggregates income and expenditures across programs (projects). In most cases, aggregation by program is in addition to, not instead of, aggregation by organizational unit. The project has its own budget. In the case of pure project organizations, the budgets of all projects are aggregated to the highest organizational level. When functional organization is used for projects, the functional department's budget will be arranged in whatever manner is standard for the organization, but the income/expense associated with each project will be shown. The physical arrangement of such budget reports varies widely, but usually takes the form of a spreadsheet with the standard budget categories listed down the left-hand side of the sheet and category totals disaggregated into "regular operations" and charges to the various projects. Project charges will be split out and spread across the page, with special columns devoted to each project. For example, the columns shown in Table 7-1 would be repeated for each project.

Two special forms of program budgeting have received considerable notoriety in the past. One is planning-programming-budgeting systems (PPBS) and the other is zero-base budgeting (ZBB). While neither PPBS nor ZBB is now widely used, both have influenced managerial thinking. We know of no organizations that currently use ZBB and only a few that have permanently adopted PPBS, mainly social service agencies. But we do know of several corporations that occasionally require PPBS-type cost–benefit analyses. We even know a few senior managers who considered preparing zero-base budgets, but none have actually done so yet. Again, because these concepts have influenced managerial thinking in ways that are important to PMs, they are briefly discussed here.

## Planning-Programming-Budgeting System (PPBS)

PPBS was developed in the late 1960s through then Secretary of Defense Robert McNamara's efforts to deal rationally with the budget of the Department of Defense. PPBS is basically a program budgeting (and planning) system oriented to identifying, planning, and controlling projects that will maximize achievement of the organization's long-run goals. The system focuses on funding those projects that will bring the greatest progress toward organizational goals for the least cost. The PPBS budgeting process entails four major steps:

1. The identification of goals and objectives for each major area of activity. This is the "planning" portion of PPBS.

2. Analysis of the programs proposed to attain organizational objectives; multi-year programs are considered as well as short-term programs. This step requires a good description of the nature of each project so that its intent and the character of its proposed contribution to the organization are understood. This is the "programming" part of PPBS.

3. Estimation of total costs for each project, including indirect costs. Time phasing of costs is detailed for multiyear projects.

4. Final analysis of the alternative projects and sets of projects in terms of expected costs, expected benefits, and expected project lives. Cost–benefit analyses are performed for each program so that the programs can be compared with one another in preparation for selecting a set of projects (i.e., a "portfolio," for funding).

PPBS was mandated by the Department of Defense for contractors, and at the time was deemed useful and effective. With the advent of cost/schedule control systems criteria (see Chapter 10) in the late 1960s, PPBS has fallen from grace and now enjoys only limited use by a few state and local government agencies and some social service organizations. Its precepts, however, have been embodied in the budgeting procedures of many organizations.

## Zero-Base Budgeting (ZBB)

ZBB came into favor in the 1970s as a reaction to the automatic budget increases given year after year to government agencies. As a form of program budgeting, the goal of ZBB was to link the level of funding directly to the achievements associated with specific programs. As opposed to making incremental changes in programs and their accompanying budget allocations, the philosophy of ZBB is that the fundamental desirability of every program should be reviewed and justified each year before the program receives any funding at all. The objective is to cut waste by culling out projects that have outlived their utility and are continuing simply because of the inertia of policymakers.

The ZBB procedure is to describe each project/program, evaluate each one, and rank them in terms of cost–benefit or some other appropriate measure. Funds can then be allocated in accordance with this ranking.

As PPBS is associated with Robert McNamara, ZBB is associated with President Jimmy Carter. He employed ZBB as governor of Georgia and promised (threatened) to do so as president. Like PPBS, ZBB has had no great success. Whereas PPBS involved difficult implementation problems, particularly in the area of measuring costs and benefits (see [30], among many other critiques), ZBB raises a different problem. The primary effect of ZBB is to challenge the existence of every budgetary unit every budget period. Any project that cannot justify continued funding is sentenced to administrative death. The threat of ZBB is so great that organizations subjected to this budget process tend to devote more and more of their energies to defending their existence.

ZBB has a great deal of opposition and little support from the people who must supply the data for the analyses. Few governments have sufficient political clout to adopt and operate a true ZBB system, but some executives employ the logic of ZBB to challenge the continuation of projects they see as inefficient or ineffective. We feel this use of ZBB has considerable merit. For most cases, we feel that use of ZBB is rarely a cost-effective means of project budget control, but the concept is useful for helping to make decisions about whether or not to terminate projects. In Chapter 13 we illustrate an approach to the termination decision based on ZBB. Please note, however, that ZBB is not applied to projects that are clearly successful or are obvious failures, but to projects that cannot be identified as belonging to either group.

# Project Management in Practice
## *Completing the Limerick Nuclear Facility under Budget*

On January 8, 1990, the Limerick nuclear power generating facility in Pennsylvania began commercial operation, thereby setting a construction record for nuclear facilities. In an era when it is common to hear of nuclear plants that massively overrun their budgets and completion schedules, Limerick was completed eight months ahead of its 49-month schedule and came in $400 million under its $3.2 billion budget. Limerick has truly set a standard for the industry.

It was no accident that Limerick was completed ahead of schedule and under budget. When construction started in February 1986, a project goal was to complete the project eight months ahead of the planned completion, which would help keep the costs under the budget limit as well. To achieve this early target, a series of innovative approaches were taken. Two of the major ones were to accelerate ramp-up staffing and to use an extensive, fully-supported second shift. The momentum of the speedy start-up set the fast pace for the remainder of the project. The second shift earned a very favorable premium, as well as having a full complement of managers and engineers to work with the manual workers. In this fashion, the second shift productivity was equal to, if not higher than, the first shift's.

Other decisions and actions further helped either the cost or the schedule. For example, it was decided that overtime would not be worked since a second shift was being used. And as a condition of the project approval, a project labor agreement with the local unions (rather than the national) had to be developed that would eliminate strikes,

*Source*: T. P. Gotzis, "Limerick Generating Station Unit 2," PM *Network*, January 1991.

Limerick Nuclear Facility contractor logos and lost-time clock.

lockouts, and delays and provide for peaceful resolution of disputes. Also, an incentive fee contract with the building contractor was signed whereby the contractor would share equally in cost/schedule overruns or underruns, with limits set.

With such attention to the goal of an early and underbudget completion, the team, numbering almost 3000 workers by June 1987, worked diligently and with high morale, meeting the goal in January 1990.

# ▶ 7.2 IMPROVING THE PROCESS OF COST ESTIMATION

The cooperation of several people is required to prepare cost estimates for a project. If the firm is in a business that regularly requires bids to be submitted to its customers, it will have "professional" cost estimators on its staff. In these cases, it is the job of the PM to generate a description of the work to be done on the project in sufficient detail that the estimator can know what cost data must be collected. Frequently, the project will be too complex for the PM to generate such a description without considerable help from experts in the functional areas.

Even with the finest of experts working to estimate resource usage, the one thing that is certain is that things will not go precisely as planned. There are two fundamentally different ways to deal with the chance events that occur on every project. The simpler and far more common way is to make an allowance for contingencies—usually 5 or 10 percent of the estimated cost. Just why these numbers are chosen in preference to $6\frac{7}{8}$ or $9\frac{1}{4}$, for instance, we do not know. We strongly prefer another method in which the forecaster selects "most likely, optimistic, and pessimistic" estimates. This method is described in detail in Chapter 8 when we cover the issue of estimating the duration of elements in the action plan. The method described in Chapter 8 is applicable, unchanged, to the estimation of resource requirements.

Turning now to the problem of estimating direct costs,* project managers often find it helpful to collect direct cost estimates on a form that not only lists the level of resource needs, but also indicates *when* each resource will be needed, and notes if it is available (or will be available at the appropriate time). Figure 7-3 shows such a form. It also has a column for identifying the person to contact in order to get specific resources. This table can be used for collating the resource requirements for each task element in a project, or for aggregating the information from a series of tasks onto a single form.

Note that Figure 7-3 contains no information on overhead costs. The matter of what overhead costs are to be added and in what amounts is unique to the firm, beyond the PM's control, and generally a source of annoyance and frustration to one and all. The allocation of overhead is arbitrary by its nature, and when the addition of overhead cost causes an otherwise attractive project to fail to meet the organization's economic objectives, the project's supporters are apt to complain bitterly about the "unfairness" of overhead cost allocation.

---

*Our emphasis on estimating direct costs and on focusing on resources that are "direct costed" in the action plan is based on our feeling that the PM should be concerned with only those items over which he/she has some control—which certainly excludes overheads. The PM, however, may wish to add some nonchargable items to the resource column of the action plan simply to "reserve" that item for use at a specific time.

Project Name _____

Date _____

Task Number _____

**RESOURCES NEEDED**

| Resources | Person to Contact | How Many/ Much Needed | When Needed | Check (✓) If Available |
|---|---|---|---|---|
| People: Managers, Supervisors | | | | |
| Professional & Technical | | | | |
| Nontechnical | | | | |
| Money | | | | |
| Materials: Facilities | | | | |
| Equipment | | | | |
| Tools | | | | |
| Power | | | | |
| Space | | | | |
| | | | | |
| | | | | |
| Special Services: Research & Test | | | | |
| Typing/clerical | | | | |
| Reproduction | | | | |
| | | | | |
| Others | | | | |
| | | | | |
| | | | | |

**Figure 7-3:**   Form for gathering data on project resource needs.

At times, firms fund projects that show a significant incremental profit over direct costs but are not profitable when fully costed. Such decisions can be justified for a number of reasons, such as:

- To develop knowledge of a technology
- To get the organization's "foot in the door"
- To obtain the parts or service portion of the work
- To be in a good position for a follow-on contract
- To improve a competitive position
- To broaden a product line or a line of business.

All of these are adequate reasons to fund projects that, in the short term, may lose money but provide the organization with the impetus for future growth and profitability. It is up to senior management to decide if such reasons are worth it.

## Learning Curves

If the project being costed is one of many similar projects, the estimation of each cost element is fairly routine. If the project involves work in which the firm has little experience, cost estimation is more difficult, particularly for direct labor costs. For example, consider a project that requires 25 units of a complex electronic device to be assembled. The firm is experienced in building electronic equipment but has never before made this specific device, which differs significantly from the items it routinely assembles.

Experience might indicate that if the firm were to build many such devices, it would use about seventy hours of direct labor per unit. If labor is paid a wage of $12 per hour, and if benefits equal 28 percent of the wage rate, the estimated labor cost for the 25 units is

$$(1.28)(\$12/hr.)(25 \text{ units})(70 \text{ hours/unit}) = \$26,880$$

In fact, this would be an underestimate of the actual labor cost because more time per unit output is used early in the production process. Studies have shown that human performance usually improves when a task is repeated. In general, performance improves by a fixed percent each time production doubles. More specifically, *each time the output doubles, the worker hours per unit decrease to a fixed percentage of their previous value.* That percentage is called the *learning rate.* If an individual requires 10 minutes to accomplish a certain task the first time it is attempted and only 8 minutes the second time, that person is said to have an 80 percent learning rate. If output is doubled again from two to four, we would expect the fourth item to be produced in

$$8(.8) = 6.4 \text{ minutes}$$

Similarly, the eighth unit of output should require

$$6.4(.8) = 5.12 \text{ minutes}$$

and so on. The time required to produce a unit of output follows a well-known formula:

$$T_n = T_1 n^r$$

*where*

$T_n$ = the time required for the nth unit of output,
$T_1$ = the time required for the initial unit of output,
$n$ = the number of units to be produced, and
$r$ = log decimal learning rate/log 2.

The total time required for all units of a production run of size N is

$$\text{total time} = T_1 \sum_{n=1}^{N} n^r$$

Tables are widely available with both unit and total values for the learning curves, and have been calculated for many different improvement ratios (learning rates—e.g., see [26]).

In the example of the electronic device just given, assume that after producing the twentieth unit, there is no significant further improvement (i.e., assembly time has reached a steady state at 70 hours). Further assume that previous study established that the usual learning rate for assemblers in this plant is about 85 percent. We can estimate the time required for the first unit by letting $T_n = 70$ hours by the unit $n = 20$. Then

$$r = \log .85/\log 2$$
$$= -.1626/.693$$
$$= -.235$$

and

$$70 = T_1(20)^r$$
$$T_1 = 141.3 \text{ hours}$$

Now we know the time for the initial unit. Using a table that shows the total time multipler (see [26, p. 347–348] for example), we can find the appropriate total time multiplier for this example—the multiplier for 20 units given a learning rate of 85 percent. With this multiplier, 12.40, we can calculate the total time required to build all 20 units. It is

$$(12.40)(141.3 \text{ hrs.}) = 1752.12 \text{ hours}$$

The last 5 units are produced in the steady-state time of seventy hours each. Thus the total assembly time is

$$1752.12 + 5(70 \text{ hrs.}) = 2102.12 \text{ hours}$$

We can now refigure the direct labor cost.

$$2102.12(\$12)(1.28) = \$32,288.56$$

Our first estimate, which ignored learning effects, understated the cost by

$$\$32,288.56 - \$26,880 = \$5,408.56$$

or about 17 percent. Figure 7-4 illustrates this source of the error.

The conclusion is simple. For any task where labor is a significant cost factor and the production run is reasonably short, the PM should take the learning curve into account when estimating costs. The implications of this conclusion should not be overlooked. We do not often think of projects as "production," but they are. Research [16] has shown that the learning curve effect is important to decisions about the role of engineering consultants on computer-assisted design (CAD) projects. The failure to consider performance improvement is a significant cause of project cost underestimation.

## Other Factors

The number of things that can produce errors in cost estimates is almost without limit, but some problems occur with particularly high frequency. Changes in resource prices is one of these. The most commonly used solution to this problem is to increase all cost estimates by some fixed percentage. A more useful approach is to identify each input that accounts for a significant portion of project cost and estimate the direction and rate of price change for each.

The determination of which inputs account for a "significant" portion of project cost is not difficult, though it may be somewhat arbitrary. Suppose, for example, that our initial, rough cost estimate (with no provision for future price changes) for

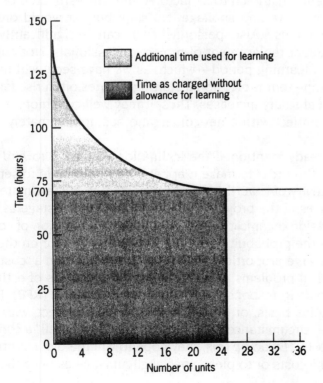

**Figure 7-4:** Effect of ignoring learning curve.

a project is $1 million and is to be spent over a three-year period in approximately equal amounts per year. If we think personnel costs will comprise about 40 percent of that total, also spread equally over time, the wage/salary bill will be about $400,000. Split into three equal amounts, we have expenditures of $133,333 per year. If we estimate that wage/salary rates will increase by 6 percent per year, our expense for the second year rises to $141,333 (an increase of $8,000), and to $149,813 in the third year (an increase of $8,480). Failure to account for wage/salary inflation would result in an underestimate of project cost of about $16,500. This is an error of slightly more than 4 percent of the personnel cost and almost 2 percent of the total project budget.

Further improvements can be made by taking into account the fact that the prices of different inputs often change at very different rates. A quick examination of the Bureau of Labor Statistics (BLS) wage and price indices, which cover a very large number of specific commodities and wage rates, will reveal that even in periods of stable prices, the prices of some things rise while others fall and still others do not change appreciably. Thus, the PM may wish to use different *inflators* for each of several different classes of labor or types of commodities.

The proper level of breakdown in estimating the impact of price changes simply depends on the organization's willingness to tolerate error. Assume that management is willing to accept a 5 percent difference between actual and estimated cost for each major cost category. In the example above, expected increases in wage/salary costs will use more than four-fifths of that allowance. That leaves less than 1 percent (about $3,500) of allowable error, and the need to add one part-time clerk to the project for a single year would more than use the remaining allowance.

Other elements that need to be factored into the estimated project cost include an allowance for waste and spoilage. No sane builder would order "just enough" lumber to build a house. Also, personnel costs can be significantly increased by the loss and subsequent replacement of project professionals. Not only must new people go through a learning period—which, as we have seen, will have a negative effect on production—but professional starting salaries often rise faster than the general rate of annual salary increases. Thus, it may well cost more to replace a person who leaves the project with a newcomer who has approximately the same level of experience.

We have already mentioned the inclination PMs have toward understating the costs of a project in order to make it appear more profitable to senior managers, as well as the proclivity of lower-level project workers to overestimate costs in order to protect themselves. If the project is in its initial planning stage as a response to an RFP from an outside organization, over- and underestimation of cost can have a serious impact on the probability of winning the contract—or on the level of profit, if a win occurs. (A large proportion of such projects are bid on a "cost plus" basis.)

Serious ethical problems may arise during the process of estimating costs and submission of bids in response to a Request for Proposal (RFP). If the job is to be paid on a cost-plus basis, or even if it is a fixed-fee project, with fee increases allowed for special circumstances, some bidders may "low ball" a contract (submit underestimated costs). By doing this, they hope to win the bid, counting on the opportunity to increase costs or to plead special circumstances once the job is underway.

At times, clients have been known to give favored bidders a "last look" at supposedly sealed bids so that the favored bidder can submit a winning bid, often with an unwritten agreement to allow some cost escalation at a later date. There is considerable opportunity for unethical behavior during cost estimation and bidding. Further, estimation and bidding practices vary widely from industry to industry.

Finally, there is plain bad luck. Delays occur for reasons that cannot be predicted. Machinery with the reliability of a railroad spike suddenly breaks down. That which has never failed fails. Every project needs an "allowance for contingencies."

Some writers and instructors differentiate four bases for estimating costs: experience, quantitative (statistical) methods, constraints, and worksheets. They discuss the advantages and disadvantages of each and then, typically, decide that one or another gives the best results. We feel strongly that all four are useful and that no approach to cost estimation should be accepted as the best or rejected out of hand. The best estimators seem to employ an eclectic approach that uses, as one said, "anything that works." The wise PM takes into account as many known influences on the project budget as can be predicted. What cannot be predicted must then, by experience, simply be "allowed for." There are two other factors, particularly common to projects involving intangible outputs such as software programming, that need to be mentioned relating to cost-estimation and the schedule. These two factors have been identified in a classic and highly-readable work—*The Mythical Man-Month*—by Brooks [7].

First, most projects involve a tangible medium that tends not to be under our control—the wood splits, the paint smears—and thus we blame implementation problems of our "good" ideas on these physical elements. So, when we are working with a purely intellectual medium that has no physical elements, such as computer code, we are highly optimistic and foolishly assume that all will go well. However, when any project consisting of a series of components can only be successful if all of the components are successful, and each component has a small probability of failing, the chances of the overall project being successful are in fact very poor. Consider, for example, a software program consisting of 1000 lines of code, each of which is 99.9 percent reliable. The chance of the program itself working is only about 36 percent! Brooks' experience has led him to the following rule of thumb for software projects. As a fraction of the total time of the project, planning consumes about $\frac{1}{3}$, coding consumes $\frac{1}{6}$, component test consumes $\frac{1}{4}$, and system test consumes $\frac{1}{4}$. Thus, if a project estimate is made based on the expected coding time (the main element for which we can derive an estimate), this in reality will usually represent only about 17 percent of the entire project time rather than the 80 to 90 percent commonly assumed.

The second factor is what Brooks calls "the mythical man month" and relates to our tendency to assume that workers and time are interchangeable. Thus, when a schedule slips, the traditional response is to add labor which is like trying to douse a fire with gasoline. Our assumption that workers and time are interchangeable is correct only when a task can be partitioned such that there is no communication needed between the workers, such as in picking cotton by hand. Most projects, however, especially computer programming, are not set up that way and the more workers that are added require even more workers to train, as well as lines of communication to coordinate their efforts. Thus, three workers require three times as much pairwise intercommunication as two, and four require six times as much, etc. This result is captured in Brooks' law: *Adding manpower to a late software project makes it later.*

## The Emanon Aircraft Corporation

Emanon Aircraft is a major manufacturer of aircraft parts, specializing in landing gear parts and assemblies. They are located in a highly industrialized midwestern state. The local area suffers from somewhat higher than average unemployment, partly because Emanon has experienced a downturn in business. In the past three years, they have lost out on a number of landing gear contracts, being underbid by competitors from other areas of the country. Senior management studied the problem, but has come to no conclusion about what can be done. They have hired a consulting team from a nearby university to study the situation and make a recommendation.

Business in the aircraft industry is not significantly different than in many other industries specializing in the building of complex machines. Aircraft builders are primarily assembly operations. They build planes from subassemblies and parts manufactured by themselves or by subcontractors who, in turn, specialize in specific subassemblies; for example, landing gear, avionics, passenger seats, heating and air conditioning, etc. When an order is received to build some number of a given type of plane, the builder (prime contractor) requests bids for the proper number of a certain part or subassembly from appropriate subcontractors. All relevant specifications for the part or subassembly are included in the RFP. The subcontractors who wish to participate in the project submit proposals that include a complete description of the proposed subassem-

bly together with price information, delivery dates, and any other pertinent conditions of sale.

The university consulting team studied three aspects of Emanon's landing gear operation: the manufacturing process, the cost structure, and the bidding behavior and profit structure on landing gear bids. They determined that the manufacturing process was reasonably efficient and not significantly different from Emanon's competitors. Second, they found that all competitors were using approximately the same level of mark-up when determining their cost-plus price. When examining the cost structure, however, they noted that in the past three years, the firm consistently ran negative cost variances in material accounts. That is, the amount of material actually used in the construction of landing gears was approximately 10 percent less than the plan indicated. The team was unsure of this finding because there were only a few winning contracts for landing gears during the past three years.

An investigation was conducted on the estimation and purchase of materials for this department. It exposed the following facts. Three and one-half years ago, Emanon was late making a delivery of landing gear parts. The firm paid a large penalty and was threatened with loss of further business with the prime contractor. The late delivery resulted when Emanon ordered an insufficient quantity of a special steel alloy used in landing gear struts, and was unable to purchase any on the open market. The steel company required a manufacturing lead time of more than 90 days, so Emanon's delivery was late.

As a result, the purchasing official who had responsibility for this contract was demoted. The new purchasing official handled the problem in a straightforward fashion by in-flating the material estimates by approximately 10 percent. The cost of material is about half of the total cost of landing gear production, which resulted in bids that were approximately 5 percent above the competition.

## On Making Better Estimates

Cost overruns are so frequent for all types of projects that senior managers often develop a cynical attitude when examining a project budget. They assume it is significantly understated. A common explanation for this phenomenon is that the PM purposely underestimates the project budget in order to improve its benefit–cost ratio, thereby increasing the probability that the project will be funded. Once the project is underway, the reasoning goes, and a monetary and psychic investment has been made in the work, the firm will not let a "good" project die and will make up for budget shortages, albeit grudgingly. It is interesting to note that in recent years computer experts (both hard- and software specialists) have replaced engineers as the people who "cannot be believed" in the industrial world. The "fact" that they will seriously underestimate both the time and cost required to do anything is taken as gospel.

Nevertheless, we will assume that budget estimation errors are not the result of a conspiracy to mislead senior managers, but rather derive from honest errors on the part of the PM, the project cost estimators, or anyone else involved in the estimation process. As we have already noted, there are a number of reasons why "honest" underestimation errors occur. Furthermore, to senior managers the job even looks easier, faster, and less expensive than it appears to the person who must do the job. Nonexpert cost estimators tend to overlook details necessary to the completion of a set of tasks. Neophyte and expert project managers alike seem to assume that Murphy's Law has been repealed in the case of their personal project.

Ambrose Bierce, in *The Devil's Dictionary*, defined "experience" as "The wisdom that enables us to recognize as an undesirable old acquaintance the folly that we have already embraced." It is axiomatic that we should learn through experience. It is a truism that we do not. Nowhere is this more evident than in project management, and yet it is not difficult to improve one's estimation/forecasting skills.

Recall that there are two generic types of estimation error. First, there is *random error* in which overestimates and underestimates are equally likely. Second, there is *bias*, which is *systematic* error. For biased estimates, the chance of over- and underestimates are not equally likely. Using the ubiquitous Lotus 1-2-3®, we can construct a spreadsheet that captures the essence of a person's performance as an estimator. Two simple statistical measures are used: the mean absolute deviation (MAD), and

|  | A | B | C | D | E | F | G |
|---|---|---|---|---|---|---|---|
| 1 | This is a template for improving one's estimating skills | | | | | | |
| 2 | | | | | | | |
| 3 | MAD = SUM (\|A(t) − F(t)\|)/n | | | | | | |
| 4 | Tracking Signal = SUM (A(t) − F(t))/MAD | | A Measure of Bias | | | | |
| 5 | | | | | | | Tracking |
| 6 | Period | Estimate | Actual | A(t) − F(t) | \|A(t) − F(t)\| | MAD | Signal |
| 7 | | | | | | | |
| 8 | 1 | 155 | 163 | 8 | 8 | | |
| 9 | 2 | 242 | 240 | −2 | 2 | 5.00 | 1.20 |
| 10 | 3 | 46 | 67 | 21 | 21 | 10.33 | 2.61 |
| 11 | 4 | 69 | 78 | 9 | 9 | 10.00 | 3.60 |
| 12 | 5 | 75 | 71 | −4 | 4 | 8.80 | 3.64 |
| 13 | 6 | 344 | 423 | 79 | 79 | 20.50 | 5.41 |
| 14 | 7 | 56 | 49 | −7 | 7 | 18.57 | 5.60 |
| 15 | 8 | 128 | 157 | 29 | 29 | 19.88 | 6.69 |
| 16 | | | | | | | |
| 17 | | | | 133 | 159 | | |
| 18 | | | | | | | |
| 19 | | | | | | | |

**Figure 7-5:** Lotus 1-2-3® template for improving cost estimation.

the tracking signal (TS). The printout* of such a Lotus 1-2-3® spreadsheet is shown in Figure 7-5. Appendix E and references [11 and 26] include information on probability, statistics, and forecasting.

Figure 7-5 assumes that for each period (Column A) someone has made an estimate of a variable (Column B), and that the actual value of that variable is, sooner or later, known (Column C). (It should be noted that Column A need not be time periods. This column simply counts the number of estimates made and links estimates with their respective actuals.) Column D calculates the difference between the actual value, A(t), and the estimate or forecast for that period, F(t). Column E contains the absolute value of that difference. We can now calculate a statistic known as the *mean absolute deviation* (MAD).

As the information in Row 3 of the spreadsheet shows:

$$\text{MAD} = \Sigma(|A(t)\text{-}F(t)|)/n$$

where $n$ is the number of differences. The MAD is therefore the arithmetic average of the absolute values of the differences—the mean absolute deviation.

Students of statistics may note that the MAD has certain logical similarities to the standard deviation. Assuming that the forecast errors are normally distributed, the MAD is approximately 80 percent of a standard deviation (see [11] and else-

---

*The data for Figures 7-5 and 7-6 were prepared using a Lotus 1-2-3® spreadsheet, transferred to Excel®, and printed. Any of the common spreadsheet programs can easily handle all of the calculations shown in this chapter. Almost all will accept the formulas and calculations from any of the others.

where). Thus, if the MAD is a sizable fraction of the variable being estimated, the average error is large and the forecast or estimate is not very accurate.

Now, consider Column D. The sum of the entries in this column for any number of periods is the sum of the forecast errors, often referred to as the "running sum of the forecast errors" (RSFE). If the estimator's errors are truly random, their sum should approach zero; that is, the RSFE should be a small number because positive errors should be offset by negative errors. If either positive or negative errors are more numerous or consistently larger than the other, the estimation process is said to be biased and the errors are not random. In Figure 7-5, RSFE = 133, so the forecast is quite positively biased.

The tracking signal measures the estimator's bias. It is easily found:

$$TS = RSFE/MAD$$

Note that it calculates the number of MADs in the RSFE (see column G in Figure 7-5, and recall the similarity between MAD and standard deviation). If the RSFE is small, approaching zero, the TS will also approach zero. As the RSFE grows, the TS will grow, indicating bias. Division of the RSFE by the MAD creates a sort of "index number," the TS, that is independent of the size of the variables being considered. We cannot say just how much bias is acceptable in an estimator/forecaster. We feel that a TS $\geq$ 3 is too high unless the estimator is a rank beginner. Certainly, an experienced estimator should have a much lower TS. (It should be obvious that the TS may be either negative or positive. Our comment actually refers to the absolute value of the TS.)

Perhaps more important than worrying about an acceptable limit on the size of the tracking signal is the practice of keeping track of it and analyzing why the estimator's bias, if there is one, exists. Similarly, the estimator should consider how to reduce the MAD, the average estimation error. Such analysis is the embodiment of "learning by experience." The Lotus 1-2-3® template makes the analysis simple to conduct, and should result in descreasing the size of both the MAD and the TS. (For those familiar with Lotus 1-2-3®, the formulas used for Figure 7-5 are shown in Figure 7-6.)

Some estimators would like to speed up the process of improving their estimation skills by grouping forecasts of different resources to generate more data points when calculating their MADs and TSs. Use of the tracking signal requires that the input data, estimates (forecasts) and actuals, be collected and processed separately for each variable being estimated. Cost estimates and actuals for different resources, for instance, would be used to find the MAD and TS for each individual resource. The reason for this inconvenience is that resources come in different units and the traditional caution about adding apples and oranges applies. (Even if all resources are measured in dollars, we still have scale problems when we mix resource costs of very different sizes.) Fortunately, there is a way around the problem.

Instead of defining the estimation error as the *difference* between actual and forecast, we can define it as the *ratio* of actual to forecast. Therefore, the new error for the first forecast (Period 1) in Figure 7-5 is not 8 units, but rather is

$$A(t)/F(t) = 163/155 = 1.052$$

| | A | B | C | D | E | F | G |
|---|---|---|---|---|---|---|---|
| 1 | | | | | | | |
| 2 | | | | | | | |
| 3 | | | | | | | Tracking |
| 4 | Period | Estimate | Actual | A(t) − F(t) | \|A(t) − F(t)\| | MAD | Signal |
| 5 | | | | | | | |
| 6 | 1 | 155 | 163 | =C62B6 | =ABS (C62B6) | | |
| 7 | 2 | 242 | 240 | =C72B7 | =ABS (C72B7) | = (SUM($E$6:E7))/A7 | =(SUM($D$6:D7))/F7 |
| 8 | 3 | 46 | 67 | =C82B8 | =ABS (C82B8) | = (SUM($E$6:E8))/A8 | =(SUM($D$6:D8))/F8 |
| 9 | 4 | 69 | 78 | =C92B9 | =ABS (C92B9) | = (SUM($E$6:E9))/A9 | =(SUM($D$6:D9))/F9 |
| 10 | 5 | 75 | 71 | =C102B10 | =ABS (C102B10) | = (SUM($E$6:E10))/A10 | =(SUM($D$6:D10))/F10 |
| 11 | 6 | 344 | 423 | =C112B11 | =ABS (C112B11) | = (SUM($E$6:E11))/A11 | =(SUM($D$6:D11))/F11 |
| 12 | 7 | 56 | 49 | =C122B12 | =ABS (C122B12) | = (SUM($E$6:E12))/A12 | =(SUM($D$6:D12))/F12 |
| 13 | 8 | 128 | 157 | =C132B13 | =ABS (C132B13) | = (SUM($E$6:E13))/A13 | =(SUM($D$6:D13))/F13 |
| 14 | | | | | | | |
| 15 | | | | =SUM (D6:D14) | =SUM (E6:E14) | | |
| 16 | | | | | | | |

**Figure 7-6:** Lotus 1-2-3® formulas for Figure 7-5.

or a 5.2 percent error. In order to produce measures similar in nature and concept to the MAD and TS, we will subtract 1 from the ratio. Thus, when the actual is *greater* than the forecast, the measure (i.e., the error ratio minus 1) will be positive, and if the actual is *less* than the forecast, the measure will be negative. Figure 7-7 shows the calculations of $\{A(t)/F(t) - 1\}$ for the data used in Figure 7-5. Column E shows the absolute value of column D, and column F lists the MAR (mean absolute ratio). The tracking signal is calculated as usual by dividing the "running sum of the forecast ratios" (RSFR) by the MAR,

$$TS = RSFR/MAR$$

| | A | B | C | D | E | F | G |
|---|---|---|---|---|---|---|---|
| 1 | | | | | | | |
| 2 | | | | | | | |
| 3 | | | | | | | Tracking |
| 4 | Period | Estimate | Actual | (A(t) / F(t))−1 | \|(A(t) / F(t))−1\| | MAR | Signal |
| 5 | 1 | 155 | 163 | 0.052 | 0.052 | | |
| 6 | 2 | 242 | 240 | −0.008 | 0.008 | 0.030 | 1.448 |
| 7 | 3 | 46 | 67 | 0.457 | 0.457 | 0.172 | 2.904 |
| 8 | 4 | 69 | 78 | 0.130 | 0.130 | 0.162 | 3.898 |
| 9 | 5 | 75 | 71 | −0.053 | 0.053 | 0.140 | 4.120 |
| 10 | 6 | 344 | 423 | 0.230 | 0.230 | 0.155 | 5.205 |
| 11 | 7 | 56 | 49 | −0.125 | 0.125 | 0.151 | 4.523 |
| 12 | 8 | 128 | 157 | 0.227 | 0.227 | 0.160 | 5.670 |
| 13 | | | | | | | |
| 14 | | | | 0.908 | 1.281 | | |
| 15 | | | | | | | |
| 16 | | | | | | | |

**Figure 7-7:** Estimation template using ratios.

| | A | B | C | D | E | F | G |
|---|---|---|---|---|---|---|---|
| 1 | | | | | | | |
| 2 | | | | | | | |
| 3 | | | | | | | Tracking |
| 4 | Period | Estimate | Actual | (A(t) / F(t))−1 | \|A(t) / F(t)−1\| | MAR | Signal |
| 5 | | | | | | | |
| 6 | 1 | 155 | 163 | =(C6/B6)−1 | =ABS((C6/B6)−1) | | |
| 7 | 2 | 242 | 240 | =(C7/B7)−1 | =ABS((C7/B7)−1) | =(SUM($E$6:E7))/A7 | =(SUM($D$6:D7))/F7 |
| 8 | 3 | 46 | 67 | =C8/B8−1 | =ABS((C8/B8)−1) | =(SUM($E$6:E8))/A8 | =(SUM($D$6:D8))/F8 |
| 9 | 4 | 69 | 78 | =C9/B9−1 | =ABS((C9/B9)−1) | =(SUM($E$6:E9))/A9 | =(SUM($D$6:D9))/F9 |
| 10 | 5 | 75 | 71 | =C10/B10−1 | =ABS((C10/B10)−1) | =(SUM($E$6:E10))/A10 | =(SUM($D$6:D10))/F10 |
| 11 | 6 | 344 | 423 | =C11/B11−1 | =ABS((C11/B11)−1) | =(SUM($E$6:E11))/A11 | =(SUM($D$6:D11))/F11 |
| 12 | 7 | 56 | 49 | =C12/B12−1 | =ABS((C12/B12)−1) | =(SUM($E$6:E12))/A12 | =(SUM($D$6:D12))/F12 |
| 13 | 8 | 128 | 157 | =C13/B13−1 | =ABS((C13/B13)−1) | =(SUM($E$6:E13))/A13 | =(SUM($D$6:D13))/F13 |
| 14 | | | | | | | |
| 15 | | | | =SUM (D6:D14) | =SUM(E6:E14) | | |
| 16 | | | | | | | |

**Figure 7-8:** Formulas for Figure 7-7.

Notice that this calculation does not suffer from unit or scale effects because the ratio of actual to forecast is a dimensionless number and we are finding the percent error rather than the "real" error.

One caution remains. While this technique will allow one to aggregate dissimilar data and, thereby, measure the degree of random error and bias faster than when using differences, care must be exercised to aggregate only data for which there is good reason to believe that the amount of bias and uncertainty is roughly the same for all resource estimations. The Lotus 1-2-3® formulas for Figure 7-7, again translated into Excel®, are shown in Figure 7-8.

A *final note*: At the beginning of this discussion, we made the assumption that estimation errors were "honest." That assumption is not necessary. If a manager suspects that costs are purposely being under- or overestimated, it is usually not difficult to collect appropriate data and calculate the tracking signal for an individual estimator—or even for an entire project team. If it is known that such information is being collected, one likely result is that the most purposeful bias will be sharply reduced.

# ▶ SUMMARY

This chapter initiated the subject of project implementation by focusing on the project budget, which authorizes the project manager to obtain the resources needed to begin work. Different methods of budgeting were described along with their impacts on project management. Then, a number of issues concerning cost estimation were discussed, particularly the effect of learning on the cost of repetitive tasks and how to use the concept of the learning curve. Finally, methods for improving cost estimation skills were described.

Specific points made in the chapter were these:

- The intent of a budget is to communicate organizational policy concerning the organization's goals and priorities.
- There are a number of common budgeting methods: top–down, bottom–up, the budget request, PPBS, ZBB.
- The intent of PPBS is to focus on cost–benefit

relative to the organization's goals for selecting projects to fund.

- The intent of ZBB is to avoid automatic percentage budgeting in each budget period by focusing on the total value of each project to the organization's goals.

- A form identifying the level of resource need, when it will be needed, who the contact is, and its availability is especially helpful in estimating costs.

- It is common for organizations to fund projects whose returns cover direct but not full-costs in order to achieve long-run strategic goals of the organization.

- If projects include repetitive tasks with significant human input, the learning phenomenon should be taken into consideration when preparing cost estimates.

- The learning curve is based on the observation that the amount of time required to produce one unit decreases a constant percentage every time the cumulative output doubles.

- A method for determining whether or not cost estimations are biased is described. The method can be used to improve any estimation/forecasting process.

- Other major factors, in addition to learning, that should be considered when making project cost estimates are inflation, differential changes in the cost factors, waste and spoilage, personnel replacement costs, and contingencies for unexpected difficulties.

In the next chapter we address the subject of task scheduling, a topic of major importance in project management. More research and investigation has probably been conducted on the subject of scheduling than any other element of project management.

## ▶ GLOSSARY

**Bottom–Up Budgeting**—A budgeting method that begins with those who will be doing the tasks estimating the resources needed. The advantage is more accurate estimates.

**Learning Rate**—The percentage of the previous worker hours per unit required for doubling the output.

**Planning-Programming-Budgeting-System (PPBS)**—A system developed in the 1960s for dealing rationally with budgeting through maximization of the chances for attaining the organization's long-run goals.

**Program Budgeting**—Aggregating income and expenditures by project or program, often in addition to aggregation by organizational unit or activity.

**Top–Down Budgeting**—A budgeting method that begins with top managers' estimates of the resources needed for a project. Its primary advantage is that the aggregate budget is typically quite accurate because no element has been left out. Individual elements, however, may be quite inaccurate.

**Variances**—The pattern of deviations in costs and usage used for exception reporting to management.

**Zero-Based Budgeting**—A budgeting method from the 1970s that was devised as an alternative to the incremental approach. Every program budget had to be totally justified every budget cycle.

## ▶ MATERIAL REVIEW QUESTIONS

1. What are the advantages of top–down budgeting? Of bottom–up budgeting? What is the most important task for top management to do in bottom–up budgeting?

2. In preparing a budget, what indirect costs should be considered?

3. What is the procedure for zero-base budgeting? Is it a good method to use in planning a state or national budget? Why, or why not?

4. List the four main steps involved in PPBS. Why has it become obsolete?

5. Describe the top–down budgeting process.

6. What is a variance?

7. Describe the learning curve phenomenon.

8. How might you determine if cost estimates are biased?

9. What is "program budgeting"?

10. What is the difference between activity- and task-oriented budgets?

# CLASS DISCUSSION QUESTIONS

1. Discuss ways in which to keep budget planning from becoming a game.

2. List some of the pitfalls in cost estimating. What steps can a manager take to correct cost overruns?

3. Why do consulting firms frequently subsidize some projects? Is this ethical?

4. What steps can be taken to make controlling costs easier? Can these steps also be used to control other project parameters, such as performance?

5. Which budgeting method is likely to be used with which type of organizational structure?

6. What are some potential problems with the top–down and bottom–up budgeting processes? What are some ways of dealing with these potential problems?

7. How is the budget planning process like a game?

8. Would any of the conflict resolution methods described in the previous chapter be useful in the budget planning process? Which ones?

9. Why hasn't ZBB caught on with project managers?

10. Why is learning curve analysis important to project management?

11. Why is it "ethically necessary to be honest" in negotiations between a superior and subordinate?

# INCIDENTS FOR DISCUSSION

## Preferred Widget Company

Larry Cole has been appointed project manager of the Preferred Widget Company's new widget manufacturing process project. Widgets are extremely price-sensitive and Preferred has done a great deal of quantitative work so it can accurately forecast changes in sales volume relative to changes in pricing.

The company president, "J. R." Widget, has considerable faith in the firm's sensitivity model and insists that all projects that affect the manufacturing cost of widgets be run against the sensitivity model in order to generate data to calculate the return on investment. The net result is that project managers, like Larry, are under a great deal of pressure to submit realistic budgets so go/no–go project decisions can be made quickly. J. R. has canceled several projects that appeared marginal during their feasibility stages and recently fired a project manager for overestimating project costs on a new model widget. The project was killed very early in the design stage and six months later a competitor introduced a similar widget that proved to be highly successful.

Larry's dilemma is how to go about constructing a budget that accurately reflects the cost of the proposed new manufacturing process. Larry is an experienced executive and feels comfortable with his ability to come close to estimating the cost of the project. However, the recent firing of his colleague has made him a bit gun-shy. Only one stage out of the traditional four-stage widget manufacturing process is being changed, so he has detailed cost information about a good percentage of the process. Unfortunately, the tasks involved in the process stage being modified are unclear at this point. Larry also believes that the new modification will cause some minor changes in the other three stages, but these changes have not been clearly identified. The stage being addressed by the project represents almost 50 percent of the manufacturing cost.

*Questions*: Under these circumstances, would Larry be wise to pursue a top–down or a bottom–up budgeting approach? Why? What factors are most relevant here?

## General Ship Company

General Ship Company has been building nuclear destroyers for the Navy for the last 20 years. It has recently completed the design of a new class of nuclear destroyer and will be preparing a detailed budget to be followed during construction of the first destroyer.

The total budget for this first destroyer is $90 million. The controller feels the initial project cost estimate prepared by the planning department was too low because the waste and spoilage allowance was underestimated. Thus, she is concerned that there may be a large cost overrun on the project and wants to work closely with the project manager to control the costs.

*Question*: How would you monitor the costs of this project?

## ▶ INDIVIDUAL EXERCISE

Use the work breakdown structure from the chapter exercise in Chapter 5 to design a project budget for that project. Organize it hierarchically by task, etc. How would a top–down budgeting process proceed for this project? Compare it to a bottom–up process.

Then consider the tasks within the WBS itself. Are any of the tasks repetitive, with a high labor content?

Might the learning curve apply here? If mechanical tasks requiring tools or machinery follow an 80 percent learning rate whereas simply memory/learning tasks follow a 60 percent learning rate, what rate would you estimate for these tasks?

## ▶ PROJECT TEAM CONTINUING EXERCISE

At this point, the team must establish the detailed project budget. Start with the work breakdown structure and then estimate, both from the bottom up and the top down, what the appropriate budget will be. Examine any discrepancies between the two budgets for errors, misunderstandings, or oversights. If any of

the tasks are repetitious, use the learning curve to predict their cost by unit. If the task is mechanical, use a 75–80 percent rate; if more mental, use a 65–70 percent rate. Finally, describe how a PPBS and ZBB approach might apply to your project.

## ▶ BIBLIOGRAPHY

1. AUSTIN, A. L. *Zero-Based Budgeting: Organizational Impact and Effects.* New York: AMACOM, 1977.

2. BACON, J. *Managing the Budget Function.* Washington, DC: National Industrial Conference Board, 1970.

3. BARTIZAL, J. R. *Budget Principles and Procedures.* Englewood Cliffs, NJ: Prentice Hall, 1940.

4. BLOCK, E. B. "Accomplishment/Cost: Better Project Control." *Harvard Business Review*, May 1971.

5. BRIGGS, G. R. *The Theory and Practice of Management Control.* New York: American Management Association, 1970.

6. BRIMSON, J. A. "Activity Product Cost." IEEE *Engineering Management Review*, Spring 1992.

7. BROOKS, F. P. *The Mythical Man-Month.* Reading, MA: Addison-Wesley, 1975.

8. BROWN, R., and J. D. SUVER. "Where Does Zero-Base Budgeting Work?" *Harvard Business Review*, Dec. 1977.

9. BUNGE, W. R. *Managerial Budgeting for Profit Improvement.* New York: McGraw-Hill, 1968.

10. BURKHEAD, J. *Budgeting and Planning.* General Learning Press, 1971.

11. CHASE, R. B., and N. J. AQUILANO. *Production and Operations Management*, 5th ed. Homewood, IL: Irwin, 1989.

12. DEAN, B. V., S. J. MANTEL, JR., and L. A. ROEPCKE.

"Research Project Cost Distributions and Budget Forecasting." IEEE *Transactions on Engineering Management*, Nov. 1969.

13. DEARDON, J. *Cost and Budget Analysis*. Englewood Cliffs, NJ: Prentice Hall, 1962.

14. EITEMAN, J. W. *Graphic Budgets*. Ann Arbor, MI: Masterco Press, 1949.

15. GAGNON, R. J. *An Exploratory Analysis of the Relevant Cost Structure of Internal and External Engineering Consulting*, Ph.D. dissertation. Cincinnati: University of Cincinnati, 1982.

16. GAGNON, R. J., and S. J. MANTEL, JR. "Strategies and Performance Improvement for Computer-Assisted Design." IEEE *Transactions on Engineering Management*, Nov. 1987.

17. HARRISON, F. L. *Advanced Project Management*. Hants, Eng: Gower, 1983.

18. HECKERT, J. B. *Business Budgeting and Control*. New York: Ronald, 1967.

19. HITCH, C. J. "Plans, Programs and Budgets in The Department of Defense." *Operations Research*, Jan.–Feb. 1963.

20. HITCH, C. J. "A Planning-Programming-Budgeting System." In F. E. Kast and J. E. Rosensweig, eds. *Science, Technology and Management*. New York: McGraw-Hill, 1963.

21. HOVER, L. D. *A Practical Guide to Budgeting and Management Control Systems: A Functional and Performance Evaluation Approach*. Lexington, MA: Lexington Books, 1979.

22. LIN, T. "Corporate Planning and Budgeting: An Integrated Approach." *Managerial Planning*, May 1979.

23. MACIARIELLO, J. A. "Making Program Management Work." *Journal of Systems Management*, July 1974.

24. MACLEAD, R. K. "Program Budgeting Works in Non-Profit Institutions." *Harvard Business Review*, Sept. 1971.

25. McKEAN, R. N. "Remaining Difficulties in Program Budgeting." In Enke, S., ed., *Defense Management*. Englewood Cliffs, NJ: Prentice Hall, 1967.

26. MEREDITH, J. R. *The Management of Operations*, 4th ed. New York: Wiley, 1992.

27. NTUEN, M. "Applying Artificial Intelligence to Project Cost Estimates." *Cost Engineering*, No. 5, 1987.

28. PYHRR, PETER A. *Zero-Base Budgeting: A Practical Management Tool for Evaluating Expenses*. New York: Wiley, 1973.

29. STEDRY, ANDREW C. *Budget Control and Cost Behavior*. Englewood Cliffs, NJ: Prentice Hall, 1960.

30. STEINER, G. "Program Budgeting: Business Contribution to Government Management." *Business Horizons*, Spring 1965.

# CASE

## AUTOMOTIVE BUILDERS, INC.: THE STANHOPE PROJECT
### Jack Meredith

It was a cold, gray October day as Jim Wickes pulled his car into ABI's parking lot in their corporate offices in suburban Detroit. The leaves, in yellows and browns, swirled around his feet as he walked into the wind toward the lobby.

"Good morning, Mr. Wickes," said his secretary as he came into the office. "That proposal on the Stanhope project just arrived a minute ago. It's on your desk."

"Good morning, Debbie. Thanks. I've been anxious to see it."

This was the day Jim had scheduled to review the 1986 supplemental capital request and he didn't want any interruptions as he scrutinized the details of the flexible manufacturing project planned for Stanhope, Iowa. The Stanhope proposal, compiled by Ann Williamson, project manager and the managerial "champion" on this effort, looked like just the type of project to fit ABI's new strategic plan, but there was a large element of risk in the project. Before recommending the project to Steve White, the executive vice president of ABI, Jim wanted to review all the details one more time.

## History of ABI

ABI started operations as the Farm Equipment Company just after the First World War. Employing new technology to produce diesel engine parts for tractors, the firm grew with the growth of farming and became a multimillion dollar company by 1940.

During the Second World War, the firm switched over to producing tank and truck parts in volume for the military. At the war's end, the firm converted its equipment over to the production of automotive parts for the expanding automobile industry. To reflect this major change in their product line, the company was renamed Automotive Builders, Inc. (ABI), though they remained a major supplier to the farm equipment market.

## A Major Capital Project

The farm equipment industry in the 1970s had been doing well but there were some disturbing trends. Japanese manufacturers had entered the industry and were beginning to take a significant share of the domestic market. More significantly, domestic labor costs were significantly higher than overseas and resulted in price disadvantages that couldn't be ignored any longer. And perhaps most important of all, quality differences between American and Japanese farm equipment, including tractors, were becoming quite noticeable.

To improve the quality and costs of their incoming materials, many of the domestic tractor manufacturers were beginning to single-source a number of their tractor components. This allowed them better control over both quality and cost, and made it easier to coordinate delivery schedules at the same time.

In this vein, one of the major tractor engine manufacturers, code-named "Big Red" within ABI, let its suppliers know that it was interested in negotiating a contract for possible 100 percent sourcing of 17 versions of special piston heads destined for a new line of high-efficiency tractor engines which were expected to replace the current conventional engines in both new and existing tractors. These were all six-cylinder diesel engines and thus would require six pistons each.

This put ABI in an interesting situation. If they failed to bid on this contract, they would be inviting competition into their very successful and profitable diesel engine parts business. Thus, to protect their existing successful business, and to pursue more such business, ABI seemed required to bid on this contract. Should ABI be successful in their bid, this would result in 100 percent sourcing in both the OEM market as well as the replacement market with its high margins. Furthermore, the high investment required to produce these special pistons at ABI's costs would virtually rule out future competition.

ABI had two plants producing diesel engine components for other manufacturers and believed they had a competitive edge in engineering of this type. These plants, however, could not accommodate the volume Big Red expected for the new engine. Big Red insisted at their negotiations that a 100 percent supplier be able to meet peak capacity at their assembly plant for this new line.

As Jim looked over the proposal, he decided to refer back to the memos which restated their business strategy and started them thinking about a new Iowa plant in the heart of the farm equipment industry for this project. In addition, Steve White had asked the following basic, yet rather difficult questions about the proposal at their last meeting and Jim wanted to be sure he had them clearly in mind as he reviewed the files.

- ABI is already achieving an excellent return on investment (ROI). Won't these investments simply tend to dilute it?
- Will the cost in new equipment be returned by an equivalent reduction in labor? Where's the payoff?
- What asset protection can we get? This proposal requires us to invest in new facilities before knowing whether we will get a long-term contract that will reimburse us for our investment.
- Does this proposal maximize ROI, sales potential, or total profit?

To address these questions adequately, Jim decided to recheck the expected after-tax profits, return on investment (internal rate of return), and the payback period for himself when he reached the financial portion of the proposals. These figures should give a clear indication of the "quality" of the investment. There were, however, other aspects of capital resource allocation to consider besides just the financial elements. One of these was certainly the new business strategy of the firm, as recently articulated by ABI's executive committee.

## The Business Strategy

A number of elements of ABI's business strategy were directly relevant to this proposal. Jim took out a note pad to jot each of them down and assign them a priority.

1. To bid only on good margin products that have the potential for maintaining their margins over a long term.

2. To pursue only those new products whose design or production process is of a proprietary nature and that lie in those areas where our technical abilities enable us to maintain a long-term position.

3. To employ, if at all possible, the most advanced technology in new projects that is either within our experience or requires the next step up in experience.

4. To foster the "project champion" approach to innovation and creativity. The idea is to encourage entrepreneurship by approving projects that individual managers are committed to and have taken on as personal "causes" because of their belief that the idea, product, or process is in our best interest.

5. To maintain small plants of no more than 480 employees. These have been found to be the most efficient and enjoy the best labor relations.

With these in mind, Jim reopened the proposal and started reading at critical sections.

## Demand Forecasts and Scenarios

For this proposal, three scenarios were analyzed in terms of future demand and financial impacts. The baseline "Scenario I" assumed that the new line would be successful. "Scenario II" assumed the Japanese would soon follow and compete successfully with Big Red in this line. "Scenario III" assumed that the new line was a failure. The sales volume forecasts under these three scenarios are shown in Table 1.

There was, however, not a lot of confidence in any of these forecasts. In the preceding few years Japan had become a formidable competitor, not only in

**Table 1**    Demand Forecasts (000s engines)*

| Year | Baseline I | Scenario II | Scenario III |
|------|-----------|-------------|--------------|
| 1987 | 69 | 69 | 69 |
| 1988 | 73 | 72 | 72 |
| 1989 | 90 | 81 | 77 |
| 1990 | 113 | 95 | 68 |
| 1991 | 125 | 87 | 62 |
| 1992 | 145 | 74 | 47 |

* Each engine requires six pistons.

price but also in more difficult areas of competition, such as quality and reliability. Furthermore, the economic situation in 1986 was taking a severe toll on American farmers and economic forecasts indicated there was no relief in sight. Thus, as stated in the proposal:

> The U.S. farm market will be a difficult battleground for world farm equipment manufacturers and any forecast of a particular engine's potential in this market must be considered as particularly risky. How much risk do we want to take on? Every effort should be made to minimize our exposure on this investment and maximize our flexibility.

## Manufacturing Plan

The proposal stressed two primary aspects of the manufacturing process. First, a learning curve was employed in calculating production during the 1000-unit ramp-up implementation period so as to not be overly optimistic. A learning rate of 80 percent was assumed. Second, an advanced technology process using a flexible manufacturing system based largely on turning centers was recommended since it came in at $1 million less than conventional equipment and met the strategy guidelines of using sophisticated technology when appropriate.

Since ABI had closely monitored Big Red's progress in the engine market, it had been anticipating the request for bids. In preparation for this, Jim had authorized a special manufacturing process study to determine more efficient and effective ways of producing piston heads. The study considered product design, process selection, quality considerations, productivity, and manufacturing system planning. Three piston manufacturing methods were considered in the study: batch manufacture via computer numerically controlled (CNC) equipment, a flexible manufacturing system (FMS), and a high volume, low-unit-cost transfer machine.

The resulting recommendation was to install a very carefully designed FMS if it appeared that the additional flexibility might be required in the future for other versions, or even other manufacturers. Though such a system would be expensive, the volume of production over the FMS' longer lifetime would offset that expense. Four preferred machine builders were contacted for equipment specifications and bids. It was ABI's plan to work closely with the selected vendor in designing and installing the equipment, thus building quality and reliability into both the product and the process and learning about the equipment at the same time.

To add further flexibility for the expensive machinery, all design features that would facilitate retool or changeover to other products were incorporated. For example, the machining centers would also be capable of machining other metals, such as aluminum or nodular iron, and would be fitted with variable feed and speed motors, feed-force monitors, pressure-controlled clamping of workpieces, and air-leveling pallets. Also, fully interchangeable chucks, spindles, pallets, tooling, and risers would be purchased to minimize the spares inventories.

## Plant Operation and Organization

As stated in the proposal, many innovative practices were also to be employed at the new plant.

- Machine operators will be trained to do almost all of their own machine maintenance.
- All employees will conduct their own statistical process control and piston heads will be subject to 100 percent inspection.
- There will only be four skill classes in the plant. Every employee in each of those classes will be trained to do any work within that class.
- There will not be any time clocks in the plant.

The organizational structure for the 11 salaried workers in the new plant is shown in Figure 1 and the complete labor summary is illustrated in Figure 2, including the shift breakdown. As can be seen, the plant will be relatively small, with 65 employees in the ratio of 1:5 salaried to hourly. The eight month acquisition of the employees during the ramp-up is illustrated in

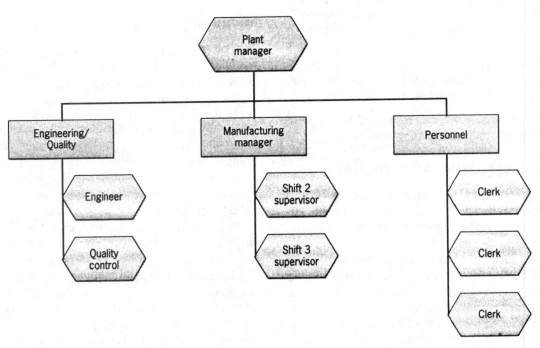

**Figure 1:** Stanhope organization.

## Salaried Labor

| | |
|---|---|
| plant manager | 1 |
| manufacturing managers (3 shifts) | 3 |
| quality control manager | 1 |
| engineering | 2 |
| personnel manager | 1 |
| clerical | 3 |
| | 11 |

## Hourly Labor

| | **Days** | **Afternoons** | **Nights** |
|---|---|---|---|
| direct | 14 | 14 | 10 |
| inspection | 1 | 1 | 1 |
| maintenance | 2 | 1 | 1 |
| tooling | 2 | 2 | 1 |
| rec./shp./mtl. | 2 | 1 | 1 |
| **total** | 21 | 19 | 14 |

## Summary

| | |
|---|---|
| salary | 11 |
| hourly | 54 |
| **total** | 65 |

**Figure 2:** Stanhope labor summary.

Figure 3, with full employment occurring by March 1987.

## Financial Considerations

Financial aspects of new proposals at ABI were considered from a number of perspectives, in part because of the interdependent nature of many proposals. The results of not investing in a proposal are normally compared with the results of investing and the differences noted. Variations on the investment assumptions are also tested, including errors in the forecast sales volumes, learning rates, productivities, selling prices, and cancellations of both current and future orders for existing and potential business.

For the Stanhope proposal, the site investment required is $3,012,000. The details of this investment are shown in Table 2. The total investment required amounts to $7,108,000 (plus required working capital of $1,380,000). The equipment is depreciated over an eight year life. ABI, under the revised tax laws, is in the 34 percent tax bracket. The price of the piston heads has been tentatively set at $25.45 apiece. ABI's expected costs are shown in Table 3.

## Some Concerns

Jim had spoken with some of his colleagues about the FMS concept after the preliminary financial results

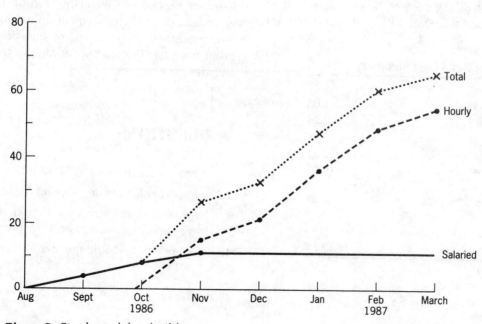

**Figure 3:** Stanhope labor buildup.

**Table 2**  Stanhope Site Capital Costs

| Land and Site Preparation | |
|---|---:|
| land | $246,000 |
| access roads/parking lot | 124,000 |
| landscaping | 22,000 |
| **Building Costs** | |
| building (67,000 sq. ft.) | 1,560,000 |
| air conditioning | 226,000 |
| power | 205,000 |
| employee services | 177,000 |
| legal fees and permits | 26,000 |
| **Auxiliary Equipment** | |
| ABI company sign | 25,000 |
| containers, racks, etc. | 33,000 |
| flume | 148,000 |
| coolant disposal | 97,000 |
| furnishings | 51,000 |
| fork lift trucks | 72,000 |
| **total** | 3,012,000 |

had been tabulated. Their concerns were what now interested him.

For example, he remembered one manager asking: "Suppose Bid Red's sales only reach 70 percent of our projections in the 1989–90 time period, or say, perhaps as much as 150 percent; how would this affect the project? Does the FMS still apply or would you

**Table 3**  Piston Head Cost Summary

| | |
|---|---:|
| material | $8.47 |
| labor | 1.06 |
| variable overhead | 2.23 |
| fixed overhead | 2.44 |
| freight | 0.31 |
| **total factory cost** | 14.51 |
| general & admin. | 1.43 |
| scrap | 0.82 |
| testing | 0.39 |
| **total cost** | 17.15 |

consider some other form of manufacturing equipment, possibly conventional or CNC with potential aftermarket application in the former case or a transfer machine in the latter case?"

Another manager wrote his thoughts down as a memo to forward to Jim. He had two major concerns:

- The "Scenario II" analysis assumes the loss of substantial volume to competition. This seems rather unlikely.

- The after-tax margins seem unreasonably high. Can we get such margins on a sole-source contract?

Jim wondered what these changes in their assumptions would do to the ROI of the proposal and its overall profitability.

## Conclusion

Jim had some concerns about the project also. He was wondering how realistic the demand forecasts were, given the weak economy and what the Japanese might do. If the demand didn't materialize, they might be very sorry they had invested in such an expensive piece of equipment as an FMS.

Strategically, it seemed like ABI had to make this investment to protect its profitable position in the diesel engine business but how far should arguments like that be carried? Were they letting their past investments color their judgment on new ones? He was also concerned about the memo questioning the high profit margins. They did seem high in the midst of a sluggish economy.

## ▶ QUESTIONS

1. What are the answers to Steve White's questions?

2. What other factors are relevant to this issue?

3. How do the changes in assumptions mentioned by the other managers affect the proposal?

4. What position should Jim take? Why?

▶ This article clearly describes the importance and impact of cost-related issues on a project. These issues can significantly alter the profitability and even success of a project. Costs are discussed from three viewpoints: that of the project manager, the accountant, and the controller. Not only are the amounts of expenditures and encumbrances important, but their timing is critical also. Perhaps most important is having a project cost system that accurately reports costs and variances in a way that can be useful for managerial decisions.

# CHAPTER

# 8

# Scheduling

The previous chapter initiated our discussion of project implementation. In this and the following three chapters, we continue with the implementation of the project plans we made in Chapter 5. In this chapter we examine some scheduling techniques that have been found to be useful in project management. We cover the Program Evaluation and Review Technique (PERT), the Critical Path Method (CPM), Gantt charts, and briefly discuss Precedence Diagramming, the Graphical Evaluation and Review Technique (GERT), and report-based methods.

In Chapter 9, we consider the special problems of scheduling when resource limitations force conflicts between concurrent projects, or even between two or more tasks in a single project. We also look at ways of expediting activities by adding resources. Following a discussion of the monitoring and information system function in Chapter 10, we discuss the overall topic of project control in Chapter 11.

## ▶ 8.1 BACKGROUND

A schedule is the conversion of a project action plan into an operating timetable. As such, it serves as a fundamental basis for monitoring and controlling project activity and, taken together with the plan and budget, is probably the major tool for the management of projects. In a project environment, the scheduling function is more important than it would be in an ongoing operation because projects lack the continuity of day-to-day operations and often present much more complex problems of coordination. Indeed, project scheduling is so important that a detailed schedule is sometimes a customer-specified requirement. In later chapters we discuss the fact that a properly designed, detailed schedule can also serve as a key input in establishing the monitoring and control systems for the project.

Not all project activities need to be scheduled at the same level of detail. In fact, there may be several schedules: the master schedule, the development and testing schedule, the assembly schedule, and so on. These schedules are typically based on the previously determined action plan and/or work breakdown structure (WBS), and it is good practice to create a schedule for each major task level in the WBS which will cover the work packages. It is rarely necessary however, to list all work packages. One can focus mainly on those that need to be monitored for maintaining adequate control over the project. Such packages are usually difficult, expensive, or have a relatively short time frame for their accomplishment.

When making a schedule, it is important that the dates and time allotments for the work packages be in precise agreement with those set forth in the project master schedule. It is also important that the work units that aggregate into work packages be in agreement with the times in the master schedule. These times are control points for the PM. It is the project manager's responsibility to insist on and maintain this consistency, but the actual scheduling of the task and work packages is usually done by those responsible for their accomplishment—after the PM has established and checked appropriate due dates for all tasks. This procedure ensures that the final project schedule reflects the interdependencies among all the tasks and departments involved in the project, and maintains consistency among them.

The basic approach of all scheduling techniques is to form an actual or implied network of activity and event relationships that graphically portrays the sequential relations between the tasks in a project. Tasks that must precede or follow other tasks are then clearly identified, in time as well as function. Such a network is a powerful tool for planning and controlling a project and has the following benefits:

- It is a consistent framework for planning, scheduling, monitoring, and controlling the project.
- It illustrates the interdependence of all tasks, work packages, and work units.
- It denotes the times when specific individuals must be available for work on a given task.
- It aids in ensuring that the proper communications take place between departments and functions.
- It determines an expected project completion date.
- It identifies so-called critical activities which, if delayed, will delay the project completion time.
- It also identifies activities with slack that can be delayed for specified periods without penalty, or from which resources may be temporarily borrowed without harm.
- It determines the dates on which tasks may be started—or must be started if the project is to stay on schedule.
- It illustrates which tasks must be coordinated to avoid resource or timing conflicts.
- It also illustrates which tasks may be run, or must be run, in parallel to achieve the predetermined project completion date.

- It relieves some interpersonal conflict by clearly showing task dependencies.
- It may, depending on the network form used, allow an estimate of the probability of project completion by various dates, or the date corresponding to a particular *a priori* probability.

# Project Management in Practice
## *Replacing the Atigun Section of the TransAlaska Pipeline*

In June of 1977, the TransAlaska Pipeline was put into service as the successful conclusion of one of the most difficult projects in history. As part of the maintenance of the 48-inch diameter pipeline, instrumented "pigs" are run along the pipeline every year to detect both internal and external corrosion. In the fall of 1988, data from the pig run indicated that excessive external corrosion had occurred in an 8.5 mile section of the pipeline located in the Atigun River flood plain, 135 miles north of the Artic Circle (see map).

Thus, in the spring of 1989 a project team was formed to take total responsibility for replacing this portion of the buried pipeline with another buried pipe that had much better external corrosion protection, fusion bonded epoxy covered with 1.25 inches of concrete, an articulated concrete mat, and then five to fifteen feet of dirt. As part of the project objectives, the oil flow of two million barrels per day at pressures exceeding 800 psi was *not* to be interrupted, and there could be absolutely no oil spills!

Polar bears at construction site—Atigun Section of TransAlaska Pipeline.

Sidebooms lower new pipe into ditch at −50°F temperatures.

This meant that a bypass system had to be constructed while the pipe was being replaced, all in a very hostile work environment. The site is subject to flooding, rockslides, avalanches, mudslides, temperatures that reach − 60° F in the winter (tires break like glass and gasoline turns to jelly at that temperature), and as little as three hours of sunshine in which to work during the winter months. To minimize exposure to the springtime avalanches, they worked in another area first and then used explosives to trigger potential avalanches and unstable snow deposits. Also, a full-time avalanche control and forecasting expert was present during construction in the danger area. Blasting was also used to dig the ditch, ironically, to protect the existing pipeline which was only 30 feet away. Another ironic aspect of the project was the constant curiosity of the wildlife in the area: "What impressed me most was completing this project right there in the middle of all these animals, and seeing that we didn't affect them at all—that was gratifying."

The project began in September of 1989 and was completed in December 1991, a 27-month duration. Scheduling was a major facet of the project, not just due to the limited hours of sunshine, but also in obtaining facilities and materials for the project. For exam-

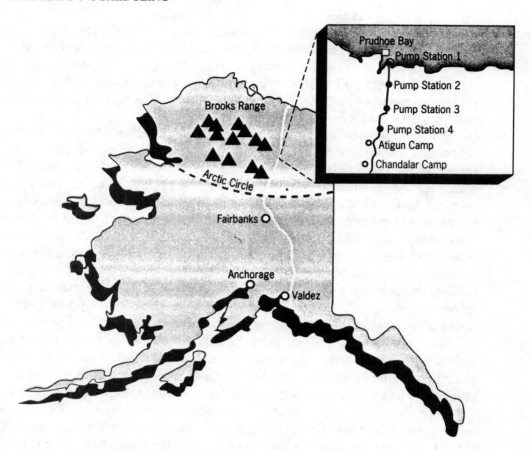

ple, some elements of the replacement pipeline had to be shipped to Saudia Arabia for corrosion treatment and then shipped back, all just prior to the Persian Gulf war. Yet, the project met or exceeded all expectations, without one oil spill. More surprisingly, the project was completed 34 percent under bud-get through careful analysis of the financial and physical risks and assignment to the most appropriate contractor.

*Source*: Project Team "Atigun Mainline Reroute Project," PM *Network*, Jan. 1993.

## ▶ 8.2 NETWORK TECHNIQUES: PERT AND CPM

With the exception of Gantt charts, to be discussed below, the most common approach to project scheduling is the use of network techniques such as PERT and CPM. The Program Evaluation and Review Technique was developed by the U.S. Navy in cooperation with Booz-Allen Hamilton and the Lockheed Corporation for the Polaris missile/submarine project in 1958. The Critical Path Method was developed by DuPont, Inc., during the same time period.

In application, PERT has primarily been used for R & D projects, the type of projects for which it was developed, though its use is more common on the "development" side of R & D than it is on the "research" side. CPM was designed for construction projects and has been generally embraced by the construction industry. (There are many exceptions to these generalities. The Eli Lilly Company, for example, uses CPM for its research projects.)

The two methods are quite similar and are often combined for educational presentation. Throughout most of this chapter we will not distinguish between them except where the differences are of direct interest to us. We will write "PERT/CPM" whenever the distinction is not important. Originally, however, PERT was strictly oriented to the time element of projects and used probabilistic activity time estimates to aid in determining the probability that a project could be completed by some given date. CPM, on the other hand, used deterministic activity time estimates and was designed to control both the time and cost aspects of a project, in particular, time/cost trade-offs. In CPM, activities can be "crashed" (expedited) at extra cost to speed up the completion time. Both techinques identified a project *critical path* whose activities could not be delayed, and also indicated *slack* activities that could be somewhat delayed without lengthening the project completion time.

We might note in passing that the *critical* activities in real-world projects typically constitute less than 10 percent of the total activities. In our examples and simplified problems in this chapter, the critical activities constitute a much greater proportion of the total because we use smaller networks to illustrate the techniques.

Before explaining the mechanics of these methods, we must note that their value in use is not totally accepted by everyone. Research on the use of PERT/CPM [11, 24, 25] conducted in the 1960s and early 1970s found that there was no significant difference in the technological performance on projects where PERT/CPM was used and where it was not. This research found, however, that there was a significantly lower probability of cost and schedule overruns when PERT/CPM was used. In our experience, the use of network scheduling techniques has increased markedly in recent years, particularly with the proliferation of project management software packages that are inexpensive and reasonably friendly to PMs who are familiar with the fundamental concepts of PERT/CPM, and who are also sensible enough to avoid trying to construct complex networks by hand.

Recent research [9] finds that a greater use of "project management techniques" (PERT/CPM among a number of others) occurs on R & D type projects, on projects with greater levels of complexity, and on projects with resource limitations, than on other types of projects or those with lower levels of complexity and fewer resource limitations. Unfortunately, this otherwise excellent research did not investigate whether or not the use of project management software influenced the number of project management techniques used. The use of project management software for scheduling projects will be discussed and illustrated in Chapter 10.

## Terminology

Let us now define some terms used in our discussion of networks.

**Activity** A specific task or set of tasks that are required by the project, use up resources, and take time to complete.

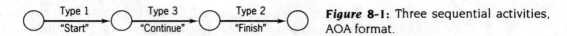

**Figure 8-1:** Three sequential activities, AOA format.

**Event**   The result of completing one or more activities. An identifiable end state occurring at a particular time.

**Network**   The combination of all activities (usually drawn as *arcs*) and events (usually drawn as *nodes* at the beginning and end of each arc) define the project and the activity precedence relationships. Networks are usually drawn starting on the left and proceeding to the right. Arrowheads placed on the arcs are used to indicate the direction of flow—that is, to show the proper precedences. Before an event can be *realized*—that is, achieved—all activities that immediately precede it must be completed. These are called its *predecessors*. Thus, an event represents an instant in time when each and every predecessor activity has been finished. Events themselves have no time duration and use no resources. They are merely points on the network, conditions of the system that can be recognized.

**Path**   The series of connected activities (or intermediate events) between any two events in a network.

**Critical**   Activities, events, or paths which, if delayed, will delay the completion of the project. A project's *critical path* is understood to mean that sequence of critical activities (and critical events) that connect the project's start event to its finish event.

To transform a project plan into a network, one must know what activities comprise the project and, for each activity, what its predecessors (and/or successors) are. An activity can be in any of these conditions: (1) it may have a successor(s) but no predecessor(s), (2) it may have a predecessor(s) but no successor(s), and (3) it may have both predecessor(s) and successor(s). The first of these is an activity that starts a network. The second ends a network. The third is in the middle. Figure 8-1 shows each of the three types of activities. Arrows are labeled with the appropriate type numbers. More than one arrow can start a network, end a network, or be in the middle. Any number of arrows can end at a node or depart from a node, as in Figure 8-2.

The interconnections depend on the technological relationships described in the action plan. For example, when one paints a room, filling small holes and cracks in the wall and masking windows and woodwork are predecessors to painting the walls. Similarly, removing curtains and blinds, as well as pictures and picture hooks

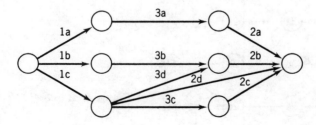

**Figure 8-2:** Activity network, AOA format.

from the wall are predecessors to spackling and masking. It is the nature of the work to be done that determines predecessor–successor relationships.

In the examples above, arrows represent activities while nodes stand for events. This is an AOA (activity-on-arrow) network. Another format for drawing networks is AON (activity-on-node). In this case, activities are represented by nodes and arrows to show the precedence relationships. In AON notation, when there are multiple activities with no predecessors, it is usual to show them all emanating from a single node called "start." Similarly, when multiple activities have no successors, it is usual to show them connected to a node called "end," as in Figure 8-3.

The choice between AOA and AON representation is largely a matter of personal preference. Our impression is that users of PERT favor AOA and users of CPM favor AON, but both approaches appear in the educational literature. Both are also used in commercially available computer packages, though AON is typically used in the most popular PC-based software. AOA networks are slightly harder to draw, but they identify events (milestones) clearly. AON networks do not require the use of *dummy* activities (defined below) and are easier to draw. Throughout most of this chapter we adopt the AOA format of PERT. In Section 8.4, we use the AON representation that is standard with that method. In this way, the reader can become familiar with both types of networks. This chapter is intended as an introduction to project scheduling at a level sufficient for the PM who wishes to use most commercial computerized project scheduling packages. For a deeper understanding of PERT/CPM, we refer the reader to [4, 12, 15, 17, 19, 37, 40, 55].

Recall the planning documents we developed in Chapter 5. In particular, the action plan contains the information we need. It is a list of all activities that must be undertaken in order to complete a specified task, the time each activity is expected to take, any nonroutine resources that will be used by the activity, and the predecessor activities for each activity. For example, we might have an action plan like that shown in Figure 8-4.

## Constructing the Network

Let us start by assuming the node numbered 1 denotes the event called "START." Activities **a** and **b** have no predecessors, so we assume their source is at START (node 1) and their destination at nodes we will number 2 and 3, respectively (Figure 8-5). As explained above, the arrowheads show the direction of flow.

Activity **c** follows **a**, activity **d** follows **b**, and activity **e** also follows **b**. Let's add these to our network in Figure 8-6. Note that we number the event nodes sequentially from left to right as we construct the network. No great damage occurs if we do not use this convention, but it is convenient.

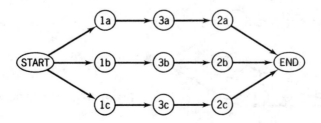

*Figure **8-3:*** Activity network, AON format.

**ACTION PLAN**

**Objective:** To complete. . . . . . . . . . . . . . . . . . . . . . . . . . . . . . . . . . . . . . . . . . . . . . . . . . . . . . . . . . . . . . . .
. . . . . . . . . . . . . . . . . . . . . . . . . . . . . . . . . . . . . . . . . . . . . . . . . . . . . . . . . . . . . . . . . . . . . . . . . . . . . . . . . . . . . . . . . . . . . . .

**Measures of Performance**. . . . . . . . . . . . . . . . . . . . . . . . . . . . . . . . . . . . . . . . . . . . . . . . . . . . . . . . . . . . .
. . . . . . . . . . . . . . . . . . . . . . . . . . . . . . . . . . . . . . . . . . . . . . . . . . . . . . . . . . . . . . . . . . . . . . . . . . . . . . . . . . . . . . . . . . . . . . .

**Constraints**. . . . . . . . . . . . . . . . . . . . . . . . . . . . . . . . . . . . . . . . . . . . . . . . . . . . . . . . . . . . . . . . . . . . . . . . . . . . . . . . .

| Tasks | Precedence | Time | Cost | Who Does |
|---|---|---|---|---|
| a | — | 5 days | — | — |
| b | — | 4 days | — | — |
| c | a | 6 days | — | — |
| d | b | 2 days | — | — |
| e | b | 5 days | — | — |
| f | c,d | 8 days | — | — |

*Figure* **8-4:** Sample action plan.

Now note that activity **f** must follow both **c** and **d**, but *any given activity must have its source in one, and only one node.* Therefore, it is clear that **c** and **d**, both of which must precede **f**, must conclude in the same node from which **f** originates. We can now redraw the network, collapsing nodes 4 and 5 (and renumbering them) as in Figure 8-7.

The action plan does not indicate any further activity is required to complete the task, so we have reached the end of this particular plan. Once again, we can redraw the network to show that the final activities (those with no successors) end in a single node, Figure 8-8.

This process of drawing and redrawing the network may seem a bit awkward, and is. If the list of activities associated with a project is long, with complicated in-

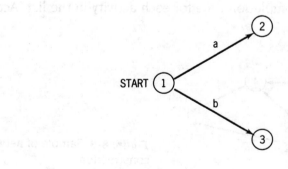

*Figure* **8-5:** Sample of network construction.

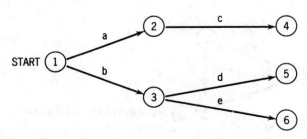

*Figure* **8-6:** Sample of network construction.

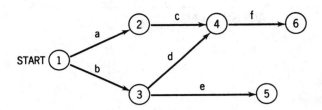

**Figure 8-7:** Sample of network construction.

terrelationships, this way of constructing the network would be too time-consuming to be practical. In Chapter 10 we will describe some computer software that can automatically generate the network.

Construction of a network may not be straightforward in some cases. For instance, there may be a need for a dummy activity to aid in indicating a particular precedence, via a dashed arc. A dummy activity has no duration and uses no resources. Its sole purpose is to indicate a technological relationship.

Figure 8-9 illustrates the proper way to use a dummy activity *if two* activities occur between the same *two* events. Figure 8-9 also shows why dummy activities may be needed for AOA networks. An activity is identified by its starting and ending nodes as well as its "name." For example, activities **a** and **b** both start from node 1 and end at node 2. Many computer programs that are widely used for finding the critical path and time for networks require the nodes to identify which activity is which. In our example, **a** and **b** would appear to be the same, both starting at node 1 and ending at node 2.

Figure 8-10 illustrates how to use a dummy activity when activities **a, b,** and **c** must precede activity **d,** but only **a** and **b** must precede activity **e.** Last, Figure 8-11 illustrates the use of dummy activities in a more complex setting.

Let us now consider a small project with ten activities in order to illustrate the network technique. Table 8-1 lists the activities, their most likely completion times, and the activities that must precede them. The table also includes optimistic and pessimistic estimates of completion time for each activity in the list. Actual activity

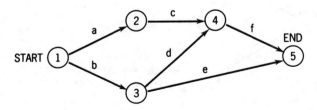

**Figure 8-8:** Sample of network construction.

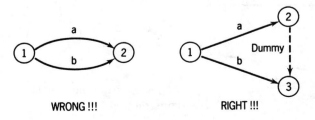

**Figure 8-9:** Networking concurrent activities.

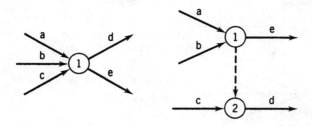

**Figure** 8-10: Activity **c** not required for **e.**

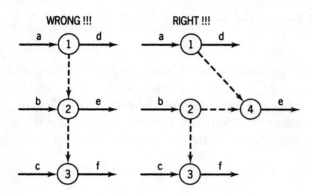

**Figure** 8-11: **a** precedes **d**; **a** and **b** precede **e**; **b** and **c** precede **f** (**a** does not precede **f**).

time is expected rarely to be less than the optimistic time or more than the pessimistic time. (More on this matter shortly.)

As described earlier, we start the network by finding those activities that have no predecessors. In the table activities **a, b,** and **c** meet the test. Therefore, they can all be drawn emerging from our starting node.

Next, we look for activities that only require **a, b,** or **c,** or some combination of **a, b,** and **c,** to precede them. Activity **d** requires that **a** be completed, and **e, f,** and **g** all require that **b** and **c** be completed. Note that a dummy will be necessary unless we begin the network from separate nodes for **b** and **c.** Last, **h** requires only that **c** be completed. To this point, the network might look like Figure 8-12.

**Table 8-1** Project Activity Times and Precedences

| Activity | Optimistic Time | Most Likely Time | Pessimistic Time | Immediate Predecessor Activities |
|---|---|---|---|---|
| a | 10 | 22 | 22 | — |
| b | 20 | 20 | 20 | — |
| c | 4 | 10 | 16 | — |
| d | 2 | 14 | 32 | a |
| e | 8 | 8 | 20 | b,c |
| f | 8 | 14 | 20 | b,c |
| g | 4 | 4 | 4 | b,c |
| h | 2 | 12 | 16 | c |
| i | 6 | 16 | 38 | g,h |
| j | 2 | 8 | 14 | d,e |

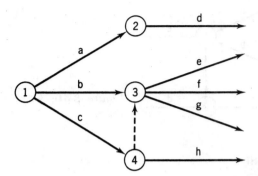

*Figure* **8-12:** Partial network.

The last two activities, **i** and **j,** are drawn in the same manner. Activity **i** requires that both **g** and **h** be completed, so **g** and **h** are directed to a single node (node 5). Similarly, activity **j** requires the completion of both **d** and **e,** which are directed to node 6. Since no activities require that **f, i,** or **j** precede them, these activities are directed to the project completion node, 7. The complete project network is shown in Figure 8-13.

## Calculating Activity Times

The next step is to calculate expected activity completion times from the data in Table 8-1. These expected completion times are found by using the three time estimates (optimistic, pessimistic, and most likely) in the table.

Once again, a short digression is helpful. Precisely what is meant by "optimistic," "pessimistic," and "most likely"? Assume that all possible times for some specific activity might be represented by a statistical distribution (e.g., the asymmetrical distribution in Figure 8-14). The "most likely" time, $m$, for the activity is the mode of this distribution. In theory, the "optimistic" and "pessimistic" times are selected in the following way. The PM, or whoever is attempting to estimate $a$ and $b$, is asked to select $a$ such that the actual time required by the activity will be $a$ or greater about 99 percent of the time. Similarly, $b$ is estimated such that about 99 percent of the time the activity will have a duration of $b$ or less. (We know of no project managers or workers who are comfortable making estimates at this level of precision, but we will delay dealing with this problem for the moment.)

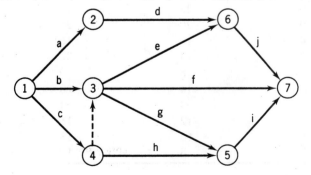

*Figure* **8-13:** The complete network from Table 8-1.

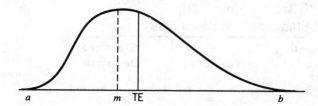

**Figure 8-14:** Distribution of all possible activity times for an activity.

The expected time, TE, is found by

$$TE = (a + 4m + b)/6$$

*where*

a = optimistic time estimate,

b = pessimistic time estimate, and

m = most likely time estimate, the mode.

Note in Table 8-1 that some activity durations are known with certainty, which is to say that a, b, and m are the same (see activity **b**, for instance). Note further that the most likely time may be the same as the optimistic time (a = m) as in activity **e,** or that the most likely time may be identical to the pessimistic time (m = b) as in activity **a.** The range about m may be symmetric where

$$m - a = b - m$$

as in activity **c,** or may be quite asymmetric, as in activities **h** and **j.**

The above formula for calculating expected times is usually said to be based on the beta statistical distribution.* This distribution is used rather than the more common normal distribution because it is highly flexible in form and can take into account such extremes as where a = m or b = m.

TE is an estimate of the mean of the distribution. It is a weighted average of a, m, and b with weights of 1-4-1, respectively. Again, we emphasize that *this same method can be applied to finding the expected level of resource usage given the appropriate estimates of the modal resource level as well as optimistic and pessimistic estimates.*

Recently, Sasieni noted [48] that writers (including himself) have been using the formula used here to estimate TE. He pointed out that it could not be derived from the formula for the beta distribution without several assumptions that were not necessarily reasonable, and he wondered about the original source of the formula. Fortunately, for two generations of writers on the subject, Littlefield and Randolph [27] cited a U.S. Navy paper that derives the approximations used here and states the not unreasonable assumptions on which they are based. Gallagher [16] makes a second derivation of the formula using a slightly different set of assumptions.

---

*We remind readers who wish a short refresher on elementary statistics and probability that one is available in Appendix E at the end of this book.

**Table 8-2**   Expected Activity Times (TE),
Variances ($\sigma^2$), and Standard Deviations ($\sigma$)

| Activity | Expected Time, TE | Variance, $\sigma^2$ | Standard Deviation, $\sigma$ |
|---|---|---|---|
| a | 20 | 4 | 2 |
| b | 20 | 0 | 0 |
| c | 10 | 4 | 2 |
| d | 15 | 25 | 5 |
| e | 10 | 4 | 2 |
| f | 14 | 4 | 2 |
| g | 4 | 0 | 0 |
| h | 11 | 5.4 | 2.32 |
| i | 18 | 28.4 | 5.33 |
| j | 8 | 4 | 2 |

The results of the expected value calculations are shown in Table 8-2 and are included on Figure 8-15 as well. Also included in the table and on the network are measures of the *uncertainty* for the duration of each activity, the *variance*, $\sigma^2$ that is given by

$$\sigma^2 = ((b - a)/6)^2$$

and the *standard deviation*, $\sigma$, which is given by

$$\sigma = \sqrt{\sigma^2}$$

This calculation of $\sigma$ is based on the assumption that the standard deviation of a beta distribution is approximately one-sixth of its range, $(b - a)/6$.

## Critical Path and Time

Consider the hypothetical project shown in Figure 8-15. Assume, for convenience, that the time units involved are days. How long will it take to complete the project?

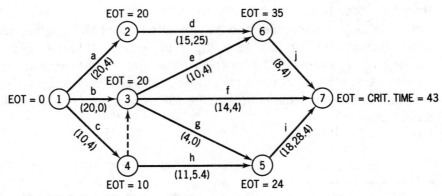

**Figure 8-15:** The complete network from Table 8-2.

(For the moment we will treat the expected times as if they were certain.) If we start the project on day zero, we can begin simultaneously working on activities **a, b,** and **c,** each of which have no predecessor activities. We will reach event 2 in 20 days, event 3 in 20 days, and event 4 in ten days. We have shown these times just above or below their respective nodes. They are labelled EOT (earliest occurrence time) because they represent the earliest times that the event can occur. Activity **d,** for example, cannot begin before event 2 has occurred, which means that all activities that precede event 2 must be completed. In this case, of course, activity **a** is the only predecessor of event 2.

Note that event 3 not only requires the completion of activity **b,** but also requires the completion of activity **c,** as shown by the dummy activity. (Refer to Figure 8-9 for a refresher.) The dummy requires neither time nor resources, so it does not affect the network time in any way. Event 3 does not occur until all paths leading to it have been completed. Therefore, the EOT for event 3 is equal to the time required by the *longest* path leading to it. The path from event 1 to event 3 requires the completion of activity **b** (20 days) *and* the completion of activities **c** and **dummy** (ten + zero days). Because the two paths may be followed simultaneously, we can reach event 3 in 20 days. Therefore, the earliest starting time (EST) for any activity emanating from event 3 is 20 days.

Proceeding similarly, we see that event 6 has two predecessor activities, **d** and **e.** Activity **d** cannot start until day 20, (EST = 20) and it requires 15 days to complete. Thus, its contribution to event 6 will require a total of 35 days from the start of the project. Activity **e** may also start after 20 days, the EOT for event 3, but it requires only ten days, a total of 30 days from the project start. Because event 6 requires the completion of both activities **d** and **e,** the EOT for event 6 is 35 days, the *longest* of the paths to it. Event 5 has an EOT of 24 days, the longest of the two paths leading to it, and event 7, the completion event of the network, has a time of 43 days. The EOTs are shown in Figure 8-15.

There are eight activity paths leading to event 7. They are

| | | |
|---|---|---|
| **a-d-j**$=20 + 15 + 8=43$ days | **c-dummy-e-j**$=10 + 0 + 10 + 8=28$ days | |
| **b-e-j**$=20 + 10 + 8=38$ days | **c-dummy-f** $=10 + 0 + 14$ $=24$ days | |
| **b-f**$=20 + !4$ $=34$ days | **c-dummy-g-i**$=10 + 0 + 4 + 18=32$ days | |
| **b-g-i**$=20 + 4 + 18=42$ days | | |
| **c-h-i**$=10 + 11 + 18=39$ days | | |

The longest of these paths is **a-d-j** using 43 days, which means that 43 days is the *shortest* time in which the entire network can be completed. This is called the *critical* time of the network, and **a-d-j** is the critical path, usually shown as a heavy line.

In a simple network such as our example, it is easy to find and evaluate every path between start and finish. Many real networks are considerably more complex, and finding all paths can be taxing. Using the method illustrated above, there is no need to worry about the problem. Every node is characterized by the fact that one or more activities lead to it. Each of these activities has an expected duration and originates in an earlier node. As we proceed to calculate the EOT of each node, beginning at the start, *we are actually finding the critical path and time to each of the nodes in the net-*

*work*. Note that event 5 has an EOT (critical time) of 24 days, and its critical path is **b-g** rather than **c-h** which requires 21 days, or **c-dummy-g** which takes 14 days.

The number of activities directly entering an event tells us the number of paths we must evaluate to find the EOT for that event. Here, *path* is defined as originating at immediate predecessor events, not at the network origin. With event 5, that number is two, so we find the EOT and activity times for the two immediate predecessors. For event 7, we have three evaluations to do, the EOT of event 6 plus the duration of activity **j** (43 days), the EOT of event 3 plus the duration of **f** (34 days), and the EOT of event 5 plus the duration of **i** (42 days). There is, therefore, no need to find, list, and evaluate all possible start-to-finish paths in the network.

Although we will assume throughout this chapter that we always employ the "as-soon-as-possible" approach to scheduling tasks ("early start"), there are situations where other approaches are sometimes used. One example is the simultaneous start, where all resources are launched at the beginning. Another is the simultaneous finish, where a facility can be moved to its next location once all the tasks are finished. Of course, delay early on in a project runs the risk of delaying the overall project if some other activities inadvertently become delayed. One important reason for using an "as-late-as-possible" approach is that it delays the use of resources as much as possible, thereby optimizing the cash flow of the project, but again at some risk of delay.

## Slack

Thus far in this discussion we have focused mostly on the events in the network. We found the EOTs for the project milestones. It is now helpful to focus on the activities by finding their earliest starting times (EST) and latest possible starting times (LST). As noted in the previous section, the EST for an activity is equal to the EOT for the event from which the activity emanates. Activity **i** cannot start until event 5 has occurred. Event 5 has an EOT of 24 days, and so activity **i** has an EST of 24 days. An important question for the PM is this: What is the latest time (LST) activity **i** could start without making the entire project late?

Refer again to Figure 8-15. The project has a critical time of 43 days. Activity **i** requires 18 days to be accomplished. Therefore, **i** must be started no later than day 25 ($43 - 18 = 25$) if the project is to be complete on day 43. The LST for activity **i** is day 25. Because **i** cannot begin until event 5 has occurred, the latest occurrence time (LOT) for event 5 is also day 25. The difference between the LST and the EST for an activity is called its *slack* or *float*. In the case of activity **i**, it *must* be started no later than day 25, but *could* be started as early as day 24, so it has one day of slack. It should be immediately obvious that all activities on the critical path have zero slack. They cannot be delayed without making the project late.

For another example, consider activity **f.** Its EST is day 20, which is equal to the EOT for event 3 from which it emanates. The LST for activity **f** is $43 - 14 = 29$. If **f** is started later than day 29, it will delay the entire project. Activity **f** has slack of LST − EST = $29 - 20 = 9$ days.

To find the slack for any activity or the LOT for any event, we make a backward pass (right to left) through the network just as we made a forward pass (left to right) to find the critical path and time and the EOTs for all events (which are also the

ESTs for successor activities). There is one simple convention we must adopt: *When there are two or more noncritical activities on a path, it is conventional to calculate the slack for each activity as if it were the only activity in the path.* Thus, when finding the slack for activity **i,** for example, we assume that none of **i**'s predecessors are delayed, and that event 5 occurred on its EOT of day 24. Of course, if some activity, **x,** had six days of slack (given a specific EOT for the immediate preceding event), and if an earlier activity was late, causing the event to be delayed say two days, then activity **x** would have only four days of slack, having lost two days to the earlier delay.

It is simple to calculate slack for activities that are immediate predecessors of the final node. As we move to earlier activities, it is just a bit more complicated. Consider activity **g.** Remembering our assumption that the other activities in the same path use none of the available slack, we see that activity **i** must follow **g,** and that **g** emanates from event 3. Starting with the network's critical time of 43 days, we subtract 18 days for activity **i** and four more days for **g** ($43 - 18 - 4 = 21$). Thus **g** can begin no later than day 21 without delaying the network. The EST for **g** (EOT for event 3) is day 20, so **g** has one day of slack.

To find the LOT for event 3, we must investigate each path that emanates from it. We have already investigated two paths, one with activity **g** and one with activity **f.** Recall that **f** could start as late as day 29. For **f** not to delay the network, event 3 would have to be complete not later than day 29. But activity **g** must start no later than day 21, so event 3 must be complete by day 21 or the **g-i** path will cause a delay. Now consider activity **e,** the only remaining activity starting from event 3. Activity **e** must be completed by day 35 or event 6 will be late and the network will be delayed. (Note that we do not have to work backward from the end of the network to find the slack for any activity that ends at a node on the critical path. All events and activities on the critical path have zero slack, so any activity ending on this path must arrive at event 6 not later than day 35.) The LST for **e** is $35 - 10 = 25$. Its EST is day 20, so activity **e** has five days of slack.

We now can see that the LOT for event 3 is day 21, the most restrictive (earliest) time required, so that no activity emanating from it will cause the network to be late. Table 8-3 shows the LST, EST, and slack for all activities, and the LOT, EOT, and slack for all events.

On occasion, the PM may negotiate an acceptable completion date for a project which allows for some slack in the entire network. If, in our example, an acceptable date was 50 working days after the project start, then the network would have a total of $50 - 43 = 7$ days of slack. This is the latest occurrence time minus the earliest occurrence time for the ending node, 7, of the network.

## Uncertainty of Project Completion Time

When discussing project completion dates with senior management, the PM should try to determine the probability that a project will be completed by the suggested deadline—or find the completion time associated with a predetermined level of risk. With the information in Table 8-2, this is not difficult.

If we assume that the activities are statistically independent of each other, then the variance of a set of activities is equal to the sum of the variances of the individual activities comprising the set. Those who have taken a course in statistics will recall that the variance of a population is a measure of the population's dispersion

**Table 8-3** Times and Slacks for Network in Figure 8-15

| Event | LOT | EOT | Slack |
|---|---|---|---|
| 1 | 0 | 0 | 0 |
| 2 | 20 | 20 | 0 |
| 3 | 21 | 20 | 1 |
| 4 | 14 | 10 | 4 |
| 5 | 25 | 24 | 1 |
| 6 | 35 | ·35 | 0 |
| 7 | 43 | 43 | 0 |
| **Activity** | **LST** | **EST** | **Slack** |
| a | 0 | 0 | 0 |
| b | 1 | 0 | 1 |
| c | 4 | 0 | 4 |
| d | 20 | 20 | 0 |
| e | 25 | 20 | 5 |
| f | 29 | 20 | 9 |
| g | 21 | 20 | 1 |
| h | 14 | 10 | 4 |
| i | 25 | 24 | 1 |
| j | 35 | 35 | 0 |

and is equal to the square of the population's standard deviation. The variances in which we are interested are the variances of the activities on the critical path.

The critical path of our example includes activities **a, d,** and **j**. From Table 8-2 we find that the variances of these activities are 4, 25, and 4, respectively; and the variance for the critical path is the sum of these numbers, 33 days. Assume, as above, that the PM has promised to complete the project in 50 days. What are the chances of meeting that deadline? We find the answer by calculating Z, where

$$Z = (D - \mu)/\sqrt{\sigma_\mu^2}$$

and

D = the desired project completion time

$\mu$ = the critical time of the project, the sum of the TEs for activities on the critical path

$\sigma_\mu^2$ = the variance of the critical path, the sum of the variances of activities on the critical path

Z = the number of standard deviations of a normal distribution (the *standard normal deviate*)

Z, as calculated above, can be used to find the probability of completing the project on time.

Using the numbers in our example, D = 50, $\mu$ = 43, and $\sigma_\mu^2$ = 33 (the square root of $\sigma_\mu^2$ is 5.745), we have

$$Z = (50 - 43)/5.745$$

$$= 1.22 \text{ standard deviations}$$

**Table 8-4** Cumulative (Single Tail) Probabilities of the Normal Probability Distribution (Areas under the Normal Curve from $-\infty$ to $Z$)

| z | 00 | .01 | .02 | .03 | .04 | .05 | .06 | .07 | .08 | .09 |
|---|---|---|---|---|---|---|---|---|---|---|
| .0 | .5000 | .5040 | .5080 | .5120 | .5160 | .5199 | .5239 | .5279 | .5319 | .5359 |
| .1 | .5398 | .5438 | .5478 | .5517 | .5557 | .5596 | .5636 | .5675 | .5714 | .5753 |
| .2 | .5793 | .5832 | .5871 | .5910 | .5948 | .5987 | .6026 | .6064 | .6103 | .6141 |
| .3 | .6179 | .6217 | .6255 | .6293 | .6331 | .6368 | .6406 | .6443 | .6480 | .6517 |
| .4 | .6554 | .6591 | .6628 | .6664 | .6700 | .6736 | .6772 | .6808 | .6844 | .6879 |
| .5 | .6915 | .6950 | .6985 | .7019 | .7054 | .7088 | .7123 | .7157 | .7190 | .7224 |
| .6 | .7257 | .7291 | .7324 | .7357 | .7389 | .7422 | .7454 | .7486 | .7517 | .7549 |
| .7 | .7580 | .7611 | .7642 | .7673 | .7704 | .7734 | .7764 | .7794 | .7823 | .7852 |
| .8 | .7881 | .7910 | .7939 | .7967 | .7995 | .8023 | .8051 | .8078 | .8106 | .8133 |
| .9 | .8159 | .8186 | .8212 | .8238 | .8264 | .8289 | .8315 | .8340 | .8365 | .8389 |
| 1.0 | .8413 | .8438 | .8461 | .8485 | .8508 | .8531 | .8554 | .8577 | .8599 | .8621 |
| 1.1 | .8643 | .8665 | .8686 | .8708 | .8729 | .8749 | .8770 | .8790 | .8810 | .8880 |
| 1.2 | .8849 | .8869 | .8888 | .8907 | .8925 | .8944 | .8962 | .8980 | .8997 | .9015 |
| 1.3 | .9032 | .9049 | .9066 | .9082 | .9099 | .9115 | .9131 | .9147 | .9162 | .9177 |
| 1.4 | .9192 | .9207 | .9222 | .9236 | .9251 | .9265 | .9279 | .9292 | .9306 | .9319 |
| 1.5 | .9332 | .9345 | .9357 | .9370 | .9382 | .9394 | .9406 | .9418 | .9429 | .9441 |
| 1.6 | .9452 | .9463 | .9474 | .9484 | .9495 | .9505 | .9515 | .9525 | .9535 | .9545 |
| 1.7 | .9554 | .9564 | .9573 | .9582 | .9591 | .9599 | .9608 | .9616 | .9625 | .9633 |
| 1.8 | .9641 | .9649 | .9656 | .9664 | .9671 | .9678 | .9686 | .9693 | .9699 | .9706 |
| 1.9 | .9713 | .9719 | .9726 | .9732 | .9738 | .9744 | .9750 | .9756 | .9761 | .9767 |
| 2.0 | .9772 | .9778 | .9783 | .9788 | .9793 | .9798 | .9803 | .9808 | .9812 | .9817 |
| 2.1 | .9821 | .9826 | .9830 | .9834 | .9838 | .9842 | .9846 | .9850 | .9854 | .9857 |
| 2.2 | .9861 | .9864 | .9868 | .9871 | .9875 | .9878 | .9881 | .9884 | .9887 | .9890 |
| 2.3 | .9893 | .9896 | .9898 | .9901 | .9904 | .9906 | .9909 | .9911 | .9913 | .9916 |
| 2.4 | .9918 | .9920 | .9932 | .9925 | .9927 | .9929 | .9931 | .9932 | .9934 | .9936 |
| 2.5 | .9938 | .9940 | .9941 | .9943 | .9945 | .9946 | .9948 | .9949 | .9951 | .9952 |
| 2.6 | .9953 | .9955 | .9956 | .9957 | .9959 | .9960 | .9961 | .9962 | .9963 | .9964 |
| 2.7 | .9965 | .9966 | .9967 | .9968 | .9969 | .9970 | .9971 | .9972 | .9973 | .9974 |
| 2.8 | .9974 | .9975 | .9976 | .9977 | .9977 | .9978 | .9979 | .9979 | .9980 | .9981 |
| 2.9 | .9981 | .9982 | .9982 | .9983 | .9984 | .9984 | .9985 | .9985 | .9986 | .9986 |
| 3.0 | .9987 | .9987 | .9987 | .9988 | .9988 | .9989 | .9989 | .9989 | .9990 | .9990 |
| 3.1 | .9990 | .9991 | .9991 | .9991 | .9992 | .9992 | .9992 | .9992 | .9993 | .9993 |
| 3.2 | .9993 | .9993 | .9994 | .9994 | .9994 | .9994 | .9994 | .9995 | .9995 | .9995 |
| 3.3 | .9995 | .9995 | .9995 | .9996 | .9996 | .9996 | .9996 | .9996 | .9996 | .9997 |
| 3.4 | .9997 | .9997 | .9997 | .9997 | .9997 | .9997 | .9997 | .9997 | .9997 | .9998 |

We turn now to Table 8-4, which shows the probabilities associated with various levels of Z. (Table 8-4 also appears as Appendix C. It is shown here for the reader's convenience.) We go down the left column until we find Z = 1.2, and then across to column .02 to find Z = 1.22. The probability value of Z = 1.22 shown in the table is .8888, which is the likelihood that we will complete the critical path of our sample project within 50 days of the time it is started. Figure 8-16 shows the resulting probability distribution of the project completion times.*

---

*Our use of the normal distribution is allowed by the Central Limit Theorem which attests to the fact that the sum of independent activity times is normally distributed if the number of activities is large.

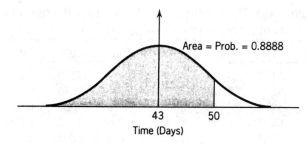

*Figure* 8-16: Probability distribution of project completion times.

We can work the problem backward, too. What deadline is consistent with a .95 probability of on-time completion? First, we go to Table 8-4 and look through the table until we find .95. The Z value associated with .95 is 1.645. (The values in the table are not strictly linear, so our interpolation is only approximate.) We know that $\mu$ is 43 days, and that $\sqrt{\sigma_\mu^2}$ is 5.745. Solving the equation for D, we have

$$D = \mu + 5.745(1.645)$$
$$= 43 + 9.45$$
$$= 52.45 \text{ days}$$

Thus, there is a 95 percent chance of finishing the project by 52.45 days.

Note that as D approaches $\mu$, Z gets smaller, approaching zero. Table 8-4 shows that for Z = 0, the chance of on-time completion is 50–50. The managerial implications are all too clear. If the PM wants a reasonable chance of meeting a project deadline, there must be some slack in the project schedule. When preparing a project budget, it is quite proper to include some allowance for contingencies. The same principle holds for preparing a project schedule. The allowance for contingencies in a schedule is network slack, and the wise PM will insist on some.

Finally, to illustrate an interesting point, let's examine a noncritical path, activities **b-g-i.** The variance of this path (from Figure 8-15) is 0 + 0 + 28.4 = 28.4, which is slightly less than the variance of the critical path. The path time is 42 days. The numerator of the fraction $(D - \mu)/\sqrt{\sigma_\mu^2}$ is larger, and in this case the denominator is smaller. Therefore, Z will be larger, and the probability of this path delaying project completion is less than for the critical path. But consider the noncritical path **c-h-i** with a time of 10 + 11 + 18 = 39 days, and a total variance of 37.8. (Remember, we are trying to find the probability that this noncritical path with its higher variance but shorter completion time will make us late, given that the critical path is 43 days.)

$$Z = (50 - 39)/6.15$$
$$Z = 1.79$$

The result is that we have a 96 percent chance for this noncritical path to allow the project to be on time.

If the desired time for the network equaled the critical time, 43 days, we have seen that the critical path has a 50–50 chance of being late. What are the chances that the noncritical path **c-h-i,** will make the project late? D is now 43 days, so we have

$$Z = \frac{(43 - 39)}{6.15}$$
$$= .65$$

Z = .65 is associated with a probability of .74 of being on time, or 1 − .74 = .26 of being late.

Assuming that these two paths (**a-d-j** and **c-h-i**) are independent, the probability that *both* paths will be completed on time is the product of the individual probabilities, (.50)(.74) = .37, which is considerably less than the 50–50 we thought the chances were. (If the paths are not independent, the calculations become more complicated.) Therefore, it is a good idea to consider noncritical paths that have activities with large variances and/or path times that are close to critical in duration (i.e., those with little slack).

Simulation is an obvious way to check the nature and impacts of interactions between probabilistic paths in a network. While this used to be difficult and time consuming, software has now been developed which simplifies matters greatly. Two excellent software packages have been developed which link to widely available spreadsheets: Crystal Ball ® which runs as a part of Excell®, and At Risk® which runs as a part of Lotus 1-2-3®. Both allow easy simulation of network interactions.

## Toward Realistic Time Estimates

The calculations of expected network times, and the uncertainty associated with those time estimates performed in the preceding sections are based, as we noted, on estimating optimistic and pessimistic times at the .99 level. That is, *a* is estimated such that the actual time required for an activity will be *a* or higher 99 percent of the time and will be *b* or lower 99 percent of the time. We then noted, parenthetically, that no project managers of our acquaintance are comfortable making estimates at that level of precision.

Fortunately, in practice it is not necessary to make estimates at the one-in-a-hundred level. Unless the underlying distribution is very asymmetric, no great error is introduced in finding TE if the pessimistic and optimistic estimates are made at the 95 percent, or even at the 90 percent levels; that is to say, only once in 20 times (or ten times for the 90 percent level) will the actual activity time be greater than or less than the pessimistic or optimistic estimates, respectively. The formula for calculating the variance of an activity, however, must be modified.

Recall that the calculation of variance is based on the assumption that the standard deviation of a beta distribution is approximately one-sixth of its range. Another way of putting this assumption is that *a* and *b* are estimated at the $-3\sigma$ and $+3\sigma$ limits respectively—roughly at the 99+ percent levels. Let the 95 percent estimates be represented by *a′* and *b′* and the 90 percent estimates by *a″* and *b″*. If we use a 95 or 90 percent estimation level, we are actually moving both *a* and *b* in from the distribution's tails so that the range will no longer represent $\pm 3\sigma$. See Figure 8-17.

It is simple to correct the calculation of variance for this error. Consider the 95 percent estimates. Referring to Table 8-4 we can find the Z associated with .95 of the area under the curve from *a′* to ∞. For .95, Z is approximately −1.65. (Of course, this applies to the normal distribution rather than to the beta distribution, but this huristic appears to work quite well in practice.) Similarly, Z = 1.65 for the area under the curve from −∞ to *b′*.

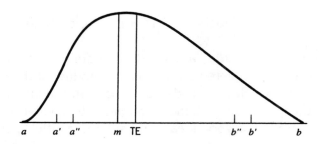

*Figure* **8-17: a, m,** and **b** estimates at the 99, 95, and 90 percent levels.

The range between $b'$ and $a'$ represents $2(1.65)\sigma = 3.3\sigma$, rather than the $6\sigma$ used in the traditional estimation of the variance. Therefore when estimating $a'$ and $b'$ at the 95 percent level, we should change the variance calculation formula to read

$$\sigma^2 = ((b' - a')/3.3)^2$$

For estimations at the 90 percent level ($a''$ and $b''$ in Figure 8-17), Z is approximately 1.3 and the variance calculation becomes

$$\sigma^2 = ((b'' - a'')/2.6)^2$$

In order to verify that this modification of the traditional estimator for the variance of a beta distribution gave good estimates of the true variance, we ran a series of trials using Statistical Analysis Systems (SAS) PROC IML for beta distributions of different shapes and estimated $a$ and $b$ at the 95 and 90 percent levels. We then compared these estimates of $a$ and $b$ with the true variance of the distribution and found the differences to be quite small, consistently under five percent.

An alternate method for approximating the mean and variance of a beta distribution when $a$ and $b$ are estimated at the 95 percent level is given in the last section of Appendix E. For the full exposition of the method, see reference 5 of Appendix E.

## Another Lotus 1-2-3® File

Just as we did in Chapter 7 on budgeting, we can construct a Lotus 1-2-3® template to do the calculations for finding the expected times, variances, and standard deviations associated with a series of three-time estimates for PERT/CPM networks. Figure 8-18 shows the file itself and Figure 8-19 shows the formulas used. Remember that the formula for calculation of variance must be modified according to the previous section unless $a$ and $b$ are estimated at the 99 + percent levels.

Most of the widely used project management software will not accept three-time estimates or do the necessary calculations to use such estimates, but a large majority of such software packages will routinely exchange information with Lotus 1-2-3,® Excel,® and similar spreadsheet software. It is therefore quite simple to enter the three-time estimates into a Lotus 1-2-3® file and enter the expected activity times, TEs, into a project management scheduling package where they can be used as if they were deterministic times in finding a project's critical path and time. Calculations of the probability of completing a project on or before some elapsed time can easily be done by hand.

|   | A | B | C | D | E | F | G |
|---|---|---|---|---|---|---|---|
| 1 | This is a template for three-time PERT schedule estimates | | | | | | |
| 2 | | | | | | | |
| 3 | *a* = optimistic time estimate | | | | | | |
| 4 | *b* = pessimistic time estimate | | | | | | |
| 5 | *m* = typical (modal) time estimate | | | | | | |
| 6 | | | | | | | |
| 7 | Activity | *a* | *m* | *b* | TE | Variance | Std. Dev. |
| 8 | | | | | | | |
| 9 | a | 5 | 6 | 8 | 6.17 | 0.250 | 0.500 |
| 10 | b | 4 | 7 | 8 | 6.67 | 0.444 | 0.667 |
| 11 | c | 6 | 8 | 12 | 8.33 | 1.000 | 1.000 |
| 12 | d | 7 | 7 | 7 | 7.00 | 0.000 | 0.000 |
| 13 | e | 6 | 7 | 8 | 7.00 | 0.111 | 0.333 |
| 14 | f | 4 | 5 | 12 | 6.00 | 1.778 | 1.333 |
| 15 | g | 4 | 6 | 9 | 6.17 | 0.694 | 0.833 |
| 16 | | | | | | | |

**Figure 8-18:** A spreadsheet template for PERT schedules.

## ▶ 8.3   GANTT CHARTS

One of the oldest and still one of the most useful methods of presenting schedule information is the Gantt chart, developed around 1917 by Henry L. Gantt, a pioneer in the field of scientific management. The Gantt chart shows planned and actual progress for a number of tasks displayed against a horizontal time scale. It is a particularly effective and easy-to-read method of indicating the actual current status for each of a set of tasks compared to the planned progress for each item of the set. As a result, the Gantt chart can be helpful in expediting, sequencing, and reallocating resources among tasks, as well as in the valuable but mundane job of keeping track of how things are going. In addition, the charts usually contain a number of special symbols to designate or highlight items of special concern to the situation being charted.

|   | A | B | C | D | E | F | G |
|---|---|---|---|---|---|---|---|
| 1 | | | | | | | |
| 2 | | | | | | | |
| 3 | Activity | *a* | *m* | *b* | TE | Variance* | Std. Dev. |
| 4 | | | | | | | |
| 5 | a | 5 | 6 | 8 | =(B5+(4*C5)+D5)/6 | =(((D5−B5)/6)^2) | =F5^0.5 |
| 6 | b | 4 | 7 | 8 | =(B6+(4*C6)+D6)/6 | =(((D6-B6)/6)^2) | =F6^0.5 |
| 7 | c | 6 | 8 | 12 | =(B7+(4*C7)+D7)/6 | =(((D7-B7)/6)^2) | =F7^0.5 |
| 8 | d | 7 | 7 | 7 | =(B8+(4*C8)+D8)/6 | =(((D8-B8)/6)^2) | =F8^0.5 |
| 9 | e | 6 | 7 | 8 | =(B9+(4*C9)+D9)/6 | =(((D9-B9)/6)^2) | =F9^0.5 |
| 10 | f | 4 | 5 | 12 | =(B10+(4*C10)+D10)/6 | =(((D10-B10)/6)^2) | =F10^0.5 |
| 11 | g | 4 | 6 | 9 | =(B11+(4*C11)+D11/6 | =(((D11-B11)/6)^2) | =F11^0.5 |
| 12 | | | | | | | |

*Adjust variance formula for level of precision (99+, 95, or 90).

**Figure 8-19:** Template formulas for PERT spreadsheet.

There are several advantages to the use of Gantt charts. First, even though they may contain a great deal of information, they are easily understood. While they do require frequent updating (as does any scheduling/control device), they are easy to maintain *as long as task requirements are not changed or major alterations of the schedule are not made.* Gantt charts provide a clear picture of the current state of a project.

Another significant advantage of Gantt charts is that they are easy to construct. While they may be constructed without first drawing a PERT diagram, there is a close relationship between the PERT/CPM network and the Gantt chart. We use the example in the previous section to illustrate this relationship and, at the same time, demonstrate how to construct such a chart.

First, the PERT/CPM network of Figure 8-15 is redrawn so that the lengths of each arc are in proportion to the respective task times. In essence, we redraw the network along a horizontal time scale. This modified network is shown in Figure 8-20. The heavy line, **a-d-j** is the critical path, and the horizontal dashed line segments indicate slack times. The vertical dashed line segments are dummy activities (as between events 3 and 4), or merely connectors (as elsewhere in the drawing). Note that to transform the network in this manner requires that we "explode" single nodes into multiple nodes when multiple activities emanate from the single node. In this modified network, each activity must originate from an individual node, although several activities still can have a common destination node.

The nodes of Figure 8-15 are placed at their EOTs (the early start times for ensuing activities), and the slack is shown *after* the activity duration. (We have used an arrowhead to separate the activity duration from its slack.) To draw the modified diagram only requires that the nodes be placed at their EOTs listed on the PERT/CPM network and the activity durations drawn out from them as solid lines. Precedence is shown by connecting the duration lines with dashed line segments, showing each specific connection to the appropriate nodes.

The Gantt chart can be drawn directly from the modified PERT/CPM diagram. A list is made of all activities required to complete the project. Activities are usually listed in alphanumeric order—which is most often the order in which they were

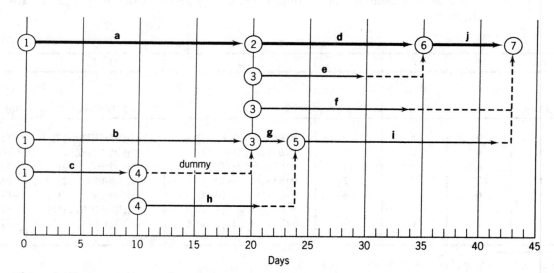

**Figure 8-20:** Gantt chart style representation of PERT/CPM network in Figure 8-15.

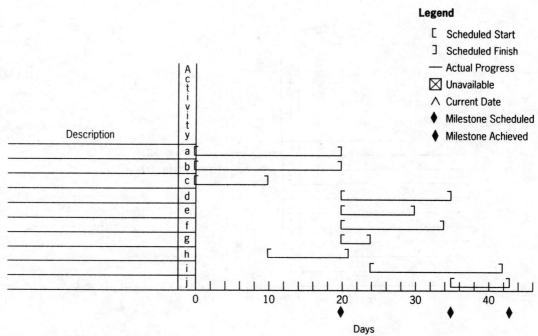

**Figure 8-21:** Gantt project chart from Figure 8-15.

listed in the action plan or whatever source document was originally used. As Figure 8-21 shows, activity times are superimposed on a linear calendar, much as in Figure 8-20. Precedence relationships are preserved by not allowing the activity line or bar for a successor activity to begin until its predecessors are complete. Scheduled activity times are drawn as light lines or hollow bars. A heavy line or a filled-in bar indicates actual progress. Color is sometimes used for easy visibility. The PM's ability to customize Gantt charts is limited only by the PM's imagination and the software being used.

Figure 8-21 transforms the modified PERT/CPM network into a Gantt chart. Note that three milestones are shown as diamonds below the baseline. These are the events that occur along the critical path. While there is no particular rule mandating the use of critical path events as project milestones, it is common for them to be chosen in this way. (If there are many critical events, some may be ignored and only the particularly noteworthy critical events are selected as milestones.) We can also see that while all precedence relationships must be preserved, it is not possible to distinguish easily their technical relationships simply by observing the chart itself. For example, activities **a** and **b** both have a duration of 20 days. Activities **d, e, f,** and **g** begin on the twentieth day. Using the Gantt chart, however, it is not possible to determine which, **a** or **b,** is predecessor to which of **d, e, f,** or **g.** If a single activity is completed at some time, it is reasonable to assume that other activities starting at that point are dependent on the first one; but if two or more activities end at the same time, the relationships between them and subsequent activities are unclear. Gantt charts, therefore, are generally inadequate for showing technological dependencies.*

---

*Actually, precedence relationships can be shown on Gantt charts, but the charts become cluttered and very difficult to read.

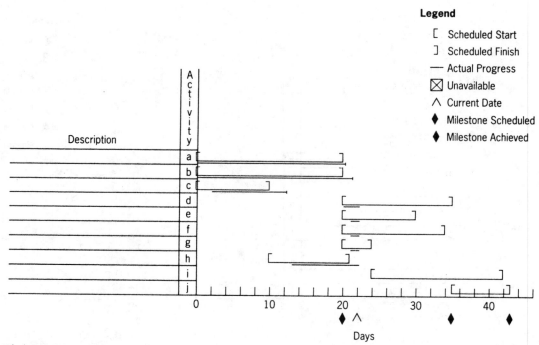

**Figure 8-22:** Gantt chart showing progress of project on Day 22.

Figure 8-22 pictures the project as it might appear on its twenty-second day. Actual progress is shown as a heavy line added just below the scheduled progress line. Activity **a** started and finished on time, while **b** started on time but was completed one day late. Activity **c** was begun two days late and finished three days late, which delayed the start of **h.** (In this case, the predecessor relationship of **c** to **h** is clear.) Activity **d** is under way and was started on time. Activities **e, f,** and **g** were all started one day late. Even with some activities starting late, nothing has happened to delay the actual critical path. While it is not clear from the Gantt chart, the network (Figure 8-15) shows that the delay in **b** means that the **b-g-i** path has gone critical.

This example illustrates both the strength and weakness of the Gantt chart. Its major strength is that it is easy to read. All popular project management software will prepare Gantt charts, and most have some options available for customization. Gantt charts are often mounted on the wall of the project office and updated frequently. Anyone interested in the project can see the state of progress easily, even if the interested party knows little about the actual nature of the work being done. The weakness of the Gantt chart is simply that one needs the PERT/CPM network (or the WBS) to interpret what appears on the Gantt chart beyond a cursory level—or to plan how to compensate for lateness.

Another advantage is the ease of construction of the chart. In our example, we converted the PERT/CPM network in Figure 8-15 to a Gantt chart by modifying the network as in Figure 8-20. In practice, this intermediate stage is not necessary, and one can easily go from network to chart in a single step. On balance, ease of construction and ease of use have made the Gantt chart the most popular method for displaying a project schedule [25]. Nonetheless, a PERT/CPM network is still needed for the PM to exercise control over the schedule.

In many ways, the Gantt chart is similar to the project master schedule described in Chapter 5. Both are types of bar charts and are used similarly. The major difference is that the Gantt chart is intended to monitor the detailed progress of work, whereas the master schedule contains only major tasks and is oriented toward overall project management rather than precise control of the detailed aspects of the project.

While PERT/CPM and Gantt charts are both scheduling techniques, they are not merely different ways of achieving the same ends; they are complementary rather than competitive. The budget can be directly related to the Gantt chart, as shown in Figure 8-23.

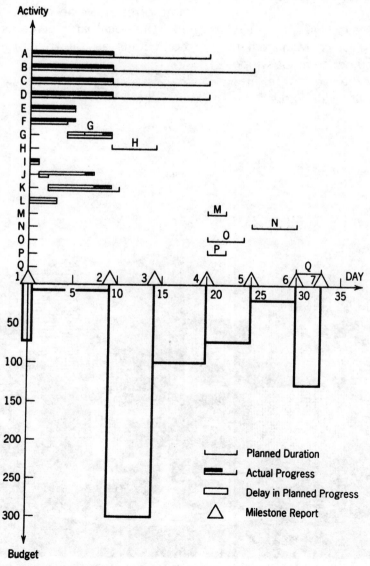

**Figure 8-23:** Relating the budget to the Gantt chart schedule.

# Project Management in Practice
## *Hosting the Annual Project Management Institute Symposium*

Planning and implementing a national conference for a society that will draw about 1000 attendees is a major project. The tasks involved in hosting such an event are considerable and involve selecting a program committee, choosing a theme, contacting exhibitors, making local arrangements, planning the program, and on and on.

Pittsburgh was selected as host city/chapter for the 1992 Project Management Institute's annual September seminar/symposium. The objectives for the event were three: (1) to deliver a high-quality, value-added pro-

gram that would be useful and last for years to come, (2) to offer a social and guest program that would reflect well on the host city, and (3) to meet strict financial criteria. The first task after selecting the city and hotel facilities was to put together the project team and chairperson. This included managers in charge of each of the tracks, the social program, the local arrangements, and all the other details as shown in the organization

Source: PMI Staff, "Catch the Spirit. . .at Pittsburgh," PM Network, May 1992.

Pittsburgh—host city for the PMI Annual Symposium.

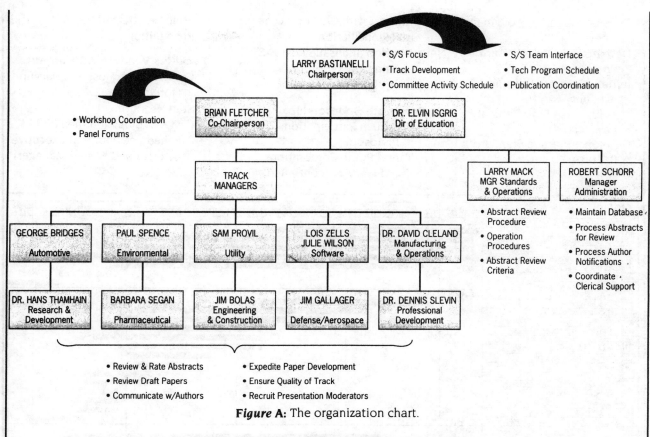

**Figure A:** The organization chart.

## WORK BREAKDOWN STRUCTURE AND TASKS

**S/S Project Management**
Recruit Project Team
Establish Organizational
Procedures
Establish CAO Support Levels
and Budget
Issue Reports to VP-Tech and
Board of Directors
Develop S/S Goals and
Objectives
Assemble and Issue Post-S/S
Report

**Technical Program**
Develop S/S Theme
Strategize Tracks and SIGs
Recruit Technical Program Team
Develop Selection Process
Procedures
Interface with Education
Committee on Workshops
Plan and Issue Call for
Papers/Panel Discussions

Recruit Invited Papers/Panel
Discussions
Recruit Moderators
Develop and Issue Master
Schedule for Presentations
Select Printer
Plan and Issue Abstract Books
and Proceedings
Organize Awards for Speakers'
Breakfasts
Identify Audio/Visual
Requirements
Develop and Issue Post-S/S
Technical Report

**Social Guest Program**
Establish Objectives
Identify Available Activities
Analyze Cost-Benefit
Identify Recommendations
Complete Contracts
Recruit Staff

**Speakers**
Identify Candidates and Related
Benefits and Costs
Make Recommendations and
Obtain Approval
Complete Contracts
Maintain Periodic Contact
Host Speakers

**Publicity/Promotion**
Theme Establishment and
Approval
Logo Development and
Approval
Video Production
Promotional Materials
Identification and Approval
Advertising: PMI, Public and
Trade Media Releases
Regional Newsletter Articles

**Finance**
Initiate Code of Accounts

**Figure B:** The work breakdown structure.

Develop Procedures of Financial Operation

Develop Independent Auditing Procedure

Initiate Separate Banking Account

Develop Cash Flow Estimates/Projections

Develop and Issue Standard Reports

Interact with CAO on Account Reconciliation

Develop and Issue Post-S/S Financial Report

**Corporate Sponsorship**
Establish Participation Philosophy

Target Prime Corporations

Solicit Participation Recognition

**Facilities Vendor/CAO Support**
Contract with Host and Backup Hotels

Staff Recruiting

(Details to be Identified and Scheduled with PMI Executive Director and Events Manager)

**Figure B:** (continued)

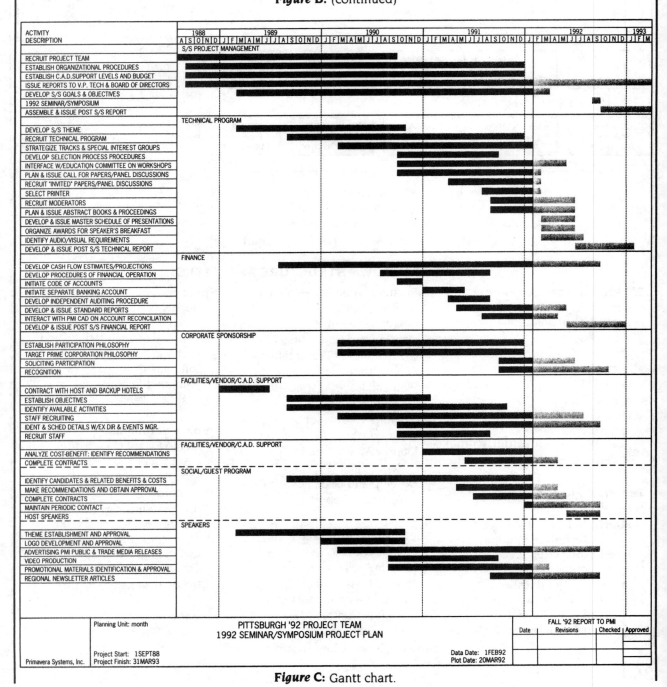

**Figure C:** Gantt chart.

structure in Figure A. The project team was organized using a functional approach. Pittsburgh PMI Chapter officers had most of the primary responsibilities, with members from nine other chapters assisting in other duties.

Next was the development of the work breakdown structure, shown in Figure B, and the Gantt chart of activity schedules, shown in Figure C. As seen in the Gantt chart, scheduling all the work for a major conference such as this is an overwhelming effort. In the WBS, the major task was the development of the technical program. For PMI '92, the technical program offered 22 workshops composed of 70 technical papers, special panel discussions, and case studies. The technical tracks included engineering and construction, pharmaceuticals, utilities, software, automotive,

R&D, defense, education, and manufacturing. The workshops included sessions on preparing for the PMI certification examinations, learning about Taguchi concepts of statistical quality control, and future practice in project management. All of these also required careful scheduling.

The vendor program included exhibits by dozens of vendors and a large number of showcase sessions for in-depth demonstrations of their wares. The social program included a golf tournament, numerous social activities to meet with colleagues, tours of Pittsburgh's attractions, and a wide variety of entertainment opportunities.

All in all, a conference such as PMI's is as difficult a project as many firms face in their competitive markets.

## ▶ 8.4   EXTENSIONS AND APPLICATIONS

There have been a large number of extensions to the basic ideas of PERT and CPM. These extensions are often oriented toward handling rather specific problem situations through additional program flexibility, computerizing some of the specific problems, fine-tuning some of the concepts for special environments, and combining various management approaches with the PERT/CPM concepts—for example, the TREND approach discussed in Chapter 5.

Another interesting extension deals with the case when it is very difficult to estimate activity times because no one has experience with the activity, or because the activity is ill-defined. In this case, the concepts of fuzzy-set theory are applied [34]. There are also opportunities for using simulation on stochastic PERT networks in order to make estimates of project finish time, as well as to examine the likelihood that noncritical paths have sufficient variance to become critical [51].

In this section we discuss some of these extensions and look at the utility of network scheduling models in general. However, we delay our coverage of extensions aimed primarily at resource allocation and formal applications of CPM until Chapter 9.

### Precedence Diagramming

One shortcoming of the PERT/CPM network method is that it does not allow for leads and lags between two activities without greatly increasing the number of subactivities to account for this. In construction projects, in particular, it is extremely common for the following restrictions to occur.

- Activity B must not start before activity A has been in progress for at least two days (Figure 8-24a).

- Activity A must be complete at least three days before activity B can be finished (Figure 8-24*b*).
- Activity B cannot begin before four days after the completion of A (Figure 8-24*c*).
- Activity B cannot be completed before eight days from the start of A (Figure 8-24*d*).

Precedence diagramming is an AON network method that allows for these leads and lags within the network. Node designations are illustrated in Figure 8-24*e*. Because of the increased flexibility regarding required lead and lag times, it must be

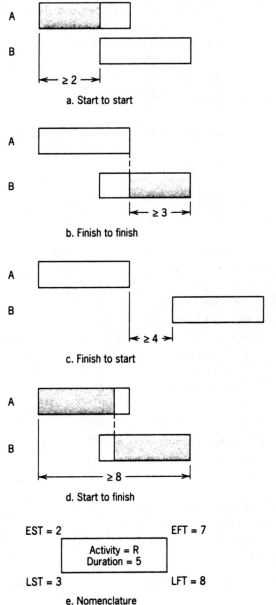

a. Start to start

b. Finish to finish

c. Finish to start

d. Start to finish

e. Nomenclature

**Figure 8-24:** Precedence diagramming conventions.

known whether each activity can be *split* or not. Splitting allows easier satisfaction of the lead and lag restrictions. If splitting is not allowed, the project may be significantly delayed.

Some anomalies tend to occur in precedence diagramming that are not encountered in PERT/CPM. For example, because of the lead and lag requirements, activities may appear to have slack when they really do not. Also, the critical path of the network will frequently go backward through an activity, with the result that increasing the activity time may actually decrease the project completion time. Such an activity is called *reverse critical*. This happens when the critical path enters the completion of an activity through a finish constraint (Figure 8-24*b* or *d*), continues backward through the activity, and leaves through a start constraint (Figure 8-24*a* or *d*).

Network node times are calculated in a manner similar to PERT/CPM times: Because of the lead and lag restrictions, it is often helpful to lay out a Gantt chart to see what is actually happening.

Precedence diagramming seems to be gaining in popularity. The richer set of precedence relationships it allows is pertinent for a variety of projects, particularly construction projects. For more details on this technique, see [1, 12 (Chapters 6 and 17), and 37]. Most current project management software will allow leads, lags, delays, and other constraints in the context of their standard AON network and Gantt chart programs.

## GERT

The Graphical Evaluation and Review Technique (GERT) is a network model developed to deal with more complex modeling situations than can be handled by PERT/CPM. GERT combines signal flowgraph theory, probabilistic networks, PERT/CPM, and decision trees all in a single framework. Its components consist of *logical nodes* (defined below) and directed arcs (or branches) with *two* parameters; the probability that a given arc is taken (or "realized") and the distribution function describing the time required by the activity. Evaluation of a GERT network yields the probability of each node being realized and the elapsed time between all nodes.

At this point, it may be useful to compare GERT and PERT/CPM in order to focus on what is different about GERT.

| **GERT** | **PERT/CPM** |
| --- | --- |
| Branching from a node is probabilistic. | Branching from a node is deterministic. |
| Various possible probability distributions for time estimates. | Only the beta distribution for time estimates. |
| Flexibility in node realization. | No flexibility in node realization. |
| Looping back to earlier events is acceptable. | Looping back is not allowed. |
| Difficult to use as a control tool. | Easy to use for control. |
| Arcs may represent time, cost, reliability, etc. | Arcs represent time only. |

While there are computer programs that optimize PERT/CPM problems, GERT and its various enhancements are computer simulations. Most of the programs (and the enhancements) are the result of work conducted by Pritsker [44]. His modeling package called Q-GERT simulates queues, or waiting lines, in the network. (There are other extensions of PERT that have some features similar to GERT and Q-GERT—VERT, for example—but GERT seems to be the most widely used extension.)

The steps employed in using GERT are these:

1. Convert the qualitative description of the project action plan into a network, just as in the use of PERT/CPM.

2. Collect the necessary data to describe the arcs of the network, focusing not only on the specific activity being modeled, but also on such characteristics of the activity as the likelihood it will be realized, the chance it might fail, any alternative activities that exist, and the like.

3. Determine the *equivalent function* of the network.

4. Convert the equivalent function of the network into the following two performance measures:

   The probability that specific nodes are realized.

   The "moment generating function" of the arc times.

5. Analyze the results and make inferences about the system.

It is not appropriate to deal here with the complex solution techniques employed for GERT networks. They make use of topology equations, equivalent functions, moment generating functions, and extensive calculation. The interested reader is urged to consult the papers of Pritsker and others [1, 44, 50] for formal descriptions of the methods involved in formulating and solving GERT networks. Instead, we will describe how to construct a GERT network of a simple situation.

The list of common GERT symbols, together with a few examples, is given in Figure 8-25. This figure describes the left, or input side of the nodes first, and then the right-hand output side next. All combinations of input and output symbols are feasible, as shown in the examples.

Now let us describe a manufacturing project situation developed by Pritsker and portray it through the GERT approach. This situation concerns the initiation of a new production process developed by manufacturing engineering for an electronic component. The resulting GERT model could just as well describe an R & D project, a government project, or a Girl Scout project.

## Sample Problem, Modeled with GERT

A part is manufactured on a production line in four hours. Following manufacture, parts are inspected. There is a 25 percent failure rate, and failed parts must be reworked. Inspection time is a stochastic variable, exponentially distributed, with a mean of 1 hour. Rework takes 3 hours, and 30 percent of the reworked parts fail the next inspection and must be scrapped. Parts that pass their original inspection or

| Symbol | Name | Explanation |
|---|---|---|
| | | **INPUT** |
| K | Exclusive—or | Any branch leading into the node causes the node to be realized, but only one branch can occur. |
| < | Inclusive—or | Any branch causes the node to be realized and at the time of the earliest branch. |
| C | And | The node is realized only after ALL branches have occurred. |
| | | **OUTPUT** |
| ) | Deterministic | All branches out must occur if the node is realized. |
| > | Probabilistic | Only one of the branches may occur if the node is realized. |

**EXAMPLES**

Beginning node with branches that must occur.

Ending node that occurs whenever **a** or **b** occurs.

Intermediate node that occurs if **a** occurs with either **b** or **c** following.

Intermediate node that occurs when all **a**, **b**, and **c** occur with either **d** or **e** following.

*Figure* **8-25**: GERT symbols.

pass inspection after rework are sent to finishing, a process that requires 10 hours 60 percent of the time and 14 hours otherwise. A final inspection rejects 5 percent of the finished parts, which are then scrapped.

We can now model this situation as a GERT network so that it can be solved for the expected percentage of good parts and the expected time required to produce a good part. This GERT network is illustrated in Figure 8-26.

Activity **a** represents the output of the four-hour manufacturing process. The outputs enter an inspection from which 75 percent are passed, **c**, and 25 percent

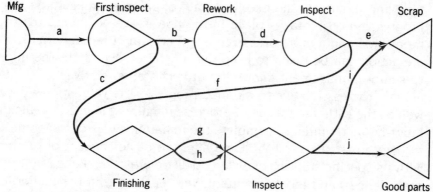

*Figure* **8-26**: Sample GERT network.

fail, **b.** The latter go to rework, with flow **d** emerging. Another inspection takes place—**e** (30 percent of 25 percent = 7.5%) flows to scrap, while the successfully reworked parts (70 percent of 25 percent = 17.5 percent), represented by **f,** go with the other good parts, **c,** to the finishing process. Sixty percent of this input requires 10 hours of work, **g,** and the remainder (40 percent) needs 14 hours, **h.** The final inspection process discards 5 percent of the output, **i** which goes to scrap, and the remainder (which is 87.875 percent of the original input) is sent to "good parts," **j.**

The time for an "average" part to proceed through the network can be found in much the same way as we calculated the output. The result of the entire analysis is therefore considerably richer than the simpler PERT/CPM. It should, however, be obvious that the input information requirements for GERT are more extensive and the computational requirements are far more extensive than for PERT/CPM, particularly for large networks. As always, the PM should adopt the simplest scheduling technique consistent with the needs of the project.

## Other Methods

Two straightforward methods for project scheduling that do not use networks or Gantt charts are employed by some agencies of the U.S. government. The Goddard Space Flight Center develops its project schedules in three phases. Phase I is advanced schedule planning, where the basic project schedule is developed directly from the work breakdown structure. Phase I lists all major elements of the project. This is used for presenting the proposed project to NASA and to the Congress and its many committees.

Phase II consists of the preparation of the operational schedule. This is the equivalent of the project master schedule. Phase III is schedule administration. In this last phase, the project is monitored and the master schedule is updated through the use of biweekly reports. Any necessary corrections and alterations to the project master schedule are made as a result of this process.

The Department of General Services uses a project scheduling system that provides planning, scheduling, and control in three distinct but closely related stages. Activity scheduling is the initial stage. At this point the planner attempts to develop optimum timing for the start and completion of all tasks associated with the project. Labor-hour and progress scheduling is carried out in the second stage. This identifies the labor (and other resources) required to initiate project activities on time and to sustain the necessary rate of progress to keep the project on schedule. Progress reporting takes place in the final stage. In this third stage, the project is monitored and a more or less constant stream of reports are filed so that appropriate action can be taken to keep the project on schedule. The information reported to senior management shows the project status relative to activity milestones and actual progress relative to planned progress. The value of the progress achieved as well as the estimated value of progress remaining is used to calculate (forecast) the labor-hours required to complete the remaining work on schedule.

Note that these methods parallel the basic concept of the project action plan with its specific steps to be taken, its estimate of resource requirements, times, and precedences, and most important, with each step in the higher-level plans broken down into lower-level action plans.

## A Mild Caveat

Many researchers, most recently Richard Schonberger [49], have exposed some interesting anomalies in PERT/CPM networks which show that deterministic times are optimistically biased. In essence, the effect comes about when one or more paths in the network have times that are close to the critical path time. If the noncritical path is delayed and becomes critical, it may extend the average completion time for the network, as we noted earlier. Schonberger develops a simple example to illustrate this finding. His critique extends to the three-time estimate method, which allows for activity time variance on a path-by-path analysis, but does not consider delays caused by path interaction. (Remember that the ability to calculate path variance as the sum of the variances of individual activities is based on the assumption of independence between activities—and paths.)

Several possible conclusions may be drawn from Schonberger's insight:

- Projects will probably be late—relative to the deterministic critical path.
- Network simulation is probably not worth the added expense.
- Deterministic time estimates should be used in place of the three time estimates.
- The network developed from these deterministic time estimates should be subjectively reevaluated for any path interaction factors that would tend to make the project late.
- Critical or near-critical activities should be intensively managed, the usual practice of project managers.

While it is helpful to be aware of these issues, we are not entirely in agreement with Schonberger's conclusions. The costs of simulation techniques are decreasing rapidly, and there are several inexpensive simulation computer programs readily available. GERT is an example of a simulation-based technique that is quite valuable *if the required information base and computational power are readily available*. GERT and other computer programs come in sufficient variety to have a great many applications in project management.

A stronger area of disagreement is our belief that three time estimates are far more informative to the PM than deterministic time estimates. The degree of activity variability is a clear indicator of the need for adaptive planning. In any case, for most project managers, the use of deterministic times does not mean that they estimate the variance of each and every activity to be zero, but rather that they assume that optimistic and pessimistic times are symmetrically distributed around the most likely times and cancel out. The distinction between a deterministic time and an average time is easily ignored by the unsophisticated. Further, this error is compounded because it leads to the false assumption that the expected time approach is the same as the deterministic approach. Clearly, the critical times would be the same in either case, which leads the unwary to the error.

As we illustrated earlier with Lotus 1-2-3®, readily available and inexpensive computer software makes the additional computational cost of three time estimates a trivial matter. Perhaps more serious is the advice to increase the calculated network time by subjective evaluation of the effects of path interaction. This will extend the network time by some arbitrary amount, usually in the form of network slack, a time-consuming but nonresource-consuming "activity" added to the end of the project, which automatically adds duration to the critical path. (In Chapter 9 we will define a similar activity as a "pseudo-activity".)

This practice makes the operation of *Parkinson's Law* a clear and present danger. The work done on project elements is almost certain to "expand to fill the additional time," as Schonberger himself and many others have observed. We favor a different way of handling the problem. If three time estimates are used, and if various completion dates with their associated probabilities are calculated, and, finally, if the PM and senior management can agree on a mutually acceptable completion date for the project, the PM can be held accountable for on-time delivery. If an additional allowance is needed for path interdependence, some mutually acceptable network slack can be added. It should not, however, make the PM any less accountable for project performance.

## Using These Tools

We have heard differing opinions on the value of each of the tools we have described, including many of the computerized project management information systems (PMISs). We have been told, "No one uses PERT/CPM/Precedence Diagramming," "No one uses three-time PERT," and "No one uses___computer package." But we have first-hand knowledge of PERT users, of CPM users, of precedence diagram users. We know PMs who collect and use three time PERT. For example, refer to the boxed Apartment Complex example (Figure 8-27).

Figure 8-27 is a portion of a 48-step action plan for the syndication of an apartment complex. Note that several of the steps are obvious composites of multistep action plans designed for a lower level (e.g., see 1-4). Figure 8-28 is an AON network of Figure 8-27. The firm also has a Gantt chart version of the network that is used for tracking each project. Figure 8-27 also contains three time estimates of the "calendar" time used for each step (in days) and of the "resource" time used for each step (in hours). The time estimate 2(10) is read, "2 days, 10 labor-hours." The duplicate data are useful for scheduling work loads.

We are reluctant to give advice about which tools to use. If the PM indulges in a bit of experimentation with the major systems, their relative advantages and disadvantages *in a given application* will become evident. We have noted Bubshait and Selen's work [9] on the use of project management techniques, and Digman and Green [14] have developed an interesting and useful framework for evaluating the various planning and control techniques. The PM should opt for the simplest method sufficient to the needs of the project and its parent firm. If a computerized PMIS is used, the problem is avoided. Most require inputs of specific form and produce their own unique outputs. Again, a thorough demonstration of the PMIS should be a prerequisite to purchase or lease. In the end, these tools are intended to help the PM manage the project. The PM should select those that seem most useful—and most comfortable. The PMISs will be discussed in more detail in Chapter 10.

| Task | *a* (days,hours) | *m* | *b* | TE (days) | $\sigma^2$ (days) | TE (hr) | $\sigma^2$ (hr) |
|------|------|------|------|------|------|------|------|
| 1. Product package received by Secy. in Real Estate (R.E.) Dept. | n/a | (.3) | (.4) | | | | |
| 2. Secy. checks for duplicates, and forwards all packages in Atlanta region (but not addressed to R.E. staff member) to Atl. via fast mail. Atl. office sends copy of submittal log to L.A. office on weekly basis. | n/a | (.2) | (.3) | | | | |
| 3. Secy, date stamps, logs, checks for duplication, makes new file, checks for contact source, adds to card file all new packages. Sends criteria letter to new source. Send duplication letter. Forwards package to Admin. Asst. (AA). | (.7) | (.7) | (.9) | | | | |
| 4. AA reviews package, completes Property Summary Form, forwards to L.A. Reg. Acquisit. Director (RAD) officer or to R.E. staff member to whom package is addressed. | (.5) | (.5) | (.7) | | | | |
| Total 1-4 | 1(1.7) | 1(1.7) | 3(2.3) | 1.3 | 0.11 | 1.8 | 0.01 |
| 5. Person to whom package forwarded determines action. (May refer to other or retain for further review.) "Passes" sent to Secy. for files. "Possibles" retained by RAD for further review. | 1(.5) | 1(.5) | 1(1) | 1.0 | | .58 | 0.01 |
| 6. RAD gets add'l data as needed, gets demographics and comparables. Rough numbers run. Looks for the "opportunities." If viable, continue. | 4(3) | 5(3) | 3(2.3) | 5.5 | 0.69 | 3.83 | 0.69 |
| &bull;   &bull;   &bull;   &bull; | | | | | | | |
| 45. Prop. Mgt./Fin. prepares for closing and take-over. At closing, prorations of taxes, rents, service contracts. | 3(4) | 5(8) | 10(24) | 5.5 | 1.36 | 10.0 | 11.11 |
| 46. PM final inspect. On-site at close. | 1(4) | 1(8) | 2(12) | 1.2 | 0.03 | 8.0 | 1.78 |
| 47. Legal closes. | 2(8) | 2(14) | 4(25) | 2.3 | 0.11 | 14.83 | 8.03 |
| 48. Legal issues Post Closing Memorandum. | 2(5) | 5(8) | 10(10) | 5.3 | 1.78 | 7.83 | 0.69 |

**Figure 8-27:** Action plan for syndication of an apartment complex.

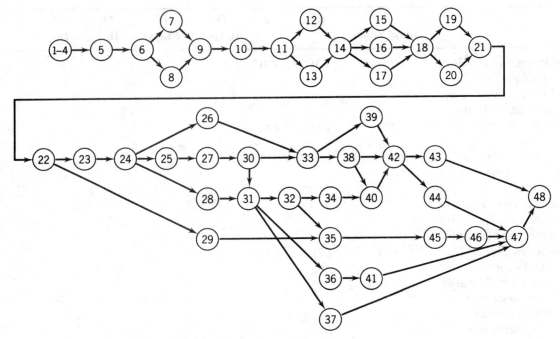

**Figure 8-28:** Apartment complex network.

## ▶ SUMMARY

In this chapter the scheduling aspect of project implementation was addressed. Following a description of the benefits of using a network for planning and controlling a project, the PERT/CPM approach was described. Next, Gantt charts were described and their relation to the PERT/CPM diagram was illustrated. Finally, precedence diagramming, GERT, and a few other extensions were discussed.

Specific points covered in the chapter were these:

- Scheduling is particularly important to projects because of complex coordination problems.
- The network approach to scheduling offers a number of specific advantages of special value for projects.
- Critical project tasks typically constitute fewer than 10 percent of all the project tasks.
- Although research indicates technological performance is not significantly affected by the use of PERT/CPM, there did seem to be a

significantly lower probability of cost and schedule overruns.

- Network techniques can adopt either an activity-on-node or activity-on-arc framework without significantly altering the analysis.
- Networks are usually constructed from left to right, indicating activity precedence and event times as the network is constructed. Through use of the network, critical activities and events are identified, early and late activity start times are found, available slacks for each activity are determined, and probabilities of project completion by various times are calculated.
- Gantt charts, a monitoring technique, are closely related to network diagrams, but are more easily understood and provide a clearer picture of the current state of the project. However, while offering some advantages, they also have some drawbacks, such as not

clearly indicating task precedence and dependencies.

- GERT is one of the more common extensions of PERT/CPM and allows:
  Probabilistic branching from nodes,
  Various probability distributions for the activity times,
  Looping in the network,

Representation of project elements other than time, such as cost or reliability.

In the next chapter we investigate the scheduling problem further when multiple projects require a set of common resources to be shared. Again, a number of techniques are useful for resource allocation and activity expediting under such circumstances.

## ▶ GLOSSARY

**Activity**—A specific project task that requires resources and time to complete.

**Activity-On-Arc (Node)**—The two ways of illustrating a network: placing the activities on the arcs or on the nodes.

**Arc**—The line connecting two nodes.

**Crash**—In CPM, an activity can be conducted at a normal pace or at an expedited pace, known as *crashed*, at a greater cost.

**Critical**—An activity or event that, if delayed, will delay project completion.

**Event**—An end state for one or more activities that occurs at a specific point in time.

**Gantt Chart**—A manner of illustrating multiple, time-based activities on a horizontal time scale.

**Milestone**—A clearly identifiable point in a project or set of activities that commonly denotes a reporting requirement or completion of a large or important set of activities.

**Network**—A combination of interrelated activities and events depicted with arcs and nodes.

**Node**—An intersection of two or more lines or arrows, commonly used for depicting an event or activity.

**Path**—A sequence of lines and nodes in a network.

**Project Management Information System (PMIS)**—The systems, activities, and data that allow information flow in a project, frequently computerized but not always.

**Trade-off**—The amount of one factor that must be sacrificed in order to achieve more or less of another factor.

## ▶ MATERIAL REVIEW QUESTIONS

1. Define *activity, event,* and *path* as used in network construction. What is a dummy activity?

2. What characteristic of the critical path times makes them critical?

3. What two factors are compared by Gantt charting? How does the Gantt chart differ in purpose from the project master schedule?

4. How is the GERT technique different from the PERT technique?

5. When is each scheduling technique appropriate to use?

6. What is the difference between activity-on-node and activity-on-arrow diagrams?

7. What does it mean to "crash" an event?

8. Briefly summarize how a network is drawn.

9. Define "late start time" and "early start time."

10. How is the critical path determined?

11. What is "slack"?

## ▶ CLASS DISCUSSION QUESTIONS

1. How do you think the network technique could be used to estimate costs for manufacturing?

2. What are some benefits of the network approach to project planning? What are some drawbacks?

**3.** What is your position on the conclusions in the Caveat section?

**4.** Why is PERT of significant value to the project manager?

**5.** How is uncertainty in project scheduling dealt with?

**6.** Are there any drawbacks to using GERT?

**7.** How are activity times estimated?

**8.** Should the critical path activities be managed differently from noncritical path activities? Explain.

## ▶ PROBLEMS

**1.** Given the following information, draw the PERT/CPM diagram:

| Activity | Immediate Predecessor |
|----------|-----------------------|
| 1 | — |
| 2 | — |
| 3 | 1,4 |
| 4 | 2 |
| 5 | 2 |
| 6 | 3,5 |

**2.** Given the diagram below, find:

(a) The critical path.
(b) How long it will take to complete the project.

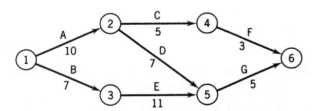

**3.** Given the following activities and precedences, draw a PERT/CPM diagram:

| Activity | Immediate Predecessor |
|----------|-----------------------|
| A | — |
| B | — |
| C | A |
| D | A,B |
| E | A,B |
| F | C |
| G | D,F |
| H | E,G |

**4.** Given the following network:
(a) What is the critical path?

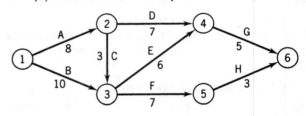

(b) How long will it take to complete this project?
(c) Can activity **B** be delayed without delaying the completion of the project? If so, how many days?

**5.** Given the estimated activity times below and the network in 4 above:

| Activity | a | m | b |
|----------|-----|-----|-----|
| A | 6 | 7 | 14 |
| B | 8 | 10 | 12 |
| C | 2 | 3 | 4 |
| D | 6 | 7 | 8 |
| E | 5 | 5.5 | 9 |
| F | 5 | 7 | 9 |
| G | 4 | 6 | 8 |
| H | 2.5 | 3 | 3.5 |

What is the probability that the project will be completed within:

(a) 21 days?
(b) 22 days?
(c) 25 days?

| **6. Activity\*** | **a** | **m** | **b** |
|-------------------|-------|-------|-------|
| AB | 3 | 6 | 9 |

---

\*The nomenclature AB means the activity *between* events A and B.

| Activity* | a | m | b |
|-----------|---|---|---|
| AC | 1 | 4 | 7 |
| CB | 0 | 3 | 6 |
| CD | 3 | 3 | 3 |
| CE | 2 | 2 | 8 |
| BD | 0 | 0 | 6 |
| BE | 2 | 5 | 8 |
| DF | 4 | 4 | 10 |
| DE | 1 | 1 | 1 |
| EF | 1 | 4 | 7 |

Find:

  (a)  the critical path;
  (b)  all event slacks;
  (c)  critical path to event D;
  (d)  probability of completion in 14 days;
  (e)  the effect if CD slips to 6 days; to 7 days; to 8 days.

**7.**

| Activity* | TE |
|-----------|----|
| AB | 1 |
| AC | 2 |
| AD | 3 |
| DC | 4 |
| CB | 3 |
| DE | 8 |
| CF | 2 |

| Activity* | TE |
|-----------|----|
| BF | 4 |
| IJ | 2 |
| CE | 6 |
| EF | 5 |
| FG | 10 |
| FH | 11 |
| EH | 1 |
| GH | 9 |
| EJ | 3 |
| GI | 8 |
| HJ | 6 |

  (a)  Draw the PERT diagram.
  (b)  Find the critical path.
  (c)  Find the completion time.

**8.** The Denver Iron & Steel Company is expanding its operations to include a new drive-in weigh station. The weigh station will be a heated/air-conditioned building with a large floor and small office. The large room will have the scales, a 15–foot counter, and several display cases for its equipment.

    Before erection of the building, the project manager evaluated the project using PERT/CPM analysis. The activities with their corresponding times were recorded in Table A:

### Table A

| # | Activity | Optimistic | Most Likely | Pessimistic | Preceding Tasks |
|---|----------|-----------|-------------|-------------|-----------------|
| 1 | Lay foundation | 8 | 10 | 13 | — |
| 2 | Dig hole for scale | 5 | 6 | 8 | — |
| 3 | Insert scale bases | 13 | 15 | 21 | 2 |
| 4 | Erect frame | 10 | 12 | 14 | 1,3 |
| 5 | Complete building | 11 | 20 | 30 | 4 |
| 6 | Insert scales | 4 | 5 | 8 | 5 |
| 7 | Insert display cases | 2 | 3 | 4 | 5 |
| 8 | Put in office equipment | 4 | 6 | 10 | 7 |
| 9 | Finishing touches | 2 | 3 | 4 | 8,6 |

*See nomenclature note in Problem 6.

Using PERT/CPM analysis, find the critical path, the slack times, and the expected completion time.

9. The Dock B Shipbuilding Company received a contract from the government to build the prototype of a new U.S. Navy destroyer. The destroyer is to be nuclear-powered, include advanced weapon systems, and have a small crew. The Dock B Shipbuilding Company has assigned to the task a project manager who, in turn, has delegated minor subprojects to subordinate managers.

   The project was evaluated using PERT/CPM analysis. Due to the extensive length of the project, many activities were combined: The following is the result.

| Activity* | Time (months) |
|-----------|---------------|
| AB | 3 |
| BC | 6 |
| BD | 2 |
| BF | 5 |
| BE | 4 |
| CD | 9 |
| DG | 20 |
| FG | 6 |
| EH | 11 |
| EI | 19 |
| GJ | 1 |
| HK | 3 |
| IL | 9 |
| LM | 12 |
| KN | 7 |
| JO | 4 |
| MN | 15 |
| NP | 13 |
| OP | 10 |

Find the critical path and expected completion date.

10. The following PERT chart was prepared at the beginning of a small construction project.

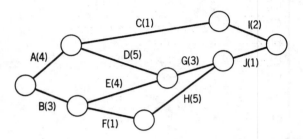

The duration, in days, follows the letter of each activity. What is the critical path? Which activities should be monitored most closely?

At the end of the first week of construction, it was noted that activity **A** was completed in 2.5 days, but activity **B** required 4.5 days. What impact does this have on the project? Are the same activities critical?

11. Given the following project, find the probability of completion by 17 weeks. By 24 weeks. By what date is management 90 percent sure completion will occur?

**Times (weeks)**

| Activity | Optimistic | Most Likely | Pessimistic |
|----------|-----------|-------------|-------------|
| 1–2 | 5 | 11 | 11 |
| 1–3 | 10 | 10 | 10 |
| 1–4 | 2 | 5 | 8 |
| 2–6 | 1 | 7 | 13 |
| 3–6 | 4 | 4 | 10 |
| 3–7 | 4 | 7 | 10 |
| 3–5 | 2 | 2 | 2 |
| 4–5 | 0 | 6 | 6 |
| 5–7 | 2 | 8 | 14 |
| 6–7 | 1 | 4 | 7 |

---

*See nomenclature note in Problem 6.

If the firm can complete the project within 18 weeks it will receive a bonus of $10,000. But if the project delays beyond 22 weeks it must pay a penalty of $5000. If the firm can choose whether or not to bid on this project, what should its decision be if the project is only a breakeven one normally?

**12.** Given a project with the following information:

| Activity | Standard Deviation | Critical? | Duration |
|---|---|---|---|
| a | 2 | yes | 2 |
| b | 1 | | 3 |
| c | 0 | yes | 4 |
| d | 3 | | 2 |
| e | 1 | yes | 1 |
| f | 2 | | 6 |
| g | 2 | yes | 4 |
| h | 0 | yes | 2 |

Find:

(a) The probability of completing this project in 12 weeks (or less).

(b) The probability of completing this project in 13 weeks (or less).

(c) The probability of completing this project in 16 weeks (or less).

(d) The number of weeks required to assure a 92.5 percent chance of completion.

**13.** Given a PERT network:

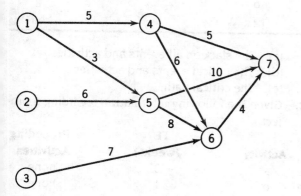

Note that three activities can start immediately. Find:

(a) The critical path.

(b) The earliest time to complete the project.

(c) The slack on activities **4-6, 5-6,** and **4-7.**

(d) Draw the network on a Gantt chart.

**14.** The events of the project below are designated as 1, 2, and so on.

(a) Draw the PERT network and the Gantt chart.

(b) Find the critical path.

(c) Find the slacks on all the events and activities.

| Activity | Prec. Evt. | Suc. Evt. | TE (weeks) | Prec. Activ. |
|---|---|---|---|---|
| a | 1 | 2 | 3 | none |
| b | 1 | 3 | 6 | none |
| c | 1 | 4 | 8 | none |
| d | 2 | 5 | 7 | a |
| e | 3 | 5 | 5 | b |
| f | 4 | 5 | 10 | c |
| g | 4 | 6 | 4 | c |
| h | 5 | 7 | 5 | d,e,f |
| i | 6 | 7 | 6 | g |

15. Given the following PERT network (times are in weeks):

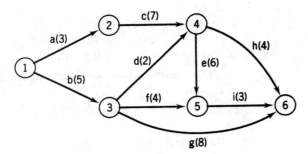

Determine:
(a) The EOT and LOT for each event.
(b) The slacks on all events and activities.
(c) The critical activities and path.

16. Given the schedule in Table B for a liability work package done as part of an accounting audit in a corporation, find:
(a) The critical path.
(b) The slack time on "process confirmations."
(c) The slack time on "test pension plan."
(d) The slack time on "verify debt restriction compliance."

## Table B

| Activity | Duration (days) | Preceding Activities |
|---|---|---|
| a. Obtain schedule of liabilities | 3 | none |
| b. Mail confirmation | 15 | a |
| c. Test pension plan | 5 | a |
| d. Vouch selected liabilities | 60 | a |
| e. Test accruals and amortization | 6 | d |
| f. Process confirmations | 40 | b |
| g. Reconcile interest expense to debt | 10 | c,e |
| h. Verify debt restriction compliance | 7 | f |
| i. Investigate debit balances | 6 | g |
| j. Review subsequent payments | 12 | h,i |

17. In the project network shown in the figure below, the number alongside each activity designates the activity duration (TE) in weeks.

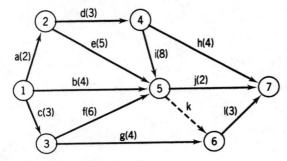

Determine:
(a) The EOT and LOT for each event.
(b) The earliest time that the project can be completed.

(c) The slack on all events and activities.
(d) The critical events and activities.
(e) The critical path.

18. Given the following information regarding a project:

| Activity | TE (weeks) | Preceding Activities |
|---|---|---|
| a | 3 | none |
| b | 1 | none |
| c | 3 | a |
| d | 4 | a |
| e | 4 | b |
| f | 5 | b |
| g | 2 | c,e |
| h | 3 | f |

(a) Draw the PERT network and the Gantt chart.

(b) What is the critical path?

(c) What will the scheduled (earliest completion) time for the entire project be?

(d) What is the critical path to event 4 (end of activities **c** and **e**)? What is the earliest time that this event can be reached?

(e) What is the effect on the project if activity **e** takes an extra week? Two extra weeks? Three extra weeks?

19. Construct a network for the project below and find its critical path.

| Activity | TE (weeks) | Preceding Activities |
|----------|------------|----------------------|
| a | 3 | none |
| b | 5 | a |
| c | 3 | a |
| d | 1 | c |
| e | 3 | b |
| f | 4 | b,d |
| g | 2 | c |
| h | 3 | g,f |
| i | 1 | e,h |

20. Construct a network for the project:

| Activity | TE (weeks) | Preceding Activities |
|----------|------------|----------------------|
| a | 3 | none |
| b | 5 | none |
| c | 14 | a |
| d | 5 | a |
| e | 4 | b |
| f | 7 | b |
| g | 8 | d,e |
| h | 5 | g,f |

(a) Draw the PERT network and the Gantt chart.

(b) Find the critical path.

(c) Assume activity **a** took five weeks. Replan the project.

(d) From where would you suggest transferring resources, and to what activities so that the original target date may be maintained?

21. Resolve part (d) of Problem 6 assuming the values of $a$ and $b$ are given at the 95 percent level. Repeat, assuming the values are given at the 90 percent level.

# ▶ INCIDENTS FOR DISCUSSION

## Yankee Chair Company

The Yankee Chair Company was anxious to get a new model rocking chair onto the market. Past efforts to introduce new models had resulted in frustrating failures. Jim Ricks, president of Yankee Chair, was determined that it would not happen again with the newest model. He had no confidence in his current management team, so he hired Jan Dymore, a local consultant, to organize and manage this project. He assigned a Yankee Chair manager, Tom Gort, to work with Dymore to start developing some talent for project management within the company. Dymore decided to set up a PERT network and guided Gort through the process of listing activities, assigning precedence, and estimating completion times. She also explained the critical path concept to Gort, who by this time had a reasonable grasp of the project direction. At the first review session with Mr. Ricks, the PERT approach was accepted enthusiastically, but toward the end of the review Dymore made some critical remarks about the product design and was subsequently released from the project.

Ricks then asked Gort if he could carry on the PERT approach by himself. Gort jumped at the chance, but later in his office he began to question whether or not he really could use the PERT network effectively. Dymore had made a guess at what the critical path would be and how long the project would take, but she had also told Gort that several other calculations had to be made in order to calculate the exact time estimates for each activity and the variances of those activity times. Gort really did not understand the mathematics involved and certainly did not want to look bad in Ricks' eyes, so he decided to take Dymore's guess at the critical path and get the best possible estimates of those activity times. By concentrating his attention on the critical path activities and ignoring the variance issues, he figured he could bring the project in on time.

*Questions*: Will Gort's approach work? How much more of a gamble is Gort taking than any project manager normally takes? What should Gort watch out for?

## Cincinnati Equipment Company

Cincinnati Equipment Company, which specializes in the manufacture of modern construction equipment, will be building a facility to house a new foundry. The company has selected a project manager and team to follow the project through to completion. The project team is very interested in selecting an appropriate scheduling technique for the project. The project manager has thus set the following guidelines for the selection process: simple; able to show durations of events, the flow of work, and the relative sequence of events; able to indicate planning and actual flow, which items may proceed at the same time, and how far they are from completion. The assistant project manager favors the Gantt chart, the finance representative likes PERT, and the construction supervisor prefers CPM.

*Question*: If you were the project manager, which method would you use, and why?

## ▶ PROJECT TEAM CONTINUING EXERCISE

The task for the project team is to formulate the schedule for the project from the work breakdown structure. Use optimistic, most likely, and pessimistic times for each activity; construct the PERT diagram; and conduct a full analysis of the data, including likelihoods of delay by certain amounts of time and 80, 90, and 99 percent likelihood of completion times. Identify the project's critical path, the critical path to each event, the slacks for each activity, and the earliest and latest occurrence times. Show the schedule as an AON and an AOA network, as well as a Gantt chart with milestones. Graph the budget from Chapter 7 on the Gantt chart to illustrate cash flow needs. Comment on the applicability of one of the other network approaches such as GERT or precedence diagramming to your project. As the project progresses, update the charts at each milestone.

## ▶ BIBLIOGRAPHY

1. AL-HAMMED, A. and S. ASSAF. "A Survey of Cost Reduction Techniques Used by Construction Firms in Saudi Arabia." *American Association of Cost Engineers Transactions*, 1988.

2. ARCHIBALD, R. D., and R. L. VILLORIA. *Network Based Management Systems (PERT/CPM)*. New York: Wiley, 1967.

3. AYERS, R. H., R. M. WALSH, and R. G. STAPLES. "Project Management by the Critical Path Method." *Research Management*, July 1970.

4. BAKER, B. N., and R. L. ERIS. *An Introduction to PERT-CPM*. Homewood, IL: Irwin, 1964.

5. BENNINGSON, L. A. TREND—*New Management Information from Networks*. Sandoz Co. Reprint, 1974.

6. BERKWITT, G. W. "Management Rediscovers CPM." *Dun's Review*, May 1971.

7. BLYSTONE, E. E., and R. G. ODUM. "A Case Study of CPM in a Manufacturing Situation." *Journal of Industrial Engineering*, Nov.–Dec. 1964.

8. BRENNAN, J. *Applications of Critical Path Techniques*. New York: Elsevier, 1968.

9. BUBSHAIT, K. A., and W. J. SELEN. "Project Characteristics That Influence The Implementation of Project Management Techniques: A Survey. "*Project Management Journal*, June 1992.

10. CLARK, C. G., D. G. MALCOM, J. H. ROSENBLOOM, and W. FAZAR. "Applications of a Technique for Research and Development Program Management." *Operations Research*, Sept.–Oct. 1959.

11. DAVIS, E. W. "Networks: Resource Allocation." *Industrial Engineering*, April 1974.

12. DEAN, B. V. *Project Management: Methods and Studies*. New York: Elsevier, 1985.

13. DECOSTER, D. T. "PERT/Cost—The Challenge." *Management Services*, May–June 1964

14. DIGMAN, L. A., and G. I. GREEN. "A Framework of Evaluating Network Planning and Control Techniques." *Research Management*, Jan. 1981.

15. EVARTS, H. E. *Introduction to PERT*. Boston: Allyn and Bacon, 1964.

16. GALLAGHER, C. "A Note on Pert Assumptions." *Management Science*, October 1987.

17. GIDO, J. *An Introduction to Project Planning*, 2nd ed. Industrial Press, 1986.

18. GOLFARB, N., and W. K. KAISER. *Gantt Charts and Statistical Quality Control*. New York: Hofstra University Press, 1964.

19. HOROWITZ, J. *Critical Path Scheduling: Management Control Through CPM and PERT*. Melbourne, FL: Krieger, 1980.

20. JENETT, E. "Experience with and Evaluation of Critical Path Methods." *Chemical Engineering*, Feb. 1969.

21 KARNS, L. A., and L. A. SWANSON. "The Effect of Activity Time Variance on Critical Path Scheduling." *Project Management Quarterly*, Dec. 1973.

22. KELLY, J. E., and M. R. WALKER. "Critical Path Planning and Scheduling." *Proceedings, Eastern Joint Computer Conference*, 1959.

23. KERZNER, H. *Project Management: A Systems Approach to Planning, Scheduling, and Controlling*, 2nd ed. New York: Van Nostrand Reinhold, 1989.

24. KIRKPATRICK, C. A., and R. C. LEVINE. *Planning and Control with PERT/CPM*. New York: McGraw-Hill, 1966.

25. LEVY, F. K., G. L. THOMPSON, and J. D. WEIST. "The ABC's of the Critical Path Method." *Harvard Business Review*, Sept–Oct. 1963.

26. LIBERATORE, M. J., and G. J. TITUS. "The Practice of Management Science in R & D Project Management." *Management Science*, Aug. 1983.

27. LITTLEFIELD, T. K., JR., and P. H. RANDOLPH. "An Answer to Sasieni's Question on PERT Times." *Management Science*, Oct. 1987.

28. LOCKYER, K. G. *An Introduction to Critical Path Analysis*. Woodstock, NY: Beckman, 1969.

29. LOWE, C. W. *Critical Path Analysis by Bar Chart*. London: Business Books, 1966.

30. MACCRIMMON, K. R., and C. R. RYAVEC. "An Analytical Study of PERT Assumptions." *Operations Research*, Jan–Feb. 1964.

31. MALLON, J. C. "Verifying Cost and Schedule During Design." *Project Management Journal*, Mar. 1992.

32. MARQUIS, D. G. "A Project Team Plus PERT= Success. Or Does It?" *Innovation*, 1969.

33. MARTINO, R. L. *Project Management and Control*, Vol. I. New York: American Management Association, 1964.

34. McCAHON, C. S. "Using PERT as an Approximation of Fuzzy Project–Network Analysis." *IEEE Transactions on Engineering Management*, May 1993.

35. MEYER, W. C., J. B. RITTER, and L. R. SHAFFER. *The Critical Path Method*. New York: McGraw-Hill, 1965.

36. MILLS, N. L. "The Development of a University Sports Complex: A Project Management Application." *Computers and Industrial Engineering*, 17:149–153, 1989.

37. MODER, J. J., C. R. PHILLIPS, and E. W. DAVIS. *Project Management with CPM, PERT, and Precedence Diagramming*, 3rd ed. New York: Van Nostrand Reinhold, 1983.

38. MORRIS, L. N. *Critical Path, Construction and Analysis*. Oxford, G.B: Pergamon Press, 1967.

39. MUTH, J. F., and G. L. THOMPSON. *Industrial Scheduling*. Englewood Cliffs, NJ: Prentice Hall, 1963.

40. NAIK, B. *Project Management: Scheduling and Monitoring by PERT/CPM*. Advent Books, 1984.

41. ORCZYK, J. J., and L. CHANG. "Parametric Regression Model for Project Scheduling." *Project Management Journal*, Dec. 1991.

42. PAZER, H. H., and L. A. SWANSON. *PERTsim, Text and Simulation*. International Textbook, 1969.

43. POWERS, J. R. "A Structured Approach to Schedule Development and Use." *Project Management Journal*, Nov. 1988.

44. PRITSKER, A. A. B. "GERT Networks." *The Production Engineer*, Oct. 1968.

45. RAITHE, A. W., ed. *Gantt on Management*. New York: American Management Association, 1961.

46. SAITOW, A. R. "CSPC: Reporting Project Progress to the Top." *Harvard Business Review*, Jan–Feb. 1969.

47. SANTELL, M. P., J. R. JUNG, and J. C. WARNER. "Optimization in Project Coordination Scheduling through Application of Taguchi Methods." *Project Management Journal*, Sept. 1992.

48. SASIENI, M. W. "A Note on PERT Times." *Management Science*, Dec. 1986.

49. SCHONBERGER, R. J. "Why Projects Are Always Late: A Rationale Based on Manual Simulation of a PERT/CPM Network." *Interfaces*, Oct. 1981.

50. SILVERBERG, E. C. "Predicting Project Completion." *Research-Technology Management*, May–June 1991.

51. TOELLE, R. A., and J. WITHERSPOON. "From 'Managing the Critical Path' to 'Managing Critical Activities.'" *Project Management Journal*, December 1990.

**52.** TURBAN, E. "The Line of Balance—A Management by Exception Tool." *Journal of Industrial Engineering*, Sept. 1968.

**53.** VAZSONYI, A. "L'Histoire de Grandeur et la Decadence de la Methode PERT." *Management Science*, April 1979.

**54.** WEIST, J. D. "A Heuristic Model for Scheduling Large Projects with Limited Resources." *Management Science*, Feb. 1967.

**55.** WEIST, J. D., and F. K. LEVY. *A Management Guide to PERT/CPM*, 2nd ed. Englewood Cliffs, NJ: Prentice Hall, 1977.

**56.** WOODGATE, H. S. *Planning by Network*. Woodstock, NY: Beckman 1977.

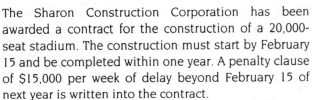

# CASE

# THE SHARON CONSTRUCTION CORPORATION
## E. Turban and Jack R. Meredith

The Sharon Construction Corporation has been awarded a contract for the construction of a 20,000-seat stadium. The construction must start by February 15 and be completed within one year. A penalty clause of $15,000 per week of delay beyond February 15 of next year is written into the contract.

Jim Brown, the president of the company, called a planning meeting. In the meeting he expressed great satisfaction at obtaining the contract and revealed that the company could net as much as $300,000 on the project. He was confident that the project could be completed on time with an allowance made for the usual delays anticipated in such a large project.

Bonnie Green, the director of personnel, agreed that in a normal year only slight delays might develop due to a shortage of labor. However, she reminded the president that for such a large project, the company would have to use unionized employees and that the construction industry labor agreements were to expire on November 30. Past experience indicated a fifty–fifty chance of a strike.

Jim Brown agreed that a strike might cause a problem. Unfortunately, there was no way to change the contract. He inquired about the prospective length of a strike. Bonnie figured that such a strike would last either eight weeks (70 percent chance) or possibly 12 weeks (30 percent chance).

Jim was not too pleased with these prospects. However, before he had a chance to discuss contingency plans he was interrupted by Jack White, the vice-president for engineering. Jack commented that an extremely cold December had been predicted. This factor had not been taken into consideration during earlier estimates since previous forecasts called for milder weather. Concrete pouring in a cold December would require in one out of every three cases (depending on the temperature) special heating that cost $500 per week.

This additional information did not please Jim at all. The chances for delay were mounting. And an overhead expense of $500 per week would be incurred in case of any delay.

The technical details of the project are given in the appendix to this case.

The management team was asked to consider alternatives for coping with the situation. At the end of the week five proposals were submitted.

**1.** Expedite the pouring of seat gallery supports. This would cost $20,000 and cut the duration of the activity to six weeks.

**2.** The same as proposal 1, but in addition, put a double shift on the filling of the field. A cost of $10,000 would result in a five-week time reduction.

**3.** The roof is very important since it precedes several activities. The use of three shifts and some overtime could cut six weeks off the roofing at an additional cost of only $9000.

**4.** Do nothing special until December 1. Then, if December is indeed cold, defer the pouring of the seat gallery supports until the cold wave breaks, schedule permitting, and heat whenever necessary. If a strike occurs, wait until it is over (no other choice) and then expedite *all* remaining activities. In that case, the duration of any activity could be cut but to no less than one third of its normal duration. The additional cost per activity for any week which is cut would be $3000.

5. Do not take any special action; that is, hope and pray that no strike and no cold December occur (no cost).

## Appendix: Technical Details of the Stadium

The stadium is an indoor structure with a seating capacity of 20,000. The project begins with clearing the site, an activity that lasts eight weeks. Once the site is clear, the work can start simultaneously on the structure itself and on the field.

The work in the field involves subsurface drainage which lasts eight weeks, followed by filling for the playing field and track. Only with the completion of the filling (14 weeks) can the installation of the artificial playing turf take place, an activity that consumes 12 weeks.

The work on the structure itself starts with excavation followed by the pouring of concrete footings. Each of these activities takes four weeks. Next comes the pouring of supports for seat galleries (12 weeks), followed by erecting pre-cast galleries (13 weeks). The seats can then be poured (4 weeks) and are ready for painting. However, the painting (3 weeks) cannot begin until the dressing rooms are completed (4 weeks). The dressing rooms can be completed only after the roof is erected (8 weeks). The roof must be erected on a steel structure which takes 4 weeks to install. This activity can start only after the concrete footings are poured.

Once the roof is erected, work can start simultaneously on the lights (5 weeks) and on the scoreboard and other facilities (4 weeks). Assume there are 28 days in February and that February 15 falls on a Monday.

## ▶ QUESTIONS

1. Analyze the five proposals and make recommendations based on expected costs.

2. What other basis might be used to make a decision besides expected costs? What then might the decision be?

3. What other factors might enter into the decision such as behavioral, organizational, and political?

4. What decision would you make as the president?

# CHAPTER
# 9
# Resource Allocation

In the previous chapter we looked at a special type of resource allocation problem, that of allocating time among project tasks, better known as *scheduling*. Now we consider the allocation of physical resources as well. Also, we are concerned with using resources in both individual and in multiple, simultaneous projects. The subject relates directly to the topic of scheduling because altering schedules can alter the need for resources and—just as important—alter the timing of resource needs. At any given time, the firm may have a fixed level of various resources available for its projects. The fixed resources might include labor-hours of various types of special professional or technical services, machine-hours of various types of machinery or instrumentation, hours of computing time, and similar scarce resources needed for accomplishing project tasks. For example, if the need for some resource varies between 70 and 120 percent of resource capacity, then that resource will be under utilized (and wasted if no alternative use exists) at one point in the project and in insufficient supply at another. If the project schedule can be adjusted to smooth the use of the resource, it may be possible to avoid project delay and, at the same time, not saddle the project with the high cost of excess resources "just to make sure."

This chapter addresses situations that involve resource problems. We discuss the trade-offs involved, the difference between allocation to one project and allocation between multiple projects, the relationship between resource loading and leveling, and some of the approaches employed to solve allocation problems, including the Critical Path Method (CPM) and several other well-known techniques. Although CPM is not actually a resource allocation method, we include it here because we view time as a resource, and trade-offs between time and other resources are a major problem in resource management. Finally, we note the major impact that current project management software has had on the PM's ability—and willingness—to deal with resource loading and leveling.

## ▶ 9.1 CRITICAL PATH METHOD

In Chapter 8 we mentioned that CPM is similar to PERT. In the original versions of CPM and PERT there was one important difference: CPM included a way of relating the project schedule to the level of physical resources allocated to the project. This allowed the PM to trade time for cost, or vice versa. In CPM, two activity times and two costs are specified, if appropriate, for each activity. The first time/cost combination is called *normal* and the second set is referred to as *crash*. Normal times are "normal" in the same sense as the *m* time estimate of the three times used in PERT. Crash times result from an attempt to expedite the activity by the application of additional resources—for example, overtime, special equipment, additional staff or material, and the like.

It is standard practice with PERT/CPM to estimate activity times under the assumption of resource loadings that are normal. To discuss a time requirement for any task without some assumption about the level of resources devoted to the task makes no real sense. At the same time, it does not make sense to insist on a full list of each and every resource that will be spent on each of the hundreds of activities that may comprise a PERT/CPM network. Clearly, there must have been some prior decision about what resources would be devoted to each task, but much of the decision making is, in practice, relegated to the common methods of standard practice and rules of thumb. The allocation problem requires more careful consideration if it is decided to speed up the accomplishment of tasks and/or the total project. We need to know what additional resources it will take to shorten completion times for the various activities making up the project.

While standard practice and rules of thumb are sufficient for estimating the resource needs for normal progress, careful planning is critical when attempting to expedite (crash) a project. Crash plans that appear feasible when considered activity by activity may incorporate impossible assumptions about resource availability. For example, we may need to crash some activities on the Wild Horse Dam Project. To do so, we have all the labor and materials required, but we will need a tractor-driven crawler crane on the project site not later than the eighth of next month. Unfortunately, our crane will be in Decatur, Illinois, on that date. No local contractor has a suitable crane for hire. Can we hire one in Decatur or Springfield and bring ours here?

And so it goes. When we expedite a project, we tend to create problems; and the solution to one problem often creates several more problems that require solutions.

Difficulties notwithstanding, the wise PM adopts the Scout's motto: "Be prepared." If deterministic time estimates are used, and if project deadlines are firm, there is a high likelihood that it will be necessary to crash the last few activities of most projects. Use of the three probabilistic time estimates of PERT may reduce the chance that crashing will be needed because they include uncertainties that are sometimes forgotten or ignored when making deterministic time estimates. Even so, many things make crashing a way of life on some projects—things such as last-minute changes in client specifications, without permission to extend the project deadline by an appropriate increment. An example of one of the problems that commonly result from the use of deterministic time estimates can be seen in the boxed example that follows.

## *Architectural Associates, Inc.*

Architectural Associates, Inc. (AAI) specializes in large, industrial, retail, and public projects, including shopping malls, manufacturing complexes, convention centers, and the like. The firm is considered to be one of the region's most effective and creative design studios. Their design facility is located in a large, midwestern city and is housed on the second floor of an old building, originally used for light manufacturing. The offices are at one end of the floor, and about two-thirds of the floor space is occupied by the design staff and technicians. The entire space devoted to design is a single, open area and workstations are laid out in such a way as to encourage communication between individuals working on a common project.

A senior executive of AAI noticed that, for the past year or two, the chance of bringing design projects in on time and on budget had decreased to the point where the only uncertainty was how late and how much over budget a project would be. Architectural projects, like computer programming and a few other creative processes, seem to be typified by the need to crash projects at the last minute, but even with the usual crash, AAI was still late and, consequently, over budget.

An examination of the workplace disclosed a large, green felt, display board mounted on the wall where it was visible to the entire design staff. The board listed the names of individual designers and technicians vertically, and design contract numbers across the horizontal axis. The times allocated for work on each project by appropriate staff members were shown at the intersections of the rows and columns. The time estimates were made by senior managers, themselves architects, based on their experience. The individuals with direct responsibility for design work generally felt that the time estimates were reasonable.

The work process was studied and the following problem was revealed. If the design of the electrical systems involved in a plan was estimated to take five days, for example, the individual(s) responsible for the work planned it in such a way that it used the five days allowed. If a problem occurred on the first day, the worker(s) simply stayed late or speeded up work the next day in order to get back on schedule. Problems on the second day, and even on the third and fourth days were handled in the same way, by crashing the work. Problems occurring on the fifth day, however, could not be handled so easily and this part of the project would be late. Because most of the different systems (the mechanicals, landscape, etc.) were designed simultaneously and staffed to require about the same number of days (rather than being sequential), and because problems were very likely to arise late in the design process of at least one of the systems, the overall design project, which required all tasks to be completed on time, was almost invariably late.

In an attempt to solve the problem, a simple check-mark to show job assignments was substituted for time allocations on the green board. Additionally, senior management made normal, optimistic, and pessimistic time estimates for each task and calculated "TE," also used to help estimate project cost. These estimates were not given to the design staff who were simply told to do the work involved as efficiently and effectively as they could. The result was that the range of task times increased slightly, but the average time required for the various tasks fell somewhat since they were now designed for efficiency rather than X days. Roughly the same number of tasks were accomplished in less than the expected time as tasks that took more than the expected time.

Consider the data in Table 9-1. First, we compute a cost/time *slope* for each activity that can be expedited (crashed). Slope is defined as follows:

$$\text{slope} = \frac{\text{crash cost} - \text{normal cost}}{\text{crash time} - \text{normal time}}$$

that is, the cost per day of crashing a project. The slope is negative, indicating that as the time required for a project or task is decreased, the cost is increased. Note that activity **c** cannot be expedited. Table 9-2 shows the time/cost slopes for our example.

A clear implication of this calculation is that activities can be crashed in increments of one day (or one period). Often, this is not true. A given activity may have only two or three technically feasible durations. The "dollars per day" slope of such activities is relevant only if the whole crash increment is useful. For example, if an activity can be carried out in either eight days or four days, with no feasible intermediate times, and if an uncrashable parallel path goes critical when the first activity is reduced from eight down to six days, then the last two days (to four days) of time reduction are useless. (Of course, there are times when the PM may expedite activities that have little or no impact on the network's critical time, such as when the resources used must be made available to another project.)

One must remember that crashing a project results in a change of the technology with which something is done. In the language of economics, it is a change in the "production function." At times, crashing may involve a relatively simple decision to increase groups of resources already being used. If the project, for instance, is to dig a ditch of a certain length and depth, we might add units of labor-shovel to shorten the time required. On the other hand, we might replace labor-shovel units with a Ditch Witch. Discontinuities in outcomes usually result. Different amounts of labor-shovel input may result in a job that takes anywhere from one to three days. Use of the Ditch Witch may require three hours. There may be no sensible combination of resources that would complete the job in, say, six hours. In some cases, technology cannot be changed, and task duration is fixed. A 30-day toxicity test for a new drug requires 30 days—no more, no less.

Not only do changes in technology tend to produce discontinuities in outcomes, they also tend to produce discontinuities in cost. As the technology is changed to speed a project, the cost curve relating input costs to time is apt to jump as we move from less to more sophisticated production systems. Not only is the curve displaced, it almost certainly will not be parallel to the earlier curve, but will change at a different rate. (For an extended treatment of this subject, see [37] (chapter 13)).

**Table 9-1**   An Example of CPM

| Activity | Precedence | Duration, Periods (normal, crash) | Cost (normal, crash) |
|---|---|---|---|
| a | – | 3,2 | $ 40,80 |
| b | a | 2,1 | 20,80 |
| c | a | 2,2 | 20,20 |
| d | a | 4,1 | 30,120 |
| e | b | 3,1 | 10,80 |

**Table 9-2** Activity Slopes—
Cost per Period for Crashing

| Activity | Slope ($/period) |
|----------|------------------|
| a | $40/-1 = -40$ |
| b | $60/-1 = -60$ |
| c | — |
| d | $90/-3 = -30$ |
| e | $70/-2 = -35$ |

To use CPM, we develop a table or graph of the cost of a project as a function of the project's various possible completion dates. This can be obtained by either of two approaches.

The first approach is to start with the normal schedule for all project activities, and then to crash selected activities, one at a time, to decrease project duration at the minimum additional cost. This approach is illustrated in Figure 9-1. The normal schedule is shown in network 9-1a. (Note the required dummy activity. We use the AOA representation to illustrate that this procedure can be used with PERT as well as with CPM.)

The critical path of network 9-1 is **a–b–e**. To reduce the total network duration, we must reduce the time required by one of the activities along this critical path. Inspecting Table 9-2 to see which critical activity can be reduced at the least cost, we find it is **e**, at a cost of $35 per day. If we crash **e** by one day, we have a seven-day project duration at a cost of $155, as shown in Figure 9-1b.

Crashing **e** by a day has created a second critical path, **a–d–dummy.** To reduce project duration further, we might cut one day off this new critical path in addition to another day from activity **e.** (Remember that the path **a–b–e** is also critical.) Activity **d** has the most favorable cost-per-day rate among the critical activities. This adds $30 to the $35 required to reduce **e,** for a total cost increment of $65. We will still have two critical paths. Another alternative, however, is to crash an activity common to both critical paths, activity **a.** Reducing **a** by one day at a cost of $40 is less expensive than crashing both **e** and **d,** so this is preferred (see Figure 9-1c). Because **a** cannot be further reduced, we now cut **e** and **d** to lower total project duration to five days, which raises the project cost to $260 (see Figure 9-1d).

Activity **e** has now been crashed to its maximum (as has **a**), so additional cuts will have to be made on **b** to reduce the **a–b–e** critical path. Cutting one day from **b** (which is expensive) and **d** results in the final network that now has a time of four days and a cost of $350, more than 200 percent of the cost for normal time. The project duration cannot be reduced further, since both critical paths have been crashed to their limits.

The second approach to CPM is to start with an all-crash schedule, compute its cost, and "relax" activities one at a time. Of course, the activities relaxed first should be those that do not extend the completion date of the project—that is, those not on the critical path. In our example, this is possible. The all-crash cost is $380, and the project duration is four days. Activity **d,** however, could be extended by one day at a cost saving of $30 without altering the project's completion date. This can be

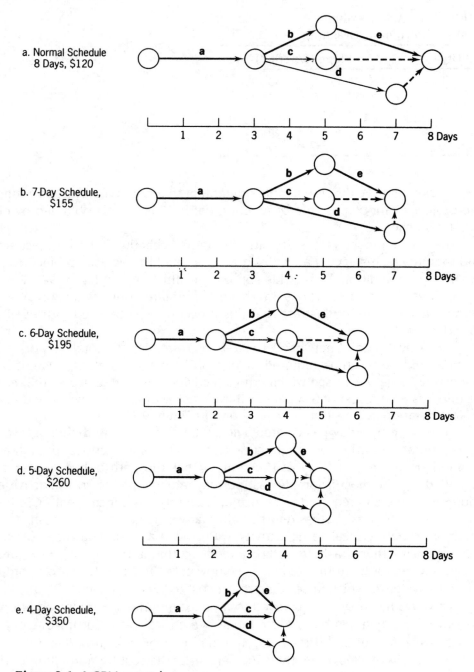

*Figure 9-1:* A CPM example.

seen in Figure 9-1e, where activity **d** is shown taking two days. Continuing in this manner would eventually result in the all-normal schedule of eight days and a cost of $120, as shown in Figure 9-1a.

The time/cost relationships of crashing are shown in Figure 9-2. Starting at the right (all-normal), note that the curve of cost per unit of duration gets steeper and

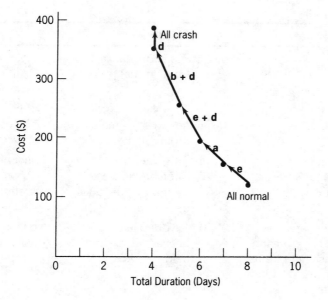

**Figure 9-2:** CPM cost-duration history.

steeper the more the project duration is reduced. It becomes increasingly costly to squeeze additional time out of the project. Economists will recognize that attempts to expedite a project are subject to decreasing marginal returns.

Charts such as the one shown in Figure 9-2 are useful to the PM in exercising control over project duration and cost. They are particularly helpful in dealing with senior managers who may argue for early project completion dates with little under-standing of the costs involved. Similarly, such data are of great benefit when clients plead for early delivery. If the client is willing to pay the cost of crashing, or if the firm is willing to subsidize the client, the PM can afford to listen with a sympathetic ear. (While we advise the PM to ignore overhead cost over which he/she has no con-trol, it should be noted that indirect costs are often altered when a project is crashed.)

Some organizations have more than one level of crashing. Table 9-3 illustrates such a case. In this example, the firm has two distinct levels of expediting a project, rush and blitz. The differences in the precedence relationships between tasks are noted in the table, as are differences in resource commitments. The last two rows of the table show the expected changes in cost and time if the project is expedited.

Finally, if a project has a penalty clause that makes the organization liable for late delivery, the cost/duration trade-off curve contains the information the PM needs to know in order to determine whether crashing the project or paying the penalty is the more economic course of action.

## ▶ 9.2 THE RESOURCE ALLOCATION PROBLEM

A shortcoming of the scheduling procedures covered in the previous chapter is that they do not address the issues of resource utilization and availability. They focus on time rather than physical resources. Also, in the discussion that follows it will not

**Table 9-3**   Official Pace of a Project

| Title | Normal | Rush | Blitz |
|---|---|---|---|
| Approved Project Definition | Full | Some abbreviations from normal pace. | Only as necessary for major management decisions, purchasing and design engineering. |
| Study of Alternates | Reasonable | Quick study of major profitable items. | Only those not affecting schedule. |
| Engineering Design | Begins near end of Approved Project Definition. | Begins when Approved Project Definition 50–75% complete. | Concurrently with such Approved Project Definition as is done. |
| Issue Engineering to Field | Allow adequate time for field to plan and purchase field items. Usually 1/2–2 months lead time between issue and field erection. | Little or no lead time between issue and field erection. | No lead time between issue and field erection. |
| Purchasing | Begins in latter stages of Approved Project Definition. | Done concurrently with Approved Project Definition. Rush purchase of all long delivery items. Many purchases on "advise price" basis. | Done concurrently with such Approved Project Definition as is done. Rush buy anything that will do job. Overorder and duplicate order to guarantee schedule. |
| Premium Payments | Negligible | Some to break specific bottlenecks. | As necessary to forestall any possible delays. |
| Field Crew Strength | Minimum practical or optimum cost. | Large crew with some spot overtime. | Large crew; overtime and/or extra shifts. |
| Probable Cost Difference Compared with Normal Pace, as a Result of: | | | |
| *Design and Development | Base | 5–10% more | 15% and up, more |
| *Engineering and Construction costs | Base | 3–5% more | 10% and up, more |
| Probable Time | Base | Up to 10% less | Up to 50% less |

be sufficient to refer to resource usage simply as "costs." Instead, we must refer to individual types of labor, specific facilities, kinds of materials, individual pieces of equipment, and other discrete inputs that are relevant to an individual project but are limited in availability. Last, we must not forget that time itself is always a critical resource in project management, one that is unique because it can neither be inventoried nor renewed.

The relationship between progress, time, and resource availability/usage is the major focus of this chapter. Schedules should be evaluated not merely in terms of meeting project milestones, but also in terms of the timing and use of scarce resources. A fundamental measure of the PM's success in project management is the skill with which the trade-offs among performance, time, and cost are managed. It is a continuous process of cost–benefit analysis: "I can shorten this project by a day at a cost of $400. Should I do it?" "If I buy 300 more hours of engineering time, I may be able to improve performance by 2 or 3 percent. Should I do it?"

Occasionally it is possible that some additional (useful) resources can be added at little or no cost to a project during a crisis period. At other times, some resources in abundant supply may be traded for scarce ones (á la M.A.S.H.'s "Radar"). Most of the time, however, these trades entail additional costs to the organization, so a primary responsibility for the PM is to make do with what is available.

The extreme points of the relationship between time use and resource use are these:

- **Time Limited:** The project must be finished by a certain time, using as few resources as possible. But it is time, not resource usage, that is critical.

- **Resource Limited:** The project must be finished as soon as possible, but without exceeding some specific level of resource usage or some general resource constraint.

The points between these two extremes represent time/resource-use trade-offs. As in Figure 9-2, they specify the times achievable at various resource levels. Equivalently, they specify the resources associated with various completion times. Clearly, the range of time or resource variability is limited.

Occasionally, both time and resources may be limited, but in this case, the specifications cannot also be fixed. If all three variables—time, cost, specifications—are fixed, the system is "overdetermined." The PM has lost all flexibility to perform the trade-offs that are so necessary to the successful completion of projects. Of course, it is possible that all three variables might be fixed at levels that allowed the PM plenty of maneuvering room, but this is most unlikely. Far more likely, our project manager acquaintances tell us, is the case in which senior management assigns budgets, schedules, and specifications without regard for the uncertainties of reality. It is the PM's responsibility, possibly with help from the project's champion, to warn senior management of the impropriety of such restrictions in spite of the chance that a senior manager might respond with "I'll get someone who can. . . !"

On occasion, it may be that one or more tasks in a project are *system-constrained*. A system-constrained task requires a fixed amount of time and known quantities of resources. Some industrial processes—heat treating, for instance—are system-constrained. The material must "cook" for a specified time to achieve the desired effect. More or less "cooking" will not help. When dealing with a system-constrained task or project, no trade-offs are possible. The only matter of interest in these cases is to make sure that the required resources are available when needed.

In the following sections we discuss approaches for understanding and using these relationships in various project situations.

## ▶ 9.3 RESOURCE LOADING

*Resource loading* describes the amounts of individual resources an existing schedule requires during specific time periods. Therefore, it is irrelevant whether we are considering a single work unit or several projects; the loads (requirements) of each resource type are simply listed as a function of time period. Resource loading gives a general understanding of the demands a project will make on a firm's resources. It is an excellent guide for early, rough project planning. Obviously, it is also a first step in attempting to reduce excessive demands on certain resources, regardless of the specific technique used to reduce the demands. Again, we caution the PM to recognize that the use of resources on a project is often nonlinear. Much of the project management software does not always recognize this fact [20].

The PERT/CPM network technique is well suited for the job of generating time-phased resource requirements. A Gantt chart could be adapted, but the PERT/CPM diagram, particularly if modified to illustrate slacks, will be helpful in the analysis used for resource leveling. Let us illustrate with the PERT/CPM network used as an example in the previous chapter. The network (Table 8-2) reappears as Figure 9-3, and resource usage is illustrated for two hypothetical resources, A and B, on the arcs. The expected activity time is shown above the arc and resource usage is shown in parentheses just below the arc, with the use of A shown first and B second—e.g., (5,3) would mean that five units of A and three units of B would be used on the activity represented by the arc. Figure 9-4 shows the "calendarized" PERT/CPM diagram, similar to the familiar Gantt chart. Resource demands can now be summed by time period across all activities.

The loading diagram for resource A is illustrated in Figure 9-5a, and that for resource B in Figure 9-5b. The loads are erratic and vary substantially over the duration of the project. Resource A, used in tasks **a, b,** and **c,** has a high initial demand that drops through the middle of the project and then climbs again. Resource B, on the other hand, has low initial use but increases as the project develops. The PM must be aware of the ebbs and flows of usage for each input resource throughout

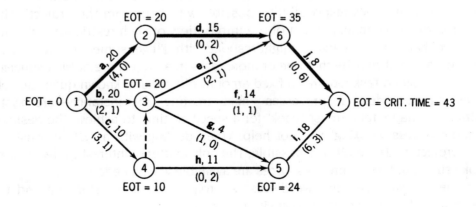

**Figure 9-3:** The complete network from Figure 8-15.

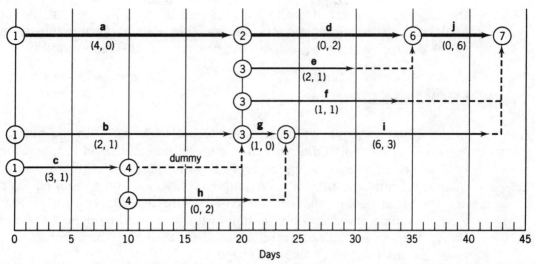

**Figure 9-4**: Modified PERT/CPM diagram showing resource usage (from Figure 9-3).

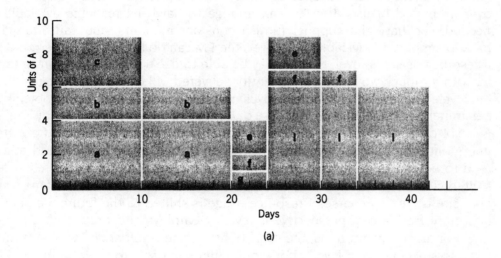

(a)

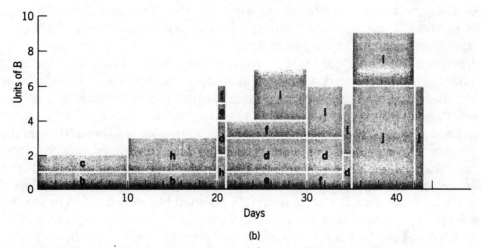

(b)

**Figure 9-5a**: Load diagram for resource A. **b**: Load diagram for resource B.

the life of the project. It is the PM's responsibility to assure that the required resources, in the required amounts, are available when and where they are needed. In the next three sections, we will discuss how to meet this responsibility.

## ▶ 9.4 RESOURCE LEVELING

In the example above, we noted that the project began with the heavy use of resource A, used smaller amounts during the middle of the project, and then continued with rising usage during the project's latter stages. Usage of B started low and rose throughout the project's life. Large fluctuations in the required loads for various resources are a normal occurrence—and are undesirable from the PM's point of view. Resource leveling aims to minimize the period-by-period variations in resource loading *by shifting tasks within their slack allowances*. The purpose is to create a smoother distribution of resource usage.

There are several advantages to smoother resource usage. First, much less hands-on management is required if the use of a given resource is nearly constant over its period of use. The PM can arrange to have the resource available when needed, can have the supplier furnish constant amounts, and can arrange for a backup supplier if advisable. Moreover, the PM can do this with little error. Second, if resource usage is level, the PM may be able to use a "just-in-time" inventory policy without much worry that the quantity delivered will be wrong. If the resource being leveled is people, leveling improves morale and results in fewer problems in the personnel and payroll offices because of increasing and decreasing labor levels.

Not only are there managerial implications to resource leveling, there are also important cost implications. When resources are leveled, the associated costs also tend to be leveled. If resource use increases as time goes by, and if resources are shifted closer to the present by leveling, costs will be shifted in the same way. The opposite is true, of course, if resource usage is shifted to the future. Perhaps most important from a cost perspective is leveling employment throughout a project or task. For most organizations, the costs of hiring and layoff are quite significant. It is often less expensive to level labor requirements in order to avoid hiring and layoff, even if it means some extra wages will be paid. In any case, the PM must be aware of the cash flows associated with the project and of the means of shifting them in ways that are useful to the parent firm.

The basic procedure for resource leveling is straightforward. For example, consider the simple network shown in Figure 9-6a. The activity time is shown above the arc, and resource usage (one resource, workers) is in parentheses below the arc. Activities **a, b,** and **c** follow event 1, and all must precede event 4. Activity **a** requires two workers and takes two days, **b** requires two workers and takes three days, and **c** needs four workers and five days. (We addressed the problem of trade-offs between labor and activity time in the first section of this chapter.) If all these tasks are begun on their early start dates, the resource loading diagram appears as shown in Figure 9-6b, steps of decreasing labor demand varying from eight workers to four workers. If, however, task **b** is delayed for two days, the full length of its slack in this particular case, the resource loading diagram is smoothed, as shown in Figure 9-6c.

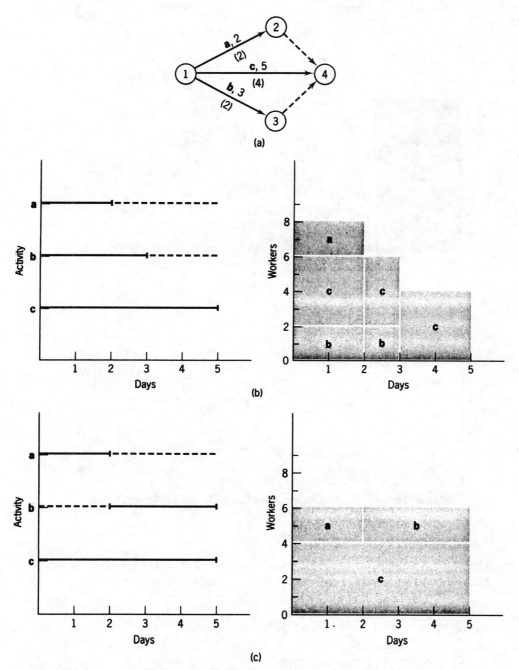

**Figure 9-6a:** The network. **b:** Before resource leveling. **c:** After resource leveling.

The same result would have occurred if **b** were started as early as possible and task **a** were delayed until day 3.

Resource leveling is a procedure that can be used for almost all projects, whether or not resources are constrained. If the network is not too large and there are only a few resources, the leveling process can be done manually. For larger networks and multiple resources, resource leveling becomes extremely complex, far be-

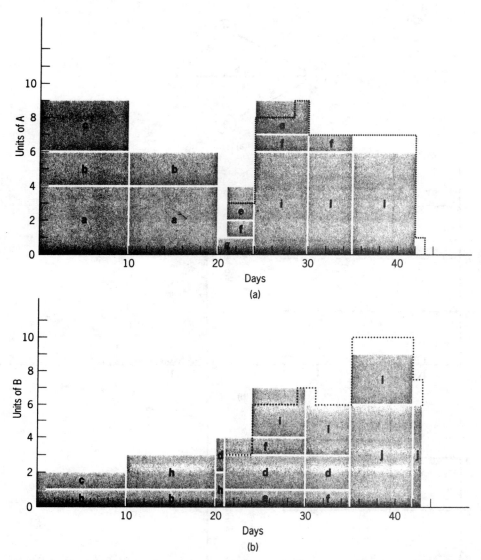

**Figure 9-7a:** Load diagram for resource A with activities **e** and **f** delayed by one day each.
**b:** Load diagram for resource B with activities **e** and **f** delayed by one day each.

yond the power of manual solutions. Fortunately, a number of computer programs can handle most leveling problems efficiently (discussed in Chapter 10).

Reconsider the load diagrams of Figures 9-5a and b. Assume it is desired to smooth the loading of resource B, which is particularly jagged. Both activities **e** and **f** can be delayed (**e** has five days of slack and **f** has nine). If we delay both for one day, we remove the peak on day 20 without increasing any of the other peaks (see Figure 9-7b). If we do this, however, it also alters the use of resource A and deepens the "valley" on day 20 (see Figure 9-7a). If we further delay **f** another seven days in order to level the use of A toward the end of the project, we would deepen the valley between days 20 and 24, and the resultant use of A would be as shown by the dotted lines on Figure 9-7a. Activity **f** would begin on day 29 (and would become critical). The effect on the usage of B is easy to see (Figure 9-7b). The change would lower usage by one unit beginning on day 21 (remember that we have already delayed **f** one day), and increase usage by one unit beginning on day 35, continuing to the end of the project. This action increases peak use of B from nine to ten units.

It is important to emphasize that if the network under consideration is more complex and the number of resources to be leveled is realistically large, a manual leveling process is out of the question. Computer-aided leveling is not only mandatory, it is also helpful because it allows the PM to experiment with various patterns of resource usage through simulation.

In the next section we raise the most general problem of minimizing resource usage while still achieving various completion dates—or the inverse problem, minimizing completion times while operating with specified limits on resources.

# Project Management in Practice
## A Resource Leveling Information System for Scheduling at Sacramento Municipal Utility District

The Sacramento Municipal Utility District had been using color-coded magnetic scheduling boards for over 20 years to keep track of line construction, meter, and service job status for its 426,000 customers and to make daily crew assignments. But with explosive population growth and increased systems maintenance requirements, the system was overloaded, resulting in a backlog of over 3000 line construction jobs. Thus, a new, computerized forecasting, planning, scheduling, and monitoring system was needed. Management dictated three requirements: (1) Keep it simple, (2) Allow for future expansion, and (3) Assure compatibility with existing information systems.

The project proceeded in phases:

*Definition*—managerial interviews and analysis of needs

*Design and approval of action plan*—work scope, resource requirements, schedule

*Information gathering*—interviews with working personnel

*Analysis and documentation*—constructing CPM schedules, process flowcharts, data dictionaries

*System specification*—specifications and programming

*Data loading and testing*—issuing status reports and meeting to resolve problems

*Documentation and training*—provide for later in-house modification ability.

Schedule construction is now a two-step process (see figure). First, CPM schedules are loaded into the system for each construction project. Second, the program reschedules the jobs based on priorities and worker availability, always maintaining customer-required dates. Any conflicts are worked out by a central planning/scheduling group with line management and the customer.

To gain scheduler acceptance, a one-month trial period was undertaken to get feedback about the system. Indeed, comments from the schedulers led to a change in the manner of scheduling on the computer, as well as some significant customization of the report-writing capabilities of the system. However, with these changes the system was well accepted by the users.

*Source:* C. J. Pospisil, "A PC-Based Scheduling System for a Transmission and Distribution Construction Department," *Project Management Journal*, Sept. 1990.

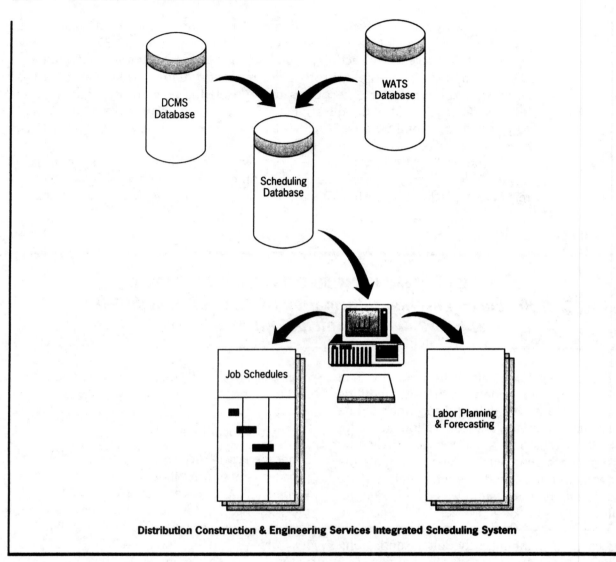

**Distribution Construction & Engineering Services Integrated Scheduling System**

## ▶ 9.5   CONSTRAINED RESOURCE SCHEDULING

There are two fundamental approaches to constrained allocation problems: heuristics and optimization models. Heuristic approaches employ rules of thumb that have been found to work reasonably well in similar situations. They seek better solutions. Optimization approaches seek the best solutions but are far more limited in their ability to handle complex situations and large problems. We will discuss each separately.

Most of the readily available PC software designed for project management will level resources and handle resource conflicts, but usually with a limited number of heuristic approaches. In leveling resources, TimeLine® gives priority to activities with earlier start dates while SuperProject® uses the least slack rule, and Primavera® will use any of several rules. In an interesting experiment, Johnson tested ten widely available project management packages for PCs against optimal solutions to a set of resource leveling problems [25]. In this particular test, Timeline® scored best with an average error of 5 percent. Figure 9-8a shows a Timeline® generated report on a resource conflict, while Figure 9-8b shows a resource-leveled solution to the conflict. (The example was extracted from a project presented in Chapter 10.)

## Heuristic Methods

Heuristic approaches to constrained resource scheduling problems are in wide, general use for a number of reasons. First, they are the only feasible methods of attacking the large, nonlinear, complex problems that tend to occur in the real world of project management. Second, while the schedules heuristics generate may not be

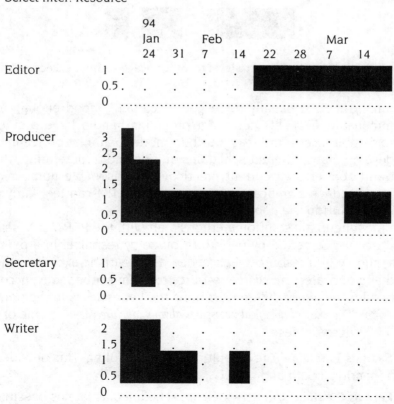

**Figure 9-8a**:   Resource conflict, two resources used beyond capacity.

Schedule Name : Producing a Video Tape
Responsible   : Project Manager
As-of Date    : 19-Jan-94  8:00a
End Date      : 29-Mar-94  5:00pm

Select filter: Resource

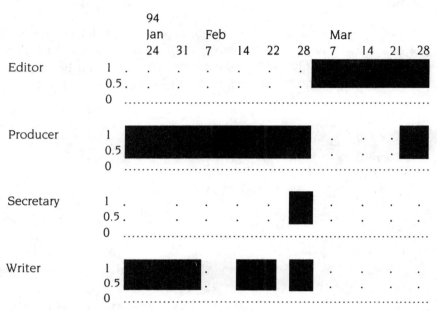

**Figure 9-8 *b***:   Rescheduling to level resource usage without exceeding capacity.

optimal, they are usually quite good—certainly good enough for most purposes. Commercially available computer programs handle large problems and have had considerable use in industry. Further, modern simulation techniques allow the PM to develop many different schedules quickly and to determine which, if any, are significantly better than current practice. If a reasonable number of simulation runs fails to produce significant improvement, the PM can feel fairly confident that the existing solution is a good one.

Most heuristic solution methods start with the PERT/CPM schedule and analyze resource usage period by period, resource by resource. In a period when the available supply of a resource is exceeded, the heuristic examines the tasks in that period and allocates the scarce resource to them sequentially, according to some priority rule. The major difference among the heuristics is in the priority rules they use. *Remember that the technological necessities always take precedence.* Some of the most common priority rules are these:

**As Soon as Possible**   The default rule for scheduling. This provides the general solution for critical path and time.

**As Late as Possible**   All activities are scheduled as late as possible without delaying the project. The usual purpose of this heuristic is to defer cash outflows as long as possible.

**Shortest Task First**  Tasks are ordered in terms of duration, with the shortest first. In general, this rule will maximize the number of tasks that can be completed by a system during some time period.

**Most Resources First**  Activities are ordered by use of a specific resource, with the largest user heading the list. The assumption behind this rule is that more important tasks usually place a higher demand on scarce resources.

**Minimum Slack First**  This heuristic orders activities by the amount of slack, least slack going first. (It is common, when using this rule, to break ties by using the shortest-task-first rule.)

**Most Critical Followers**  Tasks are arranged by number of critical activities following them. The ones with the greatest number of critical followers go first.

**Most Successors**  This is the same as the previous rule, except that *all* followers, not merely critical ones, are counted.

There are many such priority rules employed in scheduling heuristics. Most of them are simple adaptations and variations of the heuristics used for the traditional "job shop scheduling" problem of production/operations management, a problem that has much in common with multiproject scheduling and resource allocation. Also, most heuristics use a combination of rules—a primary rule, with a secondary rule used to break ties.

Several researchers [19, 28, 29] have conducted tests of the more commonly used schedule priority rules. Although their findings vary somewhat because of slightly different assumptions, the minimum slack rule was found to be best or near-best quite often and rarely caused poor performance. It usually resulted in the minimum amount of project schedule slippage, the best utilization of facilities, and the minimum total system occupancy time.

As the scheduling heuristic operates, one of two events will result. The routine runs out of activities (for the current period) before it runs out of the resources, or it runs out of resources before all activities have been scheduled. (While it is theoretically possible for the supply of resources to be precisely equal to the demand for such resources, even the most careful planning rarely produces such a tidy result.) If the former occurs, the excess resources are left idle, assigned elsewhere in the organization as needed during the current period, or applied to future tasks required by the project—always within the constraints imposed by the proper precedence relationships. If one or more resources are exhausted, however, activities requiring those resources are slowed or delayed until the next period when resources can be reallocated.

If the minimum slack rule is used, resources would be devoted to critical or nearly critical activities, delaying those with greater slack. Delay of an activity uses some of its slack, so the activity will have a better chance of receiving resources in the next allocation. Repeated delays move the activity higher and higher on the priority list. We consider later what to do in the potentially catastrophic event that we run out of resources before all critical activities have been scheduled.

The heuristic procedure just described is probably the most common. There are, however, other heuristic procedures that work in a similar manner. One works in reverse and schedules jobs from the end of the project instead of from its beginning. Activities that just precede the project finish are scheduled to be completed just barely within their latest finish times. Then, the next-to-last tasks are considered, and so on. The purpose of this approach is to leave as much flexibility as possible for activities that will be difficult to schedule in the middle and early portions of the project. This logic seems to rest on the idea that flexibility early in the project gives the best chance of completing early and middle activities on time and within budget, thereby improving the chances of being on time and budget with the ending activities.

Other heuristics use the *branch and bound* approach. They generate a wide variety of solutions, discard those that are not feasible and others that are feasible but poor solutions. This is done by a *tree search* that prunes infeasible solutions and poor solutions when other feasible solutions dominate them. In this way, the heuristic narrows the region in which good, feasible solutions may be found. If the "tree" is not too large, this approach can locate optimal solutions, but more computer search time will be required. See [55] for further details.

These heuristics are usually embedded in a computer simulation package that describes what will happen to the project(s) if certain schedules or priority rules are followed. A number of different priority rules can be tried in the simulation in order to derive a set of possible solutions. Simulation is a powerful tool and can also handle unusual project situations. Consider, for example, the following problem in *resource contouring*.

Given the network and resource demand shown in Figure 9-9, find the best schedule using a constant crew size. Each day of delay beyond 15 days incurs a penalty of $1000. Workers cost $100 per day, and machines cost $50 per day. Workers are interchangeable, as are machines. Task completion times vary directly with the number of workers, and partial work days are acceptable. The critical time for the project is 15 days, given the resource usage shown in Figure 9-9. (There are other jobs in the system waiting to be done.)

Figure 9-9 lists the total worker-days and machines per day normally required by each activity (below the activity arc). Because activity times are proportional to worker demands, path **b–c–e–i** is most demanding and this path uses 149 worker-days.

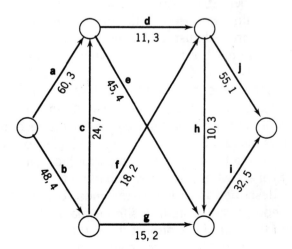

**Figure 9-9:** Network for resource load simulation. *Note:* The numbers on the arcs represent, respectively, worker-days, machines per day.

The fact that completion times vary with the number of workers means that activity **a** could be completed in 6 days with ten workers or in 10 days with six workers. Applying some logic and trying to avoid the penalty, which is far in excess of the cost of additional resources, we can add up the total worker-days required on all activities, obtaining 319. Dividing this by the 15 days needed to complete the project results in a requirement of slightly more than 21 workers–say, 22. How should they be allocated to the activities? Figure 9-10 shows one way, arbitrarily determined. Workers are shown above the "days" axis and machines below. We have 22 workers at $100 per day for 15 days ($33,000) and 128.5 machine days at $50 per day ($6425). The total cost of this particular solution is $39,425.

The "critical path" illustrated in Figure 9-10 is **a–g–i,** which takes 15 days. However, inspecting Figure 9-9, activity **g** does not follow activity **a** so how can this be a true "critical path"? The reason is: when resources are shared among activities, the resources for one activity may not be available because an earlier activity (though not necessarily a predecessor) is still using them. Thus, in theory, **g** (and **f** too) could have started at day 4 when **b** was completed but there were no workers available.

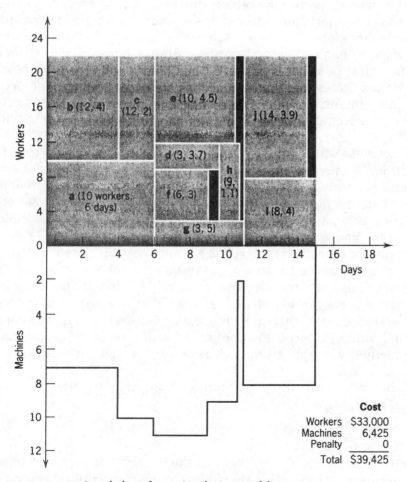

**Figure 9-10:** Load chart for a simulation problem.

The availability of workers is indicated by the shaded regions in Figure 9-10. Thus, if we use the 6 idle workers shown between activities **f** and **h** (for 0.7 days, thereby releasing 4.2 worker-days) to reduce the length of activity **g,** we could reduce it by 4.2/3 (workers) = 1.4 days, finishing now at 9.6 days. However, path **b–c–d–h** would then become critical at 10.8 days, resulting in only 0.2 days of overall project reduction. Using the 4.2 worker-days to reduce not only activity **g** but also activities **d** and **e,** would allow us to complete all of activities **e, h,** and **g** at day 10.32, thereby reducing the project time by 0.68 days. The idle labor following activity **j** could be used similarly to reduce activity **i.**

After all reallocations, it is important to recalculate the demand for machines since this will also change. Note that we have assumed that machine use depends only on time and is independent of the number of workers: if this is not the case, then a different set of calculations are required to determine the machine requirements. Finally, there may be limitations on the total number of workers or machines that are available at any one time and this can affect the solution. For example, how would the solution change if only 20 workers were available?

The purpose of reassignments is not to decrease labor cost in the project. This is fixed by the base technology implied by the worker/machine usage data. The reassignments do, however, shorten the project duration and make the resources available for other work sooner than expected. If the tradeoffs are among resources, for instance, trading more labor for fewer machines or more machines for less material input, the problem is handled in the same way. Always, however, the technology itself constrains what is possible. The Chinese build roads in the mountains by using labor. In the United States machines are used. Both nations exercise an option because either labor-intensive or machine-intensive technology is feasible. The ancient Israelites, however, could not substitute labor for straw in making bricks: No straw, no bricks.

On small networks with simple interrelationships among the resources, it is not difficult to perform these resource trade-offs by hand. But for networks of a realistic size, a computer is clearly required. If the problem is programmed for computer solution, many different solutions and their associated costs can be calculated. But, as with heuristics, simulation does not guarantee an optimal, or even feasible, solution. It can only test those solutions fed into it.

Another heuristic procedure for leveling resource loads is based on the concept of minimizing the sum of the squares of the resource requirements in each period. That is, the smooth use of a resource over a set of periods will give a smaller sum of squares than the erratic use of the resource that averages out to the same amount as the smooth use. This approach, called *Burgess's method*, was applied by Woodworth and Willie [61] to a multiproject situation involving a number of resources. The method was applied to each resource sequentially, starting with the most critical resource first.

Next, we briefly discuss some optimizing approaches to the constrained resource scheduling problem.

## Optimizing Methods

The methods to find an optimal solution to the constrained resource scheduling problem fall into two categories: mathematical programming (linear programming for the most part) and enumeration. In the 1960s, the power of LP improved from being able to handle three resources and 15 activities to four resources and 55 activities. But even with this capacity, LP is usually not feasible for reasonably large projects where there may be a dozen resources and thousands of activities. (See [18] and [41] for more detail.)

In the late 1960s and early 1970s, limited enumeration techniques were applied to the constrained resource problem with more success. Tree search and branch and bound methods [50] were devised to handle up to five resources and perhaps 200 activities. Advances in LP techniques now allow LP to be used on large constrained resource scheduling problems.

More recent approaches have combined programming and enumeration methods. Patterson and Huber [42], for example, employ an integer programming approach combined with a minimum bounding procedure to reduce the computation time for minimizing project duration. Similarly, Talbot [52] uses integer programming and implicit enumeration to formulate and solve problems where the completion time is a function of the resources allocated to the project.

One problem with even the newer combination of approaches is that the characteristics of problems that can be usefully addressed with these methods is still largely unknown. Why various methods will work on one problem and not on a similar problem is still being researched.

---

# Project Management in Practice
### *Benefits of Resource Constraining at Pennsylvania Electric*

---

Pennsylvania Electric Company, headquartered in Johnstown, PA, operates generating facilities with a capacity of 6950 megawatts to serve 547,000 customers over an area of 17,600 square miles. The Generation Division Planning Group is responsible for planning all maintenance and capital projects. In the early 1980s, the group used a manual method of planning with hand-drawn charts. The planning process has now been computerized, which is faster, allows "what-if" analyses, and controls more than just the previously monitored critical path. In bringing the planning process in-house, the group also saved $100,000 a year in service fees from an outside engineering firm who was planning their construction activities.

A special feature of the computerized system is its resource constraining module which establishes labor requirements across all jobs. In the pilot program to test the new software, $300,000 was saved when it was discovered that a job could be done with 40 percent fewer mechanics than normally used and still complete the job on time. In another application, it was found that a turbine disassembly and inspection could be added to the task list without delaying the project or exceeding the project budget.

After worker-hours are input to the program by activity, actual progress is monitored (see figure) and schedule and cost deviations are highlighted for management attention. This allows management to make adjustments to recover the schedule, slow the project down, or acquire more funds to get the

*Source*: A. J. Cantanese, "At Penelec, Project Management is a Way of Life," *Project Management Journal*, December 1990.

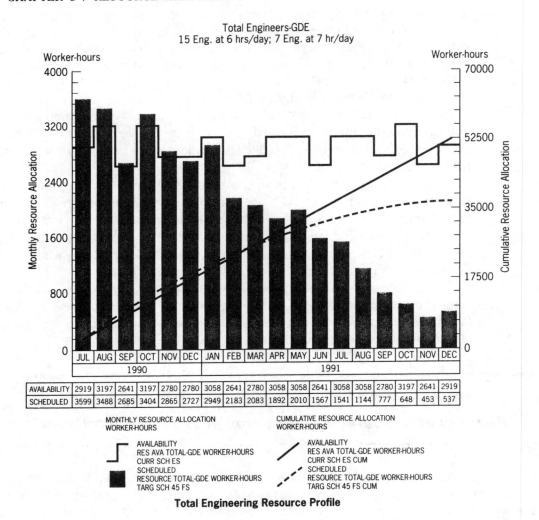

Total Engineers-GDE
15 Eng. at 6 hrs/day; 7 Eng. at 7 hr/day

|  | JUL | AUG | SEP | OCT | NOV | DEC | JAN | FEB | MAR | APR | MAY | JUN | JUL | AUG | SEP | OCT | NOV | DEC |
|---|---|---|---|---|---|---|---|---|---|---|---|---|---|---|---|---|---|---|
| AVAILABILITY | 2919 | 3197 | 2641 | 3197 | 2780 | 2780 | 3058 | 2641 | 2780 | 3058 | 3058 | 2641 | 3058 | 3058 | 2780 | 3197 | 2641 | 2919 |
| SCHEDULED | 3599 | 3488 | 2685 | 3404 | 2865 | 2727 | 2949 | 2183 | 2083 | 1892 | 2010 | 1567 | 1541 | 1144 | 777 | 648 | 453 | 537 |

MONTHLY RESOURCE ALLOCATION
WORKER-HOURS

    AVAILABILITY
    RES AVA TOTAL-GDE WORKER-HOURS
    CURR SCH ES
    SCHEDULED
    RESOURCE TOTAL-GDE WORKER-HOURS
    TARG SCH 45 FS

CUMULATIVE RESOURCE ALLOCATION
WORKER-HOURS

    AVAILABILITY
    RES AVA TOTAL-GDE WORKER-HOURS
    CURR SCH ES CUM
    SCHEDULED
    RESOURCE TOTAL-GDE WORKER-HOURS
    TARG SCH 45 FS CUM

**Total Engineering Resource Profile**

project back on schedule. Obviously, there are always some emergencies outside the plan that must be handled on an exception basis. But with this software, management knows what effect different actions will have on the basic plan and can thereby make the best use of available resources to handle the emergency with minimal impact on the plan.

## ▶ 9.6 MULTIPROJECT SCHEDULING AND RESOURCE ALLOCATION

Scheduling and allocating resources to multiple projects is much more complicated than for the single-project case. The most common approach is to treat the several projects as if they were each elements of a single large project. (A more detailed explanation is given below when we consider a specific multiproject scheduling heuristic.) Another way of attacking the problem is to consider all projects as completely independent; see [28, 29], for example. As [28] shows, these two approaches lead to different scheduling and allocation outcomes. For either approach, the conceptual basis for scheduling and allocating resources is essentially the same.

There are several projects, each with its own set of activities, due dates, and resource requirements. In addition, the penalties for not meeting time, cost, and performance goals for the several projects may differ. Usually, the multiproject problem involves determining how to allocate resources to, and set a completion time for, a new project that is added to an existing set of ongoing projects. This requires the development of an efficient, dynamic multiproject scheduling system.

To describe such a system properly, standards are needed by which to measure scheduling effectiveness. Three important parameters affected by project scheduling are: (1) schedule slippage, (2) resource utilization, and (3) in-process inventory. The organization (or the PM) must select the criterion most appropriate for its situation.

*Schedule slippage*, often considered the most important of the criteria, is the time past a project's due date or delivery date when the project is completed. Slippage may well result in penalty costs that reduce profits. Further, slippage of one project may have a ripple effect, causing other projects to slip. Indeed, expediting a project in order to prevent slippage may, and usually does, disturb the overall organization to the point where slippage due to resource shortages may then be caused in other projects. The loss of goodwill when a project slips and deliveries are late is important to all producers. As is the case with many firms, Grumman Aircraft, purchased by the Northrup Corporation in 1994, jealously guards its reputation for on-time delivery. During a project to install a new machine control system on a production line, Grumman insisted that the project be designed to minimize disturbance to operations in the affected plant and avoid late shipments. This increased the cost of the project, but the firm maintained delivery schedules.

A second measure of effectiveness, *resource utilization*, is of particular concern to industrial firms because of the high cost of making resources available. A resource allocation system that smooths out the peaks and valleys of resource usage is ideal, but it is extremely difficult to attain while maintaining scheduled performance because all the projects in a multiproject organization are competing for the same scarce resources. In particular, it is expensive to change the size of the human resource pool on which the firm draws.

While it is relatively easy to measure the costs of excess resource usage required by less than optimal scheduling in an industrial firm, the costs of uncoordinated multiproject scheduling can be high in service-producing firms, too. In the real estate syndication firm used as an example of an AON network in Chapter 8 (see Figure 8-28), the scarce resource is executive judgment time. If two deals arrived at the same time, one would have to wait. This is undesirable because other potential buyers are seeking properties, and the process must move along without delay.

The third standard of effectiveness, the amount of *in-process inventory*, concerns the amount of work waiting to be processed because there is a shortage of some resource(s). Most industrial organizations have a large investment in in-process inventory, which may indicate a lack of efficiency and often represents a major source of expense for the firm. The remedy involves a trade-off between the cost of in-process inventory and the cost of the resources, usually capital equipment, needed to reduce the in-process inventory levels. It is almost axiomatic that the most time-consuming operation in any production system involving much machining of metals is an operation called "wait." If evidence is required, simply observe parts sitting on the plant floor or on pallets waiting for a machine, or for jigs, fixtures, and tools.

All these criteria cannot be optimized at the same time. As usual, trade-offs are involved. A firm must decide which criterion is most applicable in any given situation, and then use that criterion to evaluate its various scheduling and resource allocation options.

At times, the demands of the marketplace and the design of a production/distribution system may require long production runs and sizable levels of in-process inventory. This happens often when production is organized as a continuous system, but sales are organized as projects, each customized to a client order. Items may be produced continuously but held in a semifinished state and customized in batches.

A mattress manufacturing company organized to produce part of its output by the usual continuous process; but the rest of its production was sold in large batches to a few customers. Each large order was thought of as a project and was organized as one. The customization process began after the metal frames and springs were assembled. This required extensive in-process inventories of semifinished mattresses.

As noted earlier, experiments by Fendley [19] revealed that the minimum-slack-first rule is the best overall priority rule, generally resulting in minimum project slippage, minimum resource idle time, and minimum system occupancy time (i.e., minimum in-process inventory) for the cases he studied. But the most commonly used priority rule is first come, first served—which has little to be said for it except that it fits the client's idea of what is "fair." In any case, individual firms may find a different rule more effective in their particular circumstances and should evaluate alternative rules by their own performance measures and system objectives.

Fendley found that when a new project is added to a multiproject system, the amount of slippage is related to the average resource load factor. The load factor is the average resource *requirement* during a set time period divided by resource *availability* for that time period. When the new project is added, the load factor for a resource increases and slippage rises. Analysis of resource loads is an important element in determining the amount of slippage to expect when adding projects.

Given these observations, let us examine some examples of the various types of multiproject scheduling and resource allocation techniques. We begin with a short description of one optimization method, briefly cover several heuristics, and then discuss one heuristic in greater detail.

## Mathematical Programming

Mathematical programming [16, 18, 41, 55] can be used to obtain optimal solutions to certain types of multiproject scheduling problems. These procedures determine when an activity should be scheduled, given resource constraints. In the following discussion, it is important to remember that each of the techniques can be applied to the activities in a single project, or to the projects in a partially or wholly interdependent set of projects. Most models are based on integer programming that formulates the problem using 0–1 variables to indicate (depending on task early start times, due dates, sequencing relationships, etc.) whether or not an activity is scheduled in specific periods. The three most common objectives are these:

1. Minimum total throughput time (time in the shop) for all projects

**2.** Minimum total completion time for all projects

**3.** Minimum total lateness or lateness penalty for all projects.

Constraint equations ensure that every schedule meets any or all of the following constraints, given that the set of constraints allow a feasible solution.

**1.** Limited resources

**2.** Precedence relationships among activities

**3.** Activity-splitting possibilities

**4.** Project and activity due dates

**5.** Substitution of resources to assign to specified activities

**6.** Concurrent and nonconcurrent activity performance requirements

In spite of its ability to generate optimal solutions, mathematical programming has some serious drawbacks when used for resource allocation and multiproject scheduling. As noted earlier, except for the case of small problems, this approach has proved to be extremely difficult and computationally expensive.

# Heuristic Techniques

Because of the difficulties with the analytical formulation of realistic problems, major efforts in attacking the resource-constrained multiproject scheduling problem have focused on heuristics. We touched earlier on some of the common general criteria used for scheduling heuristics. Let us now return to that subject.

There are scores of different heuristic-based procedures in existence. A great many of the procedures have been published (see [18] and [40], for example), and descriptions of some are generally available in commercial computer programs.

The most commonly applied rules were discussed in Section 9.5. The logical basis for these rules predates PERT/CPM. They represent rather simple extensions of well-known approaches to job-shop scheduling. Some additional heuristics for resource allocation have been developed that draw directly on PERT/CPM. All these are commercially available for computers, and most are available from several different software vendors in slightly different versions.

***Resource Scheduling Method*** In calculating activity priority, give precedence to that activity with the minimum value of $d_{ij}$ where

$d_{ij}$ = increase in project duration resulting when activity **j** follows activity **i**.

$= \text{Max} [0; (EFT_i - LST_j)]$

*where*

$EFT_i$ = early finish time of activity **i**

$LST_j$ = latest start time of activity **j**

The comparison is made on a pairwise basis among all activities in the *conflict set*.

***Minimum Late Finish Time*** This rule assigns priorities to activities on the basis of activity finish times as determined by PERT/CPM. The earliest late finishers are scheduled first.

***Greatest Resource Demand*** This method assigns priorities on the basis of total resource requirements, with higher priorities given for greater demands on resources. Project or task priority is calculated as:

$$\text{Priority} = d_j \sum_{i=1}^{m} r_{ij}$$

*where*

$d_j$ = duration of activity *j*

$r_{ij}$ = per period requirement of resource *i* by activity *j*

$m$ = number of resource types

Resource requirements must be stated in common terms, usually dollars. This heuristic is based on an attempt to give priority to potential resource bottleneck activities.

***Greatest Resource Utilization*** This rule gives priority to that combination of activities that results in maximum resource utilization (or minimum idle resources) during each scheduling period. The rule is implemented by solving a 0–1 integer programming problem, as described earlier. This rule was found to be approximately as effective as the minimum slack rule for multiple project scheduling, where the criterion used was project slippage. Variations of this rule are found in commercial computer programs such as RAMPS (see [35]).

***Most Possible Jobs*** Here, priority is given to the set of activities that results in the greatest number of activities being scheduled in any period. This rule also requires the solution of a 0–1 integer program. It differs from the greatest-resource-utilization heuristic in that the determination of the greatest number of possible jobs is made purely with regard to resource feasibility (and not with regard to any measure of resource utilization).

Heuristic procedures for resource-constrained multiproject scheduling represent the only practical means for finding workable solutions to the large, complex multiproject problems normally found in the real world. Let us examine a multiproject heuristic in somewhat more detail.

## A Multiproject Scheduling Heuristic

To attack this problem, recall the hierarchical approach to project planning we adopted in Chapter 5. A project plan is a nested set of plans, composed of a set of generalized tasks, each of which is decomposed into a more detailed set of work packages that are, in turn, decomposed further. The decomposition is continued until the work packages are simple enough to be considered "elemental." A PERT/CPM diagram of a project might be drawn for any level of task aggregation. A single activity (arrow) at a high level of aggregation would represent an entire network of activities at a lower level (see Figure 9-11). Another level in the planning hierarchy is shown as a Gantt chart in Figure 9-12.

If an entire network is decomposed into subnetworks, we have the equivalent of the multiproject problem where each of the projects (subnetworks) is linked to predecessor and successor projects (other subnetworks). In this case, the

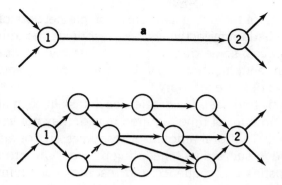

**Figure 9-11:** Task **a** decomposed into a network of subtasks.

predecessor/successor relationships depend on the technology of the parent project. In the true multiproject case, these relationships may still depend on technological relationships—for example, a real estate development project being dependent on the outcome of a land procurement project. The relationships may, however, be determined more or less arbitrarily, as when projects are sequenced on a first-come, first-served basis, or by any other priority-setting rule, or undertaken simultaneously in the hope that some synergistic side effects might occur. Or the relationship among the projects may simply be that they share a common pool of resources.

With this conceptual model, assume we have a set of projects. Each individual

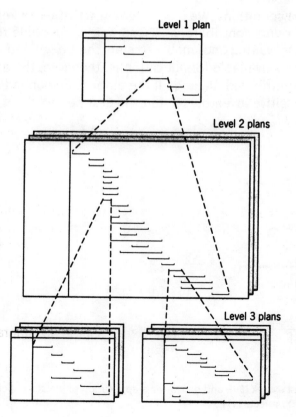

**Figure 9-12:** Hierarchy of Gantt charts.
*Source:* [23]

project is represented by a network of tasks. We can form a single network of these projects by connecting them with dummy activities (no resources, no duration) and/or pseudoactivities (no resources, some duration). Both dummy activities and pseudoactivities represent dependency relationships, but these dependencies, as noted above, may be technological or quite arbitrary.*

As usual, and excepting dummy and pseudoactivities, each task in each network requires time and resources. The amount of time required may or may not vary with the level of resources applied to it. The total amount of resources and/or amounts of individual resources are limited in successive scheduling periods. Our problem is to find a schedule that best satisfies the sequence and resource constraints and minimizes the overall duration of the entire network. The resulting schedule should indicate when to start any activity and at what level of resources it should be maintained while it is active.

Before undertaking the allocation of resources, it is proper to consider the quantity of resources available for allocation. (For the moment, we consider "resources" as an undifferentiated pool of assets that can be used for any purpose.) At the beginning of any period (hour, day, week, month, etc.) we have available any resources in inventory, $R_I$, which is to say, left over as excess from the previous allocation process. Changes in the inventory can be made from within the system of projects or by importing or exporting inventory from the outside. Excluding activities that have been completed in previous periods, every activity planned by the project is in one of four states; ongoing, stopping, waiting and technologically able to start, or waiting and technological unable to start.

Figure 9-13 illustrates these conditions. We label ongoing activities as "resource users." Those stopping are "resource contributors." Those waiting and able to start are "resource demanders." Those waiting and unable to start can be ignored for the present. The amount of resources available for allocation is, therefore, the amount in inventory plus the amount contributed, $R_I + R_C$. If the amount demanded is less than this sum, there will be a positive inventory to start the next period. If not, some demanders will go unfunded.

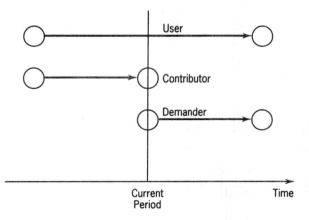

**Figure 9-13:** Sources and uses of resources.

---

*This exposition is based on Weist's work [59], and on Corwin's application of Weist's papers to resource allocation among multiple R & D projects [11].

Weist's heuristic (SPAR-1, Scheduling Program for Allocation of Resources) allocates resources to activities in order of their early start times. In the first period, we would list all available tasks and order them by their slack, from least to most. (Calculation of slack is based on the assumption that activities will be supported at *normal* resource levels.) Activities are selected for support and scheduling one by one, in order. As activities at the top of the list are supported, the relevant resource stocks are debited. Tasks are scheduled sequentially until the list of available jobs is completed, or until the stock of one or more resources is depleted. If we deplete resources before completing the task list, remaining tasks are delayed until the next period. Postponed activities lose slack and rise toward the top of the priority list.

The information requirements for this heuristic are straightforward. Each period, we need a period-by-period updating of the list of currently active tasks continued from the previous period, including the resource usage level for each active task, the current scheduled (or expected) completion date, and the current activity slack. We need to know the currently available stocks of each type of resource, less the amounts of each in use. We also need a list of all available tasks together with their slacks and normal resource requirements. As activities are completed, their resources are "credited" to the resource pool for future use.

Thus, resources are devoted to activities until the supply of available resources or activities is exhausted. If we use up the resources before all critical activities are scheduled, we can adopt one of two subheuristics. First, we may be able to borrow resources from currently active, but noncritical, tasks. Second, we may "deschedule" a currently active, noncritical task. The former presumably slows the progress of the work, and the latter stops it. In both cases, some resources will be released for use on critical tasks. Obviously, if a critical task is slowed, descheduled, or not supported, the duration of the associated project will be extended.

The decision about which of these courses of action to take, borrowing or descheduling, can be made by adopting the same logic used in Chapter 7 when we discussed the budget negotiations between subordinate and superior. The decision to borrow or deschedule depends on our estimate of the impact either action would have on the task under consideration, given its current state of completion. Figure 9-14 shows two different versions of the project or task life cycle discussed in Chapter 7. If the task is a Type 1, borrowing would minimize the damage to the task unless it is quite near completion and we are willing to accept the outcome in its current state, in which case we can deschedule. If the task is Type 2, borrowing is

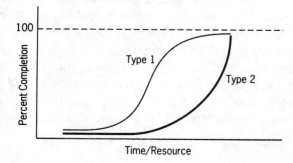

**Figure 9-14:** Project or task life cycles.

apt to have a catastrophic effect on the task and we should either deschedule it (and start it again later) or reject it as a source of resources.

If the size of the resource pool is more than sufficient for the list of active and available tasks, the extra resources may be used to crash critical activities in order to put some slack in the critical path as insurance against project delays caused by last-minute crises. In fact, it is often possible to borrow resources from tasks with plenty of slack in order to crash critical items that are frequent causes of project delay.

As a result of this scheduling process, each task from the previous period, along with any tasks newly available for support, will be:

1.  Continued as is, or newly funded at a normal level
2.  Continued or funded at a higher level of resources as a result of criticality
3.  Continued or funded at a lower-than-normal level as a result of borrowing
4.  Delayed because of a resource shortage.

If there is more than one scarce resource, a separate activity can be created for each type of scarce resource. These "created" activities must be constrained to start in the same period as the parent activity, and to have the same level of resource assignment (normal, crash, or minimal.) Figure 9-15 shows a flow diagram for SPAR-1.

As we have noted, many commercially available software packages have the ability to schedule constrained resources and deal with resource conflicts [21, 25, 57]. The *Project Management Journal* published by the Project Management Institute is an excellent source of reviews on project management software. These reviews typically include a discussion of the package's capabilities. Many will allow the user to solve the problem either automatically, using the program's heuristics, or by hand in which case the user can adopt any method desired. If a set of projects is linked together by dummy activities so that it can be treated like a single project, the software will report resource usage conflicts; that is, cases in which the scheduled utilization of a resource is greater than the supply of that resource.

In one sense this chapter's emphasis on resource shortages is misleading. The common case of shortage applies not to resources in general, but to one or two highly specific resources. For example, an insurance firm specializing in casualty insurance has a typical kind of scarce resource, a "Walt." Walter A. is a specialist in certain types of casualty losses in the firm's commerical lines business. He is the only such specialist in the firm, and his personal knowledge is required when designing new policies in the field. His knowledge is based on years of experience and an excellent, analytical mind. It is common for projects involving the modification or creation of policies in the commercial lines area to have problems associated with the fact that the firm has one, and only one Walt. Walt-capacity cannot be hired, trained, or subcontracted within an appropriate time frame. The firm's ability to extend its Walt-capacity is not sufficient to satisfy its Walt-demand. Left with no alternative, some projects must be delayed so that others can proceed.

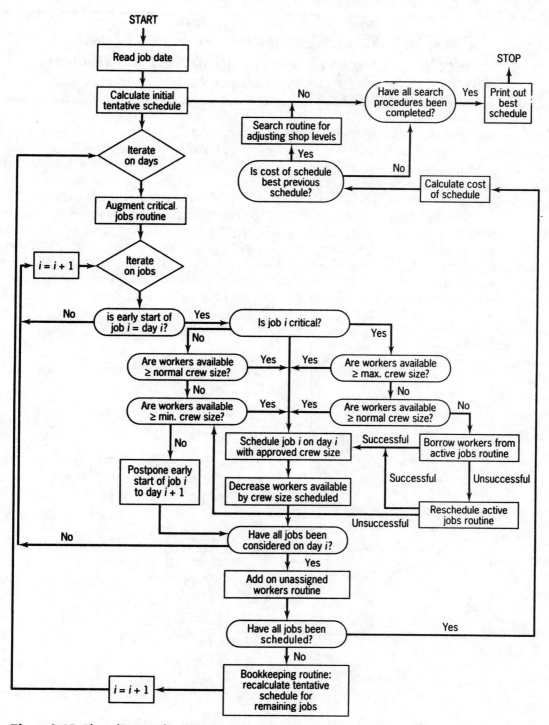

**Figure 9-15:** Flow diagram for SPAR-1. *Source*: [59]

# Project Management in Practice
## *Tying Projects to Resources and Constraints at the Minnesota Department of Transportation*

The Minnesota Department of Transportation is responsible for facility construction and maintenance for highways, bridges, airports, waterways, railroads, and even bicycle paths. At any given time, there will be approximately 1100 projects—typically, highway improvements—in active development, with a turnover of about 300 per year. These projects will range from $50,000 paint jobs to multimillion dollar freeway interchanges. The computerized Project Management and Scheduling System (PMSS) used to manage these projects is based on a work breakdown structure detailing about 100 activities involving 75 functional groups, 40 of which are in-house groups and the rest being consultants.

The PMSS encompasses three major areas: scheduling, funding, and human resource planning. It allows planning, coordination, and control of the work progress and resource requirements for multiple projects over a multiyear time span, since projects may continue

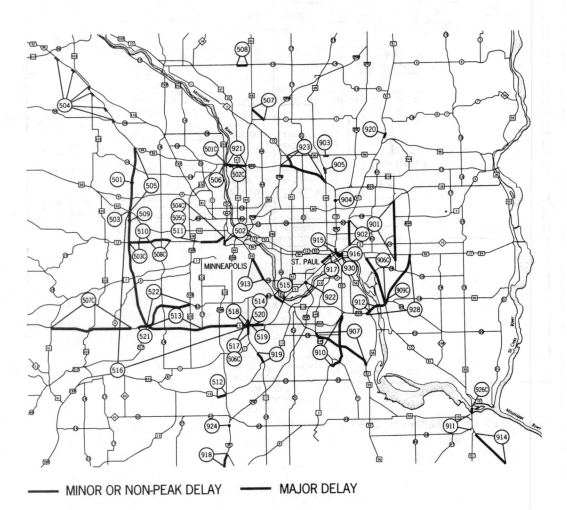

━━━ MINOR OR NON-PEAK DELAY ━━ MAJOR DELAY

for up to four years in some cases. This integration offers the capability to relate work plans to funding availability as well as human resource availability. Conversely, resource use can be planned according to the construction project schedule. Other constraints can also be included in the system and its reports, such as avoiding projects that might overly congest a high-traffic area (see figure) or properly sequencing subprojects such as grading, surfacing, and finishing.

The PMSS system gives management a "big picture" perspective of what is happening in terms of workflow over time and geography. It has also enhanced the department's ability to answer questions about activities, funding, labor, and equipment, and to present reports in a variety of configurations to satisfy the needs of many different parties.

*Source*: R. Pearson, "Project Management in the Minnesota Department of Transportation," PM *Network*, November 1988.

## ▶ SUMMARY

In this chapter we looked at the problem of allocating physical resources, both among the multiple activities of a project and among multiple projects. The continuous problem to the PM is finding the best trade-offs among resources, particularly time. We considered resource loading, allocation, and leveling, and presented methods and concepts to aid in all these tasks.

Specific points made in the chapter were these:

- The critical path method (CPM) is a network constructed in the same manner as PERT but considers the possibility of adding resources to tasks (called crashing) to shorten their duration, thereby expediting the project.

- The resource allocation problem is concerned with determining the best trade-offs between available resources, including time, throughout the duration of a project.

- Resource loading is the process of calculating the total load from project tasks on each resource for each time period of the project's duration.

- Resource leveling is concerned with evening out the demand for various resources required in a project by shifting tasks within their slack allowances. The aid of a computer is mandatory for realistic projects.

- There are two basic approaches to addressing the constrained resources allocation problem:

  Heuristic methods are realistic approaches that may identify feasible solutions to the problem. They essentially use simple priority rules, such as shortest task first, to determine which task should receive resources and which task must wait.

  Optimizing methods, such as linear programming, find the best allocation of resources to tasks but are limited in the size of problems they can efficiently solve.

- For multiproject scheduling, three important measures of effectiveness are schedule slippage, resource utilization, and level of in-process inventory.

- When a new project is added to a multiproject system, the amount of slippage is directly related to the average resource load.

- Mathematical programming models for multiproject scheduling aim either to minimize total throughput time for all projects, minimize the completion time for all projects, or minimize the total lateness (or lateness penalty) for all projects. These models are limited to small problems. There are a number of heuristic methods, such as the resource scheduling method, available for the multiproject scheduling problem.

In the next chapter we move to the ongoing implementation of the project and consider the project information systems used for monitoring progress, costs, performance, and so on. The chapter also describes some available computer packages for this function.

# ▶ GLOSSARY

Cost/Time Slope—The ratio of the increased cost for expediting to the decreased amount of time for the activity.

Followers—The tasks that logically follow a particular task in time.

Heuristic—A formal process for solving a problem, like a rule of thumb, that results in an acceptable solution.

Mathematical Programming—A general term for certain mathematical approaches to solving constrained optimization problems, including linear programming, integer programming, and so on.

Predecessors—The tasks that logically precede a particular task in time.

Priority Rules—Formal methods, such as ratios, that rank items to determine which one should be next.

Resource Leveling—Approaches to even out the peaks and valleys of resource requirements so that a fixed amount of resources can be employed over time.

Resource Loading—The amount of resources of each kind that are to be devoted to a specific activity in a certain time period.

Successors—See followers.

Tree Search—The evaluation of a number of alternatives that logically branch from each other like a tree with limbs.

# ▶ MATERIAL REVIEW QUESTIONS

1. Identify several resources that may need to be considered when scheduling projects.
2. What is resource loading? How does it differ from resource leveling?
3. What is an activity slope and what does it indicate?
4. Name four priority rules. What priority rule is best overall? How would a firm decide which priority rule to use?
5. Name three efficiency criteria that might be considered when choosing a multiproject scheduling system.

6. What is the average resource load factor? How is it used to determine project completion times?
7. What are two methods for addressing the constrained resources allocation problem?
8. What are three measures of effectiveness for multiproject scheduling?
9. What is a "system constrained" task?
10. How does the resource scheduling method heuristic work?

# ▶ CLASS DISCUSSION QUESTIONS

1. Why are large fluctuations in the demands for particular resources undesirable? What are the costs of resource leveling? How would a PM determine the "best" amount of leveling?
2. When might a firm choose to crash a project? What factors must be considered in making this decision?
3. Why is the impact of scheduling and resource allocation more significant in multiproject organizations?

4. How much should a manager know about a scheduling or resource allocation computer program to be able to use the output intelligently?
5. With the significantly increased power of today's computers, do you think the mathematical programming optimization approaches will become more popular?
6. What are some of the limitations of CPM?
7. Why is leveling of resources needed?

**8.** What are some implications of resource allocation when an organization is involved in several projects at once?

**9.** What are some of the indirect costs of crashing?

**10.** How might CPM be used for strategic planning purposes?

# ▶ PROBLEMS

**1.** Given the following network, determine the first activity to be crashed by the following priority rules:
(a) Shortest task first
(b) Minimum slack first
(c) Most critical followers
(d) Most successors.

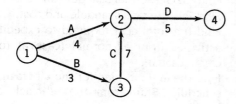

**2.** Using the network above and the additional information below, find:

(a) The crash cost per day
(b) Which activities should be crashed to meet a project deadline of 13 days at minimum cost.

| Activity | Crash Time | Normal Cost | Crashed Cost (total) | Normal Time (days) |
|---|---|---|---|---|
| A | 3 | $300 | $500 | 4 |
| B | 1 | 250 | 325 | 3 |
| C | 4 | 400 | 550 | 7 |
| D | 3 | 150 | 250 | 5 |

**3.** Consider the following network:

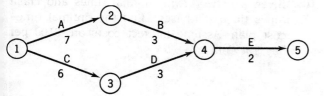

(a) Construct a schedule showing
ESTs for all activities
LSTs for all activities
EOTs for all events
LOTs for all events
Slacks for all activities and events
Critical path
(b) Given the following:

| Activity | Crash Time | Normal Cost | Crashed Cost (total) | Normal Time (days) |
|---|---|---|---|---|
| A | 4 | $500 | $ 800 | 7 |
| B | 2 | 200 | 350 | 3 |
| C | 4 | 500 | 900 | 6 |
| D | 1 | 200 | 500 | 3 |
| E | 1 | 300 | 550 | 2 |
| | | | $3100 | |

1. Find the crash cost per day.
2. Which activities should be crashed to meet a project deadline of 10 days with a minimum cost?
3. Fine the new cost.

**4.** Given the following:

| Activity | Immediate Predecessor | Activity Time (months) |
|---|---|---|
| A | —— | 4 |
| B | —— | 6 |
| C | A | 2 |
| D | B | 6 |
| E | C,B | 3 |
| F | C,B | 3 |
| G | D,E | 5 |

(a) Draw the network.
(b) Find the ESTs, LSTs, EOTs, LOTs, and Slacks.

(c) Find the critical path.

(d) If the project has a 1 1/2 year deadline, should we consider crashing some activities? Explain.

5. Given the following network with resource demands, construct a modified PERT chart with resources and a resource load diagram. Suggest how to level the load if you can split operations. The project is due at day 36.

Code: $\dfrac{\text{activity, time}}{\text{resource units}}$

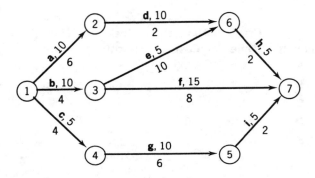

6. Reconsider Problem 14 in Chapter 8 under the constraint that the problem *must* be completed in 16 weeks. This time, however, activities **c, f, h**, and **i** may be crashed as follows.

| Activity | Crash Time (weeks) | Additional Cost per Week |
|---|---|---|
| c | 7 | $40 |
| f | 6 | 20 |
| h | 2 | 10 |
| i | 3 | 30 |

Find the best schedule and its cost.

7. The following data were obtained from a study of the times required to overhaul a chemical plant:

| | Crash Schedule | | Normal Schedule | |
|---|---|---|---|---|
| Activity | Time | Cost | Time | Cost |
| 1–2 | 3 | $6 | 5 | $4 |
| 1–3 | 1 | 5 | 5 | 3 |
| 2–4 | 5 | 7 | 10 | 4 |
| 3–4 | 2 | 6 | 7 | 4 |
| 2–6 | 2 | 5 | 6 | 3 |
| 4–6 | 5 | 9 | 11 | 6 |
| 4–5 | 4 | 6 | 6 | 3 |
| 6–7 | 1 | 4 | 5 | 2 |
| 5–7 | 1 | 5 | 4 | 2 |

*Note:* Costs are given in thousands of dollars, time in weeks.

(a) Find the all-normal schedule and cost.

(b) Find the all-crash schedule and cost.

(c) Find the total cost required to expedite all activities from all-normal (case a) to all-crash (case b).

(d) Find the *least-cost* plan for the all-crash time schedule. Start from the all-crash problem (b).

8. Given the data in Problem 7, determine the first activities to be crashed by the following priority rules:

(a) Shortest task first.

(b) Most resources first (use normal cost as the basis).

(c) Minimum slack first.

(d) Most critical followers.

(e) Most successors.

9. Consider Problem 10 in Chapter 8 again. Suppose the duration of both activities **A** and **D** can be reduced to one day, at a cost of $15 per day of reduction. Also, activities **E, G,** and **H** can be reduced in duration by one day at a cost of $25 per day of reduction. What is the least cost approach to crash the project two days? What is the shortest "crashed" duration, the new critical path, and the cost of crashing?

10. Given a network with normal times and crash times (in parentheses), find the optimal time–cost plan. Assume indirect costs are $100 per day. The data are:

| Activity | Time Reduction Direct Cost per Day |
|----------|-------------------------------------|
| 1–2 | $30 first, $50 second |
| 2–3 | $80 each |
| 3–4 | $25 first, $60 second |
| 2–4 | $30 first, $70 second, $90 third |

11. The network shown in the table has a fixed cost of $90 per day, but money can be saved by shortening the project duration. Find the least cost schedule.

| Activity | Normal Time | Crash Time | Cost Increase (1st, 2nd, 3rd day) |
|----------|-------------|------------|------------------------------------|
| 1–2 | 7 | 4 | $30, 50, 70 |
| 2–3 | 9 | 6 | 40, 45, 65 |
| 1–3 | 12 | 10 | 60, 60 |
| 2–4 | 11 | 9 | 35, 60 |
| 3–4 | 3 | 3 | — |

# ▶ INCIDENTS FOR DISCUSSION

## Bryce Power Tool Company

George Ertle is the director of engineering for the Bryce Power Tool Company. A decision was made recently to modernize Bryce's entire tool line. The president of Bryce has indicated that he expects the modernization program to result in a significant improvement in design technology. Ertle is concerned with the possibility that his department will not have adequate resources to support the modernization program. Ertle believes he has enough staff to handle the aggregate engineering requirements, but he is not too sure he will be able to supply engineering personnel at the times and quantities requested by the company's project manager.

To complicate matters further, the tool modernization program will be under the control of four different project managers. Each major market segment has been recognized as a separate business unit with the authority to modernize the key tools for that segment based on a schedule that makes sense for it.

Ertle knows a little bit about resource allocation techniques. He remembers that one of the most effective allocation techniques is to work first on the activity with the minimum slack, so he has instructed his staff to approach any tasks they are assigned as members of a project team on that basis.

*Questions*: Is this technique a reasonable way to schedule the engineering resources of Bryce? Why or why not? What complication is added by making this four separate projects?

## Critical Care Hospital

Critical Care Hospital will be purchasing a CATSCAN (computerized axial tomography scanner) in the next six months. The CATSCAN equipment will be installed in the radiology department and will require a significant renovation for the area. The scanner will arrive in about five months, but the construction project cannot be started until the unit is set in place. This will result in a project length of approximately 12 months. The hospital estimates the equipment will generate an income of $25,000 per month and is therefore in a hurry to complete the project. The project manager feels she may be able to cut the time on some aspects of the project, but at an increased cost. She has decided, in an effort to make the best decision, to use a resource allocation version of CPM.

*Questions*: What information must the project manager gather to use this method properly? How should she use this version of CPM to reduce the project time?

# ▶ PROJECT TEAM CONTINUING EXERCISE

The project team now is to address the problem of identifying and allocating resources for the project. First, determine what the resource loads are for each activity and what the resource availabilities are. Also determine whether activities can be speeded up by the allocation of additional resources; that is, the cost/time trade-offs. Conduct a CPM analysis to see where crashing may be desirable to meet an expedited completion and derive the cost-duration history graph. (If some activities have already been completed, conduct the analysis in retrospect.)

Next, plot the multiple resource needs for the project on a Gantt chart and evaluate their loadings. Use various heuristics and priority rules to level the loads and evaluate the time–resource trade-offs. Are there "natural" points of high efficiency or resource usage? What heuristics and priority rules seem to work best? Might any of the programming or optimizing methods seem applicable for your project? Might the SPAR heuristic be useful for your project? Why or why not?

# ▶ BIBLIOGRAPHY

1. ANDERSON, D. R., D. J. SWEENEY, and T. A. WILLIAMS. *An Introduction to Management Science*, 6th ed. Minneapolis, MN: West Publishing, 1991.

2. ARROW, K. J., and L. HURWICZ. *Studies In Resource Allocation Processes*. Cambridge, GB: Cambridge University Press, 1977.

3. BALAS, E. "Project Scheduling with Resource Constraints." *Applications of Mathematical Programming Techniques*, Pittsburgh: Carnegie-Mellon Univ., 1970.

4. BENSON, L. A., and R. F. SEWALL, "Dynamic Crashing Keeps Projects Moving." *Computer Decisions*, Feb. 1972.

5. BERMAN, E. B. "Resource Allocation in a PERT Network Under Continuous Activity Time–Cost Functions." *Management Science*, July 1964.

6. BILDSON, R. A., and J. R. GILLESPIE. "Critical Path Planning PERT Integration." *Operations Research*, Nov.–Dec. 1962.

7. BUFFA, E. S., and J. G. MILLER. *Production-Inventory Systems: Planning and Control*, 3rd ed. Homewood, IL: Irwin, 1979.

8. CARRUTHERS, J. A., and A. BATTERSBY. "Advances in Critical Path Methods." *Operational Research Quarterly*, Dec. 1966.

9. CHARNES, A., and W. W. COOPER. "A Network Interpretation and a Direct Subdual Algorithm for Critical Path Scheduling." *Journal of Industrial Engineering*, July–Aug. 1962.

10. CLARK, E. "The Optimum Allocation of Resources among the Activities of a Network." *Journal of Industrial Engineering*, Jan.–Feb. 1961.

11. CORWIN, B. D. "Multiple R and D Project Scheduling with Limited Resources." *Technical Memorandum No. 122*, Dept. of Operations Research, Cleveland: Case Western Reserve University, 1968.

12. CROFT, F. M. "Putting a Price Tag on PERT Activities." *Journal of Industrial Engineering*, July 1966.

13. CROWSTON, W., and G. L. THOMPSON. "Decision CPM: A Method for Simultaneous Planning, Scheduling, and Control of Projects." *Operations Research*, May–June 1967.

14. DAVIES, E. M. "An Experimental Investigation of Resource Allocation in Multiactivity Projects." *Operational Research Quarterly*, Dec. 1973.

15. DAVIS, E. W. "Networks: Resource Allocation." *Industrial Engineering*, April 1974.

16. DAVIS, E. W. *Project Management: Techniques, Applications, and Managerial Issues*, 2nd ed. Norcross, GA: Institute of Industrial Engineers, 1983.

17. DAVIS, E. W., and G. E. HEIDORN. "An Algorithm for Optimal Project Scheduling Under Multiple Resource Constraints." *Management Science*, Aug. 1971.

18. DAVIS, E. W., and J. H. PATTERSON. "A Comparison of Heuristic and Optimum Solutions in Resource-Constrained Project Scheduling." *Management Science*, April 1975.

19. FENDLEY, L. G. "Towards the Development of a Complete Multiproject Scheduling System." *Journal of Industrial Engineering*, Oct. 1968.

20. GILYUTIN, I. "Using Project Management in a Nonlinear Environment." *Project Management Journal*, Dec. 1993.

21. GLAUBER, L. W. "Project Planning With Scitor's PS5000." *Project Management Journal*, June 1985.

22. GORENSTEIN, S. "An Algorithm for Project (Job) Sequencing with Resource Constraints." *Operations Research*, July–Aug. 1972.

23. HARRISON, F. L. *Advanced Project Management.* Hants, GB Gower, 1983.

24. HASTINGS, N. A. J. "On Resource Allocation in Networks." *Operational Research Quarterly*, June 1972.

25. JOHNSON, R. V. "Resource Constrained Scheduling Capabilities of Commercial Project Management Software." *Project Management Journal*, Dec. 1992.

26. KELLEY, J. "Critical Path Planning and Scheduling: Mathematical Basis." *Operations Research*, May–June 1961.

27. KRONE, W. T. B., and H. V. PHILLIPS. "SCRAPP, a Reporting and Allocation System for a Multi-Project Situation." *Applications of Critical Path Techniques.* London: English University Press, 1968.

28. KURTULUS, I., and E. W. DAVIS. "Multi-Project Scheduling: Categorization of Heuristic Rules Performance." *Management Science*, Feb. 1982.

29. KURTULUS, I., and S. C. NARULA. "Multi-Project Scheduling: Analysis of Project Performance." *IEEE Transactions on Engineering Management*, March 1985.

30. LAMBERSON, L. R., and R. R. HOCKING. "Optimum Time Compression in Project Scheduling." *Management Science*, June 1970.

31. MARCHBANKS, J. L. "Daily Automatic Rescheduling Technique." *Journal of Industrial Engineering*, March 1966.

32. MILLS, N. L. "The Development of a University Sports Complex: A Project Management Application." *Computers and Industrial Engineering*, 1989.

33. MODER, J. J., C. R. PHILLIPS, and E. W. DAVIS. *Project Management With CPM, PERT and Precedence Diagramming*, 3rd ed. New York: Van Nostrand Reinhold, 1983.

34. MOODIE, C. L., and D. E. MANDEVILLE. "Project Resource Balancing by Assembly Lines Balancing Techniques." *Journal of Industrial Engineering*, July 1965.

35. MOSHMAN, J., J. R. JOHNSON, and M. LARSEN. "RAMPS—A Technique for Resource Allocation and Multiproject Scheduling." *Proceedings*, Spring Joint Computer Conference, 1963.

36. NAVARRE, C., and J. SCHAAN. "Design of Project Management Systems from Top Management's Perspective," *Project Management Journal*, Jun. 1990.

37. NICHOLAS, J. M. *Managing Business & Engineering Projects.* Englewood Cliffs, NJ: Prentice Hall, 1990.

38. PARNCUTT, G. "Concepts of Resource Allocation and Cost Control and Their Utility in Project Management." *Project Management Quarterly*, 1974.

39. PARRIS, T. P. E. "Practical Manpower Allocation of a Project Mix Via Zero-Float CPM Networks." *Project Management Institute Proceedings*, 1972.

40. PASCOE, T. L. "An Experimental Comparison of Heuristic Methods for Allocating Resources." Ph.D. Dissertation, Department of Engineering, Cambridge, GB: Cambridge University Press, 1965.

41. PATTERSON, J. H. "Alternate Methods of Project Scheduling with Limited Resources." *Naval Research Logistics Quarterly*, Dec. 1973.

42. PATTERSON, J. H., and W. D. HUBER. "A Horizon-Varying, Zero-One Approach to Project Scheduling." *Management Science*, Feb. 1974.

43. PRITSKER, A. A. B., L. J. WALTERS, and P. M. WOLFE. "Multi-Project Scheduling with Limited Resources: A Zero-One Programming Approach." *Management Science*, Sept. 1969.

44. ROBINSON, D. R. "A Dynamic Programming Solution to Cost-Time Trade-off for CPM." *Management Science*, Oct. 1975.

45. SAKAREV, I., and M. DEMIROV. *Solving Multi-Project Planning by Network Analysis.* Amsterdam: North-Holland, 1969.

46. SCHRAGE, L. "Solving Resource-Constrained Network Problems by Implicit Enumeration—Non-Preemptive Case." *Operations Research*, 1970.

47. SHIH, W. "A New Application of Incremental Analysis in Resource Allocations." *Operational Research Quarterly*, Dec. 1974.

48. SHIH, W. "A Branch and Bound Procedure for a Class of Discrete Resource Allocation Problems with Several Constraints." *Operational Research Quarterly*, June 1977.

49. STINSON, J. P. "A Branch and Bound Algorithm for a General Class of Resource Constrained Scheduling Problems." AIIE *Conference Proceedings*, Las Vegas, 1975.

50. STINSON, J. P., E. W. DAVIS, and B. KHUMAWALA. "Multiple Resource-Constrained Scheduling Using Branch and Bound." AIIE *Transactions*, Sept. 1978.

51. SUNAGE, T. "A Method of the Optimal Scheduling for a Project with Resource Restrictions." *Journal of the Operations Research Society of Japan*, March 1970.

52. TALBOT, F. B. "Project Scheduling with Resource-Duration Interactions: The Nonpreemptive Case." Working paper No. 200, Graduate School of Business Administration, Ann Arbor, MI: University of Michigan, Jan. 1980.

53. TALBOT, F. B., and J. H. PATTERSON. "Optimal Methods for Scheduling Under Resource Constraints." *Project Management Quarterly*, Dec. 1979.

54. TONGE, F. M. A *Heuristic Program for Assembly Line Balancing.* Englewood Cliffs, NJ: Prentice Hall, 1961.

55. TURBAN, E., and J. R. MEREDITH. *Fundamentals of Management Science*, 6th ed. Homewood, IL: Irwin, 1994.

56. WALTON, H. "Administration Aspects of Network Analysis." *Applications of Critical Path Techniques.* London: English Universities Press, 1968.

57. WEAVER, J. "Mainframe ARTEMIS: More Than a Project Management Tool." *Project Management Journal*, April 1988.

58. WHITEHOUSE, G. E., and J. R. BROWN. "GENRES: An Extension of Brook's Algorithm for Project Scheduling with Resource Constraints." *Computers and Industrial Engineering*, No. 3, 1979.

59. WEIST, J. D. "A Heuristic Model for Scheduling Large Projects with Limited Resources." *Management Science*, Feb. 1967.

60. WEIST, J. D. "Heuristic Programs for Decision Making." *Harvard Business Review*, Sept.–Oct. 1965.

61. WOODWORTH, B. M., and C. T. WILLIE. "A Heuristic Algorithm for Resource Levelling in Multi-Project, Multi-Resource Scheduling." *Decision Sciences*, 1975.

# CASE

## D. U. SINGER HOSPITAL PRODUCTS CORP.
### Herbert F. Spirer

D. U. Singer Hospital Products Corp. has done sufficient new product development at the research and development level to estimate a high likelihood of technical success for a product of assured commercial success: A long-term antiseptic. Management has instructed Singer's Antiseptic Division to make a market entry at the earliest possible time; they have requested a complete plan up to the startup of production. Marketing and other plans following startup of production are to be prepared separately after this plan has been completed.

Project responsibility is assigned to the division's Research and Development Group; Mike Richards, the project scientist who developed the product, is assigned responsibility for project management. Assistance will be required from other parts of the company: Packaging Task Force, R & D Group; Corporate Engineering; Corporate Purchasing; Hospital Products Manufacturing Group; Packaged Products Manufacturing Group.

Mike was concerned about the scope of the project. He knew from his own experience that a final formula had yet to be developed, although such development was really a "routine" function. The remaining questions had to do with color, odor, and consistency additives rather than any performance-related modification. Fortunately, the major regulatory issues had been resolved and he believed that submission of regulatory documentation would be followed by rapid approval as they already had a letter of approval contingent on final documentation.

But there were also issues in packaging that had to be resolved; development of the packaging design was one of his primary concerns at this time. Ultimately, there will have to be manufacturing procedures in accordance with corporate policies and standards: capital equipment selection and procurement, installation of this equipment and startup.

Mike was concerned about defining the project unambiguously. To that end, he obtained an interview with S. L. Mander, the group vice-president.

When he asked Mander where his responsibility should end, the executive turned the question back to him. Mike had been prepared for this and said that he would like to regard his part of the project as done when the production process could be turned over to manufacturing. They agreed that according to Singer practice, this would be when the manufacturing operation could produce a 95 percent yield of product (fully packaged) at a level of 80 percent of the full production goal of 10 million liters per year.

"But I want you to remember," said Mander, "that you must meet all current FDA, EPA, and OSHA regulations and you must be in compliance with our internal specification—the one I've got is dated September and is RD78/965. And you know that manufacturing now—quite rightly, I feel—insists on full written manufacturing procedures."

After this discussion, Mike felt that he had enough information about this aspect to start to pin down what had to be done to achieve these results. His first step in this effort was to meet with P. H. Docent, the director of research.

"You are naive if you think that you can just start right in finalizing the formula," said Docent. "You must first develop a product rationale (a).* This is a formally defined process according to company policy. Marketing expects inputs at this stage, manufacturing expects their voice to be heard, and you will have to have approvals from every unit of the company that is involved; all of this is reviewed by the Executive Committee. You should have no trouble if you do your homework, but expect to spend a good eight weeks to get this done."

"That certainly stretches things out," said Mike. "I expected to take 12 weeks to develop the ingredient formula (b) and you know that I can't start to establish product specifications (c) until the formula is complete. That's another three weeks."

"Yes, but while you are working on the product specifications you can get going on the regulatory documentation (d). Full internal specifications are not required for that work, but you can't start those documents until the formula is complete."

"Yes, and I find it hard to believe that we can push through both preparation of documents *and* get-

ting approval in three weeks, but Environmental swears it can be done."

"Oh, it can be done in this case because of the preparatory work. Of course, I won't say that this estimate of three weeks is as certain as our other time estimates. All we need is a change of staff at the Agency and we are in trouble. But once you have both the specifications and the approval, you can immediately start on developing the processing system (g)."

"Yes, and how I wish we could get a lead on that, but the designers say that there is too much uncertainty and they won't move until they have both specifications and regulatory documentation and approval. They are offering pretty fast response; six weeks from start to finish for the processing system."

"They are a good crew, Mike. And of course, you know that you don't have to delay on starting the packaging segment of this project. You can start developing the packaging concept (e) just as soon as the product rationale has been developed. If my experience is any judge, it will take a full eight weeks; you'll have to work to keep the process from running forever."

"But as soon as that is finished we can start on the design of the package and its materials (f) which usually takes about six weeks. Once that is done we can start on the packaging system (h) which shouldn't take longer than eight weeks," concluded Mike. At this point he realized that although Docent would have general knowledge, he needed to talk directly to the Director of Manufacturing.

"The first step, which follows the completion of the development of processing and packaging systems," said the Director of Manufacturing, "is to do a complete study of the facilities requirements (i). You won't be able to get that done in less than four weeks. And that must precede the preparation of the capital equipment list (j) which should take about three-quarters as long. Of course, as soon as both the process system and packaging system are completed, you could start on preparing the written manufacturing procedures (q)."

"But," said Mike, "Can I really finish the procedures before I have installed and constructed the facilities (p)?"

"No, quite right. What you can do is get the first phase done, but the last three of the ten weeks it will take to do that will have to wait for the installation and construction."

"Then this means that I really have two phases for the writing, that which can be completed without the

---

*Tasks which must be accounted for in a network plan are identified by lower-case alphabetic symbols in parentheses. Refer to Exhibit 1.

| Activity | Packaging Task Force | R & D Group | Corp. Eng. | H-P Manuf. | Pack. Prod. Manuf. | Maint. | Purchasing | Material & Other Direct Charges |
|---|---|---|---|---|---|---|---|---|
| a—prod. rationale | 1 | 12 | 1 | 1 | 2 | 0 | 0 | $ 0 |
| b—dev. formula | 0 | 16 | 4 | 2 | 0 | 0 | 0 | 500 |
| c—prod. spec. | 1 | 6 | 3 | 1 | 1 | 0 | 1 | 0 |
| d—reg. document | 0 | 12 | 4 | 2 | 0 | 0 | 0 | 0 |
| e—dev. pkg. conc. | 12 | 8 | 4 | 2 | 8 | 0 | 2 | 4000 |
| f—design pkg. | 12 | 2 | 3 | 0 | 3 | 0 | 3 | 2000 |
| g—dev. proc. sys. | 0 | 18 | 12 | 12 | 0 | 0 | 0 | 0 |
| h—dev. pkg. sys. | 24 | 8 | 8 | 0 | 8 | 0 | 2 | 0 |
| i—study fac. req. | 0 | 4 | 16 | 2 | 2 | 0 | 0 | 0 |
| j—cap. equip. list | 0 | 1 | 3 | 0 | 0 | 0 | 0 | 0 |
| k—procure proc. eqpt. | 0 | 1 | 1 | 1 | 0 | 0 | 7 | 40,000 |
| l—procure pkg. eqpt. | 1 | 0 | 1 | 0 | 1 | 0 | 9 | 160,000 |
| m—procure t. il. | 0 | 0 | 1 | 1 | 1 | 1 | 6 | 30,000 |
| n—install proc. eqpt. | 0 | 2 | 4 | 8 | 0 | 4 | 1 | 4000 |
| o—install pkg. eqpt. | 2 | 0 | 4 | 0 | 8 | 4 | 1 | 8000 |
| p—install fac. | 0 | 0 | 5 | 5 | 5 | 10 | 1 | 6000 |
| q,q'—written procedures | 5 | 5 | 5 | 10 | 15 | 10 | 0 | 5000 |
| r—pilot test | 3 | 6 | 6 | 6 | 6 | 6 | 0 | 0 |

**Exhibit 1:** Labor Requirements (Worker-weeks)

installation and construction (q), and that which has to wait for those inputs (q´)."

"True. Now you realize that the last thing you have to do is to run the equipment in a pilot test (r) which will show that you have reached a satisfactory level?"

"Yes. Since that must include debugging, I've estimated a six-week period as adequate." The director of manufacturing assented. Mike continued, "What I'm not sure of is whether we can run all the installation tasks in parallel."

"You can let the purchase orders and carry out the procurement of process équipment (k), packaging equipment (l), and facilities (m) as soon as the capital equipment list is complete. The installation of each of these types of equipment and facilities can start as soon as the goods are on hand (n,o,p)."

"What do you estimate for the times to do these tasks?" asked Mike. The director of manufacturing estimated 18, 8, and 4 weeks for the purchasing phases for each of the subsystems in that order and four weeks for each of the installations. "Then I can regard my job as done with the delivery of the procedures and when I show my 95 percent yield," said Mike, and the director of manufacturing agreed, but reminded Mike that none of the purchasing cycles could start until the capital equipment list had been prepared and approved (j) which he saw as a three-week task.

The executive committee of D. U. Singer Hospital Products Corporation set a starting date for the project of December 10 and asked Mike to project a completion date with his submission of the plan. The committee's request implied that whatever date Mike came up with was acceptable, but Mike knew that he would be expected to show how to shorten the time to complete the project. However, his task in making the schedule was clear; he had to establish the resource requirements and deal with calendar constraints as best as he could.

To this end, Mike had to get an estimate of resources which he decided to do by making a list of the activities and asking each group involved what was their level of employee input. The results of this survey are shown in Exhibit 1.

For the purposes of overall planning, the accounting department told Mike that he could estimate a cost of $600 per week per employee. This would enable him to provide a cash flow forecast along with his plan, which the chief accountant said would be expected, something that Mike had not realized.

Mike knew that it was customary at D. U. Singer to provide the following as parts of a plan to be submitted to the executive committee:

1.  Statement of Objectives.
2.  Work Breakdown Structure.
3.  A network, either activity-on-node (CPM) or event-on-node (PERT).
4.  A determination of the critical path or paths and the duration along the critical path.
5.  An Early-Start Schedule, in which every activity would be started at its Early Start, regardless of resource constraints.
6.  A period labor requirements graph for:
    a.  Each group.
    b.  Project as a whole.
7.  Cumulative labor requirements plot for:
    a.  Each group.
    b.  Project as a whole.
8.  A schedule based on the best leveling of labor requirements that could be achieved without lengthening project duration by more than 15 percent in calendar days.
9.  A cash flow requirements graph for the project when leveled, assuming that commitments for materials and other direct charges are made at the start of the activity but that arrivals of purchased goods are uniformly distributed through the first two-thirds of the activity.

## ▶ QUESTIONS

1.  Construct the nine elements of the plan identified above.
2.  Analyze the plan for potential problems.
3.  Analyze the plan for opportunities.
4.  Should the executive committee approve the plan? Why or why not?
5.  What alternatives might the executive committee suggest for analysis?

▶ This article compares a number of different PM software packages and describes their differences, particularly as regards resource leveling. The packages are then compared in terms of their ability to optimally schedule 110 projects that have over-scheduled resources.

## ▶ 10.1    THE PLANNING–MONITORING–CONTROLLING CYCLE

Throughout this book we have stressed the need to plan, check on progress, compare progress to the plan, and take corrective action if progress does not match the plan. The key things to be planned, monitored, and controlled are time (schedule), cost (budget), and performance (specifications). These, after all, encompass the fundamental objectives of the project.

There is no doubt that some organizations do not spend sufficient time and effort on planning and controlling projects. It is far easier to focus on doing, especially because it appears to be more effective to "stop all the talk and get on with the work." We could cite firm after firm that incurred great expense (and major losses) because the planning process was inadequate for the tasks undertaken.

- A major construction project ran over budget by 63 percent and over schedule by 48 percent because the PM decided that, since "he had managed similar projects several times before, he knew what to do without going into all that detail that no one looks at anyway."

- A large industrial equipment supplier "took a bath" on a project designed to develop a new area of business because they applied the same planning and control procedures to the new area that they had used (successfully) on previous, smaller, less complex jobs.

- A computer store won a competitive bid to supply a computer, five terminals, and associated software to the Kansas City office of a national firm. Admittedly insufficient planning made the installation significantly late. Performance of the software was not close to specified levels. This botched job prevented the firm from being invited to bid on more than 20 similar installations planned by the client.

The planning (budgeting and scheduling) methods we propose "put the hassles up front." They require a significantly greater investment of time and energy early in the life of the project, but they significantly reduce the extent and cost of poor performance and time/cost overruns. Note that this is no guarantee of a trouble-free project, merely an improvement in the risk of failure.

It is useful to perceive the control process as a *closed loop* system, with revised plans and schedules (if warranted) following corrective actions. We delay a detailed discussion on control until the next chapter, but the planning—monitoring—controlling cycle is continuously in process until the project is completed. The information flows for such a cycle are illustrated in Figure 10-1. Note the direction of the flows, information flowing from the bottom toward the top and authority flowing from the top down.

It is also useful to construct this process as an internal part of the organizational structure of the project, not something external to and imposed on it or, worse, in conflict with it. Finally, experience tells us that it is also desirable, though not mandatory, that the planning–monitoring–controlling cycle be the normal way of life in the parent organization. What is good for the project is equally good for the parent firm. In any case, unless the PM has a smoothly operating monitoring/control system, it will be difficult to manage the project effectively.

## Designing the Monitoring System

The first step in setting up any monitoring system is to identify the key factors to be controlled. Clearly, the PM wants to monitor performance, cost, and time but must

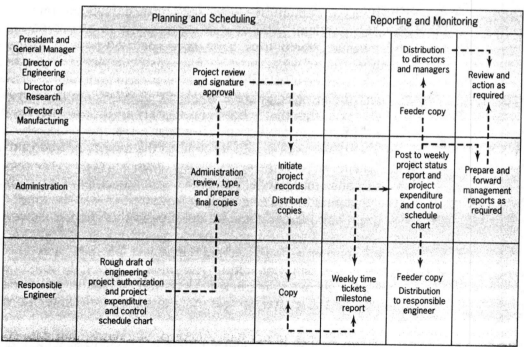

**Figure 10-1:** Project authorization and expenditure control system information flow.
*Source:* [12]

define precisely which specific characteristics of performance, cost, and time should be controlled and then establish exact boundaries within which control should be maintained. There may also be other factors of importance worth noting, at least at milestones or review points in the life of the project. For example, the number of labor hours used, the number or extent of engineering changes, the level of customer satisfaction, and similar items may be worthy of note on individual projects.

But the best source of items to be monitored is the project action plan–actually, the set of action plans that describe what is being done, when, and the planned level of resource usage for each task, work package, and work unit in the project. The monitoring system is a direct connection between planning and control. If it does not collect and report information on some significant element of the plan, control can be faulty or missing. The action plan furnishes the key items that must be measured and reported to the control system, but it is not sufficient. For example, the PM might want to know about changes in the client's attitudes toward the project. Information on the morale of the project team might be useful in preparing for organizational or personnel changes on the project. These two latter items may be quite important, but are not reflected in the project's action plans.

Unfortunately, it is common to focus monitoring activities on data that are easily gathered—rather than important—or to concentrate on "objective" measures that are easily defended at the expense of softer, more subjective data that may be more valuable for control. Above all, monitoring should concentrate primarily on measuring various facets of output rather than intensity of activity. It is crucial to remember that effective PMs are not primarily interested in how hard their project teams work. They are interested in achieving results.

The measurement of project performance usually poses the most difficult data gathering problem. There is a strong tendency to let project inputs serve as surrogate measures for output. If we have spent 50 percent of the budget (or of the scheduled time), we assume we have also completed 50 percent of the project or reached 50 percent of our performance goal. In general, this assumption is in error. Further, one must be aware of the fact that it is common to specify performance to a level of precision that is both unnecessary and unrealistic. For example, a communications software project specified that a telephone "information" system had to locate a phone number and respond to the querier in 5 seconds or less. Is 5.1 seconds a failure? Does the specification mean 5 seconds or less every time, or merely that response times should average 5 seconds or less? Is the specification satisfied if the response time is 5 seconds or less 90 percent of the time?

The monitoring systems we describe in this chapter, however, focus mainly on time and cost as measures of performance, not specifications. While we are most certainly concerned with keeping the project "on spec," and do consider some of the problems of monitoring output, the subject is not fully developed here because the software designed to monitor projects is not constructed to deal with the subject adequately. The matter will get more attention in Chapter 12 when auditing is discussed.

Given all this, performance criteria, standards, and data collection procedures must be established for each of the factors to be measured. The criteria and data collection procedures are usually set up for the life of the project. The standards themselves, however, may not be constant over the project's life. They may change as a result of altered capabilities within the parent organization or a technological breakthrough made by the project team; but, perhaps more often than not, standards and criteria change because of factors that are not under the control of the PM.

For example, they may be changed by the client. One client who had ordered a special piece of audio equipment altered performance specifications significantly when electronic parts became available that could filter out random noises.

Standards may also be changed by the community as a response to some shift in public policy—witness the changes in the performance standards imposed on nuclear power installations or automotive exhaust systems. Shifts in the prime rate of interest or in unemployment levels often alter the standards that the PM must use for making project related decisions. The monitoring process is based on the criteria and standards because they dictate, or at least constrain, the set of relevant measures.

Next, the information to be collected must be identified. This may consist of accounting data, operating data, engineering test data, customer reactions, specification changes, and the like. The fundamental problem is to determine precisely which of all the available data should be collected. It is worth repeating that the typical determinant for collecting data too often seems to be simply the ease with which they can be gathered. Of course the nature of the required data is dictated by the project plan, as well as by the goals of the parent organization, the needs of the client, and by the fact that it is desirable to improve the process of managing projects.

Perhaps the most common error made when monitoring data is to gather information that is clearly related to project performance but has little or no probability of changing significantly from one collection period to the next. Prior to its breakup, the American Telephone and Telegraph Company used to collect monthly statistics on a very large number of indicators of operating efficiency. The extent of the collection was such that it filled a telephone-book-sized volume known as "Ma Bell's Green Book." For a great many of the indicators, the likelihood of a significant change from one month to the next was extremely small. When asked about the matter, one official remarked that the mere collection of the data kept the operating companies "on their toes." We feel that there are other, more positive and less expensive ways of motivating project personnel. Certainly, "collect everything" is inappropriate as a monitoring policy.

Therefore, the first task is to examine the project plans in order to extract performance, time, and cost goals. These goals should relate in some fashion to each of the different levels of detail; that is, some should relate to the project, some to its tasks, some to the work packages, and so on. Data must be identified that measure achievement against these goals, and mechanisms designed that gather and store such data.

Similarly, the process of developing and managing projects should be considered and steps taken to ensure that information relevant to the diagnosis and treatment of the project's organizational infirmities and procedural problems are gathered and collected. A reading of the fascinating book *The Soul of a New Machine* [24] reveals the crucial roles organizational factors, interpersonal relationships, and managerial style play in determining project success.

## How to Collect Data

Given that we know *what type* of data we want to collect, the next question is *how* to collect this information. At this point in the construction of a monitoring system, it is necessary to define precisely what pieces of information should be gathered and *when*. In most cases, the PM has options. Questions arise. Should cost data be gathered before or after some specific event? Is it always mandatory to collect time and cost information at exactly the same point in the process? What do we do if a specific item is difficult to collect because the data source (human) fears reporting any information that might contribute to a negative performance evaluation? What do we do about the fact that some use of time is reported as "hours charged" to our project, and we are quite aware that our project has been charged for work done on another project (but for the same customer) that is over budget? Are special forms needed for data collection? Should we set up quality control procedures to ensure the integrity of data transference from its source to the project information system? Such questions merely indicate the broad range of knotty issues that must be handled.

A large proportion of all data collected take one of the following forms, each of which is suitable for some types of measures.

1. ***Frequency counts*** A simple tally of the occurrence of an event. This type of measure is often used for "complaints," "number of times a project report is late," "days without an accident," "bugs in a computer program," and similar items. The data are usually easy to collect and are often reported as events per unit time or events as a percent of a standard number.

2. ***Raw numbers*** Dates, dollars, hours, physical amounts of resources used, and specifications are usually reported in this way. These numbers are reported in a wide variety of ways, but often as direct comparisons with an expected or standard number. Also, "variances" are commonly reported either as the difference between actual and standard or as the ratio of actual to standard. Differences or ratios can also be plotted as a time series to show changes in system performance.

3. ***Subjective numeric ratings*** These numbers are subjective estimates, usually of a quality, made by knowledgeable individuals or groups. They can be reported in most of the same ways that objective raw numbers are, but care should be taken to make sure that the numbers are not manipulated in ways only suitable for quantitative measures. (See Chapter 2 for comments on measurements.) Ordinal rankings of performance are included in this category.

4. ***Indicators*** When the PM cannot measure some aspect of system performance directly, it may be possible to find an indirect measure or indicator. The speed with which change orders are processed and changes are incorporated into the project is often a good measure of team efficiency. Response to change may also be an indicator of the quality of communications on the project team.

When using indicators to measure performance, the PM must make sure that the link between the indicator and the desired performance measure is as direct as possible.

5.  ***Verbal measures***   Measures for such performance characteristics as "quality of team member cooperation," "morale of team members," or "quality of interaction with the client" frequently take the form of verbal characterizations. As long as the set of characterizations is limited and the meanings of the individual terms consistently understood by all, these data serve their purposes reasonably well.

---

## *Drug Counseling Program*

A social service agency applied for and received funding for a special project to counsel male drug addicts between 18 and 24 years of age, and to secure full-time employment for each client (or part-time employment for clients who were still in school). To qualify for the program, the addicts must have been arrested for a crime, but not be classed as "repeat offenders." Further, the addict must be living with at least one member of his family who is a parent or guardian. Among other conditions placed on the grant, the agency was asked to develop a measure of effectiveness for the counseling program that was acceptable to the funding agency.

The primary measure of effectiveness adopted by most drug programs was "rate of recidivism." A recidivistic incident is defined as any rearrest for a drug-related crime, or any behavior that resulted in the individual reentering the social service system after completing the program and being discharged.

While a "rearrest" is most surely recidivistic, there were several cases in which former clients contacted the agency and asked to be readmitted to the program. These voluntary readmissions resulted when a former client either began to use drugs again or was fearful that he would begin again. It seemed to the agency professionals that voluntary readmissions were successes, not failures.

A new measure of effectiveness was developed to replace "rate of recidivism." It was composed of scores on three different measures, combined with equal weighting.

1.  Number of successive weeks of "clean urines."
2.  Number of successive months of satisfactory employment (or schooling) experience.
3.  Number of successive months of satisfactory behavior at home.

Scores on the second and third measures were based on interviews with employers, teachers, and parent(s).

---

After data collection has been completed, reports on project progress should be generated. These include project status reports, time/cost reports, and variance reports, among others. Causes and effects should be identified and trends noted. Plans, charts, and tables should be updated on a timely basis. Where known, "com-

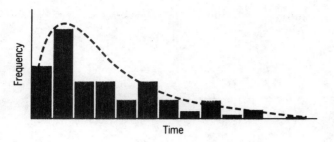

**Figure** 10-2: Number of bugs found during test of Datamix program.

parables" should be reported, as should statistical distributions of previous data if available. Both help the PM (and others) to interpret the data being monitored. Figures 10-2 and 10-3 illustrate the use of such data. Figure 10-2 shows the results of a count of "bugs" found during a series of tests run on a new piece of computer software. (Bugs found were fixed prior to subsequent tests.) Figure 10-3 shows the percent of the time a computer program retrieved data within a specified time limit. Each point represents a series of trials.

The PM can fit a statistical function to the data shown in Figure 10-2 and make a rough estimate of the number of tests that will have to be run to find some predetermined number of additional bugs in the program. By fitting a curve (formally or "by eyeball") to the data in Figure 10-3, the PM can estimate the cost and time (the number of additional trials and adjustments) required to get system performance up to the specified level.

The nature of *timeliness* will be amplified below, but it is important that the PM make sure that the PERT/CPM and Gantt charts in the project war room (office) are frequently updated. Monitoring can serve to maintain high morale on the project team as well as to alert team members to problems that will have to be solved.

The purpose of the monitoring system is to gather and report data. The purpose of the control system is to act on the data. To aid the *project controller*, it is helpful for the *monitor* to carry out some data analysis. Significant differences from plan should be highlighted or "flagged" so that they cannot be overlooked by the controller. The methods of statistical quality control are very useful for determining what size variances are "significant" and sometimes even help in determining the probable cause(s) of variances. Where causation is known, it should be noted. Where it is not

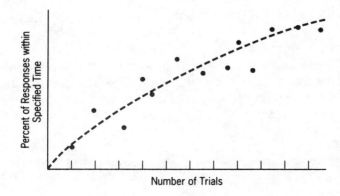

**Figure** 10-3: Percent of specified performance met during repeated trials.

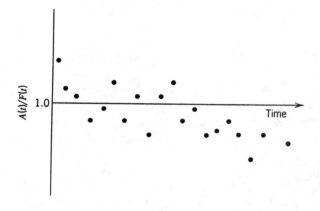

**Figure 10-4:** Ratio of actual material cost to estimated material cost, Emanon Aircraft Company.

known, an investigation may be in order. The decisions about when an investigation should be conducted, by whom, and by what methods are the prerogative of the project controller, although the actual investigation may be conducted by the group responsible for monitoring.

The Emanon Aircraft Company example presented in Chapter 7 is a case in point. While the study team collected and analyzed a great deal of cost information during the process of finding the problem, the method used for the analysis was actually quite simple. The team compared forecast or estimated cost, $F(t)$, with actual cost, $A(t)$, for each batch of output from the manufacturing system. This analysis was done for each cost center. The ratio of actual cost to estimated cost was calculated and plotted as a time series, as in Figure 10-4.* Note that $A(t)/F(t) < 1$ when the cost forecast for a cost center is greater than actual. In this case, the cost involved was "material cost." Though careful statistical analysis was not necessary in this specific case, the application of standard quality control techniques has wide application to project management (see any book on statistical quality control, [13] for example). Time series analysis can often give the PM an early warning of problems.

At base, this provides a *management by exception* reporting system for the PM. But management by exception has its flaws as well as its strengths. It is essentially an "after-the-fact" approach to control. Variances occur, are investigated, and only then is action taken. The astute PM is far more interested in preventing problems than curing them. Therefore, the monitoring system should develop data streams that indicate variances yet to come. Obviously, such indicators are apt to be statistical in nature, hinting at the likelihood of a future problem rather than predicting it with certainty. An example would be a trend in the data showing a system heading out of control. Interested readers are referred to the "2-5-7 Rule" (see [36], quality chapters). The PM may waste time and effort trying to deal with trouble that will not actually occur. This may be frustrating, but the costs of dealing with some nonproblems is usually minor when compared to the costs of dealing with real problems too late.

---

*Actual data were not used in constructing Figure 10-4, but the figure reflects the consultants' findings.

In creating the monitoring system, some care should be devoted to the issues of honesty and bias. The former is dealt with by setting in place an internal audit. The audit serves the purpose of ensuring that the information gathered is honest. No audit, however, can prevent bias. All data are biased by those who report them, advertently or inadvertently. The controller must understand this fact of life. The first issue is to determine whether or not the possibility of bias in the data matters significantly. If not, nothing need be done. Bias finding and correcting activities are worthwhile only if data with less or no bias are required.

The issue of creating an atmosphere that fosters honesty on a project is widely ignored, but it is of major importance. A set of instructions to the PM on how to do this is not beyond the scope of this book, but if such instructions exist, we do not know of them. We do, however, have some advice to offer. The PM can tolerate almost any kind of behavior except dishonesty. Projects are vulnerable to dishonesty, far more vulnerable than the ongoing operations of the parent organization. Standard operations are characterized by considerable knowledge about expected system performance. When the monitoring system reports information that deviates from expectations, it is visible, noteworthy, and tends to get attention. In the case of many projects, expectations are not so well known. Deviations are not recognized for what they are. The PM is often dependent on team members to call attention to problems. To get this cooperation, the PM must make sure that the bearer of bad news is not punished; nor is the admitter-to-error executed. On the other hand, the hider-of-mistakes may be shot with impunity—and then sent to Siberia.

There is some tendency for project monitoring systems to include an analysis directed at the assignment of blame. This practice has doubtful value. While the managerial dictum "rewards and punishments should be closely associated with performance" has the ring of good common sense, it is actually not good advice. Instead of motivating people to better performance, the practice is more apt to result in lower expectations. If achievement of goals is directly measured and directly rewarded, tremendous pressure will be put on people to understate goals and to generate plans that can be met or exceeded with minimal risk and effort.

# 11

# Project Control

In the previous chapter we described the monitoring and information gathering process that would help the PM to control the project. *Control* is the last element in the implementation cycle of planning–monitoring–controlling. Information is collected about system performance, compared with the desired (or planned) level, and action taken if actual and desired performance differ enough that the *controller* (manager) wishes to decrease the difference. Note that reporting performance, comparing the differences between desired and actual performance levels, and accounting for why such differences exist are all parts of the control process. In essence, control is the *act* of reducing the difference between plan and reality.

As has been emphasized throughout this book, control is focused on three elements of a project—performance, cost, and time. The PM is constantly concerned with these three aspects of the project. Is the project delivering what it promised to deliver or more? Is it making delivery at or below the promised cost? Is it making delivery at or before the promised time? It is strangely easy to lose sight of these fundamental targets, especially in large projects with a wealth of detail and a great number of subprojects. Large projects develop their own momentum and tend to get out of hand, going their own way independent of the wishes of the PM and the intent of the proposal.

Think, for a moment, of a few of the things that can cause a project to require the control of performance, costs, or time.

### Performance

Unexpected technical problems arise.

Insufficient resources are available when needed.

Insurmountable technical difficulties are present.

Quality or reliability problems occur.

Client requires changes in system specifications.

Interfunctional complications arise.

Technological breakthroughs affect the project.

### Cost

Technical difficulties require more resources.

The scope of the work increases.

Initial bids or estimates were too low.

Reporting was poor or untimely.

Budgeting was inadequate.

Corrective control was not exercised in time.

Input price changes occurred.

### Time

Technical difficulties took longer than planned to solve.

Initial time estimates were optimistic.

Task sequencing was incorrect.

Required inputs of material, personnel, or equipment were unavailable when needed.

Necessary preceding tasks were incomplete.

Customer-generated change orders required rework.

Governmental regulations were altered.

And these are only a few of the relatively "mechanistic" problems that can occur. Actually, there are no purely mechanistic problems on projects. All problems have a human element, too. For example, humans, by action or inaction, set in motion a chain of events that leads to a failure to budget adequately, creates a quality problem, leads the project down a technically difficult path, or fails to note a change in government regulations. If, by chance, some of these or other things happen (as a result of human action or not), humans are affected by them. Frustration, pleasure, determination, hopelessness, anger, and many other emotions arise during the course of a project. They affect the work of the individuals who feel them—for better or worse. It is over this welter of confusion, emotion, fallibility, and general cussedness that the PM tries to exert control.

All of these problems, always combinations of the human and mechanistic, call for intervention and control by the project manager. There are infinite "slips 'twixt cup and lip," especially in projects where the technology or the deliverables are new and unfamiliar, and PMs, like most managers, find control is a difficult function to perform. There are several reasons why this is so. One of the main reasons is that PMs, again like most managers, do not discover problems. Managers discover what Russell Ackoff once described as a "mess" [1]. A "mess" is a general condition of a system that, when viewed by a manager, leads to a statement that begins, "%#^@*&±#!" and goes downhill from there. It is the discovery of a mess that leads the PM to the conclusion that there is a problem(s) lurking somewhere around. In systems as complex as projects, the task of defining the problem(s) is formidable, and thus knowing what to control is not a simple task. Another reason control is difficult is because, in spite of an almost universal need to blame some person for any trouble, it is often almost impossible to know if a problem resulted from human error or from the random application of Murphy's Law.

PMs also find it tough to exercise control because the project team, even on large projects, is an "in-group." It is "we," while outsiders are "they." It is usually hard to criticize friends, to subject them to control. Further, many PMs see control as an *ad hoc* process. Each need to exercise control is seen as a unique event, rather than as one instance of an ongoing and recurring process.

Because control of projects is such a mixture of feeling and fact, of human and mechanism, of causation and random chance, we must approach the subject in an extremely orderly way. In this chapter we start by examining the general purposes of control. Then we consider the basic structure of the process of control. We do this by describing control theory in the form of a cybernetic control loop. While most projects offer little opportunity for the actual application of automatic feedback loops, this system provides us with a comprehensive but reasonably simple illustration of all the elements necessary to control any system. From this model, we then turn to the types of control that are most often applied to projects. The design of control systems is discussed as are the impacts that various types of controls tend to have on the humans being controlled. The specific requirement of "balance" in a control system is also covered, as are two special control problems: control of creative activities, and control of change.

## ▶ 11.1 THE FUNDAMENTAL PURPOSES OF CONTROL

The two fundamental objectives of control are:

1. The regulation of results through the alteration of activities.
2. The stewardship of organizational assets.

Most discussions of the control function are focused on regulation. The PM needs to be equally attentive to both regulation and conservation. Because the main body of this chapter (and much of the next) concerns the PM as regulator, let us emphasize the conservationist role here. The PM must guard the physical assets of the organization, its human resources, and its financial resources. The processes for conserving these three different kinds of assets are different.

### Physical Asset Control

Physical asset control requires control of the *use* of physical assets. It is concerned with asset maintenance, whether preventive or corrective. At issue also is the timing of maintenance or replacement as well as the quality of maintenance. Some years ago, a New England brewery purchased the abandoned and obsolete brewing plant of a newly defunct competitor. It put a project manager in charge of this old facility with the instruction that the plant should be completely "worn out" over the next five-year period, but that it should be fully operational in the meantime. This presented an interesting problem: the controlled deterioration of a plant while at the same time maintaining as much of its productive capability as possible. Clearly, both objectives could not be achieved simultaneously, but the PM met the spirit of the project quite well.

If the project uses considerable amounts of physical equipment, the PM also has the problem of setting up maintenance schedules in such a way as to keep the equipment in operating condition while minimizing interference with ongoing work. It is critical to accomplish preventive maintenance prior to the start of that final section of the project life cycle known as the Last Minute Panic (LMP). (Admittedly, the timing of the LMP is not known, which makes the planning of pre-LMP preventive maintenance somewhat difficult.)

Physical inventory, whether equipment or material, must also be controlled. It must be received, inspected (or certified), and possibly stored prior to use. Records of all incoming shipments must be carefully validated so that payment to suppliers can be authorized. The same precautions applied to goods from external suppliers must also be applied to suppliers from inside the organization. Even such details as the project library, project coffee maker, project room furniture, and all the other minor bits and pieces must be counted, maintained, and conserved.

## Human Resource Control

Stewardship of human resources requires controlling and maintaining the growth and development of people. Projects provide particularly fertile ground for cultivating people. Because projects are unique, differing one from another in many ways, it is possible for people working on projects to gain a wide range of experience in a reasonably short time.

Measurement of physical resource conservation is accomplished through the familiar audit procedures. The measurement of human resource conservation is far more difficult. Such devices as employee appraisals, personnel performance indices, and screening methods for appointment, promotion, and retention are not particularly satisfactory devices for ensuring that the conservation function is being properly handled. The accounting profession has worked for some years on the development of *human resource accounting*, and while the effort has produced some interesting ideas, human resource accounting is not well accepted by the accounting profession.

## Financial Resource Control

Though accountants have not succeeded in developing acceptable methods for human resource accounting, their work on techniques for the conservation (and regulation) of financial resources has most certainly resulted in excellent tools for financial control. This is the best developed for the basic areas needing control.

It is difficult to separate the control mechanisms aimed at conservation of financial resources from those focused on regulating resource use. Most financial controls do both. Capital investment controls work to conserve the organization's assets by insisting that certain conditions be met before capital can be expended, and those same conditions usually regulate the use of capital to achieve the organization goal of a high return on investments.

The techniques of financial control, both conservation and regulation, are well known. They include current asset controls, and project budgets as well as capital investment controls. These controls are exercised through a series of analyses and audits conducted by the accounting/controller function for the most part. Representation of this function on the project team is mandatory. The structure of the techniques applied to projects does not differ appreciably from those applied to the general operation of the firm, but the context within which they are applied is quite different. One reason for the differences is that the project is accountable to an outsider—an external client, or another division of the parent firm, or both at the same time.

The importance of proper conformance to both organizational and client control standards in financial practice and recordkeeping cannot be overemphasized. The parent organization, through its agent, the project manager, is responsible for the conservation and proper *use of* resources owned by the client or owned by the parent and charged to the client. Clients will insist on, and the courts will require the practice of, *due diligence* in the exercise of such responsibility. While some clients may not be aware of this responsibility on the part of firms with whom they contract, the government is most certainly aware of it. In essence, due diligence requires that the organization proposing a project conduct a reasonable investigation, verification, and disclosure, in language that is understandable, of every material fact relevant to the firm's ability to conduct the project, and to omit nothing where such omission might ethically mislead the client. It is not possible to define, in some general way, precisely what might be required for any given project. The firm should, however, make sure that it has legal counsel competent to aid it in meeting this responsibility.

One final note on the conservationist role of the controller. The attitude or mind-set of the conservationist is often antithetical to the mind-set of the PM, whose attention is naturally on the use of resources rather than their conservation. The conservationist reminds one of the fabled librarian who is happiest when all the books are ordered neatly on the library shelves. The PM, often the manager and controller at one and the same time, is subject to this conflict and has no choice but to live with it. The warring attitudes must be merged and compromised as best they can.

---

# Project Management in Practice
## *Formalizing the Program Control System at Battelle Laboratories*

In the late 1970s, Battelle's Pacific Northwest Laboratory made the decision to develop the Research Project Management System, including a program control segment, for projects over $100,000. As a part of the management information and support function, the program control specialists are charged with the development, implementation, and

*Source:* R. K. Johnson, "Program Control from the Bottom Up—Exploring the Working Side," *Project Management Journal*, March 1985.

maintenance of program control systems for Battelle-Northwest's research programs. These systems are not the usual monitoring systems used to provide information to top management for decision making but instead are meant for the lower-level project managers, contract administrators, personnel specialists, and others who have a direct impact on project success or failure.

The goal of the program control segment is to ensure a quality product, on schedule, within cost. In some Federal projects, such as with DOD or DOE, the implementation of a full cost/schedule control system criteria (C/SCSC) is required for control purposes, but for many other projects, particularly R&D projects, such control is not required. With a good system in place, chances of cost overruns and missed scheduled milestones are reduced, hence the need for a program control function such as Battelle's.

To date, the payoffs from incorporating this function in their project management system have been high. In the DOE's $178 million Fuels Refabrication and Development Program, Battelle's program control function is credited with achieving a high level of success and an overall performance rating of "excellent." Again, in the Seasonal Thermal Energy Program, another "excellent" performance rating was achieved. Paying attention to the control aspect of project management appears to be paying off.

# ▶ 11.2 THREE TYPES OF CONTROL PROCESSES

The process of controlling a project (or any system) is far more complex than simply waiting for something to go wrong and then, if possible, fixing it. We must decide at what points in the project we will try to exert control, what is to be controlled, how it will be measured, how much deviation from plan will be tolerated before we act, what kinds of interventions should be used, and how to spot and correct deviations before they occur, among a great many other things. In order to keep these and other such issues sorted out, it is helpful to begin a consideration of control with a brief exposition on the theory of control.

No matter what our purpose in controlling a project, there are three basic types of control mechanisms we can use: cybernetic control, go/no-go control, and postcontrol. In this section we will describe these three types and briefly discuss the information requirements of each. Remember that we describe cybernetic control systems in order to clarify the elements that must be present in any control system, as well as the information requirements of control systems.

## Cybernetic Control

Cybernetic, or steering, control is by far the most common type of control system. (*Cyber* is the Greek word for "helmsman.") The key feature of cybernetic control is its automatic operation. Consider the diagrammatic model of a cybernetic control system shown in Figure 11-1.

As Figure 11-1 shows, a system is operating with inputs being subjected to a process that transforms them into outputs. It is this system that we wish to control. In order to do so, we must monitor the system output. This function is performed by a sensor that measures one or more aspects of the output, presumably those aspects one wishes to control. Measurements taken by the sensor are transmitted to

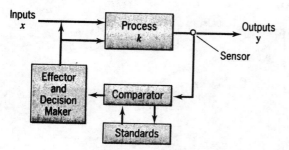

**Figure 11-1:** A cybernetic control system.

the comparator, which compares them with a set of predetermined standards. The difference between actual and standard is sent to the decision maker, which determines whether or not the difference is of sufficient size to deserve correction. If the difference is large enough to warrant action, a signal is sent to the effector, which acts on the process or on the inputs to produce outputs that conform more closely to the standard.

A cybernetic control system that acts to reduce deviations from standard is called a *negative feedback loop*. If the system output moves away from standard in one direction, the control mechanism acts to move it in the opposite direction. The speed or force with which the control operates is, in general, proportional to the size of the deviation from standard. (Mathematical descriptions of the action of negative feedback loops are widely available. See for example [48].) The precise way in which the deviation is corrected depends on the nature of the operating system and the design of the controller. Figure 11-2 illustrates three different response patterns. Response path A is direct and rapid, while path B is more gradual. Path C shows oscillations of decreasing amplitude. An aircraft suddenly deflected from a stable flight path would tend to recover by following pattern C.

**Types of Cybernetic Control Systems**    Cybernetic controls come in three varieties, or *orders*, differing in the sophistication with which standards are set. Figure 11-1 shows a simple *first-order* control system, a goal-seeking device. The standard is set and there is no provision made for altering it except by intervention from the outside. The common thermostat is a time-worn example of a first-order controller. One sets the standard temperature and the heating and air-conditioning systems operate to maintain it.

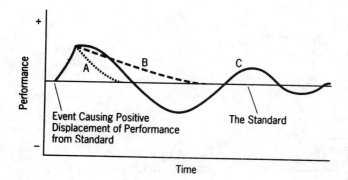

**Figure 11-2:** Typical paths for correction of deviation of performance from standard.

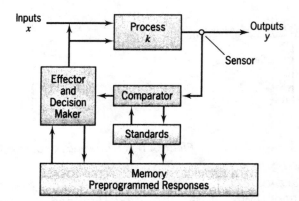

**Figure 11-3:** A second-order feedback system—preprogrammed goal changer.

Figure 11-3 shows a second-order control system. This device can alter the system standards according to some predetermined set of rules or program. The complexity of second-order systems can vary widely. The addition of a clock to the thermostat to allow it to maintain different standards during day and night makes the thermostat a second-order controller. An interactive computer program may alter its responses according to a complex set of preprogrammed rules, but it is still only a second-order system. Many industrial projects involve second-order controllers— for example, robot installations, flexible manufacturing systems, and automated record-keeping or inventory systems.

A *third-order* control system (Fig. 11-4) can change its goals without specific pre-programming. It can reflect on system performance and decide to act in ways that are not contained in its instructions. Third-order systems have reflective consciousness and, thus, must contain humans. Note that a second-order controller can be programmed to recognize patterns, and to react to patterns in specific ways. Such systems are said to "learn." Third-order systems can learn without explicit preprogramming, and therefore can alter their actions on the basis of thought or whim. An advantage of third-order controllers is that they can deal with the unforeseen and unexpected. A disadvantage is that, because they contain human elements, they may lack predictability and reliability. Third-order systems are of great interest to the PM, for reasons we now discuss.

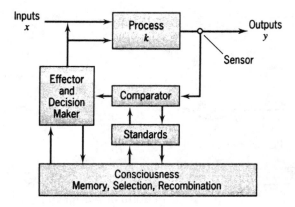

**Figure 11-4:** A third-order feedback system—reflective goal changer.

***Information Requirements for Cybernetic Controllers***   In order to establish total control over a system, the controller must be able to take a counteraction for every action the system can take. This statement is a rough paraphrase of Ashby's Law of Requisite Variety [41]. This implies that the PM/controller is aware of the system's full capabilities. For complex systems, particularly those containing a human element, this is simply not possible. Thus, we need a strategy to aid the PM in developing a control system. One such strategy is to use a cost/benefit approach to control—to control those aspects of the system for which the expected benefits of control are greater than the expected costs. We are reminded of a firm that manufactured saw blades. It set up a project to reduce scrap losses for the high-cost steel from which the blades were made. At the end of the one-year project, the firm had completed the project—cost $9700, savings $4240. (Of course, if the savings were to be repeated for several years, the rate of return on the project would be acceptable. The president of the firm, however, thought that the savings would decline and disappear when the project ended.)

Relatively few elements of a project (as opposed to the elements of a system that operates more or less continuously) are subject to automatic control. An examination of the WBS or the details of an action plan will reveal which of the project's tasks are largely mechanistic and represent continuous types of systems. If such systems exist, and if they operate across a sufficient time period to justify the initial expense of creating an automatic control, then a cybernetic controller is useful.

Given the decisions about what to control, the information requirements of a cybernetic controller are easy to describe, if not to meet. First, the PM must define precisely what characteristics of an output (interim output or final output) are to be controlled. Second, standards must be set for each characteristic. Third, sensors must be built that will measure those characteristics at the desired level of precision. Fourth, measurements must be transformed into a signal that can be compared to a "standard" signal. Fifth, the difference between the two is sent to the decision maker, which detects it, if it is sufficiently large, and sixth, transmits a signal to the effector that causes the operating system to react in a way that will counteract the deviation from standard. If the control system is designed to allow the effector to take one or more of several actions, an additional piece of information is needed. There must be built-in criteria that instruct the effector on which action(s) to take.

Knowledge of cybernetic control is important because all control systems are merely variants, extensions, or nonautomatic modifications of such controls. Because most projects have relatively few mechanistic elements that can be subjected to classic cybernetic controls, this concept of control is best applied to tracking the system and automatically notifying the PM when things threaten to get out of control.

## Go/No-go Controls

Go/no-go controls take the form of testing to see if some specific precondition has been met. This type of control can be used on almost every aspect of a project. For many facets of performance, it is sufficient to know that the predetermined specifications for project output have been met. The same is often true of the cost and time elements of the project plan.

It is, of course, necessary to exercise judgment in the use of go/no-go controls. Certain characteristics of output may be required to fall within precisely determined limits if the output is to be accepted by the client. Other characteristics may be less precisely defined. In regard to time and cost, there may be penalties associated with nonconformance with the approved plans. Penalty clauses that make late delivery costly for the producer are often included in the project contract. At times, early delivery can also carry a penalty (e.g., when a just-in-time supply system is involved). Cost overruns may be shared with the client or borne by the project. Some contracts arrange for the first $X of cost overrun to be shared by client and producer, with any further overrun being the producer's responsibility. The number and type of go/no-go controls on a project is limited only by the imagination and desire of the contracting parties.

The project plan, budget, and schedule are all control documents, so the PM has a predesigned control system complete with prespecified milestones as control checkpoints. Control can be exercised at any level of detail that is supported by detail in the plans, budgets, and schedules. The parts of a new jet engine, for instance, are individually checked for quality conformance. These are go/no-go controls. The part passes or it does not, and every part must pass its own go/no-go test before being used in an engine. Similarly, computer programs are tested for bugs. The program passes its tests or it does not.

While cybernetic controls are automatic and will check the operating systems continuously or as often as designed to do so, go/no-go controls operate only when and if the controller uses them. In many cases, go/no-go controls function periodically, at regular, preset intervals. The intervals are usually determined by clock, calendar, or the operating cycles of some machine system. Such periodicity makes it easy to administer a control system, but it often allows errors to be compounded before they are detected. Things begin to go awry just after a quarterly progress check, for instance, and by the time the next quarterly check is made, some items may be seriously out of control.

Project milestones do not occur at neat, periodic intervals; thus, *controls should be linked to the actual plans and to the occurrence of real events, not simply to the calendar*. This is not to say that periodic reports are inappropriate. All projects should be reviewed by senior management at reasonably frequent intervals. We will discuss such reports shortly, but the PM cannot control the project properly with a periodic reporting system.

The PM must keep abreast of all aspects of the project, directly or through deputies. Competent functional managers understand the importance of *follow-up*, and the project manager's work provides no exception. Control is best exerted while there is still time for corrective action. To this end, the PM should establish an *early warning system* so that potential problems can be exposed and dealt with before they metamorphose into full-fledged disasters. One way to construct such an early warning system is to set up a project forecast data sheet. On this sheet, outputs or progress are forecast by period. Actual output or progress is then checked against the forecast, period by period. Figure 11-5 illustrates such a data sheet.

For an early warning system to work, it must be clear that the messenger who brings bad news will not be shot, and that anyone caught sweeping problems and mistakes under the rug will be. As we have said before, the most important rule for

| | | | | | | | | | | | |
|---|---|---|---|---|---|---|---|---|---|---|---|

DATE

| PROD OR PROG TITLE | | | CUSTOMER | |
|---|---|---|---|---|

| DATE REC'D. | CONTRACT START DATE | SUBMISSION OR COMPLETE DATE | CUST. CONT. OR REQ. NO. | BUYER |
|---|---|---|---|---|

| CUST. - ENG. - DEPT. | T.E.P. NO. | REL. G & A PROJ. NO'S. | G & A CODE |
|---|---|---|---|

| CAPITAL EQUIPMENT | REL. ACCTG. CODE NO. | TOTAL G & A |
|---|---|---|

DESCRIPTION OF PRODUCT OR PROGRAM

REASON FOR INTEREST:

EXPLOITATION PLAN SUMMARY - (ATTACH SHEETS FOR DETAIL AND PROGRESS):

| FORECAST PERIOD | REC. G & A | TOTAL R & D | TOTAL PRODUCT | PLAN R & D | PLAN PRODUCT | PROB. FACT. | VAL. FACT. | FIG. OF MERIT | COMPETITIVE POSITION | | | | | | |
|---|---|---|---|---|---|---|---|---|---|---|---|---|---|---|---|
| | | | | | | | | | 1 | 2 | 3 | 4 | 5 | 6 | 7 |
| 1 | | | | | | | | | | | | | | | |
| 2 | | | | | | | | | | | | | | | |
| 3 | | | | | | | | | | | | | | | |
| 4 | | | | | | | | | | | | | | | |
| 1 | | | | | | | | | | | | | | | |
| 2 | | | | | | | | | | | | | | | |
| 3 | | | | | | | | | | | | | | | |
| 4 | | | | | | | | | | | | | | | |
| 1 | | | | | | | | | | | | | | | |
| 2 | | | | | | | | | | | | | | | |
| 3 | | | | | | | | | | | | | | | |
| 4 | | | | | | | | | | | | | | | |
| 1 | | | | | | | | | | | | | | | |
| 2 | | | | | | | | | | | | | | | |
| 3 | | | | | | | | | | | | | | | |
| 4 | | | | | | | | | | | | | | | |

| TOTAL BEYOND DETAILED FORECAST PERIODS | | | | | | PLAN APPROVAL | DATE | ASSIGNED TO | DATE |
|---|---|---|---|---|---|---|---|---|---|
| | | | | | | PER. | | | |
| | | | | | | SALES | | | |
| | | | | | | ENG. | | | |
| | | | | | | SUMMARY INDEX NO. | | | |

*(SEE REVERSE SIDE FOR DETAIL G & A CODE)*

**Figure 11-5:** Project forecast data sheet.

any subordinate is the Prime Law of Life on a project: Never let the boss be surprised!

Controls have a tendency to terrorize the insecure and to induce high anxiety in everyone else. The result is avoidance, and avoidance is exactly what the PM cannot tolerate. Unless deviation from plan is discovered, it cannot be corrected. Therefore, a spirit of trust between superior and subordinate at all levels of the project is a prime requisite for the effective application of control.

***Information Requirements for Go/No-Go Controls*** Most of the input information needed to operate go/no-go project control has already been referenced directly or implied by the previous discussion. The project proposal, plans, specifications, schedules, and budgets (complete with approved change orders) contain all the information needed to apply go/no-go controls to the project. Milestones are the key events that serve as a focus for ongoing control activity. These milestones are the project's deliverables in the form of in-process output or final output. If the milestones occur on time, on budget, and at the planned level of quality, the PM can take comfort from the fact that things are proceeding properly. Perhaps just as important to the PM, senior management can be equally comfortable with the project—and with the project manager as well.

Except for a few important projects, senior management usually cannot keep up with the day-to-day or week-to-week progress of work; nor should they try. Senior management does, however, need a monthly or quarterly status review for all projects. The project status report contains a list of the important milestones for each project together with the status of each. If many of the projects are similar—such as construction projects or marketing projects, for example—the milestones will be of similar type, and one table can show the status of several projects in spite of the fact that each milestone may not be applicable to each and every project. The Elanco Products Company (the agricultural products division of Eli Lilly and Company, now DowElanco) uses such a report. A generalized version of Elanco's Project Status Report is shown in Figure 11-6. The Gantt chart (see Chapter 8) is also a convenient way to present senior managers with information on project status.

Either of these report forms can be altered to contain almost any additional information that might be requested. For example, the Gantt chart can be annotated with footnotes indicating such matters of interest as the resources required to get a late milestone back on schedule, or a statement of how an activity must be changed if it is to be approved by a regulatory agency. The information requirements for such extensions of standard reports must be set on an *ad hoc* basis. For the most part,

| Task | Project | | |
|---|---|---|---|
| | #1 | #2 | #3 |
| Priorities set | C | C | C |
| PM selected | C | C | C |
| Key members briefed on RFP | C | C | C |
| Proposal sent | C | C | C |
| Proposal accepted as negotiated | C | C | C |
| Preliminary design developed | C | W/10 | C |
| Design accepted | C | W/12 | C |
| Software developed | C | NS/NR | N/A |
| Product test design | C | W/30 | W/15 |
| Manufacturing scheduled | C | NS/HR | W/8 |
| Tools, jigs, fixtures designed | W/1 | NS/HR | W/2 |
| Tools, jigs, fixtures delivered | W/2 | NS/HR | W/8 |
| Production complete | NS/HR | NS/HR | NS/HR |
| Product test complete | NS/HR | NS/HR | NS/HR |
| Marketing sign-off on product | NS/HR | NS/HR | NS/HR |

**Figure 11-6:** Sample project status report.

**Notes:**

N/A—Not applicable
C—Completed

W—Work in progress (number refers to month required)

NS—Not started
NR—Need resources
HR—Have resources

such information will be readily available within the project, but occasionally, external sources must be utilized. If the PM ensures that the status reports given to senior management contain information that is current enough to be actionable (and always is as accurate as required for control), little else can be done to furnish the decision makers with the proper data for them to exercise control. The PM is well advised to insist that status reports make clear the implications of specific conditions where those implications might be overlooked—or not understood—by senior managers. If meetings between senior management and project managers are used to report project status and progress, it is critical to remember that the process employed in such meetings should not be punitive or intimidating. As we pointed out in Chapter 10, punitive meetings do far more damage than good.

## Postcontrol

*Postcontrols* (also known as postperformance controls or postproject controls) are applied after the fact. One might draw parallels between postcontrol and "locking the barn after the horse has been stolen," but postcontrol is not a vain attempt to alter what has already occurred. Instead, it is a full recognition of George Santayana's observation that "Those who cannot remember the past are condemned to repeat it." Cybernetic and go/no-go controls are directed toward accomplishing the goals of an ongoing project. Postcontrol is directed toward improving the chances for future projects to meet their goals.

Postcontrol is applied through a relatively formal document that is usually constructed with four distinct sections.

***The Project Objectives***    The postcontrol report will contain a description of the objectives of the project. Usually, this description is taken from the project proposal, and the entire proposal often appears as an appendix to the postcontrol report. As reported here, project objectives include the effects of all change orders issued and approved during the project.

Because actual project performance depends in part on uncontrollable events (strikes, weather, failure of trusted suppliers, sudden loss of key employees, and other acts of God), the key initial assumptions made during preparation of the project budget and schedule should be noted in this section. A certain amount of care must be taken in reporting these assumptions. They should not be written with a tone that makes them appear to be excuses for poor performance. While it is clearly the prerogative, if not the duty, of every PM to protect himself politically, he or she should do so in moderation to be effective.

***Milestones, Checkpoints, and Budgets***    This section of the postcontrol document starts with a full report of project performance against the planned schedule and budget. This can be prepared by combining and editing the various project status reports made during the project's life. Significant deviations of actual schedule and budget from planned schedule and budget should be highlighted. Explanations of why these deviations occurred will be offered in the next section of the postcontrol report. Each deviation can be identified with a letter or number to index it to the explanations. Where the same explanation is associated with both a schedule and budget deviation, as will often be the case, the same identifier can be used.

***The Final Report on Project Results***   When significant variations of actual from planned project performance are indicated, no distinction is made between favorable and unfavorable variations. Like the tongue that invariably goes to the sore tooth, project managers focus their attention on trouble. While this is quite natural, it leads to complete documentation on why some things went wrong and little or no documentation on why some things went particularly well. Both sides, the good and the bad, should be chronicled here.

Not only do most projects result in outputs that are more or less satisfactory, most projects operate with a process that is more or less satisfactory. The concern here is not on what the project did but rather on how it did it. Basically descriptive, this part of the final report should cover project organization, an explanation of the methods used to plan and direct the project, and a review of the communication networks, monitoring systems, and control methods, as well as a discussion of intraproject interactions between the various working groups.

***Recommendations for Performance and Process Improvement***   The culmination of the postcontrol report is a set of recommendations covering the ways that future projects can be improved. Many of the explanations appearing in the previous section are related to one-time happenings—sickness, weather, strikes, or the appearance of a new technology—that themselves are not apt to affect future projects, although other, different one-time events may affect them. But some of the deviations from plan were caused by happenings that are very likely to recur. Examples of recurring problems might be a chronically late supplier, a generally noncooperative functional department, a habitually optimistic cost estimator, or a highly negative project team member. Provision for such things can be factored into future project plans, thereby adding to predictability and control.

Just as important, the process of organizing and conducting projects can be improved by recommending the continuation of managerial methods and organizational systems that appear to be effective, together with the alteration of practices and procedures that do not. In this way, the conduct of projects will become smoother, just as the likelihood of achieving good results, on time and on cost, is increased.

Postcontrol can have a considerable impact on the way projects are run. A large, market-driven company in consumer household products developed new products through projects that were organized in matrix form, but had a functional tie to the marketing division. PMs were almost always chosen from the marketing area. Members of the project team who represented R & D had argued that they should be given a leadership role, particularly early in the project's life. Marketing resisted this suggestion on the grounds that R & D people were not market-oriented, did not know what would sell, and were mainly interested in pursuing their own "academic" interests. After reading the perennial R & D request in a postcontrol report, the program manager of one product line decided to reorganize a project as requested by R & D. The result was not merely a successful project, but was the first in a series of related projects based on extensions of ideas generated by an R & D group not restricted to work on the specific product sought by marketing. Following this successful experiment, project organization was modified to include more input from R & D at an earlier stage of the project.

There is no need to repeat the information requirements for postcontrol here. It should be noted, however, that we have not discussed the postcontrol audit, a full review and audit of all aspects of the project. This is covered in Chapter 12.

## ▶ 11.3  COMMENTS ON THE DESIGN OF CONTROL SYSTEMS

Irrespective of the type of control used, there are some important questions to be answered when designing any control system: Who sets the standards? How realistic are the standards? How clear are they? Will they achieve the project's goals? What output, activities, behaviors should be monitored? Should we monitor people? What kinds of sensors should be used? Where should they be placed? How timely must the monitoring be? How rapidly must it be reported? How accurate must the sensors be? How great must a difference between standard and actual be before it becomes actionable? What corrective actions are available? Are they ethical? What are the most appropriate actions for each situation? What rewards and penalties can be used? Who should take what action?

If the control system is to be acceptable to those who will use it and those who will be controlled by it, the system must be designed so that it appears to be sensible. Standards must be achievable by the mechanical systems used. Control limits must be appropriate to the needs of the client—that is, not merely set to show "how good we are." Like punishment, rewards and penalties should "fit the crime."

In addition to being sensible, a good control system should also possess some other characteristics.

- The system should be flexible. Where possible, it should be able to react to and report unforeseen changes in system performance.

- The system should be cost effective. The cost of control should never exceed the value of control. As we noted above, control is not always less expensive than scrap.

- The control system must be truly useful. It must satisfy the real needs of the project, not the whims of the PM.

- The system must operate in an ethical manner.

- The system must operate in a timely manner. Problems must be reported while there is still time to do something about them, and before they become large enough to destroy the project.

- Sensors and monitors should be sufficiently accurate and precise to control the project within limits that are truly functional for the client and the parent organization.

- The system should be as simple to operate as possible.
- The control system should be easy to maintain. Further, the control system should signal the overall controller if it goes out of order.
- The system should be capable of being extended or otherwise altered.
- Control systems should be fully documented when installed and the documentation should include a complete training program in system operation.

No matter how designed, all control systems we have described use feedback as a control process. Let us now consider some more specific aspects of control. To a large extent, the PM is trying to anticipate problems or catch them just as they begin to occur. The PM wants to keep the project out of trouble because upper management often bases an incremental funding decision on a review of the project. This review typically follows some particular milestone and, if acceptable, leads to a follow-on authorization to proceed to the next review point. If all is not going well, other technological alternatives may be recommended; or if things are going badly, the project may be terminated. Thus, the PM must monitor and control the project quite closely.

The control of performance, cost, and time usually requires different input data. To control performance, the PM may need such specific documentation as engineering change notices, test results, quality checks, rework tickets, scrap rates, and maintenance activities. For cost control, the manager compares budgets to actual cash flows, purchase orders, labor hour charges, amount of overtime worked, absenteeism, accounting variance reports, accounting projections, income reports, cost exception reports, and the like. To control the schedule, the PM examines benchmark reports, periodic activity and status reports, exception reports, PERT/CPM networks, Gantt charts, the master project schedule, earned value graphs, and probably reviews the WBS and action plans.

Some of the most important analytic tools available for the project manager to use in controlling the project are variance analysis and trend projection, both of which have been discussed earlier in this book. The essence of these tools is shown in Figure 11-7. A budget, plan, or expected growth curve of time or cost for some

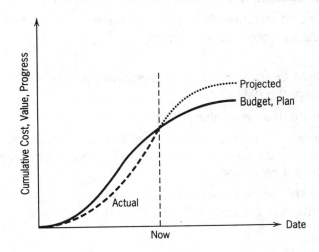

*Figure* 11-7: Trend projection.

task is plotted. Then actual values are plotted as a dashed line as the work is actually finished. At each point in time a new projection from the actual data is used to forecast what will occur in the future if the PM does not intervene. Based on this projection, the manager can decide if there is a problem, what action alternatives exist, what they will cost and require, and what they will achieve. Based on this analysis, the PM will decide what to do. Trend projection charts can even be used for combined performance/cost/time charts, as illustrated in Figure 11-8.

Earned value analysis was also described earlier. On occasion it may be worthwhile, particularly on large projects, for the PM to calculate a set of *critical ratios* for all project activities. The critical ratio is

$$\text{(actual progress/scheduled progress)} \times \text{(budgeted cost/actual cost)}$$

The critical ratio is made up of two parts; the ratio of actual progress to scheduled progress, and the ratio of budgeted cost to actual cost. (In the language of C/SCSC, the budgeted cost is the BCWP and the actual cost is the ACWP.) *Cæteris paribus*, to

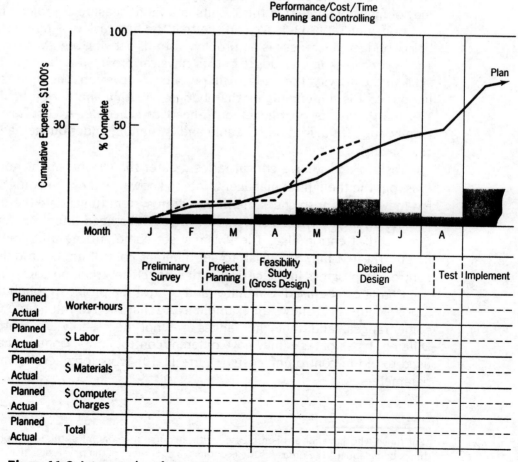

**Figure 11-8:** Integrated performance cost/time chart. *Source:* [31]

**Table 11-1**   (Actual Progress/Scheduled Progress) × (Budgeted Cost/Actual Cost)

| Task Number | Actual Progress | | Scheduled Progress | | Budgeted Cost | | Actual Cost | | Critical Ratio |
|---|---|---|---|---|---|---|---|---|---|
| 1 | (2 | / | 3) | × | (6 | / | 4) | = | 1.0 |
| 2 | (2 | / | 3) | × | (6 | / | 6) | = | .67 |
| 3 | (3 | / | 3) | × | (4 | / | 6) | = | .67 |
| 4 | (3 | / | 2) | × | (6 | / | 6) | = | 1.5 |
| 5 | (3 | / | 3) | × | (6 | / | 4) | = | 1.5 |

quote any economist who ever lived,[*] a ratio of actual to scheduled progress greater than one is "good." If the ratio is less than one, it is "bad." Similarly with the ratio of budgeted to actual cost—never forgetting *cæteris paribus*. Assuming moderately accurate measures for each element of each ratio (an assumption that rivals *cæteris paribus* for its *chutzpa*), the critical ratio is a good measure of the general health of the project. Note that the critical ratio is the product of the two separate ratios. This way of combining the two underlying ratios weights them equally, allowing a "bad" ratio for one part to be offset by an equally "good" ratio in the other. The PM may or may not agree that this results in a valid measure of project "health."

Consider Table 11-1. We can see that the first task is behind schedule but also below budget. If lateness is no problem for this activity, the PM need take no action. The second task is on budget but its physical progress is lagging. Even if there is slack in the activity, the budget will probably be overrun. The third task is on schedule but cost is running higher than budget, creating another probable cost overrun. The fourth task is on budget but ahead of schedule. A cost saving may result. Finally, the fifth task is on schedule and is running under budget, another probable cost saving.

Tasks 4 and 5 have critical ratios greater than 1 and might not concern some PMs, but the thoughtful manager wants to know why they are doing so well (and the PM may also want to check the information system to validate the unexpectedly favorable findings). The second and third activities need attention, and the first task may need attention also. The PM may set some critical-ratio control limits intuitively. The PM may also wish to set different control limits on different activities, controlling progress in the critical path more closely than on paths with high slack.

Charts can be used to monitor and control the project through the use of these ratios. Figure 11-9 shows an example. Note that the PM will ignore critical ratios in some ranges, and that the ranges are not necessarily symmetric around 1.0. Different types of tasks may have different control limits. Control charts can also be used to aid in controlling costs (Figure 11-10), work force levels, and other project parameters.

---

[*]For those who have never been blessed with a course in economics, this Latin phrase means "other things being equal." The phrase is the economist's equivalent of the physicist's frictionless plane. It does not and cannot exist in fact.

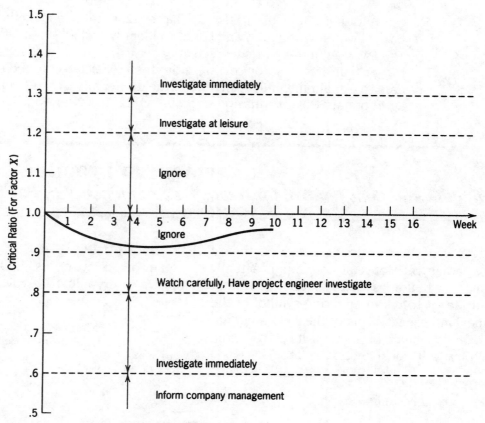

**Figure 11-9:** Critical ratio control limits.

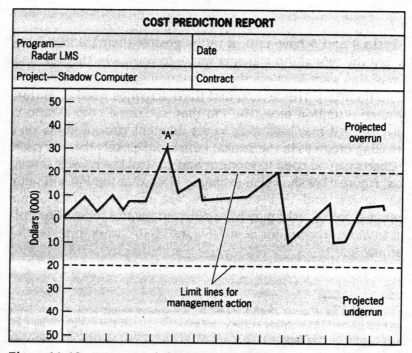

**Figure 11-10:** Cost control chart. *Source:* [17]

Auditing will be discussed in Chapter 12, but it needs a brief mention here. It is basically an investigation and count to identify and locate all elements of a project. The PM may find a particular activity perplexing or not understand why it is taking longer than it should or costing more than expected. An audit would provide the data to explain the unusual nature of the discrepancy. The PM may choose to do the audit or have the organization's accountant perform the work.

# Project Management in Practice
## Schedule and Cost Control for Australia's Immense New Parliament House

Over seven years in the making, Australia's new Parliament House at Canberra is actually a suite of buildings costing about $982 million! Meant to be an enduring symbol of the values and expectations of the Australian nation, and a source of pride for its citizens, the complex will consist of 5000 rooms, 40,000 items of furniture, 50,000 square meters of stonework, 7350 doors, and 170,000 square meters of drywall. To excavate the site, over

*Source:* T. R. Nixon, "Project Management at the New Parliament House, Canberra," *Project Management Journal,* Sept. 1987.

**Project Control Process**

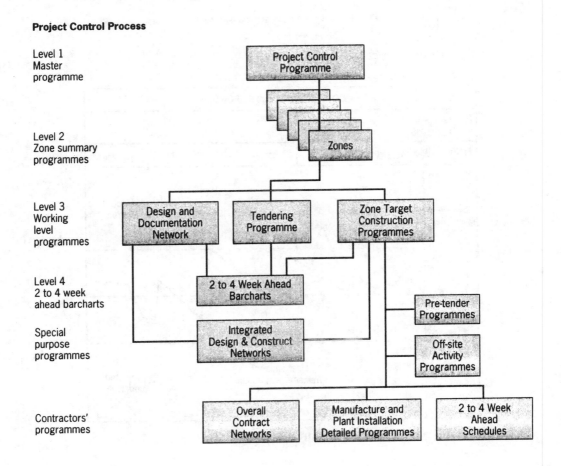

one million cubic meters of rock was moved, and 170,000 cubic meters of concrete was poured to form the foundation. At its busiest point, the complex was costing $1.2 million per working day.

Given the immensity of the project, the information systems to control its design, construction, and furnishing were equally extensive. Procedures were devised for planning, cost control, tendering, contract commencement, drawing and samples, purchasing, stores control, contracts administration, accounts, general administration, and accident prevention. In the area of contracts alone, 540 separate contracts were awarded. And 20,000 drawings were prepared, with 750,000 prints issued. Thus, computerized systems were de-

veloped for the data associated with contracts and bids, drawings, information requests, site instructions, change proposals, shop drawings, asset registers, time reporting, cost reporting, budgetary control, contracts payments, consultants' fees, and reimbursables.

Time control is based on monitoring at four levels of detail giving progressively more programming detail on aspects of the project. Special purpose programs are included for specific problems or requirements. In addition to exception reports, progress review and coordination meetings help management focus attention on the areas of concern. The overall control system is illustrated in the previous figure.

**Layout of Separate Buildings within the Parliament House**

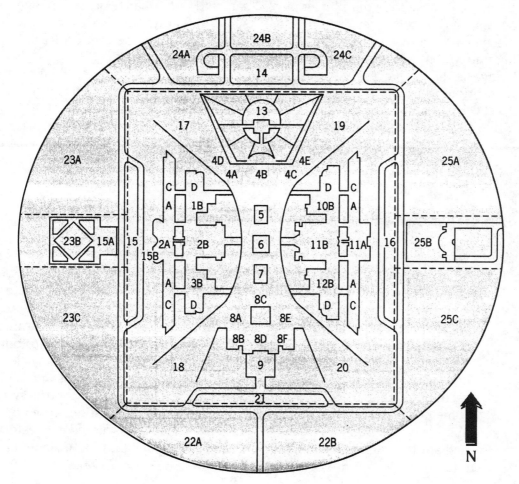

The old parliament house (foreground) and the complex of buildings that comprise the new parliament house (background) in Canberra, Australia.

Cost control is based on the philosophy that 80 percent of the cost is designed in and only 20 percent is due to construction variations. Thus, attention was focused on three points during the design process: early on, to identify allocations and deviations; halfway through to check costs again; and at the completion. Still, ongoing cost control is necessary and performance against budget is measured monthly. Forecasts are also revised every six months to check for any problems ahead.

With such attention to control, the citizens of Australia are looking forward to the completion of their new "house."

## ▶ 11.4   CONTROL AS A FUNCTION OF MANAGEMENT

With a few rare exceptions, control of projects is always exercised through people. Senior managers in the organization are governed by the CEO who is directed by such groups as the executive committee and/or board of directors/trustees. Senior managers, in turn, try to exercise governance of project managers, and project managers try to exert control over the project team and others representing functions that are involved with the project. The purpose is always the same—to bring the actual schedule, budget, and deliverables of the project into reasonably close congruence with the planned schedule, budget, and deliverables. In this and the following sections of this chapter, we discuss the design and use of control systems with some emphasis on the ways in which people respond to various types of control. A number of the points we cover in these sections are discussed at greater length in William Newman's excellent book, *Constructive Control* [33]. Its insights are as fresh today as they were two decades ago when the book was written.

Finally, it should be noted that much of the literature on total quality management (TQM), ISO 9000 standards, employee involvement (EI), and the functioning of teams is devoted to techniques for developing creativity and synergistic problem-solving through effective teamwork. What is almost never discussed is the implicit assumption that teams have a sense of direction, and are attempting to achieve some specified objectives. All of this implies control. Even the most chaotic brainstorming session (see Appendix A) is aimed at the solution of specific problems. Control is a necessary and inherent part of life in any organization. It is not helpful to think of control as coercive, though, at times, it may be. We prefer to think of control as the maintenance of ethical goal-directed behavior.

The PM is always subject to such eternal verities as the law of gravity, the laws of thermodynamics, and the brute fact that the exercise of managerial control will result in distorting the behavior of subordinates. The job of the PM/controller is to set controls that will encourage those behaviors/results that are deemed desirable and discourage those that are not. The unspoken assumption here is that control systems motivate individuals to behave in certain ways. While this may seem obvious, it is not the bland assertion it appears. The entire subject of motivation is a complex and rich field for research and there are several theories about the nature of motivation. Each has its supporters and critics. We adopt no particular theory here; we do, however, argue that the control mechanisms described in this chapter provide a context within which motivation takes place. Thus, while control does not provide a good explanation for the presence or absence of motivation, control does indicate the direction toward which the motivated person will move [28].

Though control does not ensure motivated behavior, individual reactions to the various types of control systems do affect levels of motivation. By and large, people respond to the goal-directedness of control systems in one of three general ways: (1) by active and positive participation and goal seeking, (2) by passive participation in order to avoid loss, and (3) by active but negative participation and resistance—usually not active resistance to the goal, but failure to undertake those activities that will result in goal achievement. Which of the three resemble a given individual's reaction to control depends on several variables, including such things as the specific control mechanism used, the nature of the goal being sought, the individual's self-image, assessment of the value of the goal, expectation of being able to achieve the goal, and basic tolerance for being controlled.

While human response to specific types of control is typified by its variety, some generalizations are possible.

***Cybernetic Controls***  Human response to steering controls tends to be positive. Steering controls are usually viewed as helpful rather than as a source of unwelcome pressure if the controllees perceive themselves as able to perform inside the prescribed limits. Contrary to the popular song, it is not the "impossible dream" that motivates goal-seeking behavior, but rather a moderately good chance of success.

Of course, response to steering control is dependent on the individual's acceptance of the goal as appropriate. Indeed, no control system is acceptable if the objective of control is not acceptable. Further, the source of control must be seen as legitimate for the control mechanism to be accepted.

While it appears to be true that humans respond positively to steering controls, they may not be so positive about the monitoring systems that drive the control mechanisms. Grant, *et al.* [16] have shown that computerized performance monitoring and control systems are viewed as mixed blessings and have both functional and dysfunctional effects. These monitoring systems, though not used for true cybernetic controls, are fairly common in software projects.

***Go/No-go Controls***   Response to go/no-go controls tends to be neutral or negative. The reason appears to be related to the inherent nature of this type of control system. With go/no-go control systems, "barely good enough" results are just as acceptable as "perfect" results. The control system itself makes it difficult for the worker to take pride in high-quality work because the system does not recognize gradations of quality. In addition, it is all too common to be rather casual about setting the control limits for a go/no-go control; the limits should be very carefully set. The fact that this kind of control emphasizes "good enough" performance is no excuse for the nonchalant application of careless standards.

While go/no-go control is the most frequent type of control exercised on projects, the impact of such control on the project team seems, to us, to be less negative than Newman suggests [33, pp. 41–42]. Perhaps this is because *project team performance* is the primary focus of control rather than specific items of work performed by individuals. The quality of the project taken as a whole serves as the source of satisfaction to the group, not the quality of bits and pieces. It also appears clear that the quality of the project also serves as a source of satisfaction with the *process* of doing projects. The entire subject of human response to control in a project environment is a prime area for additional research.

***Postcontrols***   Postcontrols are seen as much the same as a report card. They may serve as a basis for reward or punishment, but they are received too late to change current performance. Whether reaction to postcontrol is positive, neutral, or negative seems to depend on the "grade" received. In cases where a series of similar projects must be undertaken, postcontrols are regarded as helpful in planning for future work, but considerable care must be devoted to ensuring that controls are consistent with changing environmental conditions. To be effective, management must provide an incentive for project managers to study postcontrol reports, and to determine corrective procedures for problems exposed by the reports, as well as procedures that will replicate the techniques and systems that appear particularly helpful.

Because postcontrols are placed on the process of conducting a project, as well as on the usual time, cost, and performance standards, they may be applied to such areas as interproject communications, cooperation between the groups working on related task elements, the quality of project management, and the nature of interaction with the client. Application of control to such matters presents severe measurement problems. Often it is difficult to detect gross differences in the quality of intergroup communications, for example, or to relate these differences, if detected, to aspects of the project that can be controlled. To say that these matters are difficult to measure and control is not, of course, to obviate the need for control. The soft side of project performance is no less important in the longer run than the easier-to-measure hard side.

## ▶ 11.5   BALANCE IN A CONTROL SYSTEM

When developing a control system, it is important that the system be well *balanced*. Unfortunately, the concept of balance is fuzzy—difficult to explain, difficult to achieve, and difficult to recognize. Though precise definition is impossible, we can describe some general features of a balanced control system, and also indicate some of the things a controller can do to achieve good balance in a system.

- A balanced control system is built with cognizance of the fact that investment in control is subject to sharply diminishing returns. Costs increase exponentially as the degree of control increases.

- A balanced control system recognizes that as control increases past some point, innovative activity is more and more damped, and then finally shut off completely.

- A balanced control system is directed toward the correction of error rather than toward punishment. This requires a clear understanding of the fact that the past cannot be changed, no matter how loudly the manager yells.

- A balanced system exerts control only to the degree required to achieve its objectives. It rarely pays to spend dollars to find lost pennies, nor is it sensible to machine a part to the ten-thousandth if the client's requirements are to the tenth.

- A balanced system utilizes the lowest degree of hassle consistent with accomplishing its goals. The controller should avoid annoying those people whose cooperation is required to reach system objectives.

To sum up, a balanced control system is cost-effective, well geared for the end results sought, and not overdone. The causes of imbalance are legion. For example, the application of across-the-board controls is usually not a good idea. Treating everyone alike appeals to a naive sense of equity, but better results are usually achieved by treating everyone individually.

Across-the-board freezes on expenditures or on hiring tend to reward those who have already overspent or overhired and to penalize the frugal and efficient. The side effects of this are often quite odd. Several years ago, Procter & Gamble put a freeze on hiring into effect for an engineering development laboratory. Project managers who were shorthanded hired temporary labor, including highly skilled technicians, from Manpower and similar firms. P & G's accounting system allowed temporary labor to be charged to material accounts rather than to the salary account. The lesson to be learned is that results-oriented, creative project managers tend to see across-the-board controls as a challenge and a barrier to be circumvented.

Other common causes of imbalance are these:

1. Placing too much weight on easy-to-measure factors and too little weight on difficult-to-measure, soft factors (the so-called "intangibles").

2. Emphasizing short-run results at the expense of longer-run objectives.

3. Ignoring the changes in the structure of organizational goals that result from the passage of time or changes in the firm's circumstances. For example, high

quality and strict adherence to delivery schedules might be extremely important to a new firm. Later, perhaps, expense control might be more important.

4. Overcontrol by an aggressive executive often causes trouble. In an attempt to create a reputation for on-time delivery, one overly zealous PM put so much pressure on the project team that on-time shipments took precedence over proper test procedures. The result was serious malfunctions of the product and its subsequent recall.

5. Monitoring and controlling items may lead some people to ignore anything that is not measured. "If it isn't counted, it doesn't count," is the attitude. This factor was responsible for the failure of many attempts at management by objectives.

Achieving balance in a control system is rather easy to discuss but quite difficult to accomplish. Several principles must be simultaneously upheld. Perhaps most important is the need to tie controls directly to project objectives. Occasionally, firms establish tortuous, indirect linkages between control and objective, apparently on the theory that people should not be aware of or understand the controls under which they must operate. It is as if the firm were trying to unethically trap employees. Such control systems rarely work because they rest on two fallacious assumptions: (1) that people are generally perverse and will avoid trying to accomplish a known objective, and (2) that people are too stupid to see through the misdirection.

In addition to linking controls to objectives, controls should be closely and directly related to specific performance outcomes. Start by defining the desired results as precisely as possible. System actions that can cause deviation from the desired results are then examined and controls are designed for these actions, beginning with those that can be the source of serious deviation, particularly those that cause trouble with high frequency.

The PM should also examine all controls in terms of the probable reactions of individuals to the proposed controls. One asks, "How will the various members of the project team react to this control?" If negative reaction is likely, the control should be redesigned.

The problem of developing a good balance between long-run and short-run control objectives is delicate, not because the blending is inherently difficult, but because the PM is often preoccupied with urgent short-run problems rather than longer-run problems that can always be "temporarily" set aside no matter how important the results may be at some later date. Even the timing and sequences of monitoring and controlling can affect the likelihood of time and cost overruns [35].

A good rule for the controller is to place the control as close as possible to the work being controlled and to design the simplest possible mechanism to achieve control. Giving the worker direct control over quality has had impressive results in Japanese production processes as well as at the Lincoln Electric Company in the United States. Similar results were achieved by a major producer of housing units. Carpenters, masons, electricians, and other workers were given considerable discretion over specific production methods. Projects on which this approach was employed showed significantly improved quality when compared to projects built by standard methods.

The most important step in constructing a balanced control system must be taken far in advance of the time when control systems are usually designed. Every step of project planning must be undertaken with the understanding that *whatever work is planned will also have to be controlled*. As we have emphasized, planning and control are opposite sides of the same coin. No amount of planning can solve the current crisis, but planning combined with the design and installation of appropriate control mechanisms can go a long way toward crisis prevention.

An excellent example of integrating the planning and control functions is provided by Mead Data Central, a producer of large-scale database systems and a subsidiary of Mead Corporation. In its *Project Management Development Guide*, Mead describes six stages of the project life cycle as seen from its point of view. For each stage, the purpose is carefully explained and the deliverables for that stage are listed. For example, the list of deliverables for the feasibility stage contains these items: project description, project number, preliminary business case, project requirements document, and so forth. For each deliverable, the individual(s) and/or groups responsible are noted.

An extensive glossary of terms is included in the document so that inexperienced project workers can understand what is meant by such diverse terms as "escalation document," "functional audit," "milestone," "not-to-do list," "project cost tracking," and "release readiness statement." In addition, the *Development Guide* summarizes the tasks that must be performed by each of the functional areas or individuals during each stage of the life cycle. The work of the Idea Champion, the Market Managers, the Business Management Process Director, the Project Review Committee, and so on is well defined. The result is an effective integration of planning and control that is available to anyone working on the organization's projects.

A senior executive at a large industrial firm that carries out many projects each year sees control in a slightly different light. Noting that differences between plan and reality usually represent problems for project managers, he remarked: "If you are solving problems faster than they are arriving to be solved, you have the project under control. If not, you haven't."

## ▶ 11.6  CONTROL OF CREATIVE ACTIVITIES

Some brief attention should be paid to the special case of controlling research and development projects, design projects, and similar processes that depend intimately on the creativity of individuals and teams. First, the more creativity involved, the greater the degree of uncertainty surrounding outcomes. Second, too much control tends to inhibit creativity. But neither of these dicta can be taken without reservation. As noted in Appendix A, control is not necessarily the enemy of creativity [45]; nor, popular myth to the contrary, does creative activity imply complete uncertainty. While the exact outcomes of creative activity may be more or less uncertain, the process of getting the outcome is usually not uncertain.

In order to control creative projects, the PM must adopt one or some combination of three general approaches to the problem: (1) progress review, (2) personnel reassignment, and (3) control of input resources.

## Progress Review

The progress review focuses on the process of reaching outcomes rather than on the outcomes *per se*. Because the outcomes are partially dependent on the process used to achieve them—uncertain though they may be—the process is subjected to control. For example, in research projects the researcher cannot be held responsible for the outcome of the research, but can most certainly be held responsible for adherence to the research proposal, the budget, and the schedule. The process is controllable even if the precise results are not.

Control should be instituted at each project milestone. If research results are not as expected or desired, milestones provide a convenient opportunity to assess the state of progress, the value of accomplishment to date, the probability of valuable results in the future, and the desirability of changes in the research design. Again, the object of control is to ensure that the research design is sound and is being carried out as planned or amended. The review process should be participative. Unilateral judgments from the superior are not apt to be accepted or effective. Care must be taken not to overstress method as opposed to result. Method is controllable, and should be controlled, but results are still what count.

## Personnel Reassignment

This type of control operates in a very straightforward way. Individuals who are productive are kept. Those who are not are moved, to other jobs or to other organizations. Problems with this technique can arise because it is easy to create an elite group. While the favored few are highly motivated to further achievement, everyone else tends to be demotivated. It is also important not to apply control with too fine an edge. While it is not particularly difficult to identify those who fall in the top and bottom quartiles of productivity, it is usually quite hard to make clear distinctions between people in the middle quartiles.

## Control of Input Resources

In this case, the focus is on efficiency. The ability to manipulate input resources carries with it considerable control over output. Obviously, efficiency is not synonymous with creativity, but the converse is equally untrue. Creativity is not synonomous with extravagant use of resources.

The results flowing from creative activity tend to arrive in batches. Considerable resource expenditure may occur with no visible results, but then, seemingly all of a sudden, many outcomes may be delivered. The milestones for application of resource control must therefore be chosen with great care. The controller who decides to withhold resources just before the fruition of a research project is apt to become an ex-controller.

Sound judgment argues for some blend of these three approaches when controlling creative projects. The first and third approaches concentrate on process because process is observable and can be affected. But process is not the matter of moment; results are. The second approach requires us to measure (or at least to recognize) output when it occurs. This is often quite difficult. Thus, the wise PM will use all three approaches: checking process and method, manipulating resources, and culling those who cannot or do not produce.

## ▶ 11.7   CONTROL OF CHANGE

In Chapter 6, we discussed the fact that the original plans for projects are almost certain to be changed before the projects are completed. The changes, we noted, result from three basic causes: uncertainty about the technology on which the work of the project or its output is based, an increase in the knowledge base or sophistication of the client/user, or a modification of the rules applying to the process of carrying out the project or to its output. When either the process or output of a project is changed, there is almost always a concomitant change in the budget and/or schedule.

Conversations in recent years with more than 500 project managers have convinced us that coping with changes and changing priorities is perceived as the most important single problem facing the PM—or if not the most important, certainly the most irritating. When a senior financial officer of a toy manufacturing firm makes an offhand, negative comment about the color of a toy, and triggers a "total redesign" of the toy, thereby invalidating an already approved design, schedule, and budget, the project manager and the design artist may consider murder. (It is probable that a knowledgeable jury would find their action justifiable.)

The most common changes, however, are due to the natural tendency of the client and project team members to try to improve the product or service. New demands and performance requirements become apparent to the client which were not realized at the time of project initiation. New technologies become available or better ideas occur to the team as work progresses. As noted earlier, the later these changes are made in the project, the more difficult and costly they are to complete. Without control, a continuing accumulation of little changes can have a major negative impact on the project's schedule and cost.

There is, however, no insurance against the risks associated with project changes. Total quality management and employee involvement will help if both the deliverable and the process by which it is to be produced are carefully studied by thoughtful teams that represent the interests of the major stakeholders in any project, the client, senior management, the project team, and the community. Also, a thorough knowledge of production processes will help avoid some manufacturability-related engineering changes [38]. Since prevention of change is not possible, the PM's best hope seems to lie in controlling the process by which change is introduced and accomplished.

This is accomplished with a formal *change control system* which, in some industries, is a part of their *configuration management system* responsible for integrating and coordinating changes throughout the systems development cycle. The purpose of the formal *change control system* is to:

- review all requested changes to the project (both content and procedures)
- identify all task impacts
- translate these impacts into project performance, cost, and schedule
- evaluate the benefits and costs of the requested changes
- identify alternative changes that might accomplish the same ends

- accept or reject the requested changes
- communicate the changes to all concerned parties
- ensure that the changes are implemented properly
- prepare monthly reports that summarize all changes to date and their project impacts.

The following simple guidelines, applied with reasonable rigor, can be used to establish an effective change control procedure.

1.  All project contracts or agreements must include a description of how requests for a change in the project's plan, budget, schedule, and/or deliverables, will be introduced and processed.

2.  Any change in a project will be in the form of a *change order* that will include a description of the agreed-upon change together with any changes in the plan, budget, schedule, and/or deliverables that result from the change.

3.  Changes must be approved, in writing, by the client's agent as well as by an appropriate representative of senior management of the firm responsible for carrying out the project.

4.  The project manager must be consulted on all desired changes prior to the preparation and approval of the change order. The project manager's approval, however, is not required.

5.  Once the change order has been completed and approved, the project master plan should be amended to reflect the change, and the change order becomes a part of the master plan.

The process of controlling change is not complicated. If the project is large, Roman suggests a change control board [37, p. 274], a group representing all interested parties that processes all requests for change. For the typical small- or medium-sized project, however, the problem of handling change need not be complex. The main source of trouble is that too many project managers, in an attempt to avoid anything that smacks of bureaucracy, adopt an informal process of handling requests for change. Misunderstanding often arises from this informality, and the PM finds that the project becomes committed to deliver a changed output, but will have to swallow the additional cost involved, and will have to scramble to meet the old, unchanged schedule.

The problems associated with dealing with change orders informally are particularly severe in the case of software and information system projects. We resist the notion that computer-oriented projects are significantly different from other types of projects in this regard. (For a diametric view, see [36].) Nonetheless, the precise techniques of managing projects are not independent of the technology applied on the project. Service sector projects often require different planning and control methods than do construction projects or R & D projects.

The severity of the problem of dealing with change in software projects, it seems to us, is caused by two, interrelated factors. First, software and information systems experts too often fail to explain adequately to the client the real nature of the systems they develop. Second, clients too often fail to make an adequate effort to understand the systems that become the lifeblood for their organizations. All too often, the systems developer is preoccupied by the technical demands of the systems and ignorant of the user's needs. And all too often, the user views the systems developer as a practitioner of some arcane art that cannot be penetrated by normal minds.

Given this basic failure to communicate, the client has no real idea of what is involved in changing a software project in order to provide another useful feature not specified in the original project requirements. The software technician, eager to please the customer, agrees to provide the utility, but does not make clear to the client the level of effort and time that will be required. The project is late, over budget, and the customer is angry. This scenario is played out again and again with neither side profiting from the experience. The formal process for change suggested above tends to reduce the degree of misunderstanding—and disappointment.

Difficult as it may be, control is an important part of the PM's job on every project. Perhaps the most helpful advice we can give the PM is, in the language of the 1970s, to "hang loose." One effective project manager of our acquaintance tells his project team, "I will not accept crises after 4:30 PM. You are limited to one crisis per day. Crises are not cumulative. If you don't get yours in today, you do not get two tomorrow." All this is said, of course, with good humor. Team members understand that the PM is not serious, but his projects seem to progress with exceptional smoothness. Crises do occur from time to time, but everyone on the team works to prevent them by applying control in an effective and timely manner.

# Project Management In Practice
## Better Control of Product Development Projects at Johnson Controls

The Automotive Systems Group of Johnson Controls was having trouble controlling their product development programs with each project being managed differently, disagreements about who was responsible for what, projects failing because of rapid company growth, and new employees having trouble fitting into the culture. For a solution, they went to their most experienced and successful project managers and condensed their knowledge into four detailed procedures for managing projects. Because these procedures are now common to all projects, they can be used to train new employees, standardize practices, create a common language, tie together different company functions, create common experiences, act as implicit job descriptions, and create a positive overall project management culture.

The first procedure is project approval for authorizing the expenditure of funds and use of resources. The sales department must first provide a set of product/market information, including financial data, project scope, critical dates, and engineering resource requirements before management will approve the project. Thus, projects are now scrutinized much more closely before work is started and money spent—when more questions are asked and more people are involved, better decisions tend to be made.

The second procedure is the statement-of-work, identifying agreements and assump-

---

*Source*: W. D. Reith and D. B. Kandt, "Project Management at a Major Automotive Seating Supplier," *Project Management Journal*, September 1991.

tions for the project. Here, both the customer and top management must sign off before product design work begins, thereby reducing misunderstandings regarding not only product specifications, prices, and milestones but also intangible product requirements, explicit exclusions, and generic performance targets. Maintaining this documentation over the life of the project has helped avoid problems caused by late product changes from the customer, particularly for 3–5 year projects where the personnel rotate off the project. Customers have, however, been slow to agree to this level of documentation because it limits their ability to change timing, prices, and specifications late in the program when they are more knowledgable about their needs.

The third procedure is the work breakdown structure, consisting of nine critical life-cycle phases running from definition through production. Included in each of these nine phases are four key elements: the tasks, the timing of each task, the responsible individuals, and the meeting dates for simultaneous engineering (a formalized procedure at Johnson Controls).

The fourth procedure is a set of management reviews, crucial to successful project completion. Both the content and timing of these reviews are specified in advance and progression to the next phase of a project cannot occur until senior management has approved the prespecified requirements, objectives, and quality criteria for that phase. The procedure also specifies questions that must be answered and work that must be reviewed by senior management.

Through the use of these procedures, which are updated and improved with each new project experience, the learning that occurs in the organization is captured and made useful for future projects.

## ▶ SUMMARY

As the final subject in the project implementation part of the text, this chapter described the project control process in the planning–monitoring–controlling cycle. The need for control was discussed and the three types available were described. Then the design of control systems was addressed, including management's role, achieving the proper balance, and attaining control of creative activity as well as handling changes.

Specific points made in this chapter were these:

- Control is directed to performance, cost, and time.
- The two fundamental purposes of control are to regulate results through altering activity and to conserve the organization's physical, human, and financial assets.
- The three main types of control processes are cybernetic (either first-, second-, or third-order), go/no-go, and postcontrol.
- The postcontrol report contains four sections:
  Project objectives
      Milestones and budgets
      Final project results
      Recommendations for improvement
- The trend projection curve, critical ratios, and the control chart are useful control tools.
- Control systems have a close relationship to motivation and should be well-balanced; that is, cost-effective, appropriate to the desired end results, and not overdone.
- Three approaches to the control of creativity are progress review, personnel reassignment, and control of inputs.
- The biggest single problem facing a PM is the control of change.

In the next chapter we initiate the project termination part of the text, beginning with evaluation and auditing. This topic is closely related to the postcontrol topics in this chapter.

# ▶ GLOSSARY

**Champion**—A person with organizational clout who takes on personal responsibility (though not usually day-to-day management) for the successful completion of a project for the organization.

**Control**—Assuring that reality meets expectations or plans. Usually involves the process of keeping actions within limits to assure that certain outcomes will in fact happen.

**Control Chart**—A chart of a measure of performance—commonly a quality characteristic—over time, showing how it changes compared to a desired mean and upper and lower limits.

**Critical Ratio**—A ratio of progress (actual/scheduled) times a cost ratio (budgeted/actual).

**Cybernetic**—An automatic control system containing a negative feedback loop.

**Early Warning System**—A monitoring system that forewarns the project manager if trouble arises.

**Go/No-Go**—Initially, a type of gauge that quickly tells an inspector if an object's dimension is within certain limits. In the case of project management, this can be any measure that allows a manager to decide whether to continue, change, or terminate an activity or a project.

# ▶ MATERIAL REVIEW QUESTIONS

1. What is the purpose of control? To what is it directed?

2. What are the three main types of control systems? What questions should a control system answer?

3. What tools are available to the project manager to use in controlling a project? Identify some characteristics of a good control system.

4. What is the mathematical expression for the critical ratio? What does it tell a manager?

5. Describe the relationship between motivation and control.

6. How is creativity controlled?

7. What are go/no-go gauges?

8. What is a champion?

9. Describe a cybernetic control system.

10. What should the postcontrol report include?

11. How should change be controlled?

# ▶ CLASS DISCUSSION QUESTIONS

1. How could MBO be used in project control?

2. How might the project manager integrate the various control tools into a project control system?

3. How could a negative feedback control system be implemented in project management to anticipate client problems?

4. Compare the trend projection curve and the earned value chart. Could they be combined to aid the PM's control?

5. What other project parameters might a control chart be used for? How would their limits be set?

6. Control systems are sometimes classified into two categories, preventive and feedback. How do the three types of systems described in the chapter relate to these two categories?

7. How do internal and external controls differ?

8. What are some difficulties encountered when attempting project control?

9. How might the information required for control systems be collected?

10. How might the information collected through the control system be used on subsequent projects?

11. How does the control of creative projects differ from the control of ordinary projects?

12. Where might ethical issues arise for a PM in the stewardship of the company's resources?

13. Why is the control of change such a difficult problem for a PM?

# PROBLEMS

1. Given the following information, calculate the critical ratios and indicate which activities are on target and which need to be investigated.

| Activity | Actual Progress | Scheduled Progress | Budgeted Cost | Actual Cost |
|----------|-----------------|--------------------|---------------|-------------|
| A | 2 days | 2 days | $40 | $35 |
| B | 4 days | 6 days | $30 | $40 |
| C | 1 day | 3 days | $50 | $70 |
| D | 3 days | 2 days | $25 | $25 |

2. Calculate the critical ratios for the following activities and indicate which activities are probably on target and which need to be investigated.

| Activity | Actual Progress | Scheduled Progress | Budgeted Cost | Actual Cost |
|----------|-----------------|--------------------|---------------|-------------|
| A | 4 days | 4 days | $60 | $40 |
| B | 3 days | 2 days | $50 | $50 |
| C | 2 days | 3 days | $30 | $20 |
| D | 1 day | 1 day | $20 | $30 |
| E | 2 days | 4 days | $25 | $25 |

3. Given the following information, which activities are on time, which are early, and which are behind schedule?

| Activity | Budgeted Cost | Actual Cost | Critical Ratio |
|----------|---------------|-------------|----------------|
| A | $60 | $40 | 1.0 |
| B | $25 | $50 | 0.5 |
| C | $45 | $30 | 1.5 |
| D | $20 | $20 | 1.5 |
| E | $50 | $50 | 0.67 |

4. Design and plot a critical ratio for a project that had planned constant, linear progress from 0 to an earned value of 200 over a 100 day duration. In fact, progress for the first 20 days has been: 2, 3, 4, 6, 7, 9, 12, 14, 15, 17, 20, 21, 21, 22, 24, 26, 27, 29, 31, 33. What can you conclude about this project?

5. Design and plot a critical ratio for a project that has planned constant, linear spending from 0 to a total of 1000 over a 100 day duration. In fact, daily spending for the first 15 days has been: 11, 10, 9, 10, 11, 12, 11, 9, 8, 9, 10, 12, 14, 11, 7. What can you conclude about this project?

6. Empire State Building, Inc., has two project teams installing virtually identical buildings for a customer in two separate cities. Both projects have a planned daily cost of 100 and a planned daily earned value of 100. The first six days for each team have progressed as follows:

| Day | Team A: Earned Value | Team B: Earned Value | A: Cost | B: Cost |
|-----|----------------------|----------------------|---------|---------|
| 1 | 90 | 90 | 95 | 95 |
| 2 | 92 | 88 | 98 | 94 |
| 3 | 94 | 95 | 101 | 102 |
| 4 | 98 | 101 | 106 | 109 |
| 5 | 104 | 89 | 116 | 99 |
| 6 | 112 | 105 | 126 | 118 |

Compare the two projects in terms of general progress and according to critical ratios.

7. World Trade Building, Ltd., is also constructing an identical building for the same customer as in Problem 6 and has the following earned values and costs for the first six days: EV: 90, 88, 95, 101, 89, 105; Cost: 92, 88, 93, 98, 85, 100. Compare this project to the two in Problem 6.

# INCIDENTS FOR DISCUSSION

## Speciality Pak, Inc.

Speciality Pak, Inc., is a custom packing operation serving the chemical industry in seven states. S. P. has one operation in each state, and they vary in size from 50 to 240 employees. A disturbing trend has been developing for the last couple of years that S. P. management wishes to stop. The incidence of tardiness and absenteeism is on the increase. Both are extremely disruptive in a custom packing operation. S. P. is nonunion in all seven locations, and since management wants to keep this situation, it wants a careful, low-key approach to the problem. Roger Horn, assistant personnel manager, has been appointed project manager to recommend a solution. All seven operations managers have been assigned to work with him on this problem.

Roger has had no problem interfacing with the operations managers. They have very quickly agreed that three steps must be taken to solve the problem:

1. Institute a uniform daily attendance report that is summarized weekly and forwarded to the main office. (Current practice varies from location to location, but comments on attendance are normally included in monthly operations reports.)

2. Institute a uniform disciplinary policy, enforced in a uniform manner.

3. Initiate an intensive employee education program to emphasize the importance of good attendance.

The team has further decided that the three-point program should be tested before a final recommendation is presented. They have decided to test the program at one location for two months. Roger wishes to control and evaluate the test by having the daily attendance report transmitted to him directly at headquarters, from which he will make the final decision on whether to present the program in its current format or not.

*Questions*: Does this monitoring and control method appear adequate? What are the potential problems?

## Night Tran Construction Company

Night Tran Construction Company specializes in building small power plants, mostly for utility companies. The company was awarded a contract approximately two years ago to build such a power plant. The contract stated a project duration of three years, after which a 1 percent penalty would be invoked for each additional month of construction. Project records indicate the utility plan is only 50 percent completed and is encountering continuing problems. The owner of Night Tran Company, concerned over the potential losses, investigated the project and found the following: There were an excessive number of engineering design changes; there was a high work rejection rate; and the project was generally understaffed. As a result, she directed the project manager to develop a better system of project control and present this method to the board members in one week.

*Questions*: If you were the project manager, what characteristics would you be looking for in the new control system? Will a new control system be adequate for the problem? Explain.

## ▶ PROJECT TEAM CONTINUING EXERCISE

For this assignment, design a project control system for your team project. Determine how you will control performance, cost, and time. Will you use go/no-go, postcontrol, or cybernetic controls, and if the latter, a first-, second-, or third-order system? Are these dynamic or static controls? What will you measure? What tools will you employ: control charts, critical ratios, trend projections? Will you attempt to control

change? If so, how? Justify your control system in terms of cost effectiveness, appropriateness, and ability to motivate team members. Then apply the control system in retrospect to those activities already completed and analyze its success. Modify as appropriate and continue using it throughout the remainder of the project.

## ▶ BIBLIOGRAPHY

1. ACKOFF, R. L. "Beyond Problem Solving." *Decision Sciences*, April 1974.

2. ADAMS, J. R., S. E. BARNDT, and M. D. MARTIN. *Managing by Project Management*. Dayton, OH: Universal Technology Corp.,1979.

3. AMRINE, H. T., J. A. RITCHEY, and O. S. HULLEY.

*Manufacturing Organization and Management*, 5th ed. Englewood Cliffs, NJ: Prentice Hall, 1987.

4. ARCHIBALD, R. D. *Managing High Technology Programs and Projects*. New York: Wiley, 1976.

5. BARNES, N. M. L. "Cost Modelling—An Integrated Approach to Planning and Cost Control."

American Association of Chemical Engineers Transactions, March 1977.

6. BENT, J. A. "Project Control Concepts." Project Management Proceedings, 1979.

7. BLOCK, E. B. "Accomplishment/Cost: Better Project Control." Harvard Business Review, May 1971.

8. BOBROWSKI, P. M. "Project Management Control Problems: An Information Systems Focus." Project Management Journal, June 1989.

9. BRAZ, E. F. "Project Management Oversight: A Control Tool of Owners of Engineering and Construction Projects." Project Management Journal, March 1989.

10. BUFFA, E. S. Basic Production Management, 2nd ed. New York: Wiley, 1975.

11. CAMMANN, C., and D. A. NADLER. "Fit Control Systems to Your Management Style." Harvard Business Review, Jan.–Feb. 1976.

12. CESTIN, A. A. "What Makes Large Projects Go Wrong." Project Management Quarterly, March 1980.

13. DAVIS, S. M., and P. LAWRENCE. Matrix. Reading, MA: Addison-Wesley, 1977.

14. ELLIOTT, D. P. "Paper and Cost Control." Project Management Proceedings, 1979.

15. FRAZIER, HAUGG, and THACKERY. "Developing A Project Management Package." Journal of Systems Management, Dec. 1976.

16. GRANT, R. A., C. A. HIGGINS, and R. H. IRVING. "Computerized Performance Monitors: Are They Costing You Customers?" Sloan Management Review, Spring 1988.

17. HAJEK, V. G. Management of Engineering Projects. New York: McGraw Hill, 1977.

18. HIGGINS, J. C., and R. FINN. "Managerial Attitudes Toward Computer Models for Planning and Control." Long Range Planning, Dec. 1976.

19. HOLLANDER, G. L. "Integrated Project Control, Part II: TCP/Schedule: A Model for Integrated Project Control." Project Management Quarterly, June 1973.

20. HOROVITZ, J. H. "Strategic Control: A New Task for Top Management." Long Range Planning, June 1979.

21. HOWARD, D. C. "Cost Schedule Control Systems." Management Accounting, Oct. 1976.

22. JOHNSON, J. R. "Advanced Project Control." Journal of Systems Management, May 1977.

23. KARAA, F. A., and B. ABDALLAH. "Coordination Mechanisms During the Construction Project Life Cycle." Project Management Journal, Sept. 1991.

24. KEANE, A. "Timing for Project Management Control." Data Management, 1979.

25. KERZNER, H. "Evaluation Techniques in Project Management." Journal of Systems Management, Feb. 1980.

26. LARSEN, S. D. "Control of Construction Projects: An Integrated Approach." The Internal Auditor, Sept. 1979.

27. LIKIERMAN, A. "Avoiding Cost Escalation on Major Projects." Management Accounting, Feb. 1980.

28. LIVINGSTON, J. L., and R. RONEN. "Motivation and Management Control Systems." Decision Sciences, April 1975.

29. MARTYN, A. S. "Some Problems in Managing Complex Development Projects." Long Range Planning, April 1975.

30. MORAVEC, M. "How Organizational Development Can Help and Hinder Project Managers." Project Management Quarterly, Sept. 1979.

31. MURDICK, R. G. et al. Information Systems for Modern Management, 3rd ed. Englewood Cliffs, NJ: Prentice Hall, 1984.

32. MYERS, G. "Forms Management; Part 5—How to Achieve Control." Journal of Systems Management, Feb. 1977.

33. NEWMAN, W. H. Constructive Control. Englewood Cliffs, NJ: Prentice Hall, 1975.

34. NEWNEM, A. "Planning Ahead with an Integrated Management Control System." Project Management Proceedings, 1979.

35. PARTOVI, F. Y., and J. BURTON. "Timing of Monitoring and Control of CPM Projects." IEEE Transactions on Engineering Management, Feb. 1993.

36. ROETZHEIM, W. H. "Managing Software Projects: Unique Problems and Requirements." in P. C. Dinsmore, ed., The AMA Handbook of Project Management. New York: AMACOM, 1993.

37. ROMAN, D. D. Managing Projects: A Systems Approach. New York: Elsevier, 1986.

38. SAEED, B. I., D. M. BOWEN, and V. S. SOHONI. "Avoiding Engineering Changes through Focused

Manufacturing Knowledge." IEEE *Transactions on Engineering Management*, Feb. 1993.

39. SAITOW, A. R. "CSPC: Reporting Project Progress to the Top." In E. W. Davis, ed., *Project Management: Techniques, Applications and Managerial Issues*. Norcross, GA: American Institute of Industrial Engineers, 1976.

40. SANDERS, J. "Effective Estimating Process Outlined." *Computer World*, April 7, 14, and 21, 1980.

41. SCHODERBEK, C. G., P. P. SCHODERBEK, and A. G. KEFALAS. *Management Systems*, 4th ed. Homewood, IL: Irwin, 1989.

42. SCHOOF, G. "What Is the Scope of Project Control?" *Project Management Proceedings*, 1979.

43. SETHI, N. K. "Project Management." *Industrial Management*, Jan–Feb. 1980.

44. SNOWDON, M. "Measuring Performance in Capital Project Management." *Long Range Planning*, Aug. 1980.

45. SOUDER, W. E. "Autonomy, Gratification, and R & D Outputs: A Small-Sample Field Study." *Management Science*, April 1974.

46. TIONG, R. L. K. "Effective Controls for Large Scale Construction Projects." *Project Management Journal*, Mar. 1990.

47. TOELLNER, J. D. "Project Management: A Formula for Success." *Computer World*, Dec. 1978.

48. VAN GIGCH, J. P. *Applied General Systems Theory*, 2nd ed. New York: Harper & Row, 1978.

49. WEBER, F. M. "Ways to Improve Performance on Projects." *Project Management Quarterly*, Sept. 1981.

50. YUNUS, N. B., D. L. BABCOCK, and C. BENJAMIN. "Development of a Knowledge-Based Schedule Planning System." *Project Management Journal*, Dec. 1990.

51. ZELDMAN, M. *Keeping Technical Projects on Target*. New York: American Management Association, 1978.

# CASE

## CORNING GLASS WORKS: THE Z-GLASS PROJECT[*]
### Kim B. Clark

After several highly successful years, 1977 had been a difficult one at Corning Glass Work's Harrisburg plant. In July the yields and productivity of the Z-Glass process had begun a long decline, and the entire plant organization was working overtime trying to correct the problem. Morale was plummeting as yields continued to decline throughout the summer and fall. In December of 1977, a team of engineers from the corporate Manufacturing and Engineering (M&E) staff had been assigned to the plant; its charter was to focus on long-term process improvement while the line organization concentrated on day-to-day operations.

On the morning of March 24, 1978, Eric Davidson, leader of the M&E project team at Harrisburg, sat in his office and reflected on the group's first three months in the plant. The project had not gone well, and Davidson knew that his team members were discouraged. The technical problems they faced were difficult enough, but it seemed that the line organization had resisted almost everything the M&E team had tried to do. In addition to conflicts over responsibility and authority, there were deep disagreements about the sources of the problems and how best to deal with them. Real cooperation was almost nonexistent, and the relationships between team and line personnel in some departments were tense. Davidson felt that a change in the direction of the project had to be made immediately.

---

[*] This case has become a classic in the project implementation literature for its lessons in human behavior as well as technical analysis of laboratory data. Though somewhat dated now, the lessons are still highly relevant. Copyright 1981 by the President and Fellows of Harvard College. Harvard Business School Case 681-091. This case was prepared by Kim B. Clark as a basis for class discussion rather than to illustrate either effective or ineffective handling of an administra-tive situation. Reprinted by permission of the Harvard Business School.

As he began to sift through the comments and memos from his team, he recalled what David Leibson, vice president of Manufacturing and Engineering, had said to him shortly after he accepted the Harrisburg assignment:

Eric, this is the M&E group's first major turnaround project and the first real project of any kind in the Industrial Products division. I picked you for this job because you're the kind of guy who gets things done. This is a key one for our group, and I think a big one for the company. In situations like this, you either win big or you lose big. There's very little middle ground.

## Corning Glass Works in the 1970s

During the late 1960s and early 1970s Corning Glass Works was a corporation in transition: long a leader in the development of glass and ceramic products for industrial and commercial uses, Corning had entered several consumer goods markets during the 1960s. Under the direction of Lee Waterman, president from 1962 to 1971, Corning developed a strong marketing emphasis to go along with several new consumer products.

Although the public's perception of Corning in the 1960s was no doubt dominated by its well-known Pyrex and Ovenware cooking products, and Pyroceram dinnerware, its most successful consumer-oriented product was actually TV tube casings. Utilizing an innovative glass-forming process, Corning entered the market for TV tube funnels and front plates in 1958 and soon developed a strong market position. Throughout the mid- to late 1960s, growth in TV at Corning was rapid, and the profits at the TV division constituted the backbone of the income statement.

During the heyday of TV, Corning's organization was decentralized. The operating divisions had considerable control over marketing and manufacturing decisions, and corporate staffs in these areas were relatively small. Only in research and development did corporate staff personnel play a major role in the direction of the company. The Technical Staffs Division was responsible for all research and development activities, as well as for manufacturing engineering. New products were regarded as the lifeblood of the corporation, and the director of new product development, Harvey Blackburn, had built a creative and energetic staff. It was Blackburn's group that developed the glass-forming process that made TV tube production

possible, and it was to this group that the corporation looked when growth in the TV division and other consumer products began to slow in the late 1960s.

## Changes in TV and Corporate Reorganization

The critical year for the TV division at Corning was 1968. Up to that point, sales and profits had grown rapidly, and Corning had carved out a substantial share of the market. In 1968, however, RCA (a major Corning customer) opened a plant in Ohio to produce glass funnels and front plates. Several of the engineering and management personnel at the new RCA plant were former Corning employees. RCA's decision to integrate backward into glass production had a noticeable effect on the performance of the TV division. Although the business remained profitable, growth over the next three years was much less rapid, and Corning's market share declined.

Slower growth in TV in the 1969–72 period coincided with reduced profitability in other consumer products as costs for labor and basic materials escalated sharply. These developments resulted in weaker corporate financial performance and prompted a reevaluation of the basic direction of the company.

The outcome of these deliberations was a reemphasis of the technical competence of the company in new project development and a focus on process excellence and productivity. A major step in the new approach to operations and production was the establishment of the Manufacturing and Engineering Division (M&E) at the corporate level. This reorganization brought together staff specialists in processes, systems, and equipment under the direction of David Leibson, who was promoted from the job of director of manufacturing at the TV division and was named a corporate vice president.

Shortly after the M&E Division was formed, Thomas MacAvoy, who was the general manager of the Electronics Division and the former director of physical research on Corning's technical staff, was named president of the company. MacAvoy was the first Corning president in recent times with a technical background; he had a PhD in chemistry and a strong record in research and development. An internal staff memorandum summed up the issues facing Corning under MacAvoy:

Our analysis of productivity growth at Corning from 1960 to 1970 shows that we performed no better than the average for other glass products manufacturers (2–4 percent per year) and in the last two years have actually been below average. With prices on the increase, improved productivity growth is imperative. At the same time, we have to improve our ability to exploit new products. It appears that research output has, if anything, increased in the last few years (Z-Glass is a prime example), but we have to do a much better job of transferring products from the lab into production.

## The Manufacturing and Engineering Division

Much of the responsibility for improved productivity and the transfer of technology (either product or process) from research to production fell to the new and untried M&E division. Because of the company's historical preference for a small, relatively inactive manufacturing staff, building the M&E group into a strong and effective organization was a considerable challenge. Looking back on the early days, David Leibson reflected on his approach.

I tried to do two things in the first year:

1.  Attract people with very strong technical skills in the basic processes and disciplines in use at Corning; and
2.  Establish a working relationship with the manufacturing people in the operating divisions. I think the thing that made the difference in that first year was the solid support we got from Tom MacAvoy. It was made clear to all of the division general managers that productivity growth and cost reduction were top priorities.

From 1972 to 1977 engineers from the M&E division were involved in numerous projects throughout Corning involving the installation of new equipment and process changes. A typical project might involve four to five M&E engineers working with a plant organization to install a new type of conveyor system, possibly one designed in the M&E division. The installation project might last three to four months, and the M&E team would normally serve as consultants thereafter.

In addition to equipment products and internal consulting, the M&E group became involved in the transfer of products from R&D to production. After laboratory development and prototype testing, new products were assigned to an M&E product team which took responsibility for the design of any new equipment required and for engineering and implementing the new process. Leibson felt that successful transfer required people who appreciated both the development process and the problems of production. In many respects M&E product teams served as mediators and translators; especially in the first few projects, their primary task was to establish credibility with R&D group and with the manufacturing people in the operating divisions.

By 1976, the M&E division had conducted projects and helped to transfer new products in most of Corning's divisions, although its role in industrial products was still quite limited. The manufacturing organization in that division had been relatively strong and independent, but Leibson felt that the reputation and expertise of his staff was increasing and that opportunities for collaboration were not far off. He also felt that M&E was ready to take on a completely new kind of responsibility: a turnaround project. From time to time parts of a production process, even whole plants, would experience a deterioration in performance. In some instances, these situations would last for several months and could have serious competitive consequences. It was Leibson's view that a concentrated application of engineering expertise could shorten the turnaround time significantly and could have a measurable impact on overall corporate productivity.

## The Z-Glass Project

The opportunity for M&E involvement in a major turnaround effort and for collaboration with the Industrial Products division came in late 1977. Since June of that year, yields on the Z-Glass process at the division's Harrisburg plant had experienced a sharp decline (see Exhibit 1). Substantial effort on the part of the plant organization failed to change the downward drift in yields, and in October, Oliver Williams, director of manufacturing for industrial products, met with David Leibson to establish an M&E project at Harrisburg.

Williams, a chemical engineer with an MBA from NYU, had been named director of manufacturing in November of 1976, after 18 years of experience in various engineering and operations positions at Corning. He felt that the importance of the product (corporate expectations for Z-Glass were very high) and the seriousness of the problem warranted strong measures.

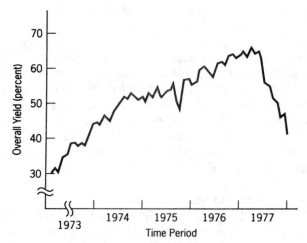

**Exhibit 1:** Overall Yield 1973–1977

The agreement he worked out with Leibson called for an M&E project team to work in the plant under the general supervision of a Review Board composed of Leibson, Williams, Martin Abramson, head of process engineering in the M&E division, and Bill Chenevert, head of M&E equipment development group. (See Exhibit 2 for an organization chart.) The team's charter was to increase yields, define and document the process and train the operating people (see Exhibit 3). A budget, the size of the team, specific goals, and timetable were to be developed in the first month of the team's operation.

While the plant manager and his staff had not been involved in the decision to bring in the M&E

team, Williams and Leibson agreed that their involvement and support were essential. A decision was made to allocate all M&E charges to the Industrial Products division in order to relieve the plant of the extra overhead expense. Moreover, M&E specialists assigned to the project would be located in the plant on a full-time basis.

Since this was M&E's first turnaround project, Leibson was personally involved in the selection of the team leader and key project engineers. He had no trouble finding people willing to work on the project. It was clear to everyone in the M&E group that "turnarounds" were the next major activity for the group and that those working on the first team would be breaking a lot of new ground. Leibson chose Eric Davidson to lead the Harrisburg project. He was 32 years old, had a masters degree in mechanical engineering from Cornell, and six years of experience at Corning. Davidson had completed several projects in the M&E division, including one in France, and had also worked as an assistant plant manager. A close friend and colleague commented on Davidson's reputation:

> To say that Eric is on the fast track is a bit of an understatement. He has been given one challenging assignment after another and has been very successful. The word around M&E is that if you have a tough problem you want solved, just give it to Eric and get out of the way.

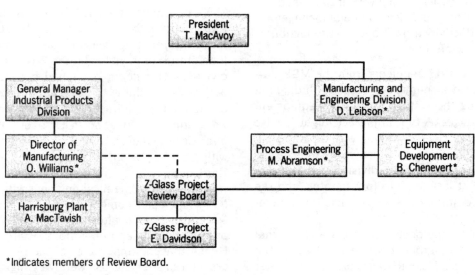

*Indicates members of Review Board.
**Exhibit 2:** Organization Chart

---

**MEMORANDUM**

To:     E. Davidson E. D.                                    November 24, 1977
From:  Harrisburg project team
Re:     Team charter

The charter of the project team is yield improvement as a top priority, definition and documentation of the process, and operator training. Enclosed is a copy of the proposed Process Definition and Documentation Program; it will serve as the framework for process diagnosis and control. Its main elements are as follows:

**Priority**

1.   Define best known *operating setpoint* for each major variable.

2.   Establish auditing system to track variables daily with built-in feedback loop.

3.   Develop and implement *process troubleshooting* guides.

4.   Write and implement *Operating Procedures*.

5.   *Train* operating personnel in procedure usage.

6.   *Audit* operating procedures on random frequency.

7.   Write and implement *Machine Specification Procedures*.

Your comments on the program are encouraged.

---

**Exhibit 3**

Working under Leibson's direction, Davidson spent the first two weeks of his assignment meeting with the plant management and selecting members of the M&E team. At the outset, he chose four specialists to work on the first phase of the project—data collection and problem definition:

*Richard Grebwell:* 35 years old, an expert in statistical process analysis with 10 years of experience at Corning. While Grebwell was considered by some to be a bit eccentric, his characteristically brilliant use of statistical analysis was vital to the project.

*Jennifer Rigby:* 28 years old, with a master's degree in industrial engineering from the University of Texas. She had worked in the Harrisburg plant for six months on her first assignment at Corning.

*Arthur Hopkins:* 40 years old, a mechanical engineer with 12 years of Corning experience. Hopkins had worked with Davidson on the French project and was, in Davidson's words, a "wizard with equipment."

*Frank Arnoldus:* 37 years old, a chemist with Corning for six years. He also had worked on the French project and had earned Davidson's admiration for his ability to solve processing problems.

Davidson's plan for the first two to three weeks was to use the small group to identify problems and then expand the team as specific tasks and subprojects were established. His objectives were focused on the long term:

I'm after increases in yields as soon as we can get them, but what I'm really shooting for is permanent improvements in the process. To do what we've go to do to define the process and document its operation. My whole approach is based on the idea of "receivership": whatever solutions we come up with have to be received, or accepted, by the plant organization. And I mean really accepted; they have to "own" the changes. That's why I will be taking a team approach—each project we do will have two co-leaders, one from M&E (the transferer) and one from the plant (the receiver).

After a brief period to get acquainted and develop a plan, Davidson and his M&E team began working in the plant on December 10, 1977.

## Z-Glass: Product and Process

Z-Glass was Corning's code name for a multilayered, compression-molded glass product which was exceptionally strong and impact-resistant for its weight. Its durability and hardness, combined with its low weight and competitive cost, made it an attractive substitute for ceramic and plastic products used in the construction and auto industries. Introduced in 1973, Z-Glass products were an immediate success. From 1973 to 1977 production capacity grew 35 to 40 percent per year and still had failed to keep up with demand (see Exhibit 4). Many people thought that the current array of products was only the beginning of Z-Glass applications.

To Corning's knowledge, no other company in the world had yet developed the capability to make a product like Z-Glass, and if one did, it was assumed that they would have to license the technology from Corning. In fact, much of this technology was still an artform in the sense that a number of the characteristics of most Z-Glass products were not completely explainable in terms of known glass technology: people knew what it could do and roughly why it could do it but were still utilizing trial-and-error methods to perfect existing products and develop new ones.

Z-Glass had been developed by Harvey Blackburn and his staff during the early 1970s. In every sense of the word, the product was Blackburn's "baby." He not only conceived of the idea, but typical of the way Corning operated before the M&E division was created, he and his staff solved numerous technical problems, built all the machinery and equipment needed for prototype production, and even worked in the plant during startup. Furthermore, Blackburn had championed the product in discussions with top management. Several times when the project was not going well, his reputation and skills of persuasion were

what kept funding going. When yields began to fall in 1977, engineers at Harrisburg had consulted Blackburn on an ad hoc basis; he still felt responsible for the product and was a walking encyclopedia of information on its nuances and subtleties.

## The Process

The production of Z-Glass products consisted of three main steps: melting, molding, and finishing, which were closely linked and had to be carried out in a fixed time sequence. The process required precise control over the composition and thicknesses of the various glass layers, as well as careful timing and monitoring during the molding and finishing operations. Maintaining this precision in a high-volume environment required continuous, tight controls as well as a "feel" for the process.

## Melting

The first step was the preparation of the different types of molten glass which composed the various layers. These mixtures were prepared in separate electrically heated vats, which were designed and built by Corning. Each vat had to be carefully monitored to ensure that the ingredients of the glass were in correct proportion, distributed evenly throughout the vat, and at the appropriate temperature.

The "base" layer was poured continuously onto a narrow (two–three foot) moving strip. The outer layers were poured on top of each other at precisely controlled intervals so that when the layered strip arrived at the molding stage each layer of the multilayered

| | Z1* | | Z4† | | Z10 | | Z35 | | Z12 | | Total | |
|---|---|---|---|---|---|---|---|---|---|---|---|---|
| | Pieces | Amount | Pieces | Amount | Pieces | Amount | Pieces | Amount | Pieces | Amount | Pieces | Amount |
| 1973 | — | — | — | — | 119 | $2,220.1 | 495 | $5,217.8 | — | — | 614 | $ 7,431.9 |
| 1974 | — | — | — | — | 232 | 4,315.2 | 549 | 6,313.5 | — | — | 781 | 10,628.7 |
| 1975 | 384 | $ 5,161.5 | — | — | 239 | 4,983.2 | 552 | 6,513.6 | — | — | 1,175 | 16,658.3 |
| 1976 | 784 | 11,514.2 | 45 | $ 552.3 | 268 | 5,831.9 | 591 | 7,541.7 | 82 | $1,213.2 | 1,770 | 26,653.3 |
| 1977 | 803 | 12,005.0 | 407 | 5,372.4 | 264 | 6,087.6 | 671 | 8,689.5 | 534 | 8,410.5 | 2,679 | 40,565.0 |
| 1978‡ | 171 | 2,565.1 | 35 | 493.5 | 145 | 1,957.5 | 250 | 2,975.2 | 61 | 988.3 | 662 | 8,979.6 |

*Introduced in early 1975.

†Introduced in late 1976.

‡Data for 1978 cover reporting periods 1–3 (i.e., first 12 weeks of 1978). Note that because of seasonal factors it is not possible to arrive at an accurate indication of annual output of a particular product by multiplying the 1978 (1–3) results by 13/3.

**Exhibit 4:** Harrisburg Plant Sales by Product Line 1973–1978 (000s)

glass sandwich was at the proper temperature and thickness for molding. Minor (and, at the beginning of process development, almost unmeasurable) deviations from the "recipe" could lead to major problems, which often could be solved only on an ad hoc basis utilizing the unprogrammable skill of the operators and technicians.

Some of these problems were clearly identifiable with the melting operations. For example, the existence of "blisters" (tiny bubbles in one or more of the glass layers), "stones" (unmelted bits of sand), and "streaks" (imperfectly melted or mixed ingredients) were observable visually and were obvious indicators of problems. Separation of the different layers, either after the molding or finishing operations, often could also be traced to improper execution during melting. But when the glass sandwich did not mold properly, there was usually some question as to which operation was at fault.

A process engineer explained the difficulty of melting control:

> The secret to avoiding problems at the melting state is maintaining its stability. Sometimes it's easy to tell when something has gone wrong there, but more often you don't find out until something goes wrong at a later stage. And usually it takes a long time to determine whether you've really solved the problem or are simply treating a symptom of a larger problem. It's tough to keep on top of what is going on in each of those melting vats because it's largely a chemical operation.

Despite the difficulty of maintaining control over the melting operation and of correcting it when problems developed, Corning had been able to achieve yields of as high as 95 percent at this stage of the process.

## Molding

In contrast to melting, molding was basically a physical operation: rectangles of the soft glass sandwich were cut off the moving strip and moved onto a series of separated conveyor belts. Each slab was inserted between the jaws of a compression-molding device which contained a number of molds for the particular parts being produced. After the parts were stamped out, they continued down the conveyor line while the glass trim was discarded. Depending on the product

mix, several conveyors might pool their contents before the parts entered the finishing stage.

Despite the apparent simplicity of this process (problems could be detected quickly and usually corrected quickly), so many different kinds of problems arose and so many different variables could be manipulated that it was generally considered to be even more of a problem to control this stage than the melting stage. Typical problems included the basic dimensional specifications of the product, its edge configuration, and "buckling" and "flattening" after molding. The occurrence of these problems, together with machine downtime associated both with correcting problems and changing the product mix, made it difficult to achieve more than an 80 percent efficiency (good output to rated machine capacity) during this stage of the process.

## Finishing

The finishing operation consisted of heat treating the molded objects, then applying one of a variety of possible coatings to them. Heat treating both stabilized the internal tensions generated by the molding operation and appeared to improve the lamination between the various layers of the glass sandwich as well. Since it required a precise sequence of temperatures and their duration, this operation took place while the objects passed through long ovens on their conveyor belts. It usually did not present a problem, but if cracks or layer separation occurred, the heat-treating operation was sometimes the cause.

The application of coatings, on the other hand, was more of a job-shop operation and could be done off-line. There were a number of possible kinds of coatings that could be applied, from either purely practical (improving the reflective, insulating, or electrical conducting properties of surface) to purely ornamental. Sometimes decals were also applied either in place of or in addition to a coating. The number of possible coatings was steadily increasing, and one process engineer characterized the process as "a continual bother: lots of short runs but a necessity to maintain high speeds." The target yield was 95 percent, but it was seldom attained.

The differing characteristics of the three stages made overall control and fine-tuning of the total process quite difficult. The backgrounds and skills of the "hot end" workers were very different from those at the "cold end," and completely different branches of engineering were involved. When problems arose, many of them were undetectable for some time and often only showed up during destructive testing of parts after they had proceeded completely through the process. Then it was often difficult to isolate which part of the process was at fault because there appeared to be a high degree of interrelation between them. And finally, once a problem and its cause were identified, it sometimes took a long period of trial-and-error fiddling until people could be convinced that it was indeed corrected.

## The Harrisburg Plant

The decision to put Z-Glass into the Harrisburg plant had been based on its availability. Long devoted to the production of headlights and other auto products (the plant was built in 1958), the plant had experienced several years of excess capacity in the late 1960s. In 1972, headlight production was consolidated in the Farwell, Ohio, plant, and Harrisburg was set up for Z-Glass production. Several of the production foremen and manufacturing staff members were transferred to Farwell and replaced by individuals who had been involved in Z-Glass prototype production. (Exhibit 5 contains a profit and loss statement for the Harrisburg plant in 1975–76.)

The plant manager at Harrisburg was Andrew MacTavish, a 54-year-old native of Scotland. He came

| | 1976 | 1977 |
|---|---|---|
| Sales* | $26,653.3 | $40,565.0 |
| Direct expenses | | |
|   Materials | 9,947.2 | 16,214.2 |
|   Labor | 3,714.3 | 6,194.7 |
| Gross profit | 12,991.8 | 18,156.1 |
| Manufacturing overhead | | |
|   Fixed† | 6,582.6 | 11,016.9 |
|   Variable‡ | 1,429.3 | 2,114.4 |
| Plant administrative expenses | 1,784.5 | 2,715.2 |
| Plant profit | $ 3,195.4 | $ 2,219.6 |

*Capacity utilization (on a nominal sales basis) was 92 percent in 1976 and 84 percent in 1977.

†Includes depreciation, insurance, taxes, maintenance, utilities, and supervision.

‡Includes fringe benefits, indirect labor and tools, and supplies.

**Exhibit 5:** Z-Glass Project, Harrisburg Plant Profit and Loss Statement, 1976–77 ($000)

to the United States shortly after World War II and began working at Corning as a helper on a shipping crew at the old main plant. Over the years, MacTavish had worked his way up through various supervisory positions to production superintendent and finally to plant manager. He was a large man with a ruddy complexion and a deep booming voice. Although his temper was notorious, most people who had worked with him felt that some of his notorious tirades were more than a little calculated. Whatever peoples' perceptions of his personality might be, there was no question as to who was in charge at Harrisburg.

In mid-1977 MacTavish had been at Harrisburg for six years. From the beginning he had developed a reputation as a champion of the "little people," as he called them. He wore what the workers wore and spent two to three hours each day on the factory floor talking with foremen, supervisors, and production workers. If he had a philosophy of plant operations, it was to keep management as close to the people as possible and to rely on the experience, judgment, and skill of his workers in solving problems.

The Harrisburg plant was organized along department lines, with a production superintendent responsible for three general foremen who managed the melting, forming, and finishing departments. Ron Lewis, production superintendent, had come to the plant in 1975 after eight years of Corning experience. He was quietly efficient and had developed a good rapport with the foremen and supervisors. Besides Lewis, three other managers reported to MacTavish: Al Midgely, director of maintenance and engineering; Arnie Haggstrom, director of production planning and inventory control; and Royce Ferguson, head of personnel.

By June of 1977 the management group at the Harrisburg plant had worked together for two years and had established what MacTavish thought was a solid organization. Speaking to a visitor in May of 1977 he commented:

> I've seen a lot of plant organizations in my time, but this one has worked better than any of them. When we sit down in staff meetings every morning, everyone is on top of their situation, and we've learned to get to the heart of our problems quickly. With the different personalities around here you'd think it would be a dog-fight, but these people really work together.

Of all the managers on his staff, MacTavish worked most closely with Al Midgely. Midgely, 46 years old, had come to the plant with MacTavish, had a B.S. in mechanical engineering, and was regarded as a genius when it came to equipment ("He can build or fix anything," MacTavish claimed). He was devoted to MacTavish:

> Ten years ago, Andy MacTavish saved my life. I had some family problems after I lost my job at Bausch and Lomb, but Andy gave me a chance and helped me pick up the pieces. Everything I have I owe to him.

Several other people in the Harrisburg plant gratefully acknowledge MacTavish's willingness to help his people.

## The M&E Project at Harrisburg

Davidson's first priority in the first two weeks of the project was to define the problem. Overall yields had declined, but there had been no analysis of available information to identify the major causes. It seemed clear to the M&E group that the plant organization had spent its time on firefighting during the past six months, and there had been little overall direction. Richard Grebwell concerned himself with analyzing the historical data collected by the production control

department. The rest of the team spent the first two weeks familiarizing themselves with the process, meeting with their counterparts in the plant organization, and meeting together to compare notes and develop hypotheses about what was going on.

One problem surfaced immediately: the relative inexperience of the department supervisors. As MacTavish explained to them, four of the six supervisors had been in the plant less than nine months. The people they replaced had been with the Z-Glass process since its prototype days. MacTavish felt that part of the explanation for the decline in yields was the departure of people who knew and understood the process extremely well. He expressed confidence in the new people and indicated that they were rapidly becoming quite knowledgeable.

Grebwell's preliminary statistical work (see Exhibit 6) pointed to the molding department as the primary source of defects, with finishing the second major source. The team identified four areas for immediate attention: overall downtime, trim settings, glass adhesion and layer separation. As Grebwell's work proceeded, other projects in other departments were identified, and additional staff members were added to the team. By the middle of January it was evident that the overall project would have to encom-

---

**MEMORANDUM**

To:     M&E Project Team
From:  R. Grebwell
Re:     Yield report for December 1977

Below are data on yields in period 13 (provided by the production control department) along with notes based on preliminary observations. Rejects are based on 100 percent inspection. Note that selecting a reason for rejection is based on the concept of "principal cause"—if more than one defect is present, the inspector must designate one as the primary reason for rejection.

Harrisburg Plant
Yield Report Period 13, 1977

| | Good Output as a Percent of Rated Capacity[a] | | | | | Downtime[b] as a Percent of Total Available Time |
|---|---|---|---|---|---|---|
| | **Z1** | **Z4** | **Z10** | **Z35** | **Z12** | |
| I. Melting: | | | | | | |
| Glass | 70.4 | 65.4 | 72.3 | 73.5 | 66.9 | — |
| Equipment downtime | — | — | — | — | — | 10.3 |

**Exhibit 6**

| | Percent Rejected by Product, Reason, and Department[c] | | | | | Downtime[b] as a Percent of total Available Time |
|---|---|---|---|---|---|---|
| | **Z1** | **Z4** | **Z10** | **Z35** | **Z12** | |
| II. Molding and finishing: | | | | | | |
| A. Molding | | | | | | |
| Trim[d] | 6.4 | 12.8 | 4.1 | 3.4 | 10.2 | — |
| Structural | 3.7 | 6.2 | 1.7 | 2.8 | 5.7 | — |
| Adhesion | 4.5 | 8.3 | 2.5 | 3.1 | 8.5 | — |
| Downtime | — | — | — | — | — | 15.2 |
| B. Finishing | | | | | | |
| Cracks | 0.8 | 4.2 | .03 | 1.2 | 3.6 | — |
| Separation | 2.6 | 3.8 | 1.5 | 2.2 | 4.4 | — |
| Coatings | 1.9 | 2.4 | 0.6 | 1.7 | 2.1 | — |
| Downtime | — | — | — | — | — | 12.6 |

| | Good Output as a Percent of Rated Capacity | | | | | |
|---|---|---|---|---|---|---|
| | **Z1** | **Z4** | **Z10** | **Z35** | **Z12** | **Total** |
| III. Summary[e]: | | | | | | |
| Melting | 70.4 | 65.4 | 72.3 | 73.5 | 66.9 | — |
| Molding | 72.4 | 61.6 | 77.8 | 76.9 | 64.1 | — |
| Finishing | 82.8 | 78.3 | 85.3 | 82.9 | 78.6 | — |
| Overall | 42.2 | 31.5 | 48.0 | 46.9 | 33.7 | 40.7 |

[a]This is overall yield and includes the effects of glass defects as well as downtime.

[b]No data are available on equipment downtime by product; the overall figure is applied to each product.

[c]The data are presented by department. They indicate the percentage of *department* output rejected and the principal reason for rejection. Total overall process yield (good output as a percent of rated capacity) depends on both product defects and downtime.

[d]The reasons for rejection breakdown as follows:

*Molding*:

Trim: This is basically two things—dimensions and edge configuration. It looks to me like the biggest problem is with the edges. The most common cause of defects in the runs I have watched is that the settings drift out of line. Apparently this depends on where the settings are established, how they are adjusted, and the quality of the glass.

Structural: Pieces are rejected if they buckle or if the surface has indentations. This one is a real mystery—it could be a problem with the equipment (not right specs) or the operating procedures. Without some testing it's hard to tell. One possibility we need to check is whether the temperature of the incoming glass is a factor.

Adhesion: If compression ratios are too low or if the glass temperature is not "just right" or the glass has stones, then the glass adheres to the surface of the molds. The operators check the ratios, but the ideal range is marked on the gauges with little bits of tape, and I suspect the margin of error is pretty large.

*Finishing*:

Cracks: Pieces sometimes develop cracks after heat treating. The principal suspect is consistency of temperature and flame zone. It is very hard to tell whether this is due to poor initial settings or changes in flames once the process starts. Inconsistencies in the material may be another source of cracks.

Layer separation: Layer separation seems to be caused by same factors as cracks.

Castings: This is almost entirely a problem of operator error—handling damage, poor settings on the equipment, inattention to equipment going out of spec, and so forth.

[e]There are four steps to calculating overall yield:

1. For a given product in a given department, add up reject rates by reason and subtract from 1.

**Exhibit 6** (*continued*)

2. Then multiply by (1 − percent downtime) to get department yield for that product (e.g., molding yield for Z12 = (1 − .244) (1 − .152) = .641).
3. Multiply department yields to get overall yield by product (e.g., yield for Z12 = .669 × .641 × .786 = .337).
4. To get overall yield, take a weighted average of product yields, with share in total output (on a total-pieces basis) as weights: in period 13 these weights were Z1 = .3, Z4 = .15, Z10 = .10, Z35 = .25, and Z12 = .2.

**Exhibit 6** (*continued*)

pass activities throughout the plant. It was decided that the only way to measure performance equitably was to use overall yield improvement. A timetable for improved yields was established and approved by the Review Board in late January of 1978.

Davidson commented on the first six weeks of the project:

Our initial reception in the plant was luke-warm. People were a little wary of us at first, but we did establish a pretty good relationship with Ron Lewis and some of the people in the production control group. I was confident that with time we could work together with MacTavish and people in other departments, but I wasn't as confident that the problems themselves could be solved. My objective was to obtain long-term improvements by defining and documenting the process, but when I arrived I found an inadequate data base and a process more complex than anyone had imagined.

Davidson also found resistance to the very idea of process documentation. The view of MacTavish and other people in the plant was aptly summarized by Harvey Blackburn, who appeared in Harrisburg off and on throughout the first three months of the M&E project. On one such visit he took Davidson into a conference room and had the following conversation:

**Blackburn** (after drawing on the blackboard): Do you know what this is? This is a corral and inside the corral is a bucking bronco. Now what do you suppose this is?

**Davidson:** It looks like a cowboy with a book in his hand.

**Blackburn:** That's right, sonny, it's a greenhorn cowboy trying to learn how to ride a bucking bronco by reading a book. And that's just what you are trying to do with all your talk about documentation. And you'll end right where the greenhorn is going to end up; flat on your face.

## The Emergence of Conflict

Following the Review Board's acceptance of the proposed timetable, it was Davidson's intent to create subproject teams, with an M&E specialist and a plant representative as co-leaders. Despite Blackburn's lecture, Davidson pressed ahead with plans for process definition and documentation. A key element of the program was the development of instrumentation to collect information on the critical operating variables (glass temperature, machine speeds, timing, and so forth). Beginning in early January, Frank Arnoldus had spent three weeks quietly observing the process, asking questions of the operators, and working on the development of instruments. He had decided to debug and confirm the systems on one production line (there were five separate lines in the plant) before transferring the instruments to other lines.

The instrumentation project was scheduled to begin on February 1, with the installation of sensors to monitor glass temperature in the molding process. However, no plant representative for the project had been designated by that time, and Davidson postponed the installation. A series of meetings between Davidson and MacTavish then followed, but it was not until two days before the next Review Board meeting on February 23 that plant representatives for each subproject were chosen. Even then, things did not go smoothly. Frank Arnoldus described his experience:

I didn't want to impose the instrumentation program on the people; I wanted them to understand that it was a tool to help them do their jobs better. But I had a terrible time getting Hank Gordel (the co-leader of the project team) to even talk to me. He claimed he was swamped with other things. The thing of it is, he *was* busy. The plant engineering group had several projects of their own going, and those people were working 15 hours a day. But I knew there was more to it than that when people stopped talking to me and even avoided me in elevators and the cafeteria.

The other subprojects suffered a similar fate. The only team to make any progress was the group working on materials control. Ron Lewis thought the program was a good one, and he supported it; he had appointed one of his better supervisors to be co-leader. In the other areas of the plant, however, little was ac-

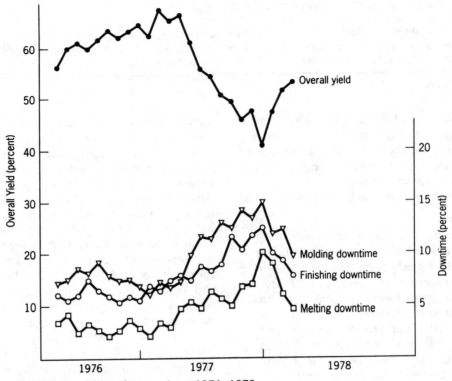

**Exhibit 7:** Yields and Downtime, 1976–1978

complished. Attempts to deal with people in the plant organization on an informal basis (lunch, drinks after work) were not successful, and Davidson's meetings with MacTavish and his requests for support were not fruitful. Indeed, it was MacTavish's view that the M&E team was part of the problem. His view was expressed forcefully in a meeting with Davidson in late March of 1978:

> I've said right from the beginning that this yield problem is basically a people problem. My experienced production people were promoted out from under me, and it has taken a few months for the new people to get up to speed. But this kind of thing is not going to happen again. I've been working on a supervisor backup training program that will give me some bench strength.
>
> I'm not saying we don't have problems. I know there are problems with the process, but the way to solve them is to get good people and give them some room. What this process needs now is some stability. Last year two new products were introduced, and this year I've got you

and your engineers out there with your experiments and your projects, fiddling around with my equipment and bothering my people.

> And then there's Blackburn. He blows in here with some crazy idea and goes right out there on the floor and gets the operators to let him try out his latest scheme. The best thing for this plant right now would be for all of you to just get out and let us get this place turned around.
>
> I am convinced we can do it. In fact, we've already been doing it. You've seen the data for the last 12 weeks.* Yields have been increasing steadily, and we're now above average for last year. While you people have been making plans and writing memos, we've been solving the problem.

## Resolving the Crisis

Eric Davidson sat at his desk in the Harrisburg plant on March 24, 1978, and reviewed the events of the last

---

*Data from the preliminary yield report are presented in Exhibits 7 and 8.

| | Product Lines | | | | | |
|---|---|---|---|---|---|---|
| **Department** | **Z1** | **Z4** | **Z10** | **Z35** | **Z12** | **Total** |
| Melting | 74.6 | 69.3 | 76.6 | 77.9 | 70.9 | — |
| Molding | 79.7 | 71.3 | 83.5 | 83.8 | 72.4 | — |
| Finishing | 85.8 | 83.7 | 88.7 | 87.6 | 84.9 | — |
| Overall | 51.0 | 41.4 | 56.7 | 57.2 | 43.6 | 53.4 |

**Exhibit 8:** Harrisburg Plant Summary of Yields, Period 3, 1978

three months. He realized that he also had been guilty of excessive firefighting and had not taken the time to step back from the situation and plot out a course of action. The situation demanded careful thought.

He was genuinely puzzled by the recent improvement in yield performance; since the M&E team had done very little beyond data analysis, the improvement must have come from somewhere else. All his training and experience supported the concept of definition and documentation, but he had never encountered such a complex process. Perhaps MacTavish was right . . . but he just couldn't bring himself to believe that.

Several options came to mind as he thought of ways to resolve the crisis; none of them were appealing. He could go to Leibson and Williams and ask (demand?) that MacTavish be replaced with someone more supportive. He could continue to try to build alliances with supporters in the plant (there were a few such people) and get a foothold in the organization. Or he could develop a new approach to the problem (perhaps new people?) and attempt to win over MacTavish. Davidson knew that his handling of this situation could have important consequences for the M&E Division, for the company, and for the careers of several people, including his own.

## ▶ QUESTIONS

1. Analyze the decline in yields to determine their cause.

2. Evaluate Davidson's approach to his assignment from Leibson's point of view.

3. Explain MacTavish's reaction to Davidson.

4. Analyze Davidson's position. What should he do now?

5. Is the M&E idea a viable concept? Is it needed?

# 13

# Project Termination

As it must to all things, termination comes to every project. At times, project death is quick and clean, but more often it is a long process; and there are times when it is practically impossible to establish that death has occurred. The skill with which termination, or a condition we might call "near termination," is managed has a great deal to do with the quality of life after the project. The termination stage of the project rarely has much impact on technical success or failure, but it has a great deal to do with residual attitudes toward the project—the "taste left in the mouth" of the client, senior management, and the project team.

At this point, the joy of discovery is past. Problems have been solved, by-passed, lived with, and/or ignored. Implementation plans have been carried out. The client is delighted, angry, or reasonably satisfied. In construction-type projects where the project cadre remains intact, the termination issue is eased because the team moves on to another challenge. For nonrecurring projects, the issue is far more akin to the breakup of a family. While the members of the family may be on the best of terms, they must now separate, go their individual ways, divide or dispose of the family property, and make plans for individual survival. The change is stressful. For projects organized as weak matrices, there will be only a few individuals, perhaps only the project manager, who "belong" to the project. This may represent an even more stressful situation than the breakup of a large project family because there is less peer group support and few or no sympathetic colleagues with whom to share the anxieties associated with transfer to a new project or back to a functional group.

The process of termination is never easy, always complicated, and, as much as we might wish to avoid it, almost always inevitable. The problem is how to accomplish one of the several levels of what is meant by project termination with a minimum of trouble and administrative dislocation.

In this chapter we examine the variety of conditions that may be generally referred to as *project termination*. As indicated above, some projects are not actually terminated, but rather are severely slowed down. We then view some decision-aiding models that can assist an organization in making the termination decision. This requires us to return to the subject of evaluation and discuss indicators of success and failure in projects. We also discuss some procedures that decrease the pain of termination, and others that reduce the administrative problems that often arise after projects have been terminated. We look into the typical causes of termination, and finally note that the preparation of a project history is an integral part of the termination process.

## ▶ 13.1    THE VARIETIES OF PROJECT TERMINATION

For our purposes, a project can be said to be terminated when work on the substance of the project has ceased or slowed to the point that further progress on the project is no longer possible, when the project has been indefinitely delayed, when its resources have been deployed to other projects, or when project personnel (especially the PM) become *personae non gratae* with senior management and in the company lunchroom. There may seem to be a spark of life left, but resuscitation to a healthy state is most unlikely. On rare occasions, projects are reborn to a new, glorious existence. But such rebirth is not expected, and project team members who "hang on to the bitter end" have allowed optimism to overcome wisdom. The PM must understand that the ancient naval tradition that the captain should go down with the ship does not serve the best interests of the Navy, the crew, the ship, and most certainly not the captain.

On the other hand, the captain must not, ratlike, flee the "ship" at the first sign of trouble. In the next section of this chapter, we note many of the signs and signals that indicate that the project may be in real trouble. At this point, it is appropriate to consider the ways in which a project can be terminated. There are four fundamentally different ways to close out a project: extinction, addition, integration, and starvation.

### Termination by Extinction

The project is stopped. It may end because it has been successful and achieved its goals: The new product has been developed and handed over to the client; the building has been completed and accepted by the purchaser; or the software has been installed and is running.

The project may also be stopped because it is unsuccessful or has been superseded: The new drug failed its efficacy tests; the yield of the chemical reaction was too low; there are better/faster/cheaper/prettier alternatives available; or it will cost too much and take too long to get the desired performance. Changes in the external environment can kill projects, too. The explosion of the Challenger stopped a number of space shuttle projects overnight. More recently, extraordinary cost escalation in the technology and materials associated with automotive racing caused the ruling bodies of both Formula I and Indy-car racing to stop (and even repeal) technological change in their respective venues.

A special case of termination by extinction is "termination by murder."* There are all sorts of murders. They range from political assassination to accidental projecticide. When senior executives vie for promotion, projects for which the loser is champion are apt to suffer. Corporate mergers often make certain projects redundant or irrelevant. NCR was forced to cancel several projects following its merger into AT&T. Two important characteristics of termination by murder, premeditated or not, are the suddenness of project demise and the lack of obvious signals that death is imminent.

When a decision is made to terminate a project by extinction, the most noticeable event is that all activity on the *substance* of the project ceases. A great deal of organizational activity, however, remains to be done. Arrangements must be made for the orderly release of project team members and their reassignment to other activities if they are to remain in the parent organization. The property, equipment, and materials belonging to the project must be disbursed according to the dictates of the project contract or in accord with the established procedures of the parent organization. Finally, the Project Final Report, also known as the *project history*, must be prepared. These subjects will be covered in greater detail later in this chapter.

## Termination by Addition

Most projects are "in-house," that is, carried out by the project team for use in the parent organization. If a project is a major success, it may be terminated by institutionalizing it as a formal part of the parent organization. NCR Corporation (now merged with AT&T and recently renamed "AT&T Global Information Solutions"), for example, uses this method of transforming a project into a division of the firm and then, if real economic stability seems assured, into an independent subsidiary. Essentially the same process occurs when a university creates an academic department out of what originally was a few courses in an existing department. For example, most software engineering and/or information systems departments began by reorganizing an engineering or business school "sub-specialty" into a full-fledged department.

When the project is made a more or less full-fledged member of the parent, it lives its first years in a protected status—much as any child is protected by the adults in the family. As the years pass, however, the child is expected gradually to assume the economic responsibilities of full adulthood.

When project success results in termination by addition, the transition is strikingly different from termination by extinction. In both cases the project ceases to exist, but there the similarity stops. Project personnel, property, and equipment are often simply transferred from the dying project to the newly born division. The metamorphosis from project to department, to division, and even to subsidiary is accompanied by budgets and administrative practices that conform to standard procedure in the parent firm, by demands for contribution profits, by the probable decline of political protection from the project's corporate "champion," indeed by a greater exposure to all the usual stresses and strains of regular, routine, day-to-day operations.

---

*The authors thank Professor Samuel G. Taylor (University of Wyoming) for noting this special case of termination by extinction.

It is not uncommon, however, for some of the more adventurous members of the project team to request transfers to other projects or to seek the chance to start new projects. Project life is exciting, and some team members are uncomfortable with what they perceive to be the staid, regulated existence of the parent organization. The change from project to division brings with it a sharply diminished sense of freedom.

This transition poses a difficult time for the PM, who must see to it that the shift is made smoothly. In Part I of this book, and especially in Chapter 3, we referred repeatedly to the indispensable requirement of political sensitivity in the PM. The transition from project to division demands a superior level of political sensitivity for successful accomplishment. Projects lead a sheltered life, for all the risks they run. The regular operating divisions of a firm are subjected to the daily infighting that seems, in most firms, to be a normal result of competition between executives.

---

## Project Management in Practice
### *Nucor's Approach to Termination by Addition*

Nucor, one of the early steel "minimills," is a highly entrepreneural firm with a compound growth rate of 23 percent per year. In 1987, its sales were $851 million with an executive staff of only 19 monitoring the operations of 23 plants and 4600 employees. As part of its strategy, Nucor in 1983 decided to move into the flat rolled steel market, the largest market for steel products. They thus initiated the construction of a major plant in Crawfordsville, Indiana, which would comprise over 20 percent of their total assets.

As another part of its strategy, Nucor does its own construction management, with most of the construction team then transitioning into permanent positions in the newly constructed plant. In this case, four managers started the conceptual team for the new facility and then brought in 19 other people from outside the company to form the rest of the construction team, none of them ever having built a steel mill before. The manager on the conceptual team for the new plant was the lead person on the site determination team and became the general manager of the facility. The field shift superintendents on the construction project will have permanent managerial responsibility for the melt shop, the hot mill, and the cold mill. The engineers will become supervisors in the mill. Even the secretary/clerk will have a position in the new facility.

Nucor also relies heavily on the services and capabilities of its suppliers in the construction process, since they are such a small firm. But it also reflects Nucor's "lean and mean" philosophy. In this case, the only error the construction team made was underestimating the engineering time required from suppliers, the time coming in at about double the estimate. Even so, the engineering costs (and probably most other labor costs, too) apparently only ran about 20 percent of what it historically costs to build this type of steel facility!

*Source*: R. Kimball, "Nucor's Strategic Project," *Project Management Journal*, Sept. 1988.

## Termination by Integration

This method of terminating a project is the most common way of dealing with successful projects, and the most complex. The property, equipment, material, personnel, and functions of the project are distributed among the existing elements of the parent organization. The output of the project becomes a standard part of the operating systems of the parent, or client.

In some cases, the problems of integration are relatively minor. The project team that installed a new machining center, instructed the client in its operation and maintenance, and then departed probably left only minor problems behind it, problems familiar to experienced operations managers. If the installation was an entire flexible manufacturing system, however, or a minicomputer complete with multiple terminals and many different pieces of software, then the complexities of integration are apt to be much more severe. In general, the problems of integration are inversely related to the level of experience that the parent organization (or client) has had with: (1) the technology being integrated and (2) the successful integration of other projects, regardless of technology.

Most of the problems of termination by addition are also present when the project is integrated. In the case of integration, the project may not be viewed as a competitive interloper, but the project personnel being moved into established units of the parent organization will be so viewed. Also, the project, which flourished so well in its protected existence as a project, may not be quite so healthy in the chill atmosphere of the "real world." The individuals who nurtured the project may have returned to their respective organizational divisions, and may have new responsibilities. They tend to lose their fervid interest in the "old" project.

Following is a list of a few of the more important aspects of the transition from project to integrated operation that must be considered when the project functions are distributed.

1. **Personnel**   Where will the project team go? Will it remain a team? If the functions that the team performed are still needed, who will do them? If ex-team members are assigned to a new project, under what conditions or circumstances might they be temporarily available for help on the old project?

2. **Manufacturing**   Is training complete? Are input materials and the required facilities available? Does the production system layout have to be replanned? Did the change create new bottlenecks or line-of-balance problems? Are new operating or control procedures needed? Is the new operation integrated into the firm's computer systems?

3. **Accounting/Finance**   Have the project accounts been closed and audited? Do the new department budgets include the additional work needed by the project? Have the new accounts been created and account numbers been distributed? Has all project property and equipment been distributed according to the contract or established agreements?

4. **Engineering**   Are all drawings complete and on file? Are operating manuals and change procedures understood? Have training programs been altered appropriately for new employees? Have maintenance schedules been adjusted for the change? Do we have a proper level of "spares" in stock?

5. **Information Systems/Software**    Has the new system been thoroughly tested? Is the software properly documented and are "comments" complete? Is the new system fully integrated with current systems? Have the potential users been properly trained to use the new system?

6. **Marketing**    Is the sales department aware of the change? Is marketing in agreement about lead times? Is marketing comfortable with the new line? Is the marketing strategy ready for implementation?

7. **Purchasing, Distribution, Legal, etc.**    Are all these and other functional areas aware of the change? Has each made sure that the transition from project to standard operation has been accomplished within standard organizational guidelines and that standard administrative procedures have been installed?

## Termination by Starvation

There is a fourth type of project termination, although strictly speaking, it is not a "termination" at all. It is "slow starvation by budget decrement." Almost anyone who has been involved with projects over a sufficient period of time to have covered a business recession has had to cope with budget cuts. Budget cuts, or decrements, are not rare. Because they are common, they are sometimes used to mask a project termination.

There may be a number of reasons why senior management does not wish to terminate an unsuccessful or obsolete project. In some firms, for example, it is politically dangerous to admit that one has championed a failure, and terminating a project that has not accomplished its goals is an admission of failure. In such a case, the project budget might receive a deep cut—or a series of small cuts—large enough to prevent further progress on the project and to force the reassignment of many project team members. In effect, the project is terminated, but the project still exists as a legal entity complete with sufficient staff to maintain some sort of presence such as a secretary who issues a project "no-progress" report each year. In general, it is considered bad manners to inquire into such projects or to ask why they are still "on the books."

## ▶ 13.2    WHEN TO TERMINATE A PROJECT

The decision to terminate a project early, by whatever method, is difficult. As we emphasized in Chapter 4, projects tend to develop a life of their own—a life seemingly independent of whether or not the project is successful. In an early article [12] on the subject of terminating R & D projects, Buell suspected that the main reason so little information was available on the subject was that it was hard to spell out specific guidelines and standards for the decision. He expressed strong doubts about the ability to "wrap everything up in a neat set of quantitative mathematical expressions," and then went on to develop an extensive set of questions that, if answered, should lead management to a decision. While these questions were aimed at R & D projects, they have wide, general applicability. Paraphrased and slightly modified to broaden and extend them beyond R & D projects, they are:

- Is the project still consistent with organizational goals?

- Is it practical? Useful?
- Is management sufficiently enthusiastic about the project to support its implementation?
- Is the scope of the project consistent with the organization's financial strength?
- Is the project consistent with the notion of a "balanced" program in all areas of the organization's technical interests? In "age"? In cost?
- Does the project have the support of all the departments (e.g., finance, manufacturing, marketing, etc.) needed to implement it?
- Is organizational project support being spread too thin?
- Is support of this individual project sufficient for success?
- Does this project represent too great an advance over current technology? Too small an advance?
- Is the project team still innovative, or has it gone stale?
- Can the new knowledge be protected by patent, copyright, or trade secret?
- Could the project be farmed out without loss of quality?
- Is the current project team properly qualified to continue the project?
- Does the organization have the required skills to achieve full implementation or exploitation of the project?
- Has the subject area of the project already been "thoroughly plowed"?
- Has the project lost its key person or champion?
- Is the project team enthusiastic about success?
- Can the potential results be purchased or subcontracted more efficiently than developed in-house?
- Does it seem likely that the project will achieve the minimum goals set for it? Is it still profitable? timely?

We could add many other such questions to Buell's list. For instance:

- Has the project been obviated by technical advances or new products/services developed elsewhere?
- Is the output of the product still cost-effective?
- Is it time to integrate or add the project as a part of the regular, ongoing operation of the parent organization?
- Would we support the project if it were proposed today at the time and cost required to complete it?
- Are there better alternative uses for the funds, time, and personnel devoted to the project?
- Has a change in the environment altered the need for the project's output?

Such questions clearly overlap, and the list could easily be extended further. Dean [16] reports that the probabilities of technical and/or commerical failure are the two most important reasons for terminating projects (see Table 13–1), according to the

**Table 13-1**   Rank-Order of Important Factors Considered in Terminating R&D Projects (36 Companies)

| Factors | No. of Companies Reporting the Factor as Being Important |
|---|---|
| *Technical* | |
| Low probability of achieving technical objectives or commercializing results | 34 |
| Technical or manufacturing problems cannot be solved with available R&D skills | 11 |
| Higher priority of other projects requiring R&D labor or funds | 10 |
| *Economic* | |
| Low profitability or return on investment | 23 |
| Too costly to develop as individual product | 18 |
| *Market* | |
| Low market potential | 16 |
| Change in competitive factors or market needs | 10 |
| *Others* | |
| Too long a time required to achieve commerical results | 6 |
| Negative effect on other projects or products | 3 |
| Patent problems | 1 |

Source: [16]

executives he surveyed. Balachandra and Raelin [9, 38] performed a discriminant analysis on 23 factors involved in terminating projects, not as a decision model, but as a way of highlighting the various factors involved and their relevance to the termination problem, as related to projects in general.

Compared to the great level of research and thought that went into the project selection decision before the 1980s (see also Chapter 2), there was relatively little research published on the termination decision. But even this bit was more than the work devoted to defining project success. As interest in project termination increased in the mid-1980s, interest in understanding project success also rose. Baker, Green, Bean, *et al.* [7,8] looked at factors associated with R & D project success and failure. Pinto and Slevin [34, 35, 36] surveyed experienced PMs and found ten factors that the managers felt to be critical to successful project implementation (see Table 13–2). Many other researchers also attacked the problem of defining success [17, 29, for example].

A particularly important finding of Baker *et al.* is that the *factors associated with project success are different for different industries.* Baker's work was restricted to R & D projects, but the Pinto and Slevin study covered many different types of projects. They found that the success-related factors differed between fundamentally different types of projects—between R & D and construction projects, for example. At the very least, the factors and their relative importance are idiosyncratic to the industry, to the project type, and, we suggest, possibly to the firm.

**Table 13-2**  Critical Success Factors in Order of Importance

1. *Project Mission*—Initial clearly defined goals and general directions.
2. *Top-Management Support*—Willingness of top management to provide the necessary resources and authority/power for project success.
3. *Project Schedule/Plan*—A detailed specification of the individual action steps for project implementation.
4. *Client Consultation*—Communication, consultation, and active listening to all impacted parties.
5. *Personnel*—Recruitment, selection, and training of the necessary personnel for the project team.
6. *Technical Tasks*—Availability of the required technology and expertise to accomplish the specific technical action steps.
7. *Client Acceptance*—The act of "selling" the final project to its ultimate intended users.
8. *Monitoring and Feedback*—Timely provision of comprehensive control information at each stage in the implementation process.
9. *Communication*—The provision of an appropriate network and necessary data to all key actors in the project implementation.
10. *Trouble-shooting*—Ability to handle unexpected crises and deviations from plan.

*Source:* [34]

Out of this work came some models that could be used to predict project success or failure, based on certain project characteristics or practices. Pinto and Mantel [33], using Pinto's work cited above, reported on factors that were associated with project failure. The factors differed for the type of project involved (R & D vs. construction), for the project's position in the life cycle, as well as for the precise way in which "failure" was defined. Green, Welsh, and Dehler found that a poor fit with the firm's existing technological expertise and/or with its existing marketing area and channels was a good early predictor of project termination [19]. Kloppenborg and Plath [25] described precursors to success and failure for projects intended to implement expert systems, and Beale and Freeman [10] modeled project success, differentiating between factors exogenous and endogenous to the project and the project team.

In the face of this diversity of success factors, it is interesting to note that there are relatively few fundamental reasons why some projects fail to produce satisfactory answers to Buell's questions.

1. **A Project Organization Is Not Required**  The use of the project form of organization was inappropriate for this particular task or in this particular environment. The parent organization must understand the conditions that require instituting a project.

2. **Insufficient Support from Senior Management**  Projects invariably develop needs for resources that were not originally allocated. Arguments between functional departments over the command of such resources are very common. Without the direct support of a champion in senior management, the project is almost certain to lose the resource battle.

3. **Naming the Wrong Person as Project Manager**  This book is testimony to the importance of the PM. A common mistake is to appoint as PM an individual with excellent technical skills but weak managerial skills or training.

4. **Poor Planning**  This is a very common cause of project failure. In the rush to get the substance of the project under way, competent planning is neglected. In such cases, crisis management becomes a way of life, difficulties and errors are compounded, and the project slowly gets farther behind schedule and over budget.

These, and a few other reasons, are the base causes of most project failures. The specific causes of failure, for the most part, derive from these fundamental items. For example:

- No use was made of earlier project Final Reports that contained a number of recommendations for operating projects in the future.
- Time/cost estimates were not prepared by those who had responsibility for doing the work.
- Starting late, the PM jumped into the tasks without adequate planning.
- Project personnel were moved without adjusting the schedule, or were reassigned during slow periods and then were unavailable when needed.
- Project auditors/evaluators were reluctant to conduct careful, detailed meaningful evaluations.
- The project was allowed to continue in existence long after it had ceased to make cost-effective progress.
- Evaluations failed to determine why problems were arising during the early phases of the project life cycle.

All these causes of failure underline the need for careful evaluation at all stages of the project. But at the same time, it is most important for the reader to note that the lion's share of the attention given to the termination issue is focused on the failing project. It is equally or more important to terminate successful projects at the right time and by proper methods. One rarely mentioned problem affecting many organizations is the inability or unwillingness of successful project managers working on successful projects to "let their projects go." This is a particularly difficult problem for in-house projects. The PM (and team) simply will not release the project to the tender care of the client department. An outstanding technical specialist and manager conducting communications projects was released from employment simply because she insisted on maintaining semi-permanent control of projects that had essentially been completed, but which were not released to the users because they "needed further testing" or "fine-tuning."

Also, little consideration has been given to *how* the termination decision is made and *who* makes it. We feel that a broadly based committee of reasonably senior executives is probably best. The broad organizational base of the committee is needed to diffuse and withstand the political pressure that accompanies all terminations—successes and failures alike. To the extent possible, the criteria used by the termination committee should be written and explained in some detail. It is, however, important to write the criteria in such a way that the committee is not frozen into a mechanistic approach to a decision. There are times when hunches should be followed (or rejected) and blind faith should be respected (or ignored). It depends on whose hunches and faith are under consideration.

# ▶ 13.3  THE TERMINATION PROCESS

The termination process has two distinct parts. First is the decision whether or not to terminate. Second, if the decision is to terminate the project, the decision must be carried out.

## The Decision Process

Decision-aiding models for the termination decision fall into two generic categories. First, there are models that base the decision on the degree to which the project qualifies against a set of factors generally held to be associated with successful (or failed) projects. Second, there are models that base the decision on the degree to which the project meets the goals and objectives set for it.

Most of the research on factors associated with success and failure can be used to "predict" project success. Pinto's work with Slevin and others [particularly 33 and 35] can be used in that way. Tadisina [46], working with a set of factors associated with project success found by Baker, *et al.* [7, 8], suggested a variety of termination-decision models that could be used if the success-related factors were monitored and used as input data in the models. Freeman and Beale [17] focused their decision model on the net present value of the project, which is determined by transforming a number of success-related factors (from the sponsor's and the project manager's points of view) into NPV equivalents. Riggs, *et al.* [39] determined a set of success-related factors pertaining to government (NASA) projects by polling experienced managers using the Delphi method. From this, they developed statistically-generated "success predictor models" for manned and unmanned space projects.

The use of models that measure project success or failure based on its achievement of present goals is subject to debate.

Balachandra and Raelin [9, 38] state that project selection models are not appropriate for the project termination decision. They argue that the data requirements for selection models are too large and costly. They also argue that the evaluation of factors in project selection models may change as projects are evaluated at different stages in their life cycles. They note that the probability of technical success of a project is usually estimated to be close to 1.0 early in the life cycle, but lower during later stages when the technical problems are known. This, they say, would bias decisions in favor of new projects and against ongoing ones.

We think [27] that the first argument is generally untrue of those selection models actually being used, which are typically of modest size. As we have remarked elsewhere in this book, the uncertainty associated with most projects is not concerned with whether or not the project objective is technically achievable, but rather with the time and cost required to achieve it.

Adopting the position that sunk costs are not relevant to current investment decisions, we hold that the primary criterion for project continuance or termination is *whether or not the organization is willing to invest the estimated time and cost required to complete the project, given the project's current status and current expected outcome.* We emphasize that this criterion can be applied to any project. Balachandra and Raelin were , of course, discussing only R & D projects.

Shafer and Mantel [42] have developed a project termination decision support system (DSS) based on the widely available Lotus 1–2–3® spreadsheet and using a constrained weighted factor scoring model (see Chapter 2). The capabilities of Lotus 1–2–3® (as well as Excel®, and several other spreadsheets), allow direct modeling of the scoring model, allow customized menus, and allow decision makers to adapt and enhance the model as they gain experience in the use of the DSS. The database requirements include data on the project, on the parent organization, and on the environment. The criteria on which projects are rated, the specifics of the scores, and the relative weights of the criteria are often developed by organizational executives using the Delphi method. (For a description of the use of the Delphi method to develop weights, see [28].) If it seems desirable, the weights may be determined through discriminant analysis, as in [9, 38, 46].

Just as decision criteria, constraints, weights, and environmental data are unique to each organization, so are the specifics of using this (or any) decision model. A detailed discussion of various potential decision rules that might be useful with such a model can be found in [42]. Figure 13–1 illustrates the structure of this model.

## The Implementation Process

Once it has been decided to terminate a project, the process by which it will be terminated must be implemented. The actual termination can be planned and orderly, or a simple hatchet job. The former is apt to have significantly better results, and so we suggest that the termination process be planned, budgeted, and scheduled just as is done for any other phase of the project life cycle. Such a project is illustrated in Figure 13–2. Archibald [4] has prepared an extensive checklist of items covering the closeout of both the administrative and substantive parts of the project (see Figures 13–3a and b).

In some organizations, the processing of the project closeout is conducted under the direct supervision of the PM, but this often raises dilemmas. For many PMs, termination signals the end of their reign as project leader. If the PM has another project to lead, the issue may not be serious; but if there is no other project and if the PM faces a return to a staid life in a functional division, there may be a great temptation to stretch out the termination process.

An examination of Figures 13–2 and 13–3a and 13–3b shows that implementing termination is a complex process. Note that in Figure 13–3b such items as A-4, B-4, C-3, and G-2, among many others, are actually small projects. It is all too easy, at this final stage of the game, to give this mountain of paperwork a "lick and a promise"—easy, but foolish. Someone must handle all the bureaucratic tasks, and if the PM leaves many loose ends, he or she will rapidly get a reputation for being slipshod, a characterization not associated with career success.

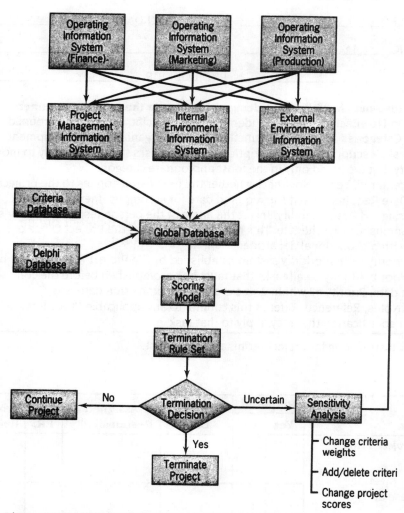

**Figure 13-1:** DSS structure for a project termination decision.

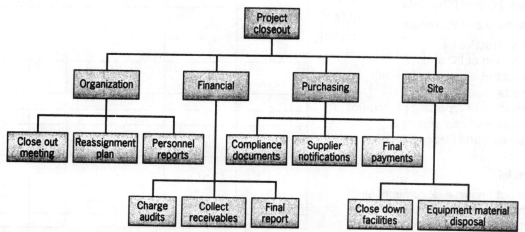

**Figure 13-2:** Design for project termination.

PROJECT TITLE _____ COMPLETION DATE _____

CONTRACT NO. _____ COST TYPE _____

CUSTOMER · _____ PROJECT MGR. _____

**The project close-out check lists are designed for use in the following manner:**

Column I—Item No.: Each task listed is identified by a specific number and grouped into categories. Categories are based on functions, not on organizations or equipment.

Column II—Task Description: Task descriptions are brief tasks that could apply to more than one category but are listed only in the most appropriate category.

Column III—Required, Yes or No: Check whether the item listed applies to the project.

Column IV—Date Required: Insert the required date for accomplishment of the task.

Column V—Assigned Responsibility: Insert the name of the person responsible to see that the task is accomplished on schedule. This may be a member of the Project Office or an individual within a functional department.

Column VI—Priority (PR): A priority system established by the Project Manager may be used here, e.g., Priority #1 may be all tasks that must be accomplished before the contractual completion date, Priority #2 within 2 weeks after the completion date, etc.

Column VII— Notes, Reference: Refer in this column to any applicable Procedures, a government specification that may apply to that task, etc.

**Figure 13-3a:** Instructions for project termination checklist.

| Item No. | Task Description | Required | | Required Date | Assigned Responsibility | PR. | Notes Reference |
|---|---|---|---|---|---|---|---|
| | | Yes | No | | | | |
| **A.** | **Project Office (PO) and Project Team (PT) Organization** | | | | | | |
| 1. | Conduct project close-out meeting | | | | | | |
| 2. | Establish PO and PT release and reassignment plan | | | | | | |
| 3. | Carry out necessary personnel actions | | | | | | |
| 4. | Prepare personal performance evaluation on each PO and PT member | | | | | | |
| **B.** | **Instructions and Procedures** | | | | | | |
| | Issue Instructions for: | | | | | | |
| 1. | Termination of PO and PT | | | | | | |
| 2. | Close-out of all work orders and contracts | | | | | | |
| 3. | Termination of reporting procedures | | | | | | |
| 4. | Preparation of final report(s) | | | | | | |
| 5. | Completion and disposition of project file | | | | | | |
| **C.** | **Financial** | | | | | | |
| 1. | Close out financial documents and records | | | | | | |
| 2. | Audit final charges and costs | | | | | | |

**Figure 13-3b:** Checklist for project termination. Source: [4]

| Item No. | Task Description | Required | | Required Date | Assigned Responsibility | PR. | Notes Reference |
|---|---|---|---|---|---|---|---|
| | | Yes | No | | | | |
| 3. | Prepare final project financial report(s) | | | | | | |
| 4. | Collect receivables | | | | | | |
| **D.** | **Project Definition** | | | | | | |
| 1. | Document final approved project scope | | | | | | |
| 2. | Prepare final project breakdown structure and enter into project file | | | | | | |
| **E.** | **Plans, Budgets, and Schedules** | | | | | | |
| 1. | Document actual delivery dates of all contractual deliverable end items | | | | | | |
| 2. | Document actual completion dates of all other contractual obligations | | | | | | |
| 3. | Prepare final project and task status reports | | | | | | |
| **F.** | **Work Authorization and Control** | | | | | | |
| 1. | Close out all work orders and contracts | | | | | | |
| **G.** | **Project Evaluation and Control** | | | | | | |
| 1. | Assure completion of all action assignments | | | | | | |
| 2. | Prepare final evaluation report(s) | | | | | | |
| 3. | Conduct final review meeting | | | | | | |
| 4. | Terminate financial, manpower, and progress reporting procedures | | | | | | |
| **H.** | **Management and Customer Reporting** | | | | | | |
| 1. | Submit final report to customer | | | | | | |
| 2. | Submit final report to management | | | | | | |
| **I.** | **Marketing and Contract Administration** | | | | | | |
| 1. | Compile all final contract documents with revision, waivers, and related correspondence | | | | | | |
| 2. | Verify and document compliance with all contractual terms | | | | | | |
| 3. | Compile required proof of shipment and customer acceptance documents | | | | | | |
| 4. | Officially notify customer of contract completion | | | | | | |
| 5. | Initiate and pursue any claims against customer | | | | | | |
| 6. | Prepare and conduct defense against claims by customer | | | | | | |
| 7. | Initiate public relations announcements re. contract completion | | | | | | |
| 8. | Prepare final contract status report | | | | | | |

**Figure 13-3b:** (continued)

| Item No. | Task Description | Required | | Required Date | Assigned Responsibility | PR. | Notes Reference |
|---|---|---|---|---|---|---|---|
| | | Yes | No | | | | |
| **J.** | *Extension-New Business* | | | | | | |
| 1. | Document possibilities for project or contract extensions, or other related new business | | | | | | |
| 2. | Obtain commitment for extension | | | | | | |
| **K.** | *Project Records Control* | | | | | | |
| 1. | Complete project file and transmit to designated manager | | | | | | |
| 2. | Dispose of other project records as required by established procedures | | | | | | |
| **L.** | *Purchasing and Subcontracting* | | | | | | |
| | For each Purchase Order and Subcontract: | | | | | | |
| 1. | Document compliance and completion | | | | | | |
| 2. | Verify final payment and proper accounting to project | | | | | | |
| 3. | Notify vendor/contractor of final completion | | | | | | |
| **M.** | *Engineering Documentation* | | | | | | |
| 1. | Compile and store all engineering documentation | | | | | | |
| 2. | Prepare final technical report | | | | | | |
| **N.** | *Site Operations* | | | | | | |
| 1. | Close down site operations | | | | | | |
| 2. | Dispose of equipment and material | | | | | | |

**Figure 13-3b:** (*continued*)

The PM also has another option, to ignore the termination process entirely. The evaluation has already been conducted and praise or censure has been delivered. Rather than deal with termination, the PM may let the project administrator handle things. Project team members may well have similar feelings and reactions, and may seek new jobs or affiliations before the project actually ends, thereby dragging out some final tasks interminably.

Special *termination managers* are sometimes useful in completing the long and involved process of shutting down a project. In such cases, the PM is transferred to another project or reassigned to a functional "home." The termination manager does not have to deal with substantive project tasks and therefore may be a person familiar with the administrative requirements of termination and the environment within which the project will be operating (if it continues to live).

If technical knowledge is required during the termination process, a member of the project team may be upgraded and assigned responsibility for the termination. This "promotion" is often a motivator and will provide development experience for the team member.

The primary duties of the termination manager are encompassed in the following eight general tasks:

1.  Ensure completion of the work, including tasks performed by subcontractors.
2.  Notify the client of project completion and ensure that delivery (and installation) is accomplished. Acceptance of the project must be acknowledged by the client.
3.  Ensure that documentation is complete, including a terminal evaluation of the project deliverables and preparation of the project's Final Report.
4.  Clear for final billings and oversee preparation of the final invoices sent to the client.
5.  Redistribute personnel, materials, equipment, and any other resources to the appropriate places.
6.  Determine what records (manuals, reports, and other paperwork) to keep. Ensure that such documents are stored in the proper places and that responsibility for document retention is turned over to the parent organization's archivist.
7.  Ascertain any product support requirements (e.g., spares, service, etc.), decide how such support will be delivered, and assign responsibility.
8.  Oversee the closing of the project's books.

It is likely that tasks 1 to 3 will be handled by the regular PM immediately before the project termination process is started. If the termination manager must handle these tasks, technical support will almost certainly be needed. Of course, many of the tasks on this list will be quite simple if the project is not large, but even with small- or medium-sized projects, the PM should make sure all items are covered.

Item 5 on this list deserves some amplification. The PM can do a great deal to reduce the problems of termination by dealing with these issues well before the actual termination process begins. As we noted in Chapter 2, arrangements for the distribution and disposal of property and equipment belonging to the project should be included in the proposal and/or in the contract with the client. Obviously, this does not stop all arguments, but it does soften the conflicts. Dealing with project personnel is more difficult.

Most PMs delay the personnel reassignment/release issue as long as possible for three main reasons: a strong reluctance to face the interpersonal conflicts that might arise when new assignments and layoffs are announced; worry that people will lose interest and stop work on the project as soon as it becomes known that termination is being considered; or concern—particularly in the case of a pure project organization—that team members will try to avoid death by stretching out the work as far as possible.

As long as the PM has access to the functional managers' ears, any team member who "quits work" before the project is completed or stalls by stretching out tasks or creating task extensions would be subject to the usual sanctions of the workplace. The PM should make it quite clear that on-the-job-resignations and tenure-for-life are equally unacceptable.

The first problem results when project leadership is held by a managerially weak PM. The height of weakness is demonstrated when the PM posts a written list of reassignments and layoffs on the project's bulletin board late Friday afternoon and then leaves for a long weekend. A more useful course of action is to speak with project members individually or in small groups, let them know about plans for termination, and offer to consult with each in order to aid in the reassignment process or to assist in finding new work. (A preliminary announcement to the entire project team is in order because the interviews may cover several weeks or months.) It is almost impossible to keep termination plans a secret, and to confront the matter immediately tends to minimize rumors.

In a large project, of course, the PM will not be able to conduct personal interviews except with a few senior assistants. The project's personnel officer, or a representative from the parent firm's personnel department, can serve instead. This may seem like an unnecessary service to the team members, but a reputation of "taking care of one's people" is an invaluable aid to the PM when recruiting for the next project.

Termination by murder makes it very difficult to follow these suggestions about dealing with project personnel. The project's death often occurs with so little warning that the PM learns of the fact at the same time as the project team—or, as sometimes happens, learns about it from a member of the project team.

There is little the PM can do in such a case except to try to minimize the damage. The team should be assembled as rapidly as possible and informed, to the best of the PM's ability, about what has happened. At this point the PM should start the reassignment/release process.

---

## Project Management in Practice
### A Smooth Termination/Transition for Suncor's Ontario Refinery

Suncor of Ontario, Canada was committed to bringing a petroleum refinery on-line quickly and by a certain date due to contractual requirements. Normally, the start-up activities of a multi-million dollar project such as this are only studied in detail after construction is well underway. However, in this situation the lead time was short and the possibilities for schedule overruns were large due to labor problems in the area.

This difficulty was approached in a number of ways. For one thing, considerable effort was expended to attain and maintain good relations and communication with the tradespeople and laborers. But equally important was the transition process devised for the facility. The nearly 200 logistical systems comprising the facility were analyzed separately in terms of handoff to operating personnel for start-up. These systems were then carefully documented in detail regarding all the requirements for handoff and start-up, and prioritized to achieve full compatability with the necessary start-up sequence. Computerized scheduling analyses were then executed to ensure that each system would be completed

*Source*: A. Rustin, "The Challenge of Project Management," *Project Management Journal*, Sept. 1985.

by its required date and in coordination with the construction schedule.

This early planning allowed the construction personnel to concentrate on the construction activities and plant operations to receive the plant in the manner and sequence that was necessary to enable a successful start-up. The end result was that all facilities were operating successfully very shortly after total construction completion.

## ▶ 13.4   THE FINAL REPORT—A PROJECT HISTORY

Good project management systems have a memory. The embodiment of this memory is the Project Final Report. The final report is not another evaluation; rather, it is the history of the project. It is a chronicle of the life and times of the project, a compendium of what went right and what went wrong, of who served the project in what capacity, of what was done to create the substance of the project, of how it was managed.

The elements that should be covered in the final report are listed below. When considering these elements it is also beneficial to consider where the source materials can be found. For the most part, the required information is contained in the project master plan, a document that includes the proposal, all action plans, budgets, schedules, change orders, and updates of the above. In addition to the master plan, all project audits and evaluations also contain required input data. Almost everything else required by the final report is reflective, based on the thoughts of the PM and others involved in the project. There is little problem in knowing where the needed documents should be kept—in the project's files. Making sure that they are, in fact, there and that they are, in fact, up-to-date is a serious concern, indeed.

The precise organization of the final report is not a matter of great concern; the content is. Some are organized chronologically, while others feature sections on the technical and administrative aspects of the project. Some are written in a narrative style and some contain copies of all project reports strung together with short commentaries. What matters is that several subjects should be addressed, one way or another, in the final report.

1. **Project Performance**   A key element of the report is a comparison of what the project achieved (the terminal evaluation) with what the project tried to achieve (the project proposal). This comparison may be quite extensive and should include explanations of all significant deviations of actual from plan. Because the report is not a formal evaluation, it can reflect the best judgment of the PM on why the triumphs and failures occurred. This comparison should be followed with a set of recommendations for future projects dealing with like or similar technical matters.

2. **Administrative Performance**   The substantive side of the project usually gets a great deal of attention, while the administrative side is often ignored until administrative problems occur. There is also a strong tendency on the part of almost everyone to treat the "pencil pushers" with grudging tolerance, at best. The administration of a project cannot solve technical problems, but it can enable good technology to be implemented (or prevent it). Administrative prac-

tices should be reviewed, and those that worked particularly well or poorly should be highlighted. It is important, when possible, to report the reasons why some specific practice was effective or ineffective. If poor administration is to be avoided and good practices adopted, it is necessary to understand why some things work well and others do not *in the environment of a particular organization*. This becomes the basis for the recommendations that accompany the discussion.

3. **Organizational Structure**    Each of the organizational forms used for projects has its own, unique set of advantages and disadvantages. The final report should include comments on the ways the structure aided or impeded the progress of the project. If it appears that a modification to the accepted form of project organization—or a change to a different basic organizational form—might be helpful for project management, such a recommendation should be made. Obviously, recommendations should be accompanied by detailed explanations and rationales.

4. **Project and Administrative Teams**    On occasion, individuals who are competent and likable as individuals do not perform well as members of a team when a high level of interpersonal communication and cooperation is required. A *confidential* section of the final report may be directed to a senior personnel officer of the parent organization, recommending that such individuals not be assigned to projects in the future. Similarly, the PM may recommend that individuals or groups who are particularly effective when operating as a team be kept together on future projects or when reassigned to the firm's regular operations.

5. **Techniques of Project Management**    The outcome of the project is so dependent on the skill with which the forecasting, planning, budgeting, scheduling, resource allocation, and control are handled that attention must be given to checking on the way these tasks were accomplished. If the forecasts, budgets, and schedules were not reasonably accurate, recommendations for improved methods should be made. The techniques used for planning and control should also be subject to scrutiny.

For each element covered in the final report, recommendations for changing current practice should be made and defended. Insofar as is possible, the implications of each potential change should be noted. Commonly ignored, but equally important, are comments and recommendations about those aspects of the project that worked unusually well. Most projects, project teams, and PMs develop informal procedures that speed budget preparation, ease the tasks of scheduling, improve forecasts, and the like. The final report is an appropriate repository for such knowledge. Once reported, they can be tested and, if generally useful, can be added to the parent organization's list of approved project management methods.

The fundamental purpose of the final report is to improve future projects. It is ultimately focused on the project itself and on the process by which the project was conducted. Data on the project and its outcomes are available in the many interim reports, audits, and evaluations conducted during the project's life. But data on the process come largely from the PM's recollections. To ensure that significant issues are included, the PM should keep a diary. The PM's diary is not an official project document, but rather an informal collection of thoughts, reflections, and commentaries on project happenings. Such a diary tends to be a rich source of unconventional wisdom when written by a thoughtful PM. It may also be a great source of learning for a young, aspiring PM. Above all, it keeps ideas from "getting lost" amid the welter of activity on the project.

Occasionally, the project diary serves a purpose not originally intended. A PM working for a Minnesota highway construction company made a habit of keeping a project diary, mostly for his own interest and amusement. The firm was sued as the result of an accident on a road under construction. The plaintiff alleged that the highway shoulder was not complete nor was it marked "Under Construction" at the time of the accident. The PM's diary noted daily progress on the road, and it showed that the relevant piece of the road had been completed several days prior to the accident. The company successfully defended its position. All company PMs keep diaries now. A vice-president of the firm mentioned that they are the same type of diary his high-school-aged daughter uses.

## ▶ SUMMARY

At last, we come to the completion of our project—termination. In this chapter we looked at the ways in which projects can be terminated, how to decide if a project should be terminated, the termination process, and the preparation of the Project Final Report.

Specific points made in the chapter were these:

- A project can be terminated in one of four ways: by extinction, addition, integration, or starvation.

- Making a decision to terminate a project before its completion is difficult, but a number of factors can be of help in reaching a conclusion.

- Most projects fail because of one or more of the following reasons:

  Inappropriate use of the project form of organization
  Insufficient top-management support
  Naming the wrong project manager
  Poor planning

- Studies have shown that the factors associated with project success are different for different industries and the various types of projects.

- Success-related factors, or any factors management wishes, can be used in termination decision models.

- Special termination managers are often used, and needed, for closing out projects. This task, consisting of eight major duties, is a proj. ect in itself.

- The Project Final Report incorporates the process knowledge gained from the project. In addition to preservation of project records, the Final Report embodies the experience from which we learn. It should include:

  Project performance comments
  Administrative performance comments
  Organizational structure comments
  Personnel suggestions, possibly a confidential section

## ▶ GLOSSARY

**Termination by Addition**—Bringing the project into the organization as a separate, ongoing entity.

**Budget Decrement**—A reduction in the amount of funds for an activity.

**Termination by Extinction**—The end of all activity on a project without extending it in some form, such as by inclusion or integration.

**Termination by Integration**—Bringing the project activities into the organization and distributing them among existing functions.

Termination by Murder—Terminating a project suddenly and without warning, usually for a cause not related to the project's purpose.

Termination by Starvation—Cutting a project's budget sufficiently to stop progress without actually killing the project.

Termination Manager—An administrator responsible for wrapping-up the administrative details of a project.

## ▶ MATERIAL REVIEW QUESTIONS

1. List and briefly describe the ways projects may be terminated.

2. What problems may occur if the project manager does not have a follow-on project when the current project nears termination?

3. What are the primary duties of a termination manager?

4. On termination of a project, what happens to the information gathered throughout the course of the project?

5. What is a budget decrement?

6. Identify the four reasons for project termination.

7. What does the Project Final Report include?

8. What factors are considered most important in the decision to terminate a project?

9. What issues should be considered when using the termination-by-integration method?

## ▶ CLASS DISCUSSION QUESTIONS

1. Discuss the impact, both positive and negative, of termination on the project team members. How might the negative impact be lessened?

2. If the actual termination of a project becomes a project in itself, what are the characteristics of this project? How is it different from other projects?

3. Discuss some reasons why a Project Final Report, when completed, should be permanently retained by the firm.

4. What elements of the termination process may be responsible for making a project unsuccessful?

5. How is discriminant analysis used in project management?

6. What are some characteristics of a good termination manager?

7. How might one choose which termination method to use?

8. Why might a failing project not be terminated?

9. How can termination for reasons other than achievement of project goals be avoided?

10. What must the project manager do in planning, scheduling, monitoring, and closing out the project?

## ▶ INDIVIDUAL EXERCISE

Using the same project used for the Chapter 12 exercise, plan a project termination by *each* of the four methods described in the chapter. How would a decision regarding early termination be made? What would the critical factors be? If the project were to become a failure, what would the most likely reason be? Does it fall within the categories given in this chapter?

# ▶ INCIDENTS FOR DISCUSSION

## Industrial Mop and Supply Co.

IMSCO began manufacturing and distributing mops and brooms to industrial customers 43 years ago. Mr. Bretting, president of IMSCO, has been toying with the idea of using IMSCO's manufacturing and distribution expertise to begin making and selling consumer products. He has already decided that he cannot sell any of his current products to consumers. Also, if IMSCO is going to go to the trouble of developing consumer markets, Mr. Bretting feels very strongly that their first product should be something new and innovative that will help establish their reputation. He thinks that the expertise required to develop a new product exists within the company, but no one has any real experience in organizing or managing such a project. Fortunately, Mr. Bretting is familiar with a local consulting firm that has a good reputation and track record of leading companies through projects such as this, so he contacted them.

Three months into the project, Mr. Bretting contacted the program manager/consultant and mentioned that he was worried about the amount of risk involved in trying to introduce such an innovative consumer product with his current organization. He was worried that the project was oriented too strongly towards R&D and did not consider related business problems in enough depth. (This was a complete about-face from his feelings three months earlier, when he had approved the first plan submitted with no changes.)

Mr. Bretting suggested that the consultant modify the existing project to include the introduction of a "me-too" consumer product before IMSCO's new product was defined and tested. Mr. Bretting thought that some experience with a "me-too" product would provide IMSCO management with valuable experience and would improve later performance with the new product. He allowed the R&D portion of the project to continue concurrently, but the "me-too" phase would have top priority as far as resources were concerned. The consultant said she would think about it and contact him next week.

*Questions:* If you were the consultant, what would you recommend to Mr. Bretting? Would you continue the relationship?

## Excel Electronics

Excel Electronics is nearing completion of a three-year project to develop and produce a new pocket computer. The computer is no larger than a cigarette pack but has all the power and features of a $5000 microcomputer. The assembly line and all the production facilities will be completed in six months and the first units will begin production in seven months. The plant manager believes it is time to begin winding the project down. He has three methods in mind for terminating the project: extinction, addition, and integration, but he is not sure which method would be best.

*Question:* Which of the three methods would you recommend, and why?

# ▶ PROJECT TEAM CONTINUING EXERCISE

This assignment marks the completion of the project team's activity. The team should prepare a Project Final Report detailing the method of project termination, the reasons for termination, and the tasks the termination manager will have to complete to terminate the project. Also include the process knowledge gained from the project concerning performance, administration, organization structure, and personnel.

Last, suggest a termination evaluation model that includes what your team considers to be the relevant project success and failure factors. Note the potential for interaction between project manager factors, organizational factors, and project factors, in particular.

# ▶ BIBLIOGRAPHY

1. ADAMS, J. R., S. E. BARNDT, and M. D. MARTIN. *Managing by Project Management.* Dayton, OH: Universal Technology Corp., 1979.

2. AMRINE, H. T. *et al. Manufacturing Organization and Management,* 5th ed. Englewood Cliffs, NJ: Prentice Hall, 1987.

3. ANDREWS, K. R. *The Concept of Corporate Strategy,* 3rd ed. Homewood, IL: Dow Jones-Irwin, 1986.

4. ARCHIBALD, R. D. *Managing High Technology Programs and Projects.* New York: Wiley, 1976.

5. AVOTS, I. "Making Project Management Work— The Right Tool for The Wrong Project Manager." *Advanced Management Journal,* Autumn 1975.

6. AVOTS, I. "Why Does Project Management Fail?" *California Management Review,* Fall, 1969.

7. BAKER, N. R., S. G. GREEN, and A. S. BEAN. A *Multivariate Analysis of Environmental Organizational and Process Variables in the Process of Organized Technological Innovation. Vol. II. Technical Summary.* Final Report on National Science Foundation Award No. ISI 7921581, College of Business Administration. Cincinnati: University of Cincinnati, Jan. 1984.

8. BAKER, N. R., S. G. GREEN, A. S. BEAN, W. BLANK, and S. K. TADISINA. "Sources of First Suggestion and Project Success/Failure in Industrial Research." *Proceedings,* Conference on the Management of Technological Innovation, Washington, D.C., 1983.

9. BALACHANDRA, R., and A. J. RAELIN. "How to Decide When to Abandon a Project." *Research Management,* July 1980.

10. BEALE, P., and M. FREEMAN. "Successful Project Execution: A Model." *Project Management Journal,* December 1991.

11. BENNINGSON, L. A. "The Strategy of Running Temporary Projects." *Innovation,* Sept. 1971.

12. BUELL, C. K. "When to Terminate a Research and Development Project." *Research Management,* July 1967.

13. CERULLO, M. J. "Determining Post-Implementation Audit Success." *Journal of Systems Management,* March 1979.

14. CLELAND, D. I., and W. R. KING. *Systems Analysis and Project Management,* 2nd. ed. New York: McGraw-Hill, 1975.

15. CONNOR, P. E. *et al.,* eds. *Dimension in Modern Management.* Boston: Houghton Mifflin, 1974.

16. DEAN, B. V. *Evaluating, Selecting, & Controlling R & D Projects.* New York: American Management Association, 1968.

17. FREEMAN, M., and P. BEALE. "Measuring Project Success." *Project Management Journal,* March 1992.

18. GRAY, C. F. *Essentials of Project Management.* Princeton, NJ: Petrocelli Books, 1981.

19. GREEN, S. G., M. A. WELSH, and G. E. DEHLER. "Red Flags at Dawn or Predicting Project Terminations at Start Up." *Research-Technology Management,* May-June 1993.

20. HOCKNEY, J. W., and K. HUMPHREYS. *Control and Management of Capital Projects,* 2nd ed. New York: McGraw-Hill, 1991.

21. HOLZMANN, R. T. "To Stop or Not—The Big Research Decision." *Chemical Technology,* 1972.

22. KEMP, P. S. "Post-Completion Audits of Capital Investment Projects." *Management Accounting,* Aug. 1966.

23. KERZNER, H. *Project Management, A Systems Approach to Planning, Scheduling, and Controlling,* 2nd ed. New York: Van Nostrand Reinhold, 1989.

24. KERZNER, H. "Evaluation Techniques in Project Management." *Journal of Systems Management,* Feb. 1980.

25. KLOPPENBORG, T. J., and D. A. PLATH. "Effective Project Management Practices during Expert Systems Implementation." *Project Management Journal,* December 1991.

26. KOONTZ, H. *Appraising Managers as Managers.* New York: McGraw-Hill, 1971.

27. LEE, W., and S. J. MANTEL, JR. "An Expert System for Project Termination." *Proceedings,* First International Conference on Engineering Management, Arlington, VA, Sept. 1986.

28. MANTEL, S. J., JR., A. L. SERVICE, *et al.* "A Social Service Measurement Model." *Operations Research,* March-April 1975.

**29.** MIGHT, R., and FISCHER, W. A. "The Role of Structural Factors in Determining Project Management Success." IEEE *Transactions on Engineering Management*, Vol. 32, 1985.

**30.** MONTGOMERY, J. L. "Appraising Capital Expenditures." *Management Accounting*, Sept. 1965.

**31.** NORTHCRAFT, G. B., and NEALE, M. A. "Opportunity Costs and the Framing of Resource Allocation Decisions." *Organizational Behavior and Human Decision Processes*, 1986, pp. 348–356.

**32.** NORTHCRAFT, G. B., and WOLF, G. "Dollars, Sense, and Sunk Costs: A Life Cycle Model of Resource Allocation Decisions." *Academy of Management Review*, No. 2 1984.

**33.** PINTO, J. K., and S. J. MANTEL, JR. "The Causes of Project Failure." IEEE *Transactions on Engineering Management*, Nov. 1990.

**34.** PINTO, J. K., and D. P. SLEVIN. "Critical Factors in Successful Project Implementation." IEEE *Transactions on Engineering Management*, February 1987.

**35.** PINTO, J. K., and D. P. SLEVIN. "Project Success: Definitions and Measurement Techniques." *Project Management Journal*, February 1988.

**36.** PINTO, J. K., and D. P. SLEVEN. "Critical Success Factors Across The Project Life Cycle." *Project Management Journal*, June 1988.

**37.** "Project Management Tasks: Wrap Up." *Design News*, April 19, 1982.

**38.** RAELIN, J. A., and R. BALACHANDRA. "R&D Project Termination in High-Tech Industries." IEEE *Transactions on Engineering Management*, Feb. 1985.

**39.** RIGGS, J. L., M. GOODMAN, R. FINLEY, and T. MILLER. "A Decision Support System for Predicting Project Success." *Project Management Journal*, September 1992.

**40.** RINGSTROM, N. H. "Making Project Management Work." *Business Horizons*, Fall 1965.

**41.** ROSENAU, M. D. *Successful Project Management*, 2nd ed. New York: Van Nostrand Reinhold, 1991.

**42.** SHAFER, S. M., and S. J. MANTEL, JR. "A Decision Support System for the Project Termination Decision." *Project Management Journal*, June 1989.

**43.** SILVERMAN, M. *Project Management: A Short Course for Professionals*, 2nd ed. New York: Wiley, 1988.

**44.** STAW, B. M., and ROSS, J. "Knowing When to Pull the Plug." *Harvard Business Review*, March-April, 1987.

**45.** STUCKENBRUCK, L. C., ed. *The Implementation of Project Management: The Professionals Handbook*. Project Management Institute, Reading, MA: Addison-Wesley, 1981.

**46.** TADISINA, S. K. "Support System for the Termination Decision in R&D Management." *Project Management Journal*, Nov. 1986.

**47.** WOLFF, M. F. "Knowing When the Horse Is Dead." *Research Management*, Nov. 1981.

# CASE I

## CINCINNATI MILACRON INC.: CASTING CLEANING
### Marianne M. Hill and James M. Comer

In early 1982 Malcolm Davis, manager of manufacturing process development of Cincinnati Milacron, Inc. faced a decision regarding the continuation of the robot-aided casting cleaning project. Although it had taken much longer than planned to tool and program the robot, it had successfully cleaned two types of castings during December 1981. There was some concern, however, about continuing the development of the cleaning applications for the remainder of the 30 castings in the foundry's medium castings line.

## Industry and Company Background

Cincinnati Milacron Inc. is engaged in the design, manufacture, and sale of process equipment and systems for industry, along with the supplies and accessories sold for use in these systems. Incorporated as Cincinnati Screw and Tap Company in 1884, the company originally sold screws, taps, and dies. After discovering a market for milling machines, the portion of the company devoted to these machines was pur-

**Table 1** Cincinnati Milacron, Inc.

| | 1974 | 1975 | 1976 | 1977 | 1978 | 1979 | 1980 | 1981 |
|---|---|---|---|---|---|---|---|---|
| | | | in thousands, except per-share amounts | | | | | |
| *Summary of Operations* | | | | | | | | |
| Sales | $424,760 | $431,225 | $420,396 | $497,073 | $592,563 | $702,120 | $816,402 | $934,395 |
| Earnings (loss) from continuing operations | 6,390 | 8,356 | 7,572 | 18,357 | 31,219 | 52,577 | 52,441 | 60,787 |
| Percent of sales | 1.5% | 1.9% | 1.8% | 3.7% | 5.3% | 7.5% | 6.4% | 6.5% |
| Percent of average shareholder's equity | 4.3% | 5.4% | 4.8% | 10.8% | 16.2% | 22.8% | 18.4% | 18.3% |
| Per common share | 0.28 | 0.37 | 0.34 | 0.83 | 1.40 | 2.34 | 2.32 | 2.68 |
| Net earnings (loss) | 10,259 | 9,946 | 9,991 | 20,869 | 33,184 | 55,439 | 75,644 | 60,787 |
| Percent of average shareholder's equity | 6.9% | 6.4% | 6.3% | 12.3% | 17.2% | 24.1% | 26.6% | 18.3% |
| Per common share | 0.47 | 0.45 | 0.45 | 0.95 | 1.49 | 2.47 | 3.35 | 2.68 |
| *Financial Position at Year End* | | | | | | | | |
| Working capital | 169,132 | 167,561 | 160,719 | 165,436 | 182,758 | 206,335 | 253,923 | 266,983 |
| Property, plant and equipment—net | 95,300 | 95,379 | 101,792 | 109,109 | 118,864 | 146,148 | 156,944 | 184,440 |
| Total assets | 421,560 | 376,891 | 393,824 | 426,422 | 482,049 | 570,562 | 626,696 | 715,779 |
| Long-term debt and lease obligations | 124,076 | 116,304 | 110,917 | 106,919 | 108,053 | 108,723 | 100,786 | 104,715 |
| Total debt | 188,449 | 149,249 | 141,635 | 136,012 | 136,908 | 139,340 | 127,343 | 126,993 |
| Shareholder's equity | 152,356 | 157,015 | 161,752 | 178,065 | 206,937 | 253,521 | 316,145 | 349,315 |
| Per common share | 6.77 | 6.99 | 7.20 | 7.86 | 9.01 | 11.03 | 13.75 | 15.17 |
| *Other Data* | | | | | | | | |
| Dividends paid to common shareholders | 5,044 | 5,047 | 5,051 | 5,809 | 7,017 | 9,902 | 14,571 | 16,283 |
| Per common share | 0.2333 | 0.2333 | 0.2333 | 0.2667 | 0.3167 | 0.4416 | 0.6467 | 0.7200 |
| Capital expenditures | 26,752 | 12,029 | 18,793 | 22,683 | 24,922 | 36,288 | 43,752 | 49,655 |
| Depreciation | 7,365 | 7,948 | 8,886 | 9,352 | 10,008 | 11,748 | 14,542 | 17,326 |
| Unfilled orders at year end | 346,226 | 216,166 | 250,082 | 320,738 | 471,231 | 673,316 | 698,288 | 476,856 |
| Employees (average) | 14,915 | 13,369 | 12,445 | 13,011 | 13,379 | 13,743 | 13,750 | 13,602 |
| U.S. plants | | | | | 16 | 18 | 17 | 19 |
| Overseas plants | | | | | 14 | 13 | 11 | 11 |

*Source:* 1983 Annual Report

**Table 2** Cincinnati Milacron, Inc. Annual Sales and Operating Earnings (in millions)

|  | 1978 | 1979 | 1980 | 1981 |
|---|---|---|---|---|
| *Machine Tool Group* | | | | |
| Sales | $374 | $449 | $563 | $640 |
| Operating Earnings | 47 | 68 | 89 | 97 |
| *Plastics Machinery Group* | | | | |
| Sales | 144 | 155 | 129 | 137 |
| Operating Earnings | 19 | 23 | 12 | 14 |
| *Industrial Specialty Products Group** | | | | |
| Sales | 75 | 99 | 125 | 158 |
| Operating Earnings | 5 | 13 | 12 | 13 |

*1980–81: robots, cutting fluids, grinding wheels, semiconductor material, printed circuit board material

1978–79 (called Industrial Products): specialty chemicals, cutting fluids, grinding wheels, semiconductor material, printed circuit board material. In these years, robots are included in "Machine Tools."

Source: 1982–1983 *Annual Reports*

chased in 1889 and named the Cincinnati Milling Machine Company. The "Cincinnati Milacron" name was adopted in 1970. In 1981 the firm had 19 plants in the United States and 11 overseas, employed over 13,000 people, and had annual sales approaching $1 billion. Financial data for the years 1974–1981 are found in Table 1.

The company has three major divisions: machine tools, plastics processing machinery, and industrial specialty products. In 1981, the machine tool group accounted for 68.5 percent of total sales and 78.1 percent of total operating earnings, and the plastics machinery group provided 14.6 percent of total sales and 11.6 percent of operating earnings. The third group, industrial specialty products, accounted for 16.9 percent of sales and 10.3 percent of operating earnings. The five product lines in this group include robots, cutting fluids, grinding wheels, semiconductor materials (silicon epitaxial wafers), and printed circuit board materials. Although industry sources rank Milacron first in dollar sales of robots in the United States, robot sales represent less than 10 percent of total company sales. Table 2 shows annual sales and operating earnings for the three product groups for the years 1978–1981.

A major component of the machine tool division is a large jobbing foundry, which has provided gray and ductile iron castings for Milacron's machine tools for over 70 years.* With recent capacity expansion and

modernization facilitating the marketing of castings to other firms, plans are currently underway to change the foundry to a cost center. There are three separate departments in the foundry served by two cupolas and an electric holding furnace producing approximately 2500 different types of castings in lot sizes from 1 to 600 in small, medium, or large sizes. The small castings range in size from 4 ounces to 200 pounds; the medium castings range from 200 to 2000 pounds and account for the largest percentage of iron poured; and, the large castings range from 2000 to 40,000 pounds.

In 1980, foundry shipments dropped significantly from 1979 levels. Even with this decline, iron foundries were the nation's fifth largest manufacturing industry in 1981 and the second largest metal producing industry (surpassed only by rolled steel). Table 3 gives gray and ductile iron shipment figures in the United States for the years 1969–1981.

## Casting and Cleaning Process

Iron castings are made in the following manner. Typically, a pattern is first made which conforms to the external shape of the casting. In the sand molding process, this pattern is then used to form a cavity in

---

*A glossary of terms used in this case is found in the case appendix.

**Table 3** Total U.S. Shipments (000 Net Tons) of Ductile
Iron and Gray Iron Castings

| | Gray Iron | | Ductile Iron | |
|---|---|---|---|---|
| | **Total** | **For Sale** | **Total** | **For Sale** |
| 1969 | 14,649 | 9,206* | 1,286 | N.A. |
| 1970 | 12,388 | 8,146* | 1,607 | N.A. |
| 1971 | 11,865 | 7,909* | 1,712 | N.A. |
| 1972 | 13,467 | 7,153 | 1,835 | 1,037 |
| 1973 | 14,801 | 7,688 | 2,246 | 1,320 |
| 1974 | 13,459 | 7,260 | 2,203 | 1,505 |
| 1975 | 10,622 | 5,235 | 1,824 | 1,202 |
| 1976 | 11,923 | 5,455 | 2,245 | 1,405 |
| 1977 | 12,371 | 5,477 | 2,736 | 1,808 |
| 1978 | 13,140 | 6,316 | 3,005 | 1,993 |
| 1979 | 12,512 | 6,084 | 2,890 | 1,865 |
| 1980 | 9,399 | 4,788 | 2,400 | 1,669 |
| 1981 | 9,610 | 5,063 | 2,191 | 1,524 |

* Includes ductile iron for sale

*Source*: Bureau of the Census

the sand which is shaped to the desired contours and dimensions of the casting. Sand is packed firmly around the pattern. After the pattern is removed, cores are set in place; the cores form the interior surface in the casting. The mold is then closed, and the casting is poured. After the iron has solidified, the casting is removed from the mold, the sand is broken away, and the casting is sandblasted. It is then sent to the casting cleaning area to remove all extraneous metal. After final cleaning, it is sent to the paint line. A flowchart of a typical foundry operation is included in Exhibit 1.

Casting cleaning is the most labor intensive operation in the foundry and one of the most difficult to staff. A casting is dumped on the floor in the cleaning area; the casting cleaners stand over it while cleaning and use crowbars and an overhead crane (which is shared among all the men) to move it and turn it over. The system of risers, runners, and gates that created a path for the molten iron to enter the mold cavity is removed. Fins and other protrusions are also trimmed with the use of chisels, grinders, etc. The casting cleaners originally worked under very difficult conditions. The position was viewed by workers primarily as an entré into a desirable organization, since one of the "incentives" of the job was the ability to transfer to another position.

## Foundry Modernization

A comprehensive internal study of the foundry was instituted in 1973. The committee investigated forecasted needs, workflows, floor plans, and health and safety concerns in order to develop an effective foundry modernization plan. The plan called for the modernization to begin first in the core room, proceed to molding, and then to the cleaning process. It was to start with the small casting line and then move on to the medium and large lines. The project began in 1976 and the scheduled completion date for the plan was 1986.

An accident in 1980 caused by a cracked wheel on an old grinder prompted an adjustment to the plan. Four grinders with improved safety features immediately replaced the remaining older ones. Also in 1980, OSHA cited Milacron for unacceptable levels of noise and respirable dust in the cleaning areas.*

The modernization project in the cleaning areas specified the installation of "cleaning booths." The

---

*Noise levels are calculated as weighted daily averages of all exposure to noise, including that produced by the worker him- or herself and other workers within hearing range.

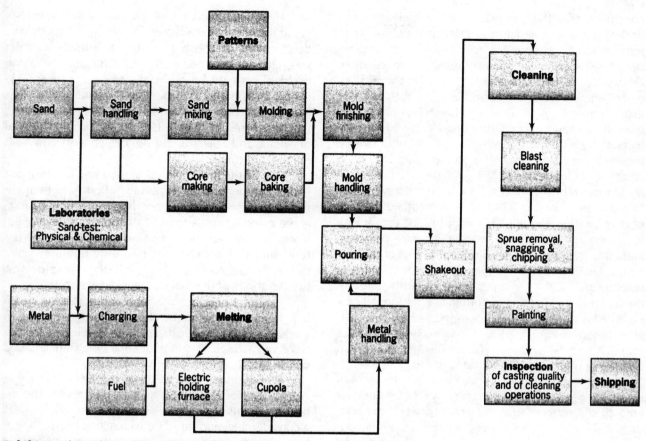

**Exhibit 1:** Flow Chart of Foundry Operations.

first booth was installed in the fall of 1980, and the twelfth was to be completed at the end of 1982, all in the small and medium castings lines. Three-sided booths for large castings are planned for 1986.

Castings enter a cleaning booth on a conveyor, and each booth has its own crane for lifting the casting onto a table. This table both rotates and elevates the casting so that the large grinders can be used. Previously, a 40–pound limit had been placed on castings that could be lifted by human operators. Castings weighing over 40 pounds were left on the floor and smaller grinders were used on them, which greatly increased the cleaning times.

In the booths, the air is circulated and cleaned. Although the air quality in the booths is such that helmet respirators are not needed, they are still worn for two reasons: they greatly reduce potential eye injury, and management wants consistency in the treatment of casting cleaners both in and out of the booths. The booths also provide isolation from noise associated with other cleaners. Although the booths and helmets did not constitute an engineering solution to the dust and noise problem, all OSHA regulations have been satisfied in these areas.

The booths result in a more orderly flow of work, improved material handling, and a decrease in tool repair. Tools are now conveniently located instead of being tossed around the cleaning area. There is also improved "housekeeping" in the booths. Management attributes this to the increased "pride of ownership" on the part of the casting cleaners. The turnover rate of cleaners has subsequently decreased dramatically.

## The Introduction of Advanced Manufacturing Technologies

During 1977–79 an executive committee reporting directly to the president was established at Cincinnati Milacron to examine the trend in manufacturing throughout the entire firm. In general, the committee concluded that the company had to modernize and update the way in which they manufactured products in order to stay competitive with the foreign competition. More specifically, studies of the future trends in the work force had indicated that workers would become unavailable for undesirable jobs, such as casting cleaning. Thus, this area was identified for a possible robotic application. Other areas targeted for new technology included the introduction of robotics into the welding shop and the implementation of a computer-aided design (CAD) system.

In early 1980 Malcolm Davis, manager of manufacturing process development, was assigned the task of investigating and implementing robotic technology for possible use in the casting cleaning process. Manufacturing process development is part of the corporate facilities and manufacturing division, which is responsible for the buildings, their contents, and the equipment used in manufacturing. In addition, all new equipment purchases must be approved by this division. Before the robot project, new technology at the foundry had been the responsibility of the group headed by the foundry technical manager.

In September 1980, a development group was physically assigned to the foundry. A robot was delivered to the foundry and the entire project was conducted there. The involvement of the foundry personnel in this project included site selection and preparation (the robot project was carried out 50 feet from the installation of a new cleaning booth) and weekly meetings between the robot development group and the foundry technical group. The superintendent of the foundry joined these meetings once a month.

A Gantt chart prepared on January 19, 1981, is shown in Exhibit 2. One of the first tasks was to provide tools for the robot. In the existing cleaning operation, air tools were the standard type used by humans. It was obvious that the robot was capable of handling tools with much greater horsepower, so the search began for existing tools with higher horsepower that could be used by the robot.

During January and February of 1981, the market and literature were searched for potential tools to be used, but nothing was available. Electric motors were ruled out because they were too heavy and the weight-to-horsepower ratio was too great. Hydraulic motors offered the most promise because the weight-to-horsepower ratio is low and the power source can be remote.

Hydraulic tools that were available on the market could not readily be adapted for use by the robot. The development of these tools by an outside supplier was ruled out because of the cost. Cincinnati Milacron decided it would be more effective to purchase hydraulic motors and then develop the tools themselves around the robot application. An outside engineering firm was hired in March 1981 to do the mechanical drawings, and Milacron did the design work and built the tools in-house.

One of the first tools developed was a chisel, but it did not perform as expected. Effort was then directed toward developing grinding tools, burr cutters, and a cutoff wheel. A total of six tools was developed. It was also necessary to develop a way to change the tools and to then transmit hydraulic power through this tool changer. This was a very extensive endeavor; two iterations of the tool changers were necessary.

Exhibit 3 descibes the robot-aided casting cleaning operation. The robot cleaned its first casting in December 1981. Applications were developed for two types of castings. Castings of each type were cleaned continuously.

The standard time to clean the first casting was 20 minutes for the worker and 16 minutes for the robot. Since this was a smaller casting, the robot spent a considerable amount of time changing tools. The robot, though, could work continuously, while the worker needed to rest. It was estimated that the robot could complete in three days what it would take the worker five days to do. Although the robot's cleaning was more consistent (e.g., grinding lines were identical on all pieces), the quality of the finished casting was not assessed as better than that done by the worker.

The second casting cleaned by the robot was larger than the first. The standard time was 36 minutes for the worker and 22 minutes for the robot. Since the amount of cleaning was greater (as opposed to tool changing), the robot could use the tool more productively over a longer period of time.

The casting cleaning robot is a point-to-point motion robot. It takes from six hours to three days to program the cleaning of each part and each operation requires a separate tape. (In comparison, 12 applications could be stored on a single tape for robot welding operations.) It is estimated that it would take one and a half to two years of programming to have enough parts programmed for the robot to function productively.

| Week/Period | Resp. | 1 | 2 | 3 | 4 | 5 | 6 | 7 | Mgmt. | Budget |
|---|---|---|---|---|---|---|---|---|---|---|
| **Program Step** | | | | | | | | | Labor or time | Money |
| 1. Layout Design | 10A | | | | | | | | | |
| 2. Site Selection | 10A | | | | | | | | | |
| 3. Site Preparation | 10A | | | | | | | | | |
| 4. Robot Installation | 92B | | | | | | | | | |
| 5. Meccana Installation | 92B | | | | | | | | | |
| 6. Tool Engineering | 92B | | | | | | | | | |
| 7. Tool Manufacturing | 92B | | | | | | | | | |
| 8. Tool Changer Installation | 92B | | | | | | | | | |
| 9. Tool Testing | 92B | | | | | | | | | |
| 10. Tool Matrix Testing | 92B | | | | | | | | | |
| 11. Adaptive Control | 92B | | | | | | | | | |
| 12. Systems Test | 92B | | | | | | | | | |
| 13. Cutting Test | 92B | | | | | | | | | |
| 14. Acceptance Test | 10A | | | | | | | | | |
| 15. Demonstration | 92B | | | | | | | | | |
| 16. Training 10A Operator | 10A | | | | | | | | | |
| 17. Release Systems to 10A | 10A | | | | | | | | | |

**Exhibit 2:** Robot-Aided Casting Cleaning—Phase 1 (1/19/81).

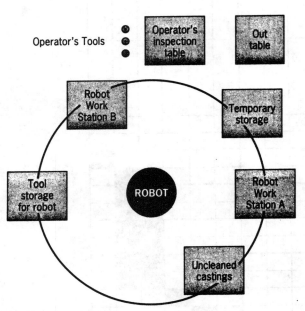

**Exhibit 3:** Casting Cleaning Robot Operation.

An operator, with the help of a crane, would pick up a raw casting and put it on Work Station A (assume a casting is already at B). The robot would clean as many sides as it could at A and then move to Work Station B and work on the one there. Meanwhile, the operator picks up the casting from A and puts it on the temporary storage table and picks up another raw casting and puts it on A. When the robot is through at B, the operator takes the casting from B to the opera-tor's inspection table, and moves the one from tempo-rary storage to Station B. The operator checks the one on the inspection table to see if anything else needs to be worked on, and if so, does it. When it is com-pleted, the operator moves it to the out table.

The robot is busy all of the time. The worker is idle about 20 percent of the time and is moving cast-ings and working 80 percent of the time. If the robot were adopted, production would be rebalanced to keep the worker busy for greater periods of time.

## Current Situation

Malcolm Davis is thus faced with drafting his recom-mendation. Although some feel that the need for the robot application is not as great now since the clean-ing booths have been installed, Malcolm views the booths as a temporary, transitional measure.

The robotic application to casting cleaning is ex-tremely attractive to management because the robot can work in any environment and would qualify as an engineering solution (required by OSHA) to the dust and noise problem. In addition, 12–16 undesirable jobs in casting cleaning could be eliminated.

Discussions with the foundry technical manager revealed that he thinks that future directions will fo-cus on improving the quality of casting in order to re-duce the amount of necessary cleaning, as well as ex-amining other methods of metal removing, such as laser cutting and plasma arc cutting.

## ▶ QUESTIONS

1. Prepare a Gantt chart for the foundry moderniza-tion project and the casting cleaning robot project that includes the activities discussed in the case. What interaction was there between the two pro-ject groups?

2. A financial feasibility study was not attempted be-fore the casting cleaning project began. Should it have been? What costs and benefits would have been included?

3. Do the cleaning booths reduce the need for the casting cleaning robot? Explain.

4. If you were Malcolm Davis, what recommenda-tions would you make? Why?

5. In June 1982, the project was discontinued. Why do you think it was terminated?

# ▶ APPENDIX

## Glossary*

**Blast Cleaning**—Removal of sand or oxide scale from castings by the impinging action of sand, metal shot, or grit projected under air, water, or centrifugal pressure.

**Captive Foundry**—One that produces castings from its own patterns for its own use.

**Casting**—(verb) Act of pouring molten metal into a mold; (noun) metal object cast to a required shape by pouring or injecting liquid metal into a mold.

**Chip**—(verb) To remove extraneous metal from a casting by hand or pneumatically operated chisels.

**Cleaning**—The process of removing all metal that does not belong on the final casting, such as gates, fins, runners, and risers; may also include the removal of adhering sand from the casting.

**Core**—A preformed sand aggregate inserted into a mold to shape the interior of the casting or that part of the casting which cannot be shaped by the pattern.

**Cupola**—A vertically cylindrical furnace for melting metal, in direct contact with coke as fuel, by forcing air under pressure through openings near its base.

**Fins**—Thin projections of excess metal on a casting resulting from imperfect mold or core joints.

**Gate**—End of the runner in a mold where the rate of flow of molten metal is controlled as it enters the casting or mold cavity.

**Gray Iron**—Cast iron which contains a relatively large percentage of the carbon present in the form of flake graphite. The metal has a gray fracture.

**Holding Furnace**—Uusually a small furnace for maintaining molten metal at the proper pouring temperature, and which is supplied from a large melting unit.

**Hydraulic Motor**—An actuator which converts forces from high pressure hydraulic fluid into mechanical shaft rotation.

**Jobbing Foundry**—One which is equipped to economically produce a single casting or in small quantities from a variety of patterns.

**Mold**—The form, made of sand, metal, or refractory material, which contains the cavity into which molten metal is poured to produce a casting of desired shape.

**Off-Line Programming**—A means of programming a robot by developing a set of instructions on an independent computer and then using the software to control the robot at a later time.

**Pattern**—A form of wood, metal, or other materials, around which molding material is placed to make a mold for casting metals.

**Point-to-Point Motion**—This is a type of robot motion in which a limited number of points along a path of motion is specified by the controller. The robot moves from point-to-point in a straight line rather than a curved path between points. The latter is often referred to as a continuous path robot and requires larger memory because more points are required.

**Respirable Dust**—Extremely fine dust; when combined with high levels of quartz silicon, it can be carcinogenic.

**Riser**—A reservoir of molten metal provided to compensate for the contraction of the metal in a casting as it solidifies.

**Robot**—A reprogrammable multifunctional manipulator designed to move material, parts, tools, or specialized devices through variable programmed motion for the performance of a variety of tasks.

**Runner**—The portion of the gate assembly that connects the downgate with the casting ingate or riser.

**Snagging**—Removal of fins and rough places on a casting by means of grinding.

**Sprue**—The vertical portion of the gating system where the molten metal first enters the mold.

**Teaching**—The process of programming a robot to perform a desired sequence of tasks.

---

*Definitions from Charles F. Walton (editor), *Iron Castings Handbook*, Iron Castings Society, Inc., 1981; and J. Gerin Sylvia, *Cast Metals Technology*, Reading, MA: Addison-Wesley Publishing Company, 1972; and *Industrial Robots*, Naperville, IL: Tech Tran Corporation, 1983.

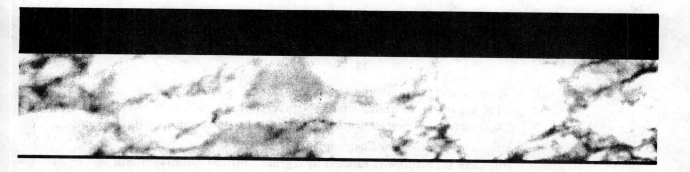

# Sourcenotes

## ▶ CHAPTER 1

J. M. Stewart: *Making Project Management Work*
© 1965 by the Foundation for the School of Business at the Indiana University. Reprinted by permission from *Business Horizons* (Fall 1965).

J. R. Meredith, M. M. Hill, and J. M. Comer: *Peerless Laser Processors*
This case research was funded by a grant entitled "Management Issues in High-Technology Manufacturing Industries," from the Cleveland Foundation of Cleveland Ohio, 1985.

## ▶ CHAPTER 2

J. R. Meredith and N. C. Suresh: *Justification Techniques for Advanced Manufacturing Technologies*
©1986 Taylor & Francis, Ltd. Reprinted by permission from *International Journal of Production Management* (Vol. 24, No. 5, pp. 1043–1057).

S. J. Mantel, Jr.: *Planning and Budgeting a Social Service System*
Presented at the 7th Annual Meeting of the American Institute for Decision Sciences, Cincinnati, Ohio, Nov. 1975. Printed by permission.

E. Filliben: *Westfield, Inc.: Packaging Alternatives*
Copyright © 1987 by the Darden Graduate Business School Foundation, Charlottesville, VA. Rev. 11/91.

## ▶ CHAPTER 3

B. Z. Posner: *What It Takes to Be a Good Project Manager*
©1987 by the Project Management Institute. Reprinted by permission from *Project Management Journal* (March 1987).

J. R. Meredith: *Geartrain International: Medina, Ohio*
This case research was funded by a grant from the Illinois Institute of Technology, Chicago, 1985.

▶ **CHAPTER 4**

E. W. Larson and D. H. Gobeli: *Matrix Management: Contradictions and Insights*
©1987 by the Regents of the University of California. Reprinted from the *California Management Review.* Vol. 29. No. 4 by permission of the Regents.

J. R. Meredith: *Oilwell Cable Company, Inc.*
This case research was funded by a grant entitled "Management Issues in High-Technology Manufacturing Industries" from the Cleveland Foundation of Cleveland, Ohio, 1985.


▶ **CHAPTER 5**

H. F. Spirer and A. G. Hulvey: *A Project Management and Control System for Capital Projects*
© 1981 Reprinted with permission from *Proceedings of* PMI, *Internet 81,* 1981, a publication of the Project Management Institute.

D. P. Slevin and J. K. Pinto: *Balancing Strategy and Tactics in Project Implementation*
Reprinted from *Sloan Management Review,* Fall 1987, pp. 33–41, by permission of the publisher. © 1987 by the Sloan Management Review Association. All rights reserved.


▶ **CHAPTER 6**

R. J. Burke: *Methods of Resolving Interpersonal Conflict*
©1969 International Personnel Management Association. Reprinted from *Personnel Administration,* July-August 1969, by permission.

J. M. Comer and M. M. Hill: *Cincinnati Milacron, Inc: Robot Welding*
This case research was funded by a grant entitled "Management Issues in High-Technology Manufacturing Industries," from the Cleveland Foundation of Cleveland, Ohio, 1985.


▶ **CHAPTER 7**

D. H. Hamburger: *Three Perceptions of Project Cost—Cost Is More Than a Four Letter Word*
©1986 by the Project Management Institute. Reprinted by permission from *Project Management Journal,* June 1986, pp. 51–58.

J. R. Meredith: *Automotive Builders, Inc.: The Stanhope Project*
This case research was funded by a grant from the Illinois Institute of Technology, Chicago, 1985.

▶ **CHAPTER 8**

E. TURBAN and J. R. MEREDITH: *The Sharon Construction Corporation*
From E. TURBAN and J. R. MEREDITH *Fundamentals of Management Science*, 6th ed., Homewood, IL: R. D. Irwin, Inc., ©1994. Reproduced by permission.

D. H. HAMBURGER: *"On-time" Project Completion—Managing the Critical Path*
This article is reprinted from *Project Management Journal*, Sept. 1987, with permission of the Project Management Institute, 130 So. State Road, Upper Darby, PA 19082, a worldwide organization for advancing the state-of-the-art of project management. Phone 215/734-3330. Fax 215/734-3266.

▶ **CHAPTER 9**

H. F. SPIRER: D. U. *Singer Hospital Products Corp.*
Reproduced with the kind permission of Herbert F. Spirer, Professor of Management and Administrative Sciences, MBA Program at Stamford, University of Connecticut. © 1980 Herbert F. Spirer.

R. V. JOHNSON *Resource Constrained Scheduling Capabilities of Commercial Project Management Software*
This article is reprinted from *Project Management Journal*, Dec. 1992, with permission of the Project Management Institute, 130 So. State Road, Upper Darby, PA 19082, a worldwide organization for advancing the state-of-the-art of project management. Phone 215/734-3330. Fax 215/734-3266.

▶ **CHAPTER 10**

P. M. BOBROWSKI: *Project Management Control Problems: An Information Systems Focus*
This article is reprinted from *Project Management Journal*, June 1989, with permission of the Project Management Institute, 130 So. State Road, Upper Darby, PA 19082, a worldwide organization for advancing the state-of-the-art of project management. Phone 215/734-3330. Fax 215/734-3266.

B. J. DIXON: *Riverview Children's Hospital*
This case was prepared by B. J. Dixon of the Western Business School. Copyright 1991, the University of Western Ontario.

▶ **CHAPTER 11**

K. B. CLARK: *Corning Glass Works: The Z-Glass Project*
© 1981 by the President and Fellows of Harvard College. Reprinted by permission of the Harvard Business School.

H. J. Thamhain and D. L. Wilemon: *Criteria For Controlling Projects According to Plan*
© 1986 by the Project Management Institute. Reprinted from *Project Management Journal*, June 1986, pp. 75–81, by permission.

## ▶ CHAPTER 12

R. D. Landel: *Delta Electronics, Inc.*
©1985 by the Darden Graduate Business School Foundation, Charlottesville, VA.

A. M. Ruskin and W. E. Estes: *The Project Management Audit: Its Role and Conduct*
© 1985 by the Project Management Institute. Reprinted from *Project Management Journal*, August 1985, pp. 64–70, by permission.

## ▶ CHAPTER 13

B. M. Staw and J. Ross: *Knowing When to Pull the Plug*
© 1987 by *Harvard Business Review*, March-April 1987, pp. 68–74.

A. Malinowski: BETA *Company: The Z15 Engine Program* (A)
© 1985 by the Colgate Darden Graduate Business School Foundation, Charlottesville, VA

M. M. Hill and J. M. Comer: *Cincinnati Milacron, Inc: Casting Cleaning*
This case research was funded by a grant entitled "Management Issues in High-Technology Manufacturing Industries" from the Cleveland Foundation of Cleveland Ohio, 1985.

## ▶ CHAPTER 14

D. I. Cleland: *The Age of Project Management*
This article is reprinted from *Project Management Journal*, March 1991, with permission of the Project Management Institute, 130 So. State Road, Upper Darby, PA 19082, a worldwide organization for advancing the state-of-the-art of project management. Phone 215/734-3330. Fax 215/734-3266.

S. J. Mantel, Jr: *Supernet* (unpublished).)

# Subject Index

Accounting data assumptions and problems, 72, 291
Action plan. *See* Planning
Activity
  activity times, 337ff.
    deterministic, 337, 390
    estimate at 95% and 90% levels, 352–353, 747
    expected time, 344–345
    normal, crash, 337, 390–395
    optimistic/pessimistic, 341–342, 343–345
    probabilistic, stochastic, 337, 390
    standard deviation of, 345, 349–351
    variance of, 345, 348–351
  definition, 337
  dummy, 339, 341–342, 418
  earliest start time (EST), 346, 347–348, 415
  latest start time (LST), 347–348, 415
  pseudoactivity, 418
Activity-on-arrow, -on-node (AOA, AON). *See* Scheduling
Airbus Industrie, 668
Allison Engine Co., 160
American Automobile Association (AAA), 60
American Telephone and Telegraph Co., 447, 613, 664
Analytical approach, 110–111
Analytic hierarchy process, 58
Artemis®, 467
Ashby's Law of Requisite Variety, 516
Ashland Oil Co., 42
AT&T Global Information Solutions (NCR Corp.), 613

Auditor/evaluator, 586
  auditor responsibilities, 576–577
  trust building, 586
Audits, 527, 567–586
  audit costs, 573
  baseline, data base, 579
  depth, 573–574
  evaluation, 205, 567–583
    goals, 568–570. *See also* Project goals
    purposes of, 568–570
  life cycle, 578–581
  measurement, 583–585
    difficulties, 584–585
    permission to enter system, 586
  reports, 574–576, 580–581
    contents, 571, 574–576
    style, 575, 583
  team, 581–582
    access to personnel, 583
    access to records, 582–583
  timing, 573
  types, 571–573
    comparison of, 571–572
Automotive Composites Consortium, 668

Bank One, 678
Baseline plan. *See* Planning, master plan
Benefit/cost, 119, 300, 397, 516
Beta distribution, 344, 352–353, 747
Bill of materials, 208
Booz-Allen Hamilton, 336
Branch and bound. *See* Resource allocation
British Petroleum, 42
Budget, 204, 287, 520–521
  activity vs. program, 297–299
  baseline, 287, 457

contingency allowance, 294
control mechanism, 287–288
cost estimation. *See* Cost estimation
decrement, 616
negotiation process, 293–296
  life cycle, 294–296
planning-programming-budgeting system (PPBS), 299–300
policy, 296–297
process, 296–297
program budget, 7
  definition, 7–8
  evaluation, 64–66
stability, 290–291, 292
top-down/bottom-up, 291–293
zero-base budgeting, 300–301
Bureau of Labor Statistics, 308

Career ladders, 115, 115fn.
  dual-track ladders, 698
CFM International, 668
Change and change orders, 126, 173, 201, 256–257
  causes for, 256, 536
  change control system, 536–538
Chartering, 255, 257, 261
Chrysler Corp., 42, 160, 161, 668, 678
Communications, 112–113
  breadth of, 126–128
*Compadre* system. *See* Multicultural project management
Comparative benefit model, 48–49
Competitive necessity model, 47
Conflict, 9, 175–177, 250ff.
  avoidance, 175, 262
  categories, 258–261
  definition, 250

intensity, 177, 261
interpersonal, 259
interproject, 260, 261–262
intraproject, 253
life cycle, 175–177, 257–264
parties-at-interest, 113, 250–251,
    258–261
project manager vs. functional
    manager, 112, 120–121,
    260, 261
reduction/resolution, 250ff.
    Pareto optimal solution, 253
sources, 175–177, 201
successful, characteristics of, 251
*Consumer Reports*, 60
Contingency plan. *See* Planning
Control, 508–538
    balance, 532–534
        causes of imbalance, 532–533
        elements of, 532
    control of change, 536–538
        causes for, 536
        change control system,
            536–538
            guidelines and process,
                537–538
            purpose, 536–537
    control of creativity, 534–535
        methods of, 535
    critical ratio, 524–526
    human response to, 529–531
        cybernetic control, 530–531
        go/no-go control, 531
        postcontrol, 531
    need for, 508–510
    purposes of, 510–512
        financial resource control,
            511–512
        human resource control, 511
        physical asset control, 510–511
    system design, 522–527
        characteristics of, 522–523
    timing, 517–518, 533
        early warning system, 517–518
    types, 513–522
        cybernetic control, 513–516
            1st order, 2nd order, 3rd
                order, 514–515
            information requirements,
                516

go/no-go control, 516–520
    information requirements,
        518–520
    postcontrol, 520–522
        elements of, 520–522
    postcontrol report, 520–522
        milestones, schedules,
            budgets, 520–521
        project objectives, 520
        project results, 521
        recommendations, 521–522
Cost
    cost shifting, 399
    direct costs, 303
    overhead costs, 302
Cost estimation, 289ff.
    allowance for waste and
        spoilage, 308
    contingency allowance, 309
    errors, 311
    ethical problems, 308–309
    improving process, 303ff.,
        311–315
        tracking signal, 312–315
            as ratio, 313–315
    learning curve, 305–307
    methods, 309
    price changes, 307–308
Cost/schedule control systems
    criteria (C/SCSC), 457,
    459–461, 469, 524
Cost/time slope. *See* Resource
    allocation
Creativity, 695–708
    barriers to, 696–698
    definition, 696
    evaluation of methods, 706–707
    group creativity, 701–706
        advantages, 702
        group composition, 702
        methods, 703–706
            bionics, 704
            brainstorming, 703–704
            Delphi, 705
            morphology, 704
            nominal group techniques,
                705
            other methods, 705–706
            storyboarding, 704–705
            synectics, 704

individual creativity, 699–701
    methods, 700–701
management, 698–699
    tweed coat management, 113,
        698
new techniques, 707
organizing for, 707–708
Critical path method (CPM). *See*
    Scheduling and Resource
    allocation
Critical ratio, 524–526

Data. *See* Monitoring
Data General, 467
Dean and Nishry's model, 62–63
Dean's profitability method, 53
Decision support systems (DSS),
    46, 622
Delphi method, 57, 59, 67, 621, 622,
    705, 726–728
Department of Defense, 74, 300, 459
Department of General Services,
    367
Digital Equipment Corp. (DEC), 467
Due diligence, 512, 573
DuPont, Inc., 336

Earned value. *See* Monitoring
Elanco Products Co., 519
Eli Lilly Co., 115fn., 337, 519, 698
Employee Involvement (EI), 174,
    530
Environmental impact on project
    management, 666–670
    business cycle environment,
        669–670
    definition, 666
    legal environment, 667–669
    socioeconomic environment,
        666–667
    technological environment, 670
ESPRIT, 668
Ethics, 131, 253–254, 308–309, 452
    code of, 130
Evaluation. *See* Audits
Event, node
    definition, 338
    earliest occurrence time (EOT),
        346–347, 355

Event (*continued*)
latest occurrence time (LOT), 347–348
Excel®(Microsoft), 43, 312fn., 315, 352, 353, 622
Expediting projects, 390–395

Facilitator. *See* Project manager
Factor scoring models. *See* Project
Fiat, 668
Float. *See* Scheduling, slack
Ford Motor Co., 668
*Fortune* 500, 66
Functional project organization. *See* Organization

Gantt chart. *See* Scheduling
General Electric Co., 7, 668, 678
General Motors Corp., 668
Goal programming, 63–64
Goddard Space Flight Center, 367
Goodyear Aircraft Co., 290
Gozinto chart, 208, 210
Graphical Evaluation and Review Technique (GERT). *See* Scheduling
Grumman Aircraft Co., 413

Harvard negotiation project, 267
Hewlett Packard, 467
Hierarchical planning, 207ff., 292
Holistic approach, 155, 157. *See also* Systems approach

IBM, 42, 467
Idea generation. *See* Creativity
Information system. *See* Project Management Information System
Interdependencies, 8
Interface management, 221–224
Interfaces, 263
International Aero Engines, 668
ISO 9000, 530

Japan Aero Engines, 668
J. C. Penney Co., 573

Learning curves, 305–307
Life cycle, 8
alternate cycle, 294–296
conflict, 257–264
project goals, 14–15, 124–125
stages, 13–16
Lincoln Electric Co., 533
Linear responsibility charts, 217ff.
Lockheed Corp., 156, 336
Lotus 1-2-3® (Lotus Development Corp.), 43, 59, 311, 312, 313, 315, 352, 353, 368, 622
LTV Corp., 47

Management of change. *See* Change and change orders
Management by exception, 451
Management by objectives (MBO), 174
Manpower Temporary Services, 532
Materials requirements planning (MRP), 208
Mathematical programming, 63–64, 410–411, 414–416
Matrix multiplication, 65–66, 735–736
Matrix organization. *See* Organization
McDonnell Douglas Automation Corp., 468
MCI, 678
Mead Corp. 534
Mead Data Corp. project development guide, 534
Mean absolute deviation (MAD), 311–314
Mean absolute ratio (MAR), 314
Measurement, 72–73
difficulties, 584–585
quantitative/qualitative, 73
reliable/unreliable, 73
subjective/objective, 73, 446
valid/invalid, 73
Meetings, 455–456
Merck, 678
Merrill Lynch, 678
Micromanagement, 112, 213
Microsoft, 678

Microsoft Project®, 18, 461, 469, 472
Milestones, 76, 339, 356, 446, 453–454, 467, 517, 518–519, 520–521, 584
reports, 463–465
Models. *See* Project selection models
types of, 40–41
Monitoring, 441ff., 513
accounting data, 72
data collection procedures, 446–447, 448–452
definition, 441
earned value, 457–459, 524
value completed, 457
variances, 457–459
of work performed, 457
ethical issues, 452
human factors, 450
measurement problems and issues, 446, 447
planning, monitoring, controlling cycle, 444–452
closed loop information flow, 445
purposes of, 442
reports, 449–455, 469
benefits of, 454
common problems, 456–457
final report, 521
frequency, 450
milestone reports, 465, 520–521
project status or progress, 449–452, 519–520, 521
timing of, 450, 452–453
types of, 454–455
schedule, 332–333
standards and criteria, 446–447
changes in, 447
system design, 445–448
types of data, 448–449
Motivation, 120–122, 155, 156, 173–175
MTU, 668
Multicultural project management, 661–678
*compadre* system, 663, 663fn., 667
culture impact on project, 663–664

definition of culture, 662
elements of culture, 662–663
managerial behavior, 675–677
microcultures, 664–665
multicultural communication,
674–678
structure and style of
communications, 674–675
psychosocial needs of project
team, 677–678
Multiproject scheduling. *See*
Resource allocation

NASA, 1, 121, 367, 621
National Cooperative Research Act
(1984), 668
National Science Foundation, 48
NCR Corp., 613
Negotiation, 128, 162, 172, 173,
213, 250ff.
budget, 293–296
definition, 252–253
ethics of, 253–254
nature of, 266
positional, 267
principled, 266–267
requirements, 266
style, 265ff.
win-win, 251, 266–268, 294
Networks. *See* Scheduling
Normal probability distribution,
350, 734
North American Free Trade
Agreement (NAFTA), 669
Northrup Corp., 413
Not-invented-here (NIH) syndrome,
696

Objective/subjective measures, 73
Office of Naval Research, 48, 159
Office of Technology Assessment,
714
Operating necessity model, 47
Organization, 150ff.
choosing form, 165–167
functional, 153ff.
advantages/disadvantages,
153–155

matrix, 158ff.
advantages/disadvantages,
161–162
authority conflicts, 258ff.
strong/weak, 158–159,
172–173, 262
mixed form, 163–165
advantages/disadvantages,
164–165
pure project, 155ff.
advantages/disadvantages,
156–158

Pacifico's method, 53
Parkinson's Law, 369
Parties-at-interest, 9, 113, 126,
250–251, 258–261,
661–662
Partnering, 254–255, 257, 261
Peer review, 48
Personnel, acquiring and
motivating. *See* Motivation
Peter Principle, 679
Planning, 196ff.
action plan, 174, 207–213, 332,
339–340, 446, 459, 469,
516
form of, 208ff.
contingency plan, 76, 126
effectiveness, 206
elements of, 203–205
importance of, 210
master plan, 200, 201, 288, 459
phases, sequences, 196–197
sign-offs, 213, 255
Planning programming budgeting
system (PPBS), 299–300
PMBOK. *See* Project management
body of knowledge
Portfolio selection, 64–66
Pratt & Whitney, 7, 668
Precedence diagramming, 362–364
Primavera®, 404
Priorities, 256–257, 260, 262–264
Probability and statistics, 738–747
event relationships and
probability laws, 739–741
addition rule, 741
definitions, 739–740
multiplication rule, 740–741

probability, 738–739
experimental probability, 739
logical probability, 739
subjective probability, 739
standard probability
distributions, 747
statistics, 742–747
definitions, 742ff.
descriptive vs. inferential
statistics, 743
inferential statistics, 745–746
measures of central tendency,
743–744
measures of dispersion,
744–745
Procter & Gamble, 62, 114, 532, 678
Product line extension model, 48
Profit/profitability models, 50ff.
advantages/disadvantages, 53–54
average rate of return, 50
Dean's profitability method, 53
discounted cash flow, 50–51
internal rate of return, 52
Pacifico's method, 53
payback period, 50
profitability index, 52
Program budgeting. *See* Budget
Program evaluation and review
technique (PERT). *See*
Scheduling
Project
champion, 120, 613, 699
coordination, 200ff.
definition, 7–9
deliverables, objectives, 3, 200,
204, 519, 520, 568–570
evaluation, 39ff.
failure, 127
effect on morale, 126
fear of, 125–126
reasons for, 126
final report, 613. *See also*
Termination
goals, 3, 14–15, 43–46, 568–570
ancillary, 568–570
identification problems,
569–570
direct, 568
threshold values, 46
master plan, 200

Project (*continued*)
　master schedule, 204, 218,
　　520–521
　meetings, 455–456
　portfolio, 39
　predicting success or failure,
　　618–621
　　causes of failure, 619–621
　proposals, 41, 48, 74–76, 520
　　executive summary, 74–75
　　implementation plan, 75–76
　　logistic support, 76
　　technical approach, 75
　purpose, 8, 9–10, 127
　selection, 39ff., 260
　　information base, 71ff.
　　models,
　　　choice, 66–67
　　　criteria, 41–43
　　　nature of, 40–41, 41–47
　　　nonnumeric models, 47–49
　　　numeric models, 49ff.
　　　types, 40–41, 43–44, 49ff.
　　under uncertainty, 67ff.
Project budgeting. *See* Budget
Projectitis, 157–158, 165
Project management
　advantages/disadvantages, 9–10
　definition, 4
　forces for, 1–2
　limitations, 10
　professionalization of, 4, 14,
　　679–680
　unsolved problems, 678–680
　　conflict resolution in matrix
　　　organizations, 678–679
　　rewarding excellence, 679–680
　　universal information system,
　　　678
Project management body of
　　knowledge (PMBOK), 4,
　　114
Project management information
　　system (PMIS), 369,
　　466–480
　desirable capabilities, 470, 471
　large PMIS capabilities, 466,
　　467–469
　management errors, 466–467
　selection process, 471–480

　small PMIS capabilities, 466,
　　469–480
Project Management Institute
　　(PMI), 4, 114, 131, 420
Project manager, 108ff.
　authority, 9, 258ff.
　career, 4, 10, 113–115, 679–680
　credibility, 129
　demands on, 119–128
　diary, 630–631
　ethics, 130, 131, 452
　facilitator vs. functional manager,
　　110–112
　firefighting, 122–123
　information network, 127
　initial tasks, 108–109
　interpersonal sensitivity, 176
　leadership, 131
　orientation, problem vs.
　　discipline, 109, 122
　political sensitivity, 122, 127, 129
　responsibilities, 112–113, 156,
　　159, 162, 221, 264, 333,
　　398, 413, 450, 452, 517,
　　523, 530, 534, 627, 667,
　　677
　role of, 110ff.
　selection of, 128–132
　stress, 129, 131–132
Project office, war room, 170–171,
　　450, 570
Project organization. *See*
　　Organization
Project planning. *See* Planning
Project review committee, 456
Project scheduling. *See* Scheduling
Project team, 113, 170ff., 531
　characteristics, 121–122
　composition, 171–172
　human factors, 173ff.
　interpersonal conflict, 175–177.
　　*See also* Conflict
　morale, 126
　motivation, 156, 173–175
　psychosocial needs in
　　multicultural project,
　　677–678
　team building, 174–175
Project termination. *See*
　　Termination

Project/2®, 467
Proposals. *See* Project, proposals

Quattro Pro® (Borland), 43
Q-sort, 48–49

Rand Corp., 57
Reliance Electric Co., 74
Reports. *See* Monitoring
Republic Steel Corp., 47
Request for proposal (RFP), 39,
　　74–75, 308, 467, 695
Resource acquisition, 119–120
Resource allocation, 389ff. *See also*
　　Trade-offs
　constrained resource allocation,
　　404–412
　　branch and bound approach,
　　　408, 411
　　Burgess's method, 410
　　hueristic methods, 405–410
　　　priority rules, 406–407
　　optimizing methods, 410–411
　critical path method (CPM),
　　390–395
　　cost/time slope, 392
　multiproject scheduling resource
　　constrained, 412–421
　　effectiveness measures,
　　　413–414
　　hueristic methods, 415–421
　　　descheduling/borrowing,
　　　　419–420
　　　effect of alternate life cycles,
　　　　419–420
　　　RAMPS, 416
　　　SPAR-1, 419–421
　　　Walt-capacity, 420
　　optimizing methods, 414–415
Resource allocation for multiple
　　project scheduling
　　(RAMPS), 416
Resource contouring, 408–410
Resource leveling, 399–403
Resource loading, 398–399
Resource scarcity, 397, 420
Responsibility matrix, 217ff.
Risk
　analysis, 68–71
　avoidance, 696–697
Rolls Royce, 160, 668

Sacred cow model, 47
Scheduling, 332ff. *See also* Activity
  control mechanism, 332
  critical path, 337, 338, 345–347
    reverse critical path, 364
  critical path method (CPM),
    336ff., 389, 398
  critical time, 345–347
  distinction between PERT and
    CPM, 337, 339, 390
  Gantt chart, 354–358, 398, 416,
    450, 469, 471, 472
    advantages/disadvantages,
      354–355, 356, 357
    relation to PERT/CPM, 355
  graphical evaluation and review
    technique (GERT),
    364–367, 368
    comparison with PERT/CPM,
      364
    definition of symbols, 366
    methods, 365
    Q-GERT, VERT, 365
  master schedule, 204, 218,
    520–521
  networks, 333ff., 450, 469, 470,
    471, 472
    activity-on-arrow, on-node,
      (AOA, AON), 339, 363,
      369, 393, 470
    benefits, 333, 334
    construction of, 338–343
    definition, 333
    terminology, 337–338
  other scheduling methods, 367
  program evaluation and review
    technique (PERT), 336ff.,
    353–354, 398
    potential bias, 368
  project completion time,
    348–352
  slack, 337, 347–348, 355, 399
Scheduling program for allocation
  of resources (SPAR-1),
  419–421
Scientific Advisory Board, 713
Scoring models, 55ff., 585
  advantages/disadvantages, 63–64
  constrained weighted factor,
    61–62

Dean and Nishry's model, 62–63
  goal programming, 63
  unweighted factor, 55–57
  unweighted 0-1 factor, 55
  weighted factor, 57–61
Selection. *See* Project, selection
SEMATECH, 668
Simulation, 71, 352, 362, 368
  At Risk®, 352
  Crystal Ball®, 352
  Monte Carlo, 68
  risk analysis, 68–70
Slack. *See* Scheduling
Snecma, 668
Stakeholders. *See* Parties-at-interest
Statistical bias, 311–315
Statistics. *See* Probability and
  statistics
Suboptimize, 9, 155
Supermanager, 4
SuperProject®, 404
Support from senior management,
  127, 203, 210, 287
Systems approach, 110–111,
  160–161
Systems integration, engineering,
  205–206

Task, 7
Team building. *See* Project team
Technical change procedure. *See*
  Change and charge orders
Technical proposal requirements
  (TPR), 74–75
Technological forecasting, 711–731
  definition, 711
  forecasting methods, 714–728
    judgment-based methods,
      721–728
      cross-impact analysis, 728
      Delphi method, 726–728
      monitoring, 721–722
      morphological analysis, 725
      network analysis, 722–724
      relevance trees, 726
      scenarios, 724–725
    numeric data-based methods,
      714–721
      envelope curves, 719–720
      growth curves, 718–719

limit analysis, 715–716
    multivariate trend
      correlation, 716–717
    statistical curve fitting, 715
    substitution model, 720–721
    trend correlation, 716
    trend extrapolation, 714
    trend extrapolation,
      qualitative, 717–718
  history of, 713–714
  innovation vs. invention, 713
  nature of, 712–713
  purpose, 711–712
  selecting method, 728–731
Technological shock, 73–74
Technology Assessment Act (1972),
  714
Termination, 611ff.
  decision, 616–621
    major questions, 616–617
    mathematical/statistical
      models, 621–622
  decision support system (DSS),
    622
  process, 621–628
    implementation, 622–628
  project final report, history, 613,
    620, 629–631
    content, 629–630
  special considerations, 615–616
  termination manager, 626–628
    duties of, 627–628
  types of termination, 612–618
    by addition, 613–614
    by extinction, 612–613
    by integration, 615–616
    by starvation, 616
Texas Instruments, 164, 699
3M, 678, 699
TimeLine® (Symantec), 18, 404,
  405, 461, 469, 472
Top management support. *See*
  Support from senior
  management
Total quality management (TQM),
  174, 254, 257, 294, 530
Tracking signal, 312–315
  as ratio, 313–315
Trade-offs, 4, 123–125, 253, 263,
  337, 389ff., 397, 413–414

Trade-offs (*continued*)
   and life cycle, 124–125, 263
   time/cost trade-offs, 390–395
     cost shifting, 399
TRAK®, 467
TREND, 221–224, 362
Tweed coat management, 113, 698

Uncertainty, 15–16, 46, 222–223,
     256, 289–290

project completion time,
    348–352
United Way, 48
University of California, 2
University of Cincinnati, 153, 154
U.S. Air Force, 7
U.S. Navy, 1, 336, 344
U.S. Patent Bureau, 713

Value engineering, 206, 294

Walt Disney Studios, 704
War room, 170–171, 450, 570
Work breakdown structure (WBS),
    172, 215ff., 288, 291, 292,
    333, 452, 459, 467, 469,
    472, 516
   design of, 216–221
Work packages, units, 7, 213

Zero-base budgeting, 300–301

# Photo Credits